AFTER
the
BALL

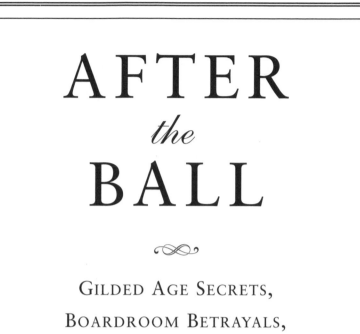

AFTER *the* BALL

Gilded Age Secrets,
Boardroom Betrayals,
and the Party That Ignited
the Great Wall Street
Scandal of 1905

PATRICIA BEARD

HarperCollins*Publishers*

HarperCollins books may be purchased for educational, business, or sales promotional use. For information, please write: Special Markets Department, HarperCollins Publishers Inc., 10 East 53rd Street, New York, NY 10022.

FIRST EDITION

Designed by Elliott Beard

Printed on acid-free paper

Library of Congress Cataloging-in-Publication Data
    After the ball : Gilded Age secrets, boardroom betrayals, and
the party that ignited the great Wall Street scandal of 1905 / by
Patricia Beard.—1st ed.
      p. cm.
    Includes bibliographical references.
    ISBN 0-06-019939-3
    1. Hyde, James Hazen, 1876–1959. 2. Businessmen—United
States—Biography. 3. Equitable Life Insurance Company—
History. 4. Wall Street—History. I. Title.
HC102.5.H94B43   2003
368.32'0092—dc21
   [B]   2003044987

03 04 05 06 07 ❖/RRD 10 9 8 7 6 5 4 3 2 1

With thanks to Lorna Hyde Graev, who stimulated my interest in her grandfather, and provided encouragement, inspiration, hospitality, and friendship

And in memory of Henry B. Hyde, 1915–1997

"Mr. Hyde's ball . . . served his enemies as an excuse for making an overt attack upon him. . . . [Y]et as regards its artistic side, its perfection of detail, its correctness in costume, its novelty and color, nothing has been attempted on this side of the water which could be compared with it."

—*Metropolitan Magazine*, June 1905

"Well, you know that most of the people read headlines . . . and they get their impressions through headlines, and there are headline manufacturers in connection with the Press."

—E. H. Harriman,
testimony before the Legislative Insurance Investigating Committee,
December 15, 1905

"[M]any insurance secrets are also Wall Street secrets, and Wall Street secrets are deeply buried and bear no headstones announcing names and dates."

—*New York Times*, October 15, 1905

"I will furnish your paper with full particulars of the greatest business scandal this country has ever known and what I will give you will tear hitherto unblemished reputations and smear many men with the mud of their own iniquity."

—Gage Tarbell, second vice president, Equitable Life Assurance Society,
later quoted by a reporter for *The World*

"For a time, while a thousand groundless reports were set in motion, the impression was given to the public that the management of great fiduciary institutions . . . of all the corporations or companies or individuals which carried on great business operations, was rotten to the core. . . . [As] the result of bitter personal quarrels. . . . The public good seemed to be almost entirely forgotten."

—Thomas Fortune Ryan,
"Why I Bought the Equitable," *North American Review* (August 1913)

Contents

Part Four

AFTER THE BALL

A Note on the Portrait

James Hazen Hyde, oil on canvas, painted by Théobald Chartran, 1849–1907. (Courtesy of the New-York Historical Society, gift of the subject, 1848.1)

JAMES HAZEN HYDE

James Hazen Hyde was just twenty-four when the artist Théobald Chartran captured his dark beauty. Chartran showed him as he was in 1901: socially prominent, cultured, and innocent of the ugly attentions good fortune can attract. It was an act of some arrogance for a man so young to commission Chartran, who was among the most sought-after portraitists in France, England, and the United States. He already had one important picture hanging in the White House, President William McKinley and the signing of the Treaty of Paris—a gift from Henry Clay Frick. In 1902, the year after Chartran painted James Hyde, he was called back to Washington to do the portrait of the new First Lady, Edith Roosevelt.

Chartran portrayed James in a style that could be called International Aristocratic. The painting might be mistaken for a work by John Singer Sargent, or by Sargent's master, the Parisian Emile Carolus-Duran, whose portrait of the society leader known as "The Mrs.

Astor" glowers from the wall of the Metropolitan Museum of Art in New York City.

James stands like a Velázquez prince against a rich, dark background the color of the well-burnished saddles in his stables. He rests one hand on a hip, arm akimbo, jacket open. Heavy gold rings weight the little fingers of his long, graceful hands. The small leather-bound volume that dangles casually from one hand is a symbol of his passion for collecting books. He had recently received the Légion d'Honneur from the government of France; perhaps it was that honor which inspired him to commission a portrait of himself. In those early days, his valet threaded the narrow red ribbon, the everyday symbol of the award, in his buttonhole each morning. That was before he thought of having the ribbon sewn into all his suits; and before he imagined that he might become the youngest American minister to France—he would have been more than a decade younger than Thomas Jefferson was when he succeeded Benjamin Franklin in Paris. James would live in Paris for nearly four decades, but it would be as an exile.

Impatiently alive, swaggering, and sexual, James seems certain that nothing will ever go wrong. But even those who do not know what happened to the man in the picture can feel the unsettling sense that if the paint were scraped off, bit by bit, an underdrawing would emerge.

Many years later, when everything important in his life had been fixed in legend and he was beginning to give things away, James Hyde donated the Chartran portrait to the New-York Historical Society. As recently as the spring of 2002, it hung in the society's Masterworks of American Painting exhibition, but that was only temporary. The Hyde portrait now sits in storage somewhere in New Jersey.

PART ONE

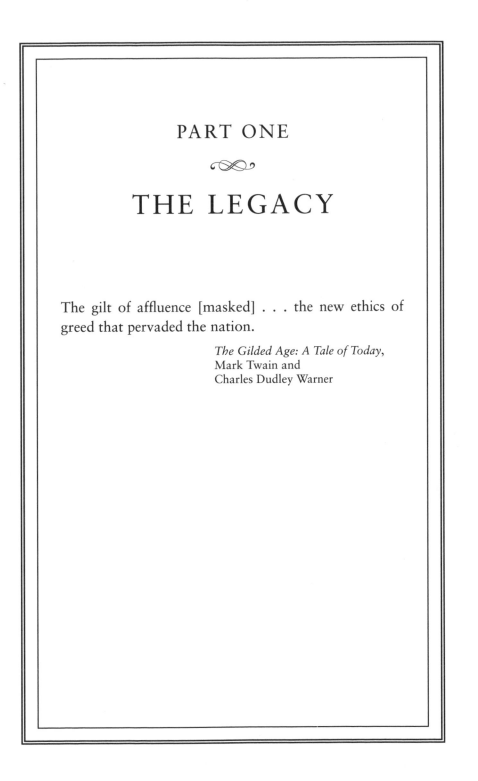

THE LEGACY

The gilt of affluence [masked] . . . the new ethics of greed that pervaded the nation.

The Gilded Age: A Tale of Today,
Mark Twain and
Charles Dudley Warner

Prologue

Hic situs est Phaëton, currus auriga paterni,
Quem si non tenuit, magnis tamen excidit ausis
                    —Ovid

Here lies Phaëton, the driver of his father's chariot,
which if he failed to manage, yet he fell in a great
undertaking.[1]

$\mathcal{L}$et us first acknowledge the power of glamour.

Glamour has its own reality, but sometimes it is so dazzling that it obscures the facts.

James Hazen Hyde was the handsomest man in any room, the most dramatically dressed, and, at nearly six foot four, usually the tallest. He was often referred to as the richest bachelor in New York, even though his friend Alfred Gwynne Vanderbilt inherited forty times as much when both their fathers died in 1899. What was true was that as heir to the majority shares in the Equitable Life Assurance Society, he controlled an investment fund of hundreds of millions of dollars, more than the reserves of the Bank of England at the height of its empire.

Newspapers liked James Hyde's dash; or at least they liked to write about him, and the stories they printed had an eccentric, racy quality. A favorite rumor was that he traveled with three valets, and trunks of black draperies, black silk sheets, and black carpets to refit his rooms in even the grandest houses so he could sleep in absolute darkness. He did wear a black mask when he went to bed, to protect his sensitive eyes, and he favored black silk pajamas. He was well into his sixties when a nephew glanced into his bedroom and saw the pajamas laid out on the bed with its lustrous black sheets. Thinking of James's reputation as a ladies' man, he commented wryly, "Uncle's working clothes."

In 1905, when James was twenty-eight, he gave one of the great balls of the Gilded Age, a French eighteenth-century-themed costume party for which he would be known all his life, and long after his death. The ball was cited as a marker of the age before the Metropolitan Opera orchestra played the first note. It was held at society's gathering place, Sherry's Hotel in New York, in two floors of gilt-and-mirror ballrooms, decorated to evoke the gardens of Versailles. The six hundred guests wore costumes embroidered with emeralds and pearls, and jewels that had belonged to empresses. The centerpiece of the evening was a play set in the eighteenth century, written especially for the party, to feature the famous French actress, Réjane.

The next morning, the Hyde Ball was reported in admiring detail in every newspaper in the city, giving James's enemies the excuse they had been waiting for to claim that he was too frivolous to run the "sacred trust" of a life insurance company. This was not a small matter; life insurance was a linchpin of the economy, and the most reliable form of protection a man could offer his family in the eventuality of his death. Hyde was more of a financier than an insurance man—that had been his father's fiefdom—and the public understood that he had the controlling power in the company. The policyholders were concerned with their own security, and when the rumor spread that the ball cost $200,000, and that James had charged it to the Equitable, the story caused widespread alarm. The putative price tag and the canard that the Equitable paid the bill are still published as fact in histories of the Gilded Age. A government investigation established that James paid for the ball himself, but even he did not know exactly what the price was: $50,000 would be a reasonable guess.

In other respects, the cost was enormous.

The Hyde Ball set off a business brawl that entangled the most famous railroad entrepreneurs, industrialists, and financiers of the era. The spectacular fight surrounding one of the three most powerful insurance companies in the world commanded 115 front page articles in the *New York Times* and 122 in *The World* in a single year.[2] To read those newspapers is to open a window onto financial, political, and social behavior at a time when the rules were just being made, and the laws that did exist were often ignored without penalty.

James's father was one of the pioneers of that vigorous period. Henry Baldwin Hyde founded the Equitable Life Assurance Society in 1859, when he was twenty-five. Forty years later, the company had a billion dollars of insurance in force. It has never been fashionable to consider Gilded Age businessmen like Henry as idealists, and public opinion was irreversibly influenced against them after the loaded phrase "robber barons" melted into the vernacular in 1934,[3] yet many of them entertained visions of great deeds, and often they were as voracious for growth as they were rapacious for wealth. In their own ways, they were fathers of their country. They created its infrastructure, and their conviction that opportunities were limitless became the armature of the national ethos. With the nostalgia of hindsight, they can seem almost naive in their certainty that they were working for the greater good.

In Henry Hyde's case, that was correct: more than three hundred thousand Americans, as well as others served by the Equitable's seventy-seven foreign offices, counted on insurance to protect their families. Death could grab a young father who was in robust health when he left for work and plant him in a coffin in the parlor within days. If a man could do nothing else, during much of the nineteenth century he could buy a policy on his life to provide for his widow and children.

Gilded Age entrepreneurs expected to pass their empires along, and most of them did. Few sons could match their fathers' drive and talent, but the dynastic instinct is hard to resist. When Henry Hyde bequeathed the majority shares in the Equitable to his only surviving son, James inherited the authority to select the company's directors. That power threw him in with tycoons like E. H. Harriman and J. Pierpont Morgan, who were a generation older, and who had succeeded because they had also failed and knew how to recover. By the time James knew them, they were at the top of their careers, and many of them had taken on the patina of financial statesmen. They seemed infinitely wise to a man one year out of Harvard, inexperienced, overprotected, underprepared, and absorbed by his own interests.

James was a devoted student of French culture, and as an undergraduate, he established a $30,000 fund to finance the exchange of professors between France and the United States. It was that gift that earned him his first Legion d'Honneur in his early twenties. Given a choice, he would have become a patron of the arts and lived a transatlantic life, principally in Paris. Instead, weeks after Henry's death, he was elected first vice president of the Equitable, in training to take over the presidency on his thirtieth birthday.

Henry had so thoroughly dominated his son's life that he chose the books James read as a child, and arranged for the placement of the hooks in his bathroom when he went to college. Now James was free from Henry's oversight—although it is easy to underestimate the influence of the dead. James rebelled by seeking social prominence. It was a pleasant form of insurrection, and one that contravened his father's inflexible credo that personal publicity was undignified and inappropriate for the leader of a business devoted to protecting the vulnerable.

The life of a vaunted socialite suited the exuberance of the early-twentieth-century boom. The country had been battered by the Civil War and a series of financial crises; and between 1893 and 1897, just as recovery seemed established, the economy was crushed by one of the worst depressions in American history. When prosperity finally returned, the public was ready to embrace evidence that any American could realize grand ambitions. Newspaper readers were fascinated by that new breed, the millionaire, and most of them knew who the press was referring to when they wrote of "Jupiter" (J. P. Morgan) and "Mephistopheles" (the railroad tycoon, Jay Gould).

Newspapers celebrated the titans and their families, printing the smallest details of their lives. Gossip writers met ocean liners returning from Europe, reporting such tidbits as how much a woman paid in import duties for her Paris clothes. Journalists even noted who rode where in the field at a fox hunt. One woman, waiting outside to see the swells arrive at a ball, bragged to a reporter that she had saved the clod of mud she scavenged from a wheel of the carriage that took Consuelo Vanderbilt to the church where she married the Duke of Marlborough.[4] When the sixteen-year-old Cornelia Martin married the Earl of Craven at Grace Church in New York, a mob stormed the church, not in protest against the public reports that she had received millions of dollars in diamond jewelry as wedding gifts, but to see the glorious spectacle. The uninvited audience crushed guests, ripped their gowns, and tore down the floral arrangements to take home.[5] There were pockets of class resentment, anarchists, socialists, unionists, privileged reformers, and political leaders who were outraged by what a writer nearly one hundred years later would call "contemptuous consumption."[6] But most Americans were convinced that the rich had a special kind of grace.

James demonstrated the pleasures money could buy. As he later admitted, "I got too much power when I was young." In his twenties, he owned a brownstone in New York, a house in Paris, a private railroad car, and a four-hundred-acre estate, The Oaks, on Long Island. He enlarged his dining room to seat one hundred—more informal dinners were sometimes held in the stables, where a staff of eighty attended the horses and carriage collection. He was famous as one of the premier drivers of four-in-hand coaches in the United States, a sport that was almost unparalleled for its expense. A supremely eligible bachelor, he was rumored to date pretty young actresses who were looking for patrons, although he was most famously a beau of Alice Roosevelt, the beautiful, audacious daughter of the president of the United States.

But while James played hard, he also had ambition and intelligence, and he was interested in finance. He recognized the change in the business climate, and he understood that the Equitable, with an investment pool edging up toward $400 million, was well positioned to profit from volatile economic conditions. Railroaders and financiers were in a phase of mergers and acquisitions, looking for capital, and the men who ran Wall Street were eager to ingratiate themselves with the young heir whose majority shares gave him the power to choose the company's directors, who, in turn, decided how the money would be invested.

Ninety percent of the Equitable's portfolio was in railroad stocks, bonds, and loans. Railroads and the industries that depended on them were at the heart of nearly every financial maneuver of consequence, and they were well represented on the board. Among the directors were E. H. Harriman of the Union Pacific; James J. Hill of the Great Northern; Alexander Cassatt of the Pennsylvania; Alfred Vanderbilt and Chauncey Depew of the New York Central; George J. Gould of the Missouri Pacific; Henry Clay Frick, who became one of the world's largest individual stockholders in railroads after U.S. Steel absorbed the Carnegie companies; and two of the era's principal financiers, Jacob Schiff of Kuhn, Loeb; and August Belmont, the Rothschilds' banker. The tycoons encouraged James to think of himself as one of them, and within a couple of years, he had been invited to serve on forty-eight boards. Through them, the Equitable took part in deals that caused turmoil in the stock market and bought blocks of bonds that helped finance wars, supporting the Japanese against Russia and the British in the Boer War. On the whole, the Equitable made money on these transactions, and so did its directors.

James's father had loved and protected him, and led him to believe that other successful men of his generation would take the same benevolent, if despotic, interest in his welfare. Above all, James expected that he could count on James W. Alexander, the Equitable's president, who was his trustee and official mentor. In 1905, Alexander was sixty-five and had been with the company for forty years. Alexander's father, a Presbyterian minister, had helped Henry Hyde assemble the company's original investors and directors; and Henry and JWA lived in the same boardinghouse when they were young.

JWA seemed like a suitable interim leader, a company man and a loyalist, who could keep the Equitable on a steady track until James was thirty and could take over. JWA was apparently kindly and upright; if he had a fault, it was that he was a little weak. But that might be just as well; at least he didn't want to usurp James's future position. No one could have anticipated that he would launch the fight for control of the Equitable, or that he would have the cunning to time his challenge so it would coincide with the headline stories about James's ball, to prove that James was unsuited to head a company with such a serious mission.

Alexander claimed to believe that he was acting in the best interests of the policyholders, but beneath the surface, he was gripped by the tension between a righteous self-image and a history of participating in murky financial dealings with Henry Hyde. After Henry died, JWA, as president, was more exposed, and as James Hyde gained social notoriety, his expensive lifestyle increased the risk that someone might wonder about the source of the money he was spending. If that happened, the truth could emerge that Alexander had led his protégé to participate in deals that would be embarrassing, if not illegal. One approach would have been for JWA to take a firm stand, insisting that James maintain a lower public profile to deflect unwelcome attention. Instead he allowed James to flaunt his wealth, only occasionally admonishing him; then made the situation worse by attacking James publicly, declaring that he was too extravagant. That accusation virtually ensured that someone would, indeed, begin to wonder where the money came from, and that the path would eventually lead to Alexander.

Instead of trying to keep James's excesses under control, Alexander exposed and exaggerated them, throwing an internal fight into the public forum. With the Equitable racked by internal dissension, powerful financiers entered the picture, tempted by the hope that, with James discredited, they might be able to pick up his stock like change lying in the gutter. The *New York American* summed up the situation in a front-page headline that read: EQUITABLE FIGHT REALLY IS ONE FOR CONTROL BY GREAT MONEY BORROWERS OF WALL STREET. MORGAN GROUP IS FIGHTING HARRIMAN FOR SUPREMACY.[7]

President Theodore Roosevelt took the opportunity to add the insurers to his list of "malefactors of great wealth," and the potential for serious damage certainly existed, if only because the Equitable's reach was so long. The failure of any major corporation could cause a loss of confidence in the economy, but the collapse of a major life insurance company posed a special danger. In 1900, half of all American savings were held in life insurance or annuities,[8] and if one of the insurers fell, it could impact the others and rip apart the security net on which millions of people relied. The threats to Wall Street were equally serious: The combined assets of the Equitable, New York Life, and Mutual Life amounted to $1.2 billion,[9] and insurance companies were among the most important backers of American corporations.[10]

The Equitable's investment capacity was indispensable, but James was not. On nearly the last day of 1905, at the end of the worst year of his life, the *New York American* published an editorial referring to the financial leaders who had misled him, tossed him back and forth among themselves, and nearly ruined him. The *American* called them "the hoary rascals who stole for him at first, and afterward stole from him."[11] James had recognized that their business tactics were suspicious at the beginning of his career, but as he explained, while "I was shocked by some things when I first went into business, it is easy to go along when you are 23."

The greatest betrayal was posthumous. Henry Hyde left a tangle of investments that embroiled the Equitable, its executives, directors, and his son in dealings that would not bear public scrutiny, and were so byzantine that it took years of investigation to trace the route of millions of dollars.

The practices that caught them up are mirrored in the early twenty-first century, when, once again, the promise of great lashings of money have led even those who think of themselves as upright to participate in wrongdoing, markets to plummet, investors to lose their stakes, and companies to fail. The major insurers at the peak of the Gilded Age provided modern-day businesses with models of shape-shifting investments, self-dealing, insider trading, accounting malpractice, price-fixing, and corporate funding of private pleasures.

But in the age of the original moguls, most of the transgressions were legal—if not legitimate. They operated within a barely regulated free-for-all that was contemporaneous with the Wild West. Today, the corporate scoundrels are not "cowboys"; they are criminals. This time, once-lionized business leaders are slightly more likely to be sent to jail; although they seem to be able to hold on to enough cash to live quite well when they return to society, chastised, but rarely shunned.

In 1905, as the details of the Equitable scandal spread across the front pages of countless newspapers, it caused public outrage, confusion, and fear, and led to a government investigation. That autumn, the New York State Legislature's counsel, Charles Evans Hughes, called the most renowned business leaders in the country onto the witness stand. His role as chief inquisitor catapulted him into the governor's mansion in Albany, less than a year after the Hyde Ball. By the time he was elected in 1906, the legislature had substantially tightened the laws governing the interaction between insurance companies and Wall Street.

When the investigation was over, James sailed to Paris, on the first leg of a long, lavish exile. A year earlier, he had been planning his party; now he had sold his country estate, his carriages and horses, his railroad car, and his majority interest in the Equitable. For the next thirty-five years he did not set foot in the United States even once. He stayed in Paris after the city fell to the Germans in June 1940, but finally, in 1941, he was forced to flee. During the remaining eighteen years of his life, he lived in New York, still attracting attention when he walked along Fifth Avenue in his cape and spats, honored by the French as a man of exceptional culture, a member of Harvard University's Romance Languages and Literatures Visiting Committee, and a charming dinner guest—but no longer a force in the social and financial life of the city.

Every story is shaped by the inclination to fit the narrative to the needs of the moment, and, for most of a century, James's party was the clothesline on which cautionary tales were hung. His stunning rise and precipitous fall were recounted to exemplify outrageous extravagance, a party gone wrong, and a patrimony lost. The tale could all be reduced to one word, hubris, elaborated by a single notion: A spoiled young man gave a ball that threatened to destroy a financial empire. It is a story that will be played out again and again wherever wealth is amassed, fathers try to pass their success along to their sons, sons want to please their fathers, and envy and greed parade as admiration and ambition.

The gossip has grown cold after a hundred years, but the party still glitters in its grandeur, and stings in its poignancy. It resonates with the irony of an event whose effect, disgrace, is the opposite of its intention to solidify and parade position. That can happen anywhere, but James's tale has a peculiarly American appeal. While English dramas tend to be rooted in a sense of place, their "green and pleasant land," and the French are partial to sex and intrigue, many of the great American sagas are founded upon a national belief in the transforming power of money. Yet Americans take a perverse satisfaction in the reversal of fortunes, a tendency that reflects a curious ambivalence about wealth and democracy. It is a basic tenet that anyone can become a millionaire or, in the twenty-first century, a billionaire, but the Puritan heritage and the immigrant work ethic are always in reserve. At a certain point, individuals, social classes, or nations come to seem too rich, and ostentation no longer appears entertaining, but wasteful, elitist, and insulting to the common human condition. Then values are reassessed, rules are changed, and callow youths are forced to mature. That cycle, too, will gradually fall into desuetude, as the prevailing philosophical truths become stale, time dulls the memory that too much luxury can be tiresome, and another dramatic host gives a wonderful party.

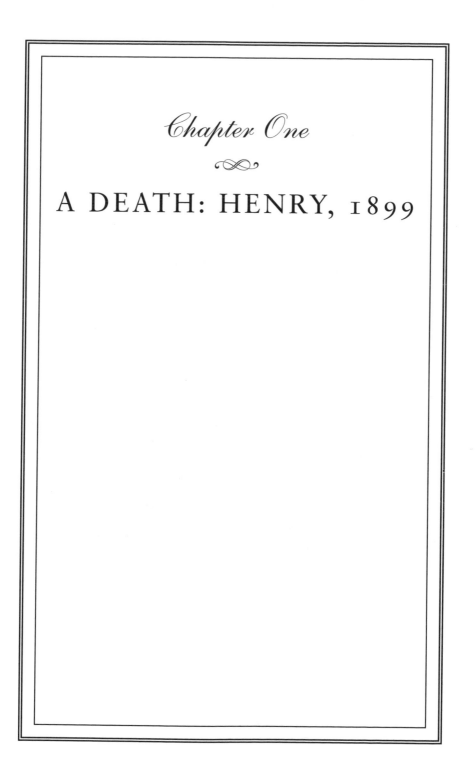

Chapter One

A DEATH: HENRY, 1899

The Equitable Building.

Henry Baldwin Hyde was the first businessman to install elevators in an office building, and the building he erected in 1870 at 120 Broadway was the model for the New York skyscraper. It attracted astonished tourists, who rode up and down in the elevators to observe the view from the roof. *(Courtesy AXA Financial Archives)*

At 120 Broadway, on the third of May, 1899, the work-men were out at dawn. It was their task to drape the Equitable Life Assurance Society in mourning, from the Quincy granite stoop to the mansard roof, all 110 feet of a building that was the protoype of the skyscraper. The fabric was crape—not the French dress material called crêpe, but a dull gauze scrim that made the world seem dusky to those looking out the windows, and hid the face of the company like a widow behind a veil. In 1899, people knew how to use the color black.

Henry Baldwin Hyde, the handsome, hypnotic entrepreneur whom contemporaries described as being "tall as a pine," with "the eyes of an eagle," was dead.[1] The flags of the United States of America and of the Equitable Life Assurance Society flew at half-mast, as did the flags atop the Mutual and New York Life Insurance companies. Their competition was so fierce that the three were called "the racers," yet New York Life's president had instructed that the headquarters he had just completed, a building eleven stories high and a block long, also be swathed in crape.

Henry Hyde had three obsessions: his company, his son, and his buildings. The home office at 120 Broadway stood on one full acre of land in the heart of Manhattan's business district, and other grand edifices housed his employees in Paris, Madrid, Vienna, Berlin, Melbourne, and Yokohama. Everyone in downtown Manhattan looked at the seven-story-Beaux-Arts-cum-Greek-temple monolith each day, not only because it was magnificent, but to check the weather report communicated by flags from a weather station on the roof. The view was so wide that it was possible to see the sunset across the river in New Jersey, or storm clouds massing north in Harlem. Other signals were

commonly recognized, too. When the president of the Equitable sailed
to Europe, the company's flags were dipped and raised three times, and
the ship replied by blasting its whistle and lowering and raising its colors.[2] This time the flags would stay at half-mast for a week.

Henry Hyde referred to his appetite for architectural grandeur as
"building for glory."[3] His offices were an interesting contrast to his
own consciously modest stance. He boasted, "I can start from my
house uptown in the morning, go to the elevated station and take the
train to Rector Street, pass through the Arcade to Broadway and up
that street to my office and not be recognized by a single person."[4]
He refused interviews, declined to be included in *Who's Who in
America*, never gave permission for his photograph to be published,
and believed that seeking or even permitting personal publicity was a
lapse in the appearance of rectitude necessary for a man in such a
serious business. But he was not reticent about the first important
building to represent his company. He fought the appalled directors
in 1867 at the end of the Civil War, when the Equitable was worth a
little more than $5 million, and spent 80 percent of it to erect his
splendid landmark, which took three years to complete.

Until Henry came along, no one had dared to use passenger elevators in an office building. He began with two: They were powered by
steam, paneled in tulipwood, decorated with gilt and mirrors,[5] and cost
$29,657. The elevators enabled him to build two stories higher than
the previous five-story maximum, so he could rent out offices on the
top floors. The Equitable Building was such a sensation that, in 1885,
the *Real Estate Record and Guide* recalled, "People came from far and
wide to ascend its roof and look down from the dizzy height upon the
marvelous stretch of scenery taking in the Bay, the Narrows, Staten
Island, the North and East Rivers, and the major portion of New York
and Brooklyn."[6] Even the elevator guard towered above other men:
John Seaton, the descendant of two of George Washington's slaves,
was over six and a half feet tall, although his height was generally
described as seven feet. Henry had noticed Seaton in 1874 when he
was part of the honor guard that escorted the abolitionist senator
Charles Sumner's body to New York, tracked Seaton down, and hired
him for his impressive dimensions.[7]

The porticoed and pedimented entrance to the home office had originally been decorated by a John Quincy Adams Ward statue group representing the Goddess of Protection, the Equitable's icon.[8] Over time, the stone began to crumble, and the sculpture had to be removed, which Henry saw as a disappointment, but not an augur. Inside, a two-story-high, two-hundred-foot-long, domed central hall was dominated by a floor-to-ceiling stained-glass window with a center medallion of "the Protection Group," a sweet-faced, classically robed woman standing with a spear in one hand and a shield held like an umbrella in the other, sheltering a young mother and child. The implication was that their husband and father had left them sorrowful but insured. The window was made in France in 1879; a year later, Henry Hyde's beloved first son, little Henry, died at age eight of complications of scarlet fever. When the stained glass was installed, a medallion surrounding a head-and-shoulders portrait of the boy with freshly combed hair and an Eton-style collar and tie was placed at the bottom center of the window. Little Henry was a handsome, dark-haired child; even rendered in glass he looked bright, merry, and good. If he had lived, he would have been brought up to run the Equitable. Instead, his father transferred his love and, ultimately, his stock to James, his younger son.

With both Henry Hydes dead, James would become the majority shareholder. But until he turned thirty the Equitable would be headed by his trustee, James Alexander, and run like a regency, subject to the intrigues, flatteries, and struggles for control that such an arrangement invites.

Henry Hyde's heart finally failed on May 2, 1899, at four in the afternoon, in the sudden heat that sometimes breaks out in the spring. His wife, Annie Fitch Hyde, sat at his deathbed with their children, James and his older sister, Mary Hyde Ripley, some of Henry's closest business associates, and a trained nurse. No privacy there, for either the dying or the bereaved. The time between each breath stretched to minutes, and then the room was shockingly quiet, until Annie cried out, and Mary bustled her off to her bedroom. The nurse drew the blinds and asked one of the servants hovering outside the door to close the curtains throughout the house while James retreated to the adjoining brownstone. The Hydes lived at 11 East Fortieth Street, and Henry had annexed its neighbor, number 9, for his home office and a small, private museum of Equitable memorabilia. When James came home from college, Henry designed an apartment for him at 9 East Fortieth, to give him a place of his own under the family roof.

That afternoon, as was the custom, the undertaker came to lay out the body on a rubber-sheeted embalming board on top of the bed. He suctioned out the blood, washed it down the drain, and replaced it by injecting formalin, the newest innovation in embalming, into the veins. Finally, he extracted the viscera, dropped them into a pail, covered it, and took it out by the service entrance. By the time he left, the doorbell had been hung with black streamers, indicating that the household was in mourning and warning callers not to ring too loudly.

Two days later, Henry lay in his parlor, neatly packaged in a black coat and striped trousers—the only person not dressed in deep mourning was the deceased. He appeared healthier than he had for months, but not quite like himself, as though he had been polished and the life had been scrubbed off. At least now his expression was peaceful. In the months before he finally succumbed to heart disease, he had been considerably disturbed in his mind.

His agitation at the end had a darker quality than the disruptive but episodic depressions that had plagued him for decades. Something unfinished gnawed at him. He had written James at the end of his Harvard career, "I want to see you in the Equitable with all your interests guarded and protected while I am alive and can attend to you." But by the time James came home, Henry was too weak to start the training he had postponed. He spent the last of his strength talking about the insurance business, and although James caught on quickly, his father would never have allowed anyone else who had so little experience to take a position of such responsibility in the most powerful company in its field.

The morning Henry was to be eulogized, prayed for, sung over, and buried, James slid his arms into a black frock coat, custom made in Paris, and attached a serge mourning band to the left sleeve. Then he popped open his black silk top hat, fastened another wide mourning band above the brim, and tried the hat on. The elegant James Hazen Hyde, Harvard, A.B. 98, *cum laude*, looked well in whatever he wore.

He joined his mother and sister and a few close friends in the parlor for a brief, private service, and looked into the open casket, and saw Henry for the last time before the lid was shut. Then he put on his public face and set off for the Fifth Avenue Presbyterian Church. There, the last honors would be held for a man whom the obituary writers called great, who loomed over his son as absolutely as 120 Broadway had once dominated Wall Street, and who would be nearly forgotten in fifty years.

Henry Hyde might have been right when he claimed that no one recognized him on his way to work, but anyone who saw his funeral cortege with its imposing line of black coaches drawn by black horses and driven by coachmen wearing black broadcloth coats, black kid gloves, and black top hats, would know that someone important had died. The carriages clattered decorously past the mansions along Fifth Avenue, one massive, magnificent, if faux, French château after another—every one of them grander than the Hydes' brownstones. There was the Morton Plant house, soon to be inhabited by the jeweler Cartier,⁹ and half-a-dozen buildings in what was called "Vanderbilt Row" in the low and mid-Fifties. The most famous was the French Gothic mansion Richard Morris Hunt designed for William K. Vanderbilt and his then-wife, Alva. It was there, in 1883, that she gave the costume ball that was said to complete the Vanderbilts' acceptance into the stratosphere of society. The most magnificent and largest private palace in New York was another Vanderbilt establishment, 1 West Fifty-seventh Street, Cornelius II's vigorous late Gothic, early Renaissance, and decidedly French brick and limestone establishment of 137 rooms, including a ballroom and a double-height Moorish smoking room with mother-of-pearl inlaid walls.

A police captain commanding fifteen patrolmen attempted to maintain order as thousands of mourners assembled at the Fifth Avenue Presbyterian Church. Among them were three hundred Equitable employees, dignitaries, official deputations from the other two major insurance companies, banks, railroads, and industrial megaliths. Onlookers waited to catch sight of the celebrated, awe-inspiring millionaires—people traveled to watch the rich pay their respects to the dead. Just months after Henry's funeral, when Cornelius Vanderbilt II lay dying at 1 West Fifty-seventh Street, hundreds gathered outside his house. When his widow emerged en route to the funeral, an even larger crowd assembled, grew silent, and the men held their hats in their hands.[10]

Henry's black-plumed hearse drew up, with the coffin on view through glass sides decorated with the symbols of grief: a drooping cypress tree and a torch turned upside down and extinguished. It was ten o'clock when the bells tolled, and the Reverend Dr. Henry Van Dyke[11] descended the steps and helped Annie from her carriage.

In the majestic open space of the sanctuary, not a single column obscured the view, and every seat was taken. The congregation rose and turned toward the pallbearers as they proceeded in single file, led by Henry's friend, Chauncey Depew, president of the New York Central Railroad. Depew had been in Detroit when Henry died, and ran a special train to get to New York for the funeral. One newspaper remarked, "The list of pallbearers is a notable one . . . several hundred millions of dollars being represented . . . by the seven men selected."[12] The Hydes took their seats just below the altar, where the thick, drowsy scent of lilies of the valley, roses, violets, orchids, sweet peas, and greenery soaked the air. Wreaths, crosses, and sheaves of flowers were packed together, banked six feet high. Up in the pulpit, Dr. Van Dyke looked as though he were emerging from a huge, colorful, ball-gown skirt.

Henry's death had transformed James from a boy just out of Harvard, whose chief distinction was his rich father, to one of the most interesting young men in New York. Businessmen at the service made a note to get to know him better; some had already offered advice. But on that May morning, the only guidance James wanted was from the father who had assured him when he started at Harvard, "If anything goes wrong or anyone gives you any trouble let me know as I am sure I can fix it."[13]

James Alexander, the man Henry had designated as his son's protector, sat with the pallbearers, just behind the family. A contemporary described JWA as "the handsomest and the most polished gentleman I ever came in contact with."[14] He had the aspect of a career diplomat in his final post, the second man in one of the more civilized embassies. His hair was white and silky, matching his fluffy white mustache, he spoke with the phrasing of an ecclesiastic and the deliberation of a lawyer, which he was; and he had the manners of a consummate clubman: He was president of the Society of the Virginians in New York, and of the University and Princeton Clubs. He and the Equitable had done well together. He owned a large house at 4 East Sixty-fourth Street, and, soon after Henry's death, his salary was raised to $100,000, worth about $2 million in 2000 dollars, making him one of the highest-paid executives in the United States— in 1900, the average American earned less than $750 a year.

JWA had often served as acting president when Henry was traveling, and he had been running the company during Henry's illness, so he was prepared for the responsibility. He had never wanted to be president himself, but now that it was inevitable, it would be a nice way to end the career he had spent in the service of a single company.

The big job would be to train the young man who stood in front of him. James had been modest enough to turn down a salary when he started to work. Now he would be paid; in five days the directors would promote him to first vice president, directly under JWA, at a generous $25,000 a year. He had a lot to learn, but his trust wouldn't expire for another seven years; Henry Hyde had been even younger when he started the Equitable.

A few rows farther back, but still well toward the front of the church, Gage Tarbell, the Equitable's third vice president and head of sales, was seated with his fellow directors. Now forty-three, Tarbell had arrived from upstate New York via the Midwest in 1893, and he was the liaison with the thousands of agents in the field. No one used the Equitable's private railroad car more; he was on the road visiting agencies four months out of twelve.[15] When he bounced off the train and into action, with his thick, seal-brown center-parted hair, eyes crinkling behind his rimless glasses, and a big smile under an enormous mustache, he gleamed like Teddy Roosevelt. Tarbell loved managing the agents, and he was born to sell, but he was pushy. Three years after he came to New York, Henry pulled him up short in a scorching seventeen-page handwritten letter. He wrote, "You have at times a most disagreeable, overbearing, imperious manner which makes people dislike you." When Tarbell defended himself, Henry shot back, "You came from Chicago about three years ago. I organized the Equitable about the time you were born."[16] Tarbell would never become an honorary Hyde family member like James Alexander, but he would be promoted to second vice president at next week's board meeting. At one time, Henry had led Tarbell to believe that he would be made first vice president, perhaps in tandem with James, and Tarbell was disgruntled by the change in plans.

Funerals, like concerts, have a way of loosening the mind so it ambles away from the matters at hand, and it would not have been surprising if Tarbell reflected on business at the service for his boss. But by the time the sixteen members of the choir sang "Lead Kindly Light," and the minister spoke the benediction, most of the congregation recalled why they were assembled. Henry Hyde had been more powerful than most, but he was mortal like the rest of them.

At eleven-thirty in the morning on May 5, 1899, in a sober and sorrowful mood, James and his mother and sister, James W. Alexander, Gage Tarbell, and a few hundred select mourners proceeded in their carriages down Fifth Avenue to Grand Central Terminal, to accompany Henry's coffin on a special train of four cars. Their destination was society's graveyard, Woodlawn Cemetery, in the still-countrified Bronx, where the mausoleums looked like miniatures of the mansions that housed New York's prominent families. There, Henry was buried next to his first son, who would have been twenty-eight if he had lived to attend his father's funeral.

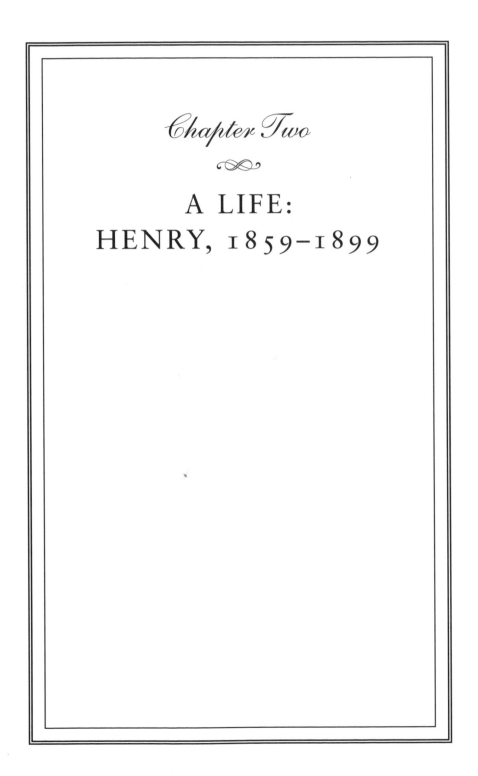

Chapter Two

A LIFE:
HENRY, 1859–1899

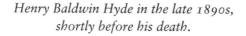

Henry Baldwin Hyde in the late 1890s,
shortly before his death.

Henry Hyde's famous eagle glance softened in his last years, but he never lost the awe-inspiring stature that had enabled him to raise $100,000 from near-strangers to start the Equitable when he was twenty-five. *(Courtesy AXA Financial Archives)*

*I*n 1859, Henry Hyde had rented an office for the incipient Equitable, but four people crowded the space. To make his presentation to prospective investors, he borrowed a boardroom and with the help of his patron, the Reverend James Waddell Alexander of the Fifth Avenue Presbyterian Church, assembled some of most established men in New York. Henry may have been impressed, but he was uncowed and refreshingly attractive. His dark hair was luxuriant and wavy, his sideburns were lavish, and his deep-set eyes flashed. He stood straight, thrust his cleft chin forward, tucked a thumb in his vest pocket, and began to talk. Because of the minister's urging, men with names like Auchincloss, Biddle, Low, and Lord listened carefully. The Reverend Alexander, whose son James Alexander would soon come to work at the Equitable, had met Henry nearly ten years earlier when Henry, age sixteen, arrived in the city from upstate New York. Henry's first job was at a dry goods merchant, but he soon moved to the Mutual Life Insurance Company, where his father, Henry Hazen Hyde, was the top agent for the Boston area. The senior Henry Hyde was deeply religious, and his son looked for and found a church, Fifth Avenue Presbyterian, where he attended services and taught Sunday School. By the time he approached the Reverend Alexander to ask his advice about starting his own insurance company, the minister had come to admire the young man's ability and confidence. Thanks to the Reverend Alexander, seventeen of the original fifty-two Equitable directors would be members of the Fifth Avenue Presbyterian Church.

Until the winter of 1859, Henry had been the cashier at the Mutual. But when he approached his boss, president Frederick S. Winston, and suggested that, together, they open a new business to sell policies with a greater value than the Mutual's current cap, Mr. Winston fired him. Henry rented an empty room in the Mutual's building, borrowed furniture, and bought a box of cigars to create an illusion of prosperity, or at least of hospitality. Before a week had passed, his sign was attached to the front of the building, although his office was squashed in the back. The sign read EQUITABLE LIFE ASSURANCE SOCIETY, and it hung directly above the smaller Mutual sign, like a cocked eyebrow.

President Winston was annoyed, but not worried: Henry might have an office, but Winston doubted that he could get a charter. Since 1853, the New York legislature had required that any new life insurance company raise $100,000 in paid capital stock to back up policyholders' claims. Many of the events that threatened to destroy the Equitable in the disastrous year of 1905 can be traced back to that requirement, which set the company apart from the other major insurers who were purely "mutuals."

Mutual life insurance companies were solely owned by their policyholders, who shared in a portion of the profits. The most important companies had been established prior to the 1853 regulations, so they did not have to raise capital. But for Henry to start the Equitable, he would have to create another layer of interested parties, the investors, to whom he would have to issue shares. He could not give them part ownership of the company, or a graduated portion of the profits, like a publicly held company. Instead, he would offer shareholders two incentives: interest on their investment, and a place on the board. The interest was modest: 7 percent per annum, fixed to the amount of the initial investment, so an investor who put in $10,000 would receive $700 a year, no matter how successful the company became. As for membership on the board, in the early days, there was neither prestige nor power attached to association with Henry's new company. It would be many years before a directorship would be a source of financial clout.

As the Equitable grew, so did the pot of money held in reserve to cover claims, a fund that was available for long-term capital investment. Board members who served on the executive and finance committees determined how the money was apportioned, and the more shares a director held, the more votes he controlled. Forty years after

Henry founded the Equitable, when the reserve amounted to nearly $400 million, it had become an irresistible resource for Wall Street and industry, and the majority shareholder could virtually dictate how the money was invested.

The 1905 fight for control, the scandal, the investigation, and the abrupt reversal of James Hyde's fortunes were rooted in the hybrid mutual/stock structure, because Henry's stock allowed him to pass the deciding votes along to his son. If the Equitable had been a pure mutual, James would not have been tied to his father's company, or become a target for the titans and their bankers.

In 1859, that scenario was far from Henry's mind: he was twenty-five years old, he had limited contacts, he needed to find investors, and the rewards he could offer were meager. Yet the nature of the business mitigated in his favor. The idea that life insurance was a trust with an elevated social purpose was deeply ingrained in the culture, and would remain so for the next century. On the Equitable's twenty-fifth anniversary, the worldly Chauncey Depew, one of the most famous after-dinner speakers of the age, declaimed, apparently without irony, that the founding of the company was the third most important event in the history of the world. Even in 1905, when scandals rocked the industry, former U.S. president Grover Cleveland declared, "Life insurance has to do with the most sacred things that stir the human affections . . . its management involves a higher duty and more constant devotion than we associate with a mere business enterprise."[1] As late as the 1960s, the Equitable historian, Carlyle R. Buley, would write that life insurance is "a materialization of the doctrine of duty . . . an instrument of the ethical code practiced by civilized man . . . the most reliable system of economic security which has yet been devised."[2]

The philosophy that, as the historian Alan Trachtenberg explained, "a corporate charter was a privilege to be granted only by a special act of a state legislature, and then for purposes clearly in the public interest," fit life insurance, and insurers were among the first to receive state charters.[3]

Henry sold the Equitable's stock, met the filing deadline, and after five months, he reported insurance in force of $1,144,000.[4] The Reverend Alexander did not have the opportunity to buy insurance from the new company; he died four days after the Equitable received its charter.

Henry drove the business, but Reverend Alexander's brother, William, former speaker of the New Jersey Senate, and a respected elder statesman, had the title of president until he died in 1874: at twenty-five, Henry had seemed too young to inspire the average policyholder's confidence. Henry was soon joined by two of the Reverend's three sons; another William Alexander joined the company in 1860 and worked there for sixty-eight years: He was secretary from 1880 to 1937, and became the company historian. James W. Alexander graduated from Princeton and from law school, and in 1866 he, too, came to work for the Equitable.

Henry was original as well as energetic. The Equitable was the first large insurance company to train its agents, and Henry hounded them with personal letters, even when he had thousands of men and women working for him. To be sure he saw them all personally, he convened what may have been the first sales conference. Even the perceived will of the Almighty did not deter him. He fought the prejudice that taking out life insurance was a sign that the purchaser did not trust in God's beneficence, hiring the famous preacher, the Reverend Henry Ward Beecher, to write columns for his magazine, *Our Mutual Friend*. Its slogan warned, "The Tale of Life Is Not to Be Continued. Each Day We Turn a Leaf; Tomorrow May Bring the End."[5]

One of Beecher's essays, "Truth in a Nutshell," opened with an engraving of the Equitable Building and a line instructing, "Read this carefully, and hand it to your wife." Beecher described what might follow the death of a family man: "The income would cease; the children must be withdrawn from school; the mother and elder children must resort to every expedient merely to sustain the family . . . [but] if a man has insured a sum of five or ten thousand dollars upon his life, this anxiety and foreboding is removed."

Calling life insurance "a moral duty," Beecher addressed the issue, "Can a Christian man rightfully seek such assurance?" The question, he wrote, should be "Can a Christian man justify himself in neglecting such a duty?" In his last sentence, the Reverend Beecher revealed, "We have insured our own life in the Equitable Life Assurance Society of New York. We should select it again if we were to choose again."[6]

Henry Hyde had been in business for five years, and was a successful thirty-year-old bachelor, when he first saw Annie Fitch. He was seated behind her at the theater, and during the play he gazed at her back and profile and was distracted by her beauty. Her features were regular, her eyes were bright, and her skin was lovely and fair. As she turned toward her companions he saw that her plump bosom rose above a tiny waist. After the play, he discreetly followed her home and set out to discover who she was. Annie lived with her upper-middle-class parents, Mr. and Mrs. Simeon Fitch, in a charming limestone house at 6 East Thirty-sixth Street; they had enough common acquaintances that Henry soon found someone to introduce them, after which he courted her the way he did everything— with determination and contagious enthusiasm. They were married on March 29, 1864, and their first baby, a girl named Annie, was born less than a year later. She died before she took her first steps, but three more children followed.

Henry worked compulsively and traveled extensively, but like many of the toughest men of the period, he was devoted to his family. In an extreme version of the custom followed by a wealthy late-nineteenth-century paterfamilias, he ran the households. He saw to the decorations in New York and Bay Shore, down to the wallpaper and the repairs. He hired the baby nurse and chose the children's toys, and he ordered the provisions—every day one loaf of fresh bread was delivered to Fortieth Street, along with flowers, fresh milk, butter, and vegetables from The Oaks in Bay Shore, and nine lemons a week from the grocer.[8] The Oaks occupied even more of his attention. The house, designed by the architect Calvert Vaux—who, with Frederick Law Olmstead, designed Central Park—was the center of a working farm. Henry sold his chickens and produce to the Café Savarin and the Lawyers' Club, both of which he had established in the Equitable Building.

The Hydes lived a conservative Victorian life, and Henry established a strict regime. At seven each morning, the barber arrived to shave him, and at exactly twenty past seven, Henry held prayers for the family and servants. In the evenings, he was usually at home for dinner. When he was invited to join the Lotos Club in 1896, he declined, explaining, "I now belong to the Union Club and the Union League Club, but I so rarely go out of an evening that I do not go into them once a year, and when I do go the man who sits at the door looks upon me with suspicion and rushes into the office to find out if I am a member, which is very disagreeable."[9]

Annie Hyde had one pleasure that was hers alone; she drew well in crayons and made engravings, but very little distinguished her from other women of her class. Much of her time was spent in the usual rituals, chief of which was paying calls. In 1899, the *Social Register* published its first Visiting Index, which organized New York by neighborhoods, noting the day for "at homes" when ladies received visitors or their visiting cards. Annie's "at home" was Wednesday; by coincidence, that was when *Town Topics* came out, which gave the ladies something extra to talk about.

Everyone read the weekly gossip sheet with a circulation of 150,000. *Town Topics'* owner, and the author of many of its articles, Col. William D'Alton Mann, reported on anything that might be of interest to its readers—clothes, parties, travel, friendships, feuds, and romances. Some of his stories were true, many were fabricated, and others were blatantly scandalous. But when Henry and Annie were soiled by gossip, Colonel Mann was not the culprit; the editor of an insurance magazine published the accusation in 1876 that

> Henry Hyde . . . has found time . . . to provide for the widow and orphans . . . life tenants of a fine dairy farm in Orange County, New York, purchased by Mr. Hyde for the purpose, and where Mr. Hyde retires, when wearied with the cares of business, to rest himself in the bosom of his family No. 2 . . . She was once the wife of a policyholder in the Equitable; the policy lapsed, and he died; but her piteous pleadings so affected the tender heart of Mr. Hyde, that he purchased the farm aforesaid, installed her as mistress, and on its income she is enabled to live with comfort, educate her children, and fit them to become worthy representatives of their putative father,

never forgetting to instill in their minds the beneficence of life insurance. [10]

There was no evidence that the allegation had any basis in fact, but the story spread. Annie was humiliated, and Henry instituted a court action for libel. After a couple of unpleasant, embarrassing months, the publisher backed off, admitting, "while the remarks are true they do not apply to Mr. Hyde, but to another man." [11]

The words most commonly used to describe Henry were "rugged," "indomitable," and "hard-driving," and he was known to have a ferocious temper; but he also suffered long, debilitating spells of "neurasthenia," the contemporary catchall term that covered depression, anxiety, and neurosis. Neurasthenia was a common complaint among nineteenth-century leaders of finance and industry. Like Henry, many of them were born in the 1830s, hit their stride around the Civil War, and created empires within a couple of decades. The journeys that brought them from little country towns to mansions in New York and castles in Europe took a toll. No one cowed them, but they were frightened by the fragility of their own bodies. Often, they were hypochondriacs, or were sick so frequently that even when they felt well, they were anticipating the next illness.

Henry's neurasthenia was probably caused by a combination of pressure and genetics. His sister, Lucy B. Hyde, was institutionalized in Bloomingdale's Insane Asylum; Henry was awarded a citation for guardianship of an insane person and managed the $35,000 trust fund their father had set aside for her. In 1875, Henry was told that she was temporarily improved, and making an effort to keep her hysteria in check, but that she was almost certain to suffer a relapse. The evidence that Henry had episodes of instability includes a 1905 newspaper report that he had "supported" a private clinic on Long Island that specialized in "rest cures," and that he and James had both stayed there. [12]

When Henry was depleted and depressed, he went away, sometimes for long periods. The first such trip, which lasted for months in 1870, was an outdoorsman's expedition to the American West to recover from the rigors of building 120 Broadway. Eight years later, he bolted again, this time for a year. He left his growing business, his wife, and their three small children, and traveled around the world with a secretary, the housekeeper's son. His letters, written in large, scrawling, but legible handwriting, reflected the way his moods bounced around; some were cheerful travelogues, others were melancholy threnodies. For some months in the late fall and early winter of 1878, the correspondence between him and Annie was anguished. From Egypt, he wrote,

> After the trouble we have been through, and I don't see how we could have avoided it after the first cause, any man that loved his wife as I love you must have suffered deeply down into the bottom of his heart, and of course you have for the first time in your life found out what trouble was—*now it is over forever* . . . it seemed as if I should die, if I was in future to be expecting from you what I was never to receive, and that was your first affection. and the only was [sic] was to cut loose and go away some where and not expect any thing from any body [*sic*]." . . . [I am] "recovered from all my past difficulties, and hope to return home a new man" . . . "Now, dear Ma, be brave Come to Europe . . . we will begin new lives together. . . . I have neglected you in the past and you shall have my first love and devotion in future. . . . I shall be changed and improved by this foreign travel.[13]

The "first cause" could have been the foul rumor about his "second family," his obsessive work schedule, or the difficulty for Annie of living with a self-absorbed autocrat who swung between manic energy, depression, and mild paranoia. He was almost certainly exaggerating when he wrote in 1897, "I have kept a record of the men who have treated me badly during my life and it amounts to 47,983, so you see I am used to it,"[14] but the remark conveyed a fear that he was surrounded by people he could not trust.

Even letters to his young children were flyspecked with complaints about sleeplessness and "dyspepsia," which referred to intestinal disorders. From Cairo, on Christmas morning, 1878, he wrote Henry, Mary, and James that he awoke alone, and "couldn't run into your room and say Merry Christmas [so] I wished myself Merry Christmas, and shook hands with myself, and did the best I could."

His dark moods seemed minor when compared with the depression that settled over the house two years later, after little Henry died. The next summer, reluctant to leave their two surviving children behind, Henry and Annie went to Europe and took James and Mary with them. James saw Paris for the first time when he was only five.

Henry never fully recovered from his grief, which was the underpinning of his obsession with his second son, whom he took over, molding him into a replacement child. Equitable secretary William Alexander wrote, "The father was broken-hearted and did not recover from the blow for a long time. He had expected to bring the boy [Henry] up to take his place at the head of the Equitable . . . [instead] Mr. Hyde transferred his hopes and affection to the younger, James Hazen Hyde, with the result that the boy was pampered and indulged. He was at the same time brought up with the idea that he would ultimately succeed his father as the Equitable's head." Henry crowded Annie out as a parent; she may have resented being a margin note to the intimacy between father and son, or she may have stepped aside willingly. Not every mother is maternal, and not every parent and child are well suited. Whatever the reason, she and James did not develop a bond that would carry them through the many years after Henry's death, when she was James's only surviving parent, and nearly his only relative.

James's older sister, Mary, was almost thirteen in September 1880 when little Henry died, still childish enough to hope that she might become first in her father's affections. But it soon became clear that even though James was only four years old, Henry would never be as interested in a daughter as he was in his son. Perhaps that influenced her decision to marry when she was seventeen. Henry and Annie told her she was too young, but she was determined, and the man she chose, Sidney Dillon Ripley, was suitable. He was socially prominent, good-looking, blond, indolent in a sporting way, and rich; his grandfather, Sidney Dillon, was president of the Union

Pacific Railroad. The Ripleys lived near the Hydes on Long Island, and as a favor to Sidney's parents Henry had hired Sidney to assist the manager of the Lawyers' Club at 120 Broadway.

It was Henry, not Annie, who planned their daughter's wedding, held at The Oaks at noon on October 14, 1885. A special five-car train transported more than four hundred guests, including the president of Mexico, Señor Porfirio Diaz; two former New York governors; U.S. senators; socialites; and financiers. The local station was too small to accommodate the crowd, so Henry had a temporary station built, and arranged for fifty stages and carriages to bring guests to the house.

The great hall was set up for a ceremony performed by two Episcopal priests, under a bower of autumn leaves, flanked by panels of red, white, and yellow roses. Henry escorted his daughter down the oak staircase in her white satin dress with a tulle veil. For a large society wedding, there were relatively few attendants: four bridesmaids, wearing pearl-studded moiré; four ushers; and a best man. Mary and Sidney received their guests for an hour, then left for their honeymoon, and the reception continued. The weather was fine, but to be sure a storm or cold snap didn't spoil the day, Henry had the broad verandas enclosed in glass so the entire first floor could be set with tables for the luncheon, catered by Delmonico's.[15]

An uncle for whom Sidney was named bought the young couple their first house, at 38 West Fifty-third Street. Henry proposed tiger skins for the parlor floor, ordered Royal Berlin china from Germany, and assembled antique furnishings, some provided by agents who had been scouring sources in Boston and Philadelphia for him for years. Sidney was consulted, Mary was expected to agree, and her father paid the bills.

Henry was generous, but he was also critical. After the wedding, he wrote a cousin that Mary, who was feeling pleased with herself, "has not yet found out that her doll is stuffed with sawdust. It will come in time." The "doll" may have been Sidney, whom Henry didn't like. Nevertheless, he appointed him cashier of the Equitable, and, along with Sidney's grandfather, secured the $50,000 bond.[16] A place on the board came with the position, but Sidney was only mildly interested in working. He foxhunted with the Meadow Brook Hunt near their estate, The Crossways, on Long Island; he bred Brown Swiss cattle; indulged his new passion, the automobile; and studied mushrooms and other fungi with the New York Mycological Society.[17] When his grandfather died in 1892, leaving a $6 million estate, he received an annual income of $50,000, the equivalent of $1 million in 2002 dollars, and bought a handsome neo-Georgian town-house at 16 East Seventy-ninth Street, where he and Mary brought up four children.

The guest list at Mary and Sidney's wedding was an indication of the Equitable's standing in the mid-1880s. The company had drawn up alongside New York Life and the Mutual, as Henry expanded fearlessly, traveling everywhere, opening offices in places he might never see again. With its seventy-seven foreign offices, the Equitable was the first truly international life insurance company. He led the industry in changing practices, simplifying policy contracts, replacing baffling legal language, and making policies indisputable after three years. He was famous for paying a $40,000 claim to the heirs of a man who bought more than $250,000 of life insurance from different companies. That claim was mentioned decades later in most of Henry's obituaries.

The expansion of the late 1880s halted abruptly in 1893, when the United States Treasury went off the gold standard, foreign investors withdrew their gold from U.S. reserves, and the economy plummeted. By 1894, some five hundred banks, more than fifteen thousand businesses, and nearly a third of the railroads had failed.[18] Instead of retrenching, Henry doubled agents' bonuses[19] so his sales force would be in place to take advantage of the recovery when it came.

The depression rolled on, stronger businesses absorbed weaker ones, and bankers and railroad men scurried to finance acquisitions. They turned to the big insurance companies, with portfolios worth hundreds of millions of dollars, to buy their bonds. The insurers and Wall Street strengthened their connections, and Henry augmented his board. George J. Gould, who had become president of Western Union and the Missouri Pacific Railroad when his father died, was elected a director in 1893. John Jacob Astor IV, whose personal fortune approached $100 million, joined in 1898; and Alexander Cassatt, president of the Pennsylvania, in 1899. Among the first directors Henry added were such prominent international bankers as August Belmont, who came on in 1892, and the German-born Jacob Schiff of Kuhn, Loeb, who joined in 1893, and, as an Equitable director, sold the company bonds that Kuhn, Loeb was underwriting.

Henry had cultivated an image for the Equitable that made it seem as ethical as a church. But true propriety eluded him. The financial writer Michael Lewis asked rhetorically in a *New York Times Magazine* article in 2002, "Is it possible that scandal is somehow an essential ingredient in capitalism? That a healthy free-market economy must tempt a certain number of people to behave corruptly, and that a certain number of these will do so. . . . After all, a market economy is premised on a system of incentives designed to encourage an ignoble human trait: self-interest."

Henry's temptations were exacerbated by the hybrid stock/mutual structure. As a young man earning $1,500 a year, he often paid business expenses out of his own pocket, and did not always bother to reimburse himself. Yet, when the Equitable surpassed every other life insurer, he had no more share in its growth than any other stockholder. To balance what seemed like an inequity, an informal "consensus [evolved] that the Hydes should be permitted to use some of the company's money as their own,"[20] and Henry did; he borrowed at will, repaid casually, mixed personal and corporate affairs, and failed to recognize that, if he died, no one else would have the dexterity to keep the act going.

In the 1890s, despite the dismal economy, Henry spent more time away from the office. He had a new obsession: the Jekyll Island Club in Georgia, founded in 1888 and nicknamed "the millionaires club" because its members included J. P. Morgan, James J. Hill, William Rockefeller, Joseph Pulitzer, Pierre Lorillard, William K. Vanderbilt, and Marshall Field. One historian called it "the most elite and inaccessible social club in the United States,"[21] but the atmosphere was simple by comparison to that in other resorts. To maintain its rustic atmosphere, the club did not install electricity until 1903; dinner featured game shot by tycoons on holiday; and the roads were paved with crushed seashells. (One year, before Henry sent his horses down to Georgia, he checked to find out if his coachman would look too fancy if he wore livery.[22]) Henry's health had been damaged by overwork, and he was attracted to the salubrious climate during the brief winter season—when he became Jekyll's greatest booster, he arranged to have a temperature report wired to New York three times a week and published in the *Herald*.[23]

Members invested in one another's deals, gleaned information early, and developed the kind of trust that evolves between gentlemen who shoot and fish together. But it wasn't only health or business that tied Henry to the island; it was also his penchant for building. He had finished erecting Equitable buildings, and he craved another project. In 1892, he stacked the board with his friends and earned the title the "Czar of Jekyll Island." He advanced his own money to remodel the clubhouse and build a stable with stalls to be leased to the members. In 1896, he oversaw and helped finance Jekyll's distinctive "apartment house," the Sans Souci, where he and a few other members, including William Rockefeller, had flats. When J. P. Morgan bought an apartment in Sans Souci, he asked Henry to furnish it, and he duplicated his own decorations, "down to the chair coverings and the last print on the wall."[24] Annie Hyde was less enthusiastic; she rarely went down to Jekyll, and when she did, she complained "continually" about the smell from the club's gas lamps.

Henry barraged the manager with letters about the right way to hang pictures, the cost per head of feeding the servants, and how much coffee each of them should be allotted. Even when he was in precarious health in his last season, 1898, he barely "managed to resist trying to run every activity on the island."[25]

Despite Henry's prolonged absences, the Equitable survived the depression and thrived. By 1898, when James graduated from Harvard, the company had paid $307 million to beneficiaries, had more than $300 million in reserve, and had some three hundred thousand policyholders. Henry knew every catch and quirk of the insurance business, had invented some of them himself, and could leave for weeks or even months at a time and be confident that his business would run smoothly. He taught his son none of this.

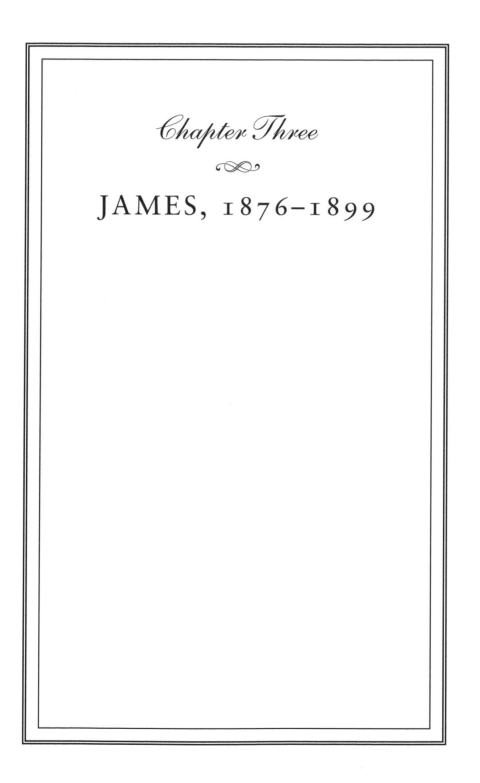

Chapter Three

JAMES, 1876–1899

James Hyde's Harvard Graduation Picture, 1898.

Shortly before James graduated from Harvard, he wrote his father, "I am a hot house flower, edition de luxe, limited on fine paper, morocco binding, and I fear you never can make anything else out of me." It was not a promising start for a young man destined to take over a life insurance company. *(Courtesy Lorna Hyde Graev)*

*J*ames's sister, Mary, was married when James was only nine, and he became the only child at home, the object of Henry's doting, hovering attention, and his generosity. The little boy's first financial connection with the Equitable was an allowance, paid when he was eleven by the company's cashier.[1] He received three dollars a week, stacked the way he liked it: a silver dollar at the bottom; next, the slightly smaller fifty-cent pieces and finally, a little tower of four quarters. When he collected stamps, Equitable agents all over the globe helped with his hobby. He became interested in toy soldiers, so his father had sets shipped from Paris and Hamburg. Henry subscribed to children's magazines from England, chose the books James read, and the day on which he read them, which was Sunday.[2] When he was old enough to go to dancing class with girls his age, Henry hired a private ballroom dancing master to teach him the steps and the proper etiquette.

The small, elite Cutlers School James attended adjusted his schedule so he could skip classes to spend long weekends at Bay Shore, but he did not fall behind; Henry hired tutors in general studies, drawing, French, and German. In the summer of 1894, he engaged the professor in charge of the Harvard Physical Training Department to spend August and September at The Oaks, coaching James to improve his strength and coordination before he went to college.[3]

When James entered Harvard, it was the first time he had lived away from home, but Henry wrote or telegraphed nearly every day. He missed his favorite child so badly that when he left James in Cambridge, he was sick with grief and took to his bed. "I don't expect ever to get used to being away from you or suffering when you go away from me," he wrote.[4] James understood. In his second year, he wrote his parents a letter signed, "your sad, solitary, silent son."[5] That was more than a momentary low point. A professor, the philosopher George Santayana, said he was "rich and isolated." His classmates saw him more superficially; one observed that he possessed "a self-confidence surpassing anything . . . even in the Harvard undergraduate world."[6]

Henry, who had not gone to college, was eager to participate in James's Harvard life, to the extent of decorating his lodgings. He dispatched an Equitable engineer to electrify the rooms, another to hang hooks in the bathroom, and sent James a pair of curtains, instructing him to have shot put in the hems so they would hang properly.

Equitable director George Gould gave James passes for free Western Union services; and in the fall of his freshman year, Henry prevailed on Chauncey Depew to lend James his private railroad car to take a group of friends to the Harvard-Yale football game in Springfield, Massachusetts. Henry even arranged what the boys would eat. On Saturday evening, October 26, 1894, he wrote James,

> I thought about you as soon as I woke up this morning "parlor car" "cold dinner" "Cold Supper" "cold day," and felt sure you would be sick as a result. So I called on Chauncey, and he was very nice about it and said you could have his car. I don't think you will have to pay any fares but don't say so. You better have $100 in your pocket any way [sic] but put away so it can't be stolen and don't take your gold watch . . . This is different than if you hired a private car—this might be "<u>too</u>" tony, but . . . better let every one know he's given you—Buy a big bottle of Powell Estra, bath your feet night and morning and wash your self [sic] a little with it and you will like it. I will make up your menu for dinner and supper and send it to you. How many boys do you expect to go, and who? . . . A buffet car would be better than a parlor car as you could have a hot cup of tea—I could pick out an extra fine piece of beef and leg of mutton and have them roasted and kept nearly a week . . . and Savarin bread and Darlington Butter. . . . However we will see after I have had a talk with the car men—I will take good care of you any where [sic]. . . .
>
> I think of you always, your affectionate father. H. B. Hyde[7]

Henry made sure James had a large allowance and a $5,000 line of credit at a Cambridge bank, and when James ran out of money, he wired home for more; in one letter he referred to his financial condition as "dull, stupid poverty."[8] He bought three horses for $850, and did not have enough in his account to pay for them, so he borrowed $250 from James Alexander to cover the shortfall because Henry and Annie were in Europe.[9] He also began to collect rare books, which required frequent infusions of capital. In his senior year he was asked to fill out a form that asked about the range of his college expenses. Harvard's categories started with "(a) under $500," with a maximum of "(d) above $1000." James wrote "d" for his freshman year, "e" for his sophomore, "f" for his junior, and "g" for his senior year. It was a carelessly arrogant gesture, and along with such visible symbols of wealth as the jogging cart, sleigh, and horses Henry sent to Cambridge, it fed the outrageous myths that his allowance was $25,000 a year, and that he paid a barber ten dollars a day to shave him.

When journalists later tried to piece together the kind of man James had been in college, some of them came up with the theory that he had arrived a "hayseed" and left a dandy. An inventive reporter claimed that he was so unsophisticated his classmates called him "Caleb," a country boy's name. The rumor was based on the misinterpretation of a family nickname Henry had bestowed on him, after favorite uncle, Caleb J. Camp; it was unclear whether James reminded him of the older Caleb, or Henry simply wanted to honor his uncle. The name stuck; even when James was an old man, his sister Mary's children and grandchildren called him "Uncle Caleb."

Henry spoiled James, but he also fussed, particularly about his health. His letters were filled with admonitions about ways to avoid falling ill. He warned James that if he met a friend on the street when the weather was cold and windy, he should not linger to talk, so he would not get a sore throat. When James went to a football game, Henry wrote to remind him to wear a scarf and not to talk too much because the wind might blow down his throat. His concern was extreme, but not irrational. Henry and his sister, Lucy, were the only survivors of four siblings, his mother had died when he was twelve, and he and Annie lost the two children they named after themselves.

Even in the late nineteenth century, one child in three failed to reach the age of twenty-one.

Wealth was no protection against childhood death. One of E. H. Harriman's sons, Harry, succumbed to diphtheria at age four. Henry Clay Frick lost two children—his beloved daughter, Martha, who was five at her death, and a boy who died shortly after he was born. Many years later, Frick bought a George Romney portrait that looked the way Martha might have if she had lived to be a young woman; it hung in his bedroom, and he gazed at it when he lay dying. Leland Stanford, the Western Railroad magnate, was in Florence, Italy, with his wife and their only son, Leland Jr., when the fifteen-year-old boy fell ill and died of typhoid fever. The grieving parents founded Stanford University to honor his memory.

J. P. Morgan's brother was eleven when he died of an infection in his hip socket; and Morgan's father, Junius, worried about health to the extent of writing Morgan when he was at school in Europe, "You are altogether too rapid in disposing of your meals . . . and then there is the great irregularity in the matter I so often spoke to you of when in New York. You may depend upon it you can have no health if you go on in this way. I would urge of you to correct it at once—[if you do not] . . . dyspepsia with all attendant evils is sure to be upon you."[10] When James went to Harvard, Henry was reminded of his own older brother's death at Yale, a generation earlier.

James may have been coddled, but he took his studies seriously. His favorite course was French literature, and he took French for four years, English and German for three, history twice, as well as Italian, economics, government, and philosophy. He hired three tutors at a time to help him with his work. The French club, the Cercle Français, aroused his interest and then an overriding enthusiasm, and he was elected president in his junior and senior years. When the club gave its annual French plays, James asked his father's secretary, William McIntyre, to press newspapers in New York and Boston to cover the performances. In his senior year, he used money from his trust fund to pay for a series of lectures by Réné Doumic, an important French author, and held a series of dinners for him. His final gesture as an undergraduate was to establish a French-American exchange of professors; the $30,000 endowment was a gift from Henry, but the idea and organization were James's, and earned him his first Légion d'Honneur in 1900.

The Cercle Français members included students from Radcliffe, where James met the kind of intelligent women he would seek out all his life. He also attended Boston cotillions and New York debutante parties, but the only woman he regularly mentioned in letters to his father was Grace Norton, the older, bluestocking sister of the distinguished Harvard art history professor and cofounder of *The Nation,* Charles Eliot Norton. Other men his age courted suitable girls, or ran wild, or both, but James was inexperienced and idealistic. He was twenty-two when he wrote Henry that when he watched the harvest moon from the piazza at The Oaks, "It made me feel as sentimental as a sick cow and I would have very much liked to have played Romeo to some fair Juliet."[11]

When James filled out the same Harvard form that inquired about his spending money, he left a blank in response to "Have you pursued any remunerative occupation during your summer vacations?" but when asked if he had "a plan for work after . . . college," he wrote, "Intend to enter Equitable Life Assurance Society." His intentions and affinities were at war, and as graduation approached, he began to hint more insistently that he was not the man his father wanted him to be. Only eighteen months before Henry died, James wrote him, in a passionate jumble of metaphors, mostly drawn from his book-collecting hobby, "I am a hot house flower, edition de luxe, limited on fine paper, morocco binding, and I fear you never can make anything else out of me."[12] Yet he was pliant and ambivalent. He did not want to give up the power his father was handing him; he just hoped to postpone the time when he would have to do the job. He asked his father to allow him to stay in Cambridge to take a graduate degree in French, but Henry was ready for him to come home. "I could not stand another year," he wrote.[13]

Henry had always made it clear that a hothouse was not his son's ultimate destination. In 1896, he wrote, "I want you to regard it as your greatest duty in life to take care of the Equitable and it may require an iron man and a strong hand and a fighter all the way through. I know I can depend on you, with your mind and heart in the work you will take your place by, as it were, divine right. I know what you are made of."[14]

James was elected a director of the Equitable in his sophomore year, and if he ever had a momentary doubt about his place in the corporate constellation, he could go to the lobby of the Boston office and look at the oval bronze medallion of himself, nearly two feet high. Henry commissioned it in multiples from the famous sculptor, John Quincy Adams Ward,[oo] who made *Indian Hunter,* the first sculpture for Central Park, and the majestic statue of President James Garfield in Washington, D.C. In the medallion, James is shown in profile, looking handsome and boyish, with bow tie and wing collar, his wavy short hair brushed back from a center part. Henry sent copies of the medallions to be installed in prominent locations in other Equitable offices.

James had no regularized apprenticeship, but he believed that proximity to the chief executive was a form of training. As he explained,

> I had always been brought up to consider my legitimate life work to succeed my father in the Equitable, and my education from my earliest youth, both at home and abroad, had tended in that direction. I had traveled with my father all over Europe for a good many years, had translated much French and German business for him, and have been present at many important conferences for the transaction of business, had kept, when it was possible, an elementary run of his correspondence, and have translated for many of the people whom he had seen.
>
> Then I have been all over this country previous to my going into the business with my father. . . . He had instilled in me his theories about the business of life insurance. . . . A year or more before graduating from college . . . I became a director of the Society and attended its annual meetings. . . . I had lived in what might be called a life insurance atmosphere from my earliest youth.[15]

In the "life insurance atmosphere," Henry impressed on James "the sacredness of the trust" and the concept that the Equitable had a soul, which would be his "solemn duty" to protect. Yet even in 1898, when Henry was failing, his letters to his son rarely mentioned business; they were filled with reports on the $50,000 stable he was building for him at 216 West Fifty-eighth Street, to make up for refusing to allow him to stay on at Harvard. Henry engaged the Equitable's superintendent of construction to oversee the stable project, ordered an elevator to be installed, had a monogram designed to go over the door, and proposed that the stable's colors match the ones he was using to redecorate James's rooms at home.

Henry was desperate to have his son back. He told James, "I want to see you in the Equitable with all your interests guarded and protected while I am alive and can attend to you." He wrote, "My thoughts continually wander to you and I cannot express the love that I have for you." Recognizing that he was mortally ill, he added, "I cannot go on much longer this way."[16] In a melancholy letter, he had remarked that "the way of the World" was "to live alone in the end," but he was not planning to die alone.

When James came back to New York in June, and moved into his newly refurbished apartment in the family brownstones, he still did not go to work. Henry allowed him to enjoy a languid summer at The Oaks, riding, traveling to parties, and occupying himself with incidental details of landscaping; but at last, in November, James finally went downtown to the Equitable office. He was isolated from the first; far above anyone else his age in rank, he lagged behind every other officer in experience, and he was not certain he wanted to be there at all. Perhaps he felt guilty about his ambivalence when Henry wrote, "I love you better than anyone in the world—more than everybody and everything combined."[17]

James's circumstances followed ancient patterns: he was the son of an old king who would not relinquish his power soon enough; he was the prince who would rather support the arts than run a kingdom; he was surrounded by advisers who tried to control an underage heir; and he was oppressed by a parent's strangling love. Uneasy, unready, and alone, he looked for a place to make his mark. Wisely, he chose finance, the field in which there was the most room for growth and originality. He began well, but when he lost his bearings, he did what spoiled and frightened princelings often do: he played when it was most important to work.

Chapter Four

THE FIRST MENTOR: JAMES ALEXANDER

James Waddell Alexander,
president of the Equitable, 1899–1905.

James Alexander had worked at the Equitable nearly all his life when Henry Hyde chose him as his son's trustee. Henry's intention was that Alexander would be the company president until James turned thirty. At first, he seemed to be an unimpeachable mentor, but he later became an implacable enemy. *(Courtesy AXA Financial Archives)*

*I*n November 1898, Henry's visits to 120 Broadway were becoming rarer, but some days he was strong enough to spend time in his full-story-high office on the third floor, warmed by the fire in his fireplace. There were now twelve elevators, and Mr. Hyde had his own private car, in which he rode to have lunch in his private dining room. The best view was in his hideaway under the mansard roof, which the Mutual Life Insurance Company's magazine had enviously and unfairly described as "the highest and most sumptuous boudoir in town."[1] If Henry felt well, he could lunch at the Lawyers' Club on the fifth and sixth floors, among a selection of its fourteen hundred members (dues payable to the Equitable), or in the elegant Café Savarin.

When he entered the dining room, he looked worn, but still imposing. His hair was thick and white, smoothed off a center part, his overhanging eyebrows and up-curled mustache were luxuriant, and the dimple in his chin had become so deep it looked like a battle scar. At sixty-five, he had the air of the powerful elder lion in a pride.

But by early 1899, his appearances downtown were largely ceremonial. His fragile health was attributed to overwork, and his doctors insisted that he limit his involvement in the business, so even before Henry died, James was guided by James Alexander. He took a great deal on faith. As he said, "I did not make it my business to examine into everything that was being done, as that would have been absolutely impossible—I would have been swamped in detail; and I assumed that everything being done was being rightly done and had the sanction of the proper authorities, and the sanction of tradition and custom."[2]

In the first months after Henry's death, James was soothed to hear Alexander pronounce the old litanies. JWA defined the ideal company as "first of all, one whose officers and directors are high-minded, honorable, experienced and skillful men, who have no aims in the business other than to subserve the interests of the policyholders."[3] James believed him, and JWA believed his own words, despite his decades of serving special interests. He tried to uphold the "sacred trust," while managing the investments to which Henry had committed the company, but the wires that connected the conflicting parts of his character twanged with tension.

Henry's former secretary, William McIntyre, also participated in Equitable transactions that crossed the line between business and personal affairs, and he knew everything about Henry's affairs—he was so close to the boss that Henry called him his "red-haired Mercury." Willie had started as an office boy at the Equitable in 1879 when he was fourteen, and within four years, he was serving as Henry's secretary and virtual manservant. His tasks could be as mundane as buying a pair of suspenders, a half-dozen toothbrushes, a brass ring for the nose of a bull at The Oaks, a gallon of "javelle water" to remove spots from linens, or a dozen boxes of matches for the parlor fire. He took Henry's eyeglasses to be repaired, and he paid the household staff when Henry was abroad. He knew the workings of the brownstones on Fortieth Street as well as Henry did, and better than Annie. As Henry's right hand at the office, his knowledge was exhaustive; even JWA was not as well informed. Willie deposited Henry's paycheck, signed his letters, and prepared financial reports.[4] The *Insurance Press* was not exaggerating when it stated, in November 1900:

> Henry B. Hyde . . . gave [McIntyre] . . . his unreserved confidence . . . [which] had no counterpart in the Equitable office. . . . McIntyre was exactly fitted by temperament, as well as qualifications, to be Mr. Hyde's trusted man of details and chief aide. He was always ready, always cool and always exact. . . . The man most useful to him [Henry] was one who knew intuitively what to do, saw what was coming before it arrived . . . never got rattled and never shrank from assuming responsibility because an undertaking meant hard work or was on a large scale.[5]

After Willie became an Equitable vice president, he continued to do the sort of errands for Henry that other men asked of their valets, and he provided similar services for James. While James was at Harvard, Willie wrote him that he "was ever ready to 'jump at your call—no previous notice necessary. Please do not hesitate one instant in sending for me if you want me. Nothing will stand in my way.'"[6] Slight and unobtrusive, he even hovered at stage doors to ask for the autographs of actresses for James's collection.

Willie had been promoted to assistant secretary in 1898, and he was made a director when Henry died. Henry's legacies to him were $5,000, the largest bequest to anyone outside the family, and a bank of knowledge no one could match. Although Willie had started training a young man, Charles Williamson, to become James's private secretary two years before James graduated from college, Willie would be James's confidant and ally. He would protect him, speak for him, and balance his checkbook. When it was necessary, he would fill him in on the company's shadowed dealings—but he was too loyal to Henry to reveal everything he knew.

On July 24, 1899, three months after Henry died, four hundred members of the Equitable "family" came to New York for a three-day gala celebration of the company's fortieth anniversary.[7] The opening event was a reception at the Waldorf, followed by a lively boating excursion, highlighted by a minstrel show and a baseball game on shore. Gage Tarbell was given a bat that was longer than he was tall, and the umpire was presented with a cabbage. On the way back to the city, William Alexander, an unlikely entertainer with his professorial appearance, pince-nez, long salt-and-pepper beard, and stooped shoulders, played the snare drums and made quick sketches of the agents.

During the next morning's speeches, JWA informed the agents that their compensation package would be revised, reducing the first year's commissions, but increasing the percentage paid for renewals. Those new terms would become a point of extreme vulnerability before the end of the year. The highlight of the day was JWA's announcement that the Equitable had attained a billion dollars in sales. Everyone already knew it, and the other two "racers"—New York Life and the Mutual—hit the mark that year, too, but it was exciting to hear when they were all together.

At a banquet on the third night, July 26, JWA declared that his administration would "be marked by justice, equity and the conscientious regard for what is right and best in the conduct of such a sacred calling. . . . Our investments shall be made first for permanence, and next for productiveness."

When he introduced James, he acknowledged "the satisfaction I personally feel in having by my side the son of my old and life-long friend, Mr. Hyde . . . there never has been a longer or more sincere or harmonious friendship . . . he and I have stood side by side and shoulder to shoulder." Although Mr. Hyde's "hope and expectation that he would be able himself to see his son introduced into the business" was thwarted, JWA was proud to "take his place . . . in inculcating the views which we had in common about the sacredness of this business . . . assisting [James] . . . in making his entry into business life . . . so that he might guard that thing which Mr. Hyde felt was a sacred thing—the Equitable Life Assurance Society." Henry's heir, he said, "has come into our Society with that modesty, with that intention to help, with that serious feeling about business and with that grave sense of responsibility . . . in your first vice-president you have a man who has got the stuff of his father in him, and who . . . will give his best ability, his integrity, his zeal, his intelligence to do what is right."

When James stood up to speak, he had a solemn air of bereavement, a clean-shaven face, and an earnest expression. He began by quoting Lord Chatham, who said, "The atrocious crime of being a young man I shall neither attempt to palliate nor deny, but content myself with wishing that I may be one of those whose follies may cease with their youth, and not of that number who are ignorant in spite of experience." With boyish enthusiasm, he embellished JWA's theme: "To my mind corporations have a soul. . . . They are the embodiment of an ideal, and an ideal which is a vision—a beautiful vision which will lead us onward and upward and forward to the great and golden future, not for a day, but for all time."[8]

That evening, JWA had promised to "avoid . . . pyrotechnic and clap-trap movements which do not tend for permanency . . . No rush for temporary popularity shall seduce us from doing what goes for safety, economy and ultimate strength."[9] James, too, believed that the Equitable was a sacred trust because it was his father's legacy, but he wanted to be popular, and he liked fireworks. It took only five years for the rockets to go off.

PART TWO

CXO

THE RICHEST YOUNG
MAN IN NEW YORK

In the Gilded Age, "The worship of success was actually
a social cult. It was a crusade."

Van Wyck Brooks[1]

"[T]he middle class American of [the 1950s] . . . is best
thought of not as the normal state of our society, but as
an interregnum between Gilded Ages. America before
1930 was a society in which a small number of very rich
people controlled a large share of the nation's wealth."

Paul Krugman, "The Class Wars,"
New Tork Times Magazine[2]

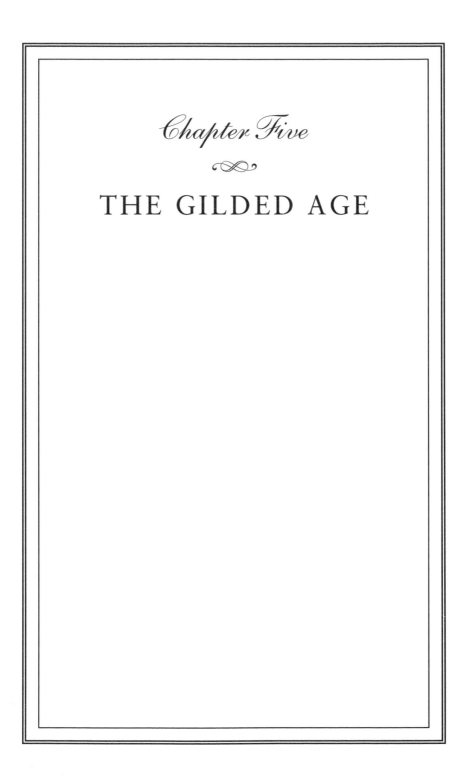

Chapter Five

THE GILDED AGE

James Hyde on the box of a four-in-hand road coach,
in front of The Oaks.

At Bay Shore, Long Island, James built miles of coach roads
on his four-hundred-acre estate, and took guests on outings.
Here, Mrs. Patrick Campbell, mistress of King Edward VII, is
on the box with James; in the second row, the crown prince of
Siam is seated next to Mrs. Otto Kahn. Even at the height of
the Gilded Age, few men in their twenties could host such a
party. *(Courtesy Lorna Hyde Graev)*

The Gilded Age, in which James flourished, was named before he was born. Two journalists in Hartford, Connecticut—Samuel Clemens, known by his pen name, Mark Twain, and Charles Dudley Warner, the publisher and associate editor of the *Hartford Courant*—were having dinner with their wives and making fun of popular "sentimental," "feminine" books. When their husbands took exception to Louisa May Alcott's *Little Women* and *Little Men*, the women challenged them to write their own novel. Within three months Clemens and Warner had a draft of *The Gilded Age*. It was Twain's first book, and it named an era. Published in 1873, it sold thirty-five thousand copies in the first few months.

The characters they created were in the early stages of accumulating and displaying wealth, and their excess had a crude frontier quality. But by 1900, the Gilded Age had matured, and rich Americans styled themselves after Continental aristocrats. James came into his inheritance in the midst of a golden era of architecture, collecting, and travel that heralded the beginning of American internationalism. Only an ascetic or a man with great self-control could have resisted the lifestyle he was handed in his early twenties.

Versailles represented the apex of grandeur and taste, and between the end of the Civil War and the beginning of World War I, Americans built mansions that would have suited Marie Antoinette and Louis XVI. Such blatant opulence was a recent development in the United States. Until the mid-nineteenth century, the richest Americans were baronial landholders, especially in New York and Virginia; or local manufacturers and bankers. They lived well, but they were often based on large estates and had to travel some distance to see one another. In the cities, too, they entertained privately. New

Englanders, in particular, disapproved of ostentation; even the rich righteously worked six days a week, took care of their families, helped their neighbors, and went to church on Sundays. It would not have been especially amusing to read about them in the newspapers.

The shift to sources of greater capital accumulation had begun in 1848, when John Jacob Astor died. He was the richest man in the history of the country, with an estate estimated to be in excess of $20 million, one-fifteenth of the money then in circulation in the United States.[1] Astor, a butcher's son who emigrated from Germany as a young man, made his first fortune in the fur trade, then had the foresight to buy swaths of New York City real estate. In the next half century, others leapt past him. "Commodore" Cornelius Vanderbilt died in 1877, leaving $100 million; in 1885, when his principal heir died, that sum had doubled. By the early 1890s, millionaires were counted in the thousands—there were 4,047 Americans with 1 million dollars or more in 1892, according to the United States Bureau of the Census.

As the first generation of industrialists and financiers died, it was possible to learn how much they were worth. In 1905, the *New-York Herald's* European edition announced on the front page that John D. Rockefeller's annual income was $30 million; at his death in 1913, Rockefeller left nearly a billion dollars. The same year, J. P. Morgan, who, as one of his contemporaries commented, was not nearly as rich as everyone thought, left an estimated $80 million, about $1.5 billion in 2000 dollars. It wasn't just money that made millionaires celebrities; the late nineteenth century subscribed to the "great man" theory, based on the belief that men made history, rather than the other way around.[2]

Houses were the most visible emblems of wealth. In Newport, Marble House, which Alva and William K. Vanderbilt Sr. built in 1892, was said to have cost $2 million, with $9 million more for furnishings. There were no knobs on the outside of the doors in the principal reception rooms, to make the point that there were footmen to open them from the inside. Houses the size of ducal palaces were going up as fast as architects could design them. George Vanderbilt's Biltmore, which may still be the largest private home in the United States, was located amid 140,000 acres of woodlands near then remote Asheville, North Carolina. It cost $5 million to build and supported its own village, where 750 of the 2,000 inhabitants were employed by the estate.[3]

Social figures talked so much about what they spent that an English observer wryly asked whether everything in America had a price tag on it. Money was a focus of gossip. One Newport family, the Pembroke Joneses, confessed that they budgeted $300,000 each summer for "extra entertainment." Henry Clewes was a financial legend; his book, *Fifty Years in Wall Street*, was published in 1908; but long before that his wife grabbed the headlines, telling a reporter that she "set aside $10,000 for mistakes in her clothes." Her son, Henry (later noted for wearing white silk socks, even with evening clothes) was one of James's childhood friends, and they remained close all their lives. The first time James visited a friend overnight was when he went to stay with the Cleweses in Newport.

The recently rich accumulated land as well as houses; they often had working farms and hothouses for their own use, and like British landowners, they were apt to have hampers of food sent to town by train so they could enjoy their own out-of-season fruits and cream from their own cows. Dr. William Seward Webb and his wife, Eliza, one of William Henry Vanderbilt's seven children, who lived in a forty-four-thousand-square-foot house on Shelburne Farms in Vermont, ran a model working operation, with a breeding barn, an indoor riding ring the size of a polo field, and such a fine dairy herd that every pat of butter used in the New York Central's dining cars came from Shelburne, embossed with the farm's initials.[4] The Webbs also owned a forty-seven-thousand-acre preserve surrounded by a sixty-three-mile-long fence in the Adirondacks. Their neighbors, the William C. Whitneys, owned ninety thousand acres there; another ten thousand acres and a mansion near Lenox, Massachusetts; and houses in Newport; Westbury, Long Island; Aiken, South Carolina; Florida; London; and on Fifth Avenue.[5]

August and Eleanor Belmont had a surfeit of real estate, including two Long Island houses, one to breed horses, another for polo; a stud farm in Lexington, Kentucky; a cottage for the races in Saratoga; a shooting box in South Carolina; a Newport cottage; and a house on

Fifth Avenue. Arden, E. H. Harriman's private park in Orange County, New York, had its own village and power plant, and occupied twice as much terrain as Manhattan Island.[6]

Modes of conveyance have a long history as symbols of wealth and status, and much prestige was attached to the private railroad car, the yacht, and the sporting coach. It was not unusual to own a railroad car, but George F. Baker of National City Bank had his own siding constructed under his house on Park Avenue in New York. Regardless of who else was aboard, the trains stopped in his basement when he wanted his car to be hitched on. Members of the Tuxedo Park Club in Orange County, New York, wore gold oak-leaf pins that they showed to the local stationmaster, who arranged for the Erie trains to make unscheduled stops at the Tuxedo Station.[7] After James Hyde got his own car, the "Bay Shore," local newspapers mentioned that he inconvenienced passengers on the Long Island Railroad who had to wait for the car to be hooked up to the train, and then for him to arrive at the station to board.

As for yachting, it was not unusual for families to take off for a year and sail around the world on their own ships, with a crew of dozens, and a staff of valets, ladies' maids, nurses, and governesses. The largest American yacht was said to be Robert Goelet's *Nahma*, which weighed 1,506 tons and required sixty-seven in crew; the most exotic was Col. Francis L. Leland's *Safa-el-Bahr*, which he bought from the Khedive of Egypt, and ran with the khedive's fez-capped crew. When William K. Vanderbilt took his family as far as India on his massive 1,400-ton yacht, *Alva*, it was mistaken for a warship when it tried to enter the Dardanelles at Constantinople, and the Turks fired warning shots across its bow.

Many of these details of the elite world were published in *Town Topics*, where society's official gossip-and-scandal monger, Col. William D'Alton Mann, relished every nuance of dress, jewels, and property. Mann was a midwesterner with a lively background. He organized the Seventh Michigan Cavalry in the Civil War, then followed postwar opportunity to Alabama, building a cotton-seed oil mill and refinery. He invented a sleeping car for trains, and built one for King Leopold II of Belgium. George M. Pullman bought him out, but not for enough to make him rich. In 1885, Mann's brother purchased a slim little magazine, renamed it *Town Topics,* and ran it as a scandal sheet. When he was convicted of sending obscene matter through the mails, Colonel Mann took over. Under his regime, which started in 1891, the scandals were only slightly less vulgar. He was apt to print such items as, "I wonder if a certain dashing little Kenwood divorcee would continue wasting her devotions on the debonair bachelor whose suite of rooms at the Hotel Metropole is the scene of much lavish hospitality if she knew that often at his side, when he telephones her, is an attractive blonde, with whom he thinks he is making a big hit by allowing her to listen to the gross widow's lovesick protestations."[8] Mann was a staunch defender of the world he wrote about, but his friendly attentions were a market commodity, exchanged for cash and flattery.

Henry Hyde had been helpful to Mann, although his goal was to keep his name out of print, and according to one source, "James Hazen Hyde's . . . Equitable Life Assurance Society had made a loan of $165,000 on the real estate owned by Mann and the Ess Ess Publishing Company (the initials stood for 'smart set')."[9] James was not the only benefactor; Mann later admitted to having taken loans of more than $184,000 from twelve luminaries. By 1900, at sixty-one, with his flowing white mustache, clerical frock coat, and red bow ties, Mann gave the misleading impression that he was the archetype of a kindly gentleman who could be found on a veranda sipping mint juleps and reminiscing. In 1906, legal actions inevitably brought him down, but at the peak of his power, he lionized James and made sure he was posted in the *Town Topics* office as one of the privileged few socialites exempt from the magazine's barbs. Other society columnists took their lead from *Town Topics,* and soon James's secretary, Charles Williamson, was underlining James's name in blue pencil, clipping the articles, and pasting them into scrapbooks. Henry Hyde would have hated it.

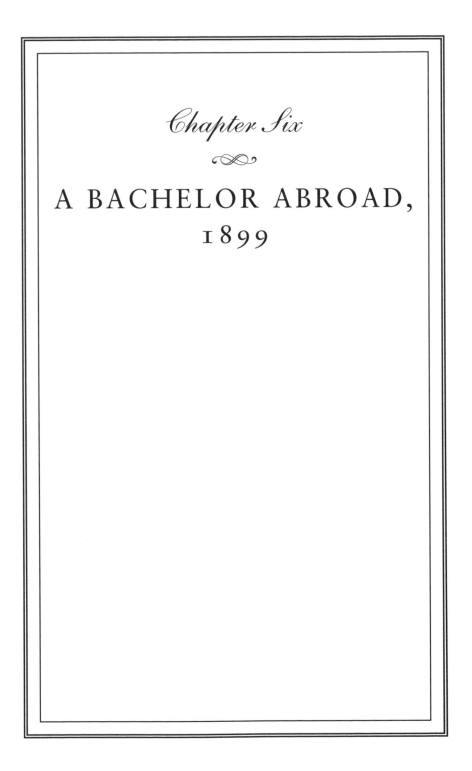

Chapter Six

A BACHELOR ABROAD,
1899

James's Parisian life was lampooned in this newspaper cartoon published in 1905.

The Francophilia James espoused covered both high and low culture and was very much in style. As one historian of the Gilded Age explained, "France was a magic word in America at the end of the nineteenth century." *(Courtesy AXA Financial Archives)*

*L*ate Victorian America was a bleak time and place to be in mourning. For James, the six-month "deep mourning" period men observed on the death of a father stretched ahead until November 1899, when it would felicitously end in time for the opening of the winter social season at the opera and the National Horse Show. Until then, the last big social events he could expect to attend were Henry's funeral and the Equitable's fortieth-anniversary celebrations. As June and July unfolded, James sat at home with his mother on Fortieth Street and in Bay Shore, or went downtown to 120 Broadway, and watched James Alexander try to take his father's place.

But Paris was another matter. On July 27, the day after the Equitable's fortieth anniversary celebrations were over, James sailed for Cherbourg, and did not return until September 24. In those two months he attended to Equitable business, but above all, he was a budding boulevardier.

He could have been the model for the young American in Edith Wharton's novella *Madame de Treymes*, who "was always struck by the vast and consummately ordered spectacle of Paris; by its look of having been boldly and deliberately planned as a background for the enjoyment of life, instead of being forced into grudging concessions to the festive instincts, or barricading itself against them in unenlightened ugliness, like his own lamentable New York."[1]

James did not find New York dreary, but he was enchanted by Paris. He shared the upper-class-American attraction to everything French: design, culture, manners, cuisine. Rich Americans collected French furniture, art, and sometimes châteaux, which they had dismantled, shipped across the ocean, then reconstructed. Those who did not import their castles were apt to hire architects trained at the

Ecole des Beaux Arts in Paris, where their style was influenced by the French eighteenth century.

Women went to Paris twice a year to have their clothes made by the dressmakers on the rue de la Paix—Worth, Doucet, Poiret, and Rouff—and settled in for a month to have their fittings. Many Americans stayed at the venerable Hôtel de Crillon, the Bristol, or the Continental, and when César Ritz opened the Hôtel Ritz in 1898, he attracted his own devoted clientele. At the Ritz every bedroom had its own bathroom, a luxury Ritz determined to offer after he walked by another hotel where the Prince of Wales, the future King of England, was staying, and saw a copper tub with two large pots of water being delivered so the prince could take a bath.

The guest list at the Ritz's opening night party in the summer of 1898 was a sampling of the circle that would open its drawing rooms to James. There were marquises and vicomtesses and comtesses, ducs and duchesses, two Russian grand dukes, Marcel Proust, and the most prominent courtesans in Paris. Among the Americans were Anthony Drexel, known as the "Beau Brummel of the American Colony," a few Vanderbilts, and the heiress Anna Gould and her husband Count Boniface de Castellane, a great-nephew of Prince de Talleyrand.

Anna Gould, the youngest child of the financier Jay Gould, had married Boni in 1895, the same year Consuelo Vanderbilt married the Duke of Marlborough. Consuelo's marriage inspired the legislature of the state of Illinois to make what one newspaper called "an official entreaty to nubile heiresses to bestow themselves, or, rather, their inheritances, upon Americans only."[2] Like Consuelo, Anna was only eighteen when she married. Both her parents had died, and she had inherited an enormous fortune—the newspapers said she had $17 million in 1895, and revised it upward to $75 million five years later. Although she was shy and homely (it was said that she had black hair growing on her back), she was engaged to a nephew of E. H. Harriman's, and she was in Paris acquiring her trousseau when she met Boni. He was handsome, an aesthete of the highest order, and was said to have been one of the inspirations for Proust's beautiful young hero, St-Loup. Anna, swept away, broke her engagement. The family settled $2 million on her husband when they were married at the Paris house of her brother, George Gould. Boni spent it all, and more.

He redesigned his wife from hair to wardrobe, and on a one-acre lot on the avenue du Bois de Boulogne, he oversaw the building of a rose-colored marble replica of Madame de Maintenon's Grand Trianon at Versailles. There, Anna slept in Marie Antoinette's ostrich-feather-trimmed bed, while Boni reverted to his preferred pattern and took mistresses.

In the summer of 1899, when James arrived, Paris was still talking about the twenty-first birthday party Boni had given Anna two years earlier. Held in the Bois de Boulogne by special permission of the city, it was illuminated by eighty thousand Murano glass lamps from Venice, which hung in the trees. Five dozen footmen were dressed in scarlet livery and arranged decoratively around the scene for "a patch of colour in the right place"; and amid "fountains of fire" (a poetic description of fireworks) guests danced to an orchestra with two hundred musicians.[3]

Eventually, Anna divorced Boni and married his cousin, the Prince de Sagan, but at the turn of the century she was enchanted by her husband's style and attentions and still oblivious to his affairs. James was introduced to the de Castellanes by Anna's brother, George, and became a friend. He later saved some of Anna's letters, and they indicate that there may have been something more between them when her marriage was collapsing.[4]

Many wealthy Americans had residences in Paris, even those not married to Europeans. The George Vanderbilts' pied à terre was in an eighteenth-century Louis XIV town house. Edith Wharton came and went until 1907, when she moved to France for good. Caroline Astor, the doyenne of New York and Newport, spent as much as five months abroad. Her apartment, at 146, avenue des Champs Elysées, was filled with contemporary (but not modern) French art, and she held a regular salon.

The Champs Elysées was a favorite street for Americans, who often rented full-floor, eight-bedroom flats in the creamy Beaux-Arts apartment houses. Consuelo Vanderbilt made her debut on the avenue at a bal blanc at the Duc de Gramont's house—"white" balls were for debutantes; the balls were called "pink" when young married women were invited.

James attended the large, lavish parties, but he particularly relished the salons where Americans mixed with the circle the French called *le gratin*, colloquial for "upper class," referring to a crusty broiled cheese topping. Edith Wharton wrote in her memoirs, "The whole raison d'être of the French salon is based on the national taste for general conversation . . . social intercourse is a perpetual exchange, a market to which everyone is expected to bring his best for barter."[5] Some salons were mostly social, others intellectual and artistic, like those held by the artist Jacques-Emile Blanche, who hung his portraits of Thomas Hardy and Marcel Proust alongside new work by Dégas, Manet, and Whistler. At M. Blanche's one could meet André Gide, Jean Cocteau, and Diaghilev.

The Belle Epoque was the French version of the Gilded Age, but frothier. Money carried less weight as a social credential in Paris, and pleasures were pursued less earnestly than in America. Among the delights of the Belle Epoque was the institution of the courtesan— chief among them were the rivals La Belle Otéro, dramatic and dark as a gypsy, and the elegant Liane de Pougy. In Monte Carlo, they both took up residence at the Hôtel de Paris, where innocent young American women were cautioned not to look at them as they swooshed by.[6] Nightly, they arrived to gamble at the tables at the Casino, making a spectator sport of outshining each other. On one memorable evening, Otéro appeared covered from hair to shoe buckles with precious jewels from her admirers. The next night, Pougy wore a plain white dress without a single ornament; her jewels bedecked her maid, who paraded behind her. James was not sophisticated enough to become a patron of women like these, but he was often in the audience at the French theater, and met some of the younger beauties who played ingenue roles but were who not as chaste offstage.

He was having a very good time.

It wasn't only James's charm that made him popular. The Equitable wrote millions of dollars of insurance in France each year, and its headquarters were superbly located at 36 and 36 *bis* avenue de l'Opéra. Just down the street, at number 49, the *New-York Herald*'s business office was one of the first stops for visiting Americans who went by to meet friends and pick up mail. In 1890, more than one hundred thousand visitors registered there.

Tiffany and Company installed its Paris shop on the Equitable Building's ground floor, with floor-to-ceiling arched windows on the rue de la Paix and the place de l'Opéra. Tiffany's was equipped with an ultra-modern "ventilating plant for the renewal of the atmosphere three times an hour," and Paris's first Edison storage battery. Even if the city's power went down, the vaults would be secure.

The building enhanced the Equitable's image and brought in revenues from rents, but the French business was in a perilous state. Problems had been brewing for many years; in 1897, Henry Hyde wrote James Alexander, "France will drive us out eventually."[7] The Chambre des Députés had been threatening to pass a law that would cripple American insurance companies, and JWA urged James to work on the legislative issues and to cultivate anyone who could speak on the Equitable's behalf. James took the responsibility seriously, and he was an important symbol of the connection between past and future success.

In August, he crossed the Channel to attend the London dinner in honor of the fortieth anniversary, and read a heavy-handed cablegram from JWA, who declared, "Every Equitable Englishman, Scotchman, Irishman, and Welshman will do his duty." Then James held up a pair of little American and English flags, waved them, and intoned the company motto, "Not for a day, but for all time." In Paris, James was the host of the anniversary dinner and gave a speech in fluent French to a prestigious guest list. He missed the Australian party with its "fortune tellers, phonographs, and a cinematograph which showed Samoans engaging in dances, pillow fights, and real fights."[8]

That summer, James found a passion that would consume him and bring him pleasure and notoriety; it was in Paris that he learned to drive a four-in-hand coach. Local transportation in the early years of the twentieth century was still dominated by horse-

drawn conveyances, but long-distance stagecoaches had been super-
seded by the railroads. Large coaches like the ones that fascinated
James were mostly private, used principally for sport by the few who
could afford them. Coaching required elegance, formality, show, pro-
tocol, and skill—nearly everything that he liked.

A well-kept coach was a magnificent object. The bodies gleamed
with the lacquered shine of as many as twenty layers of paint, usually
crow's-wing black, trimmed in contrasting shades. Most notable
families had their own colors. The Vanderbilt coachmen and footmen wore maroon, which went well with their black horses. The
Belmonts' carriages were maroon, with a scarlet stripe on the wheels,
and the Belmont livery matched. Coachmen wore black top hats for
dress; everyone knew when the owners were driving, because their
hats were gray. When James began to collect his own coaches, he
chose burgundy for the panels, and added jaunty, bright red wheels
and poles, and red leather upholstery.

Appearance was a priority, but comfort was not. The coachman,
called "the whip," sat on a tufted leather seat that was backless, so he
could lean against the reins. A three-thousand-pound road coach was
an enormous conveyance; its wheels were some four feet in diameter,
and the seats were nine feet above the ground, which made mounting
awkward for corseted women in their layered skirts. The seating
arrangement was as precise as the *placement* at a dinner party. The
most prestigious guest sat on the box with the "whip," or driver, and
the other passengers rode behind, on gammon seats, covered in leather,
wool, or cord, with cushioned metal backs. Some faced forward, others backward. Servants usually rode inside the small, airless cabins,
where they could not hear the passengers' conversation. Regardless of
the weather, virtually no one wanted to sit inside; one passenger compared the experience to being in a barrel, wheeling down a road at top
speed. When the weather was extremely cold, men and women who
rode above sometimes packed themselves in straw, drawing leather
robes and furs over their laps; in the rain, they used oilskins, and in the
summer, cotton robes against the dust.

Many drivers came to Paris to sharpen their skills with Edwin
Howlett, a Paris-based Swiss, the author of an 1894 book called *Dri-*

ving Lessons, and whose stable leased coaches and teams. James became one of his pupils. He had the requisite athleticism, strength, and coordination, a sensitive hand on the "ribbons," as the reins were called, and the nerve to handle five tons of horseflesh, moving at a snappy trot. Soon he was driving in the Bois de Boulogne with M. Howlett's son, Morris, and inviting parties of friends to join him on excursions to the Parisian suburbs for lunch or dinner.

In September, James asked Howlett if he could organize an eight-day trip from Paris to Cherbourg, where he was scheduled to sail home on the *Deutschland*. Howlett said, "Yes, if you have enough money," and, as he later recalled, James "assured me that he had."[9] As guests, James invited three other young men from New York, who were leaving on the same ship. They were Lawrence Gillespie, Bradish Johnson, who turned twenty-one on the trip, and Richard T. Wilson.

The Wilson family was an example of the mobility of the New York society in which James was planted after only one generation of wealth and prominence. Richard's father, R. T. Wilson, married the daughter of a Tennessee grocer, who started R.T. in the grocery business. He was so successful that, at the start of the Civil War, he was appointed commissary general of the Confederacy, based in Atlanta. There, it was said that he sold cotton blankets to the Confederate Army and charged them for wool. As the war drew to a close, he and his family ran the sea blockade and reached London. One story claimed that he cashed in the Confederate bonds he had been banking in England while they were still negotiable; another that he collected the money the British owed plantation owners for cotton shipments, and kept it. However the Wilsons came by their riches, it was understood when they arrived in New York after the war that they were millionaires many times over. Despite R. T. Wilson's unsavory reputation, he had such southern charm that he was later rumored to have been the model for Rhett Butler in *Gone With the Wind*.[10] His children inherited his attractive manner, and the family slipped into New York social circles through them, although one daughter, the spirited and beautiful Grace, had a more difficult time. When she and Cornelius Vanderbilt III, known as Neily, became engaged, Neily's father, the conservative, pious Cornelius II, was implacably opposed to Grace; and when Neily married her, promptly slashed his inheritance to $500,000, plus a $1 million trust. Only three years later, in 1899, shortly after James and his friends returned from Europe, Cornelius died at fifty-six, leaving Neily's younger brother, Alfred, $42 million. Alfred gave Neily $6 million of that, a generous gesture unless you believed that the original agreement between the brothers had been that Neily would get $10 million. The Vanderbilt inheritance fracas was an indication of where James fell in the hierarchy of wealth. He was probably worth $1 million at most in 1899, not counting the Equitable stock, whose value was hard to calculate.

The 1899 Paris-to-Cherbourg run had the lighthearted air of young men on a lark. The coach was packed with baggage and hampers of food and drink; James, Howlett, and the three guests slung themselves aboard; the groom blew a blast on the hunting horn and the horses trotted off. The "enthusiasts," who, James wrote, typically gathered, "follow[ed] to catch the last glimpse as we disappear[ed] in the distance."[11] Howlett had arranged for horses to be shipped ahead by rail, so the team could be changed three or four times a day; the coach could then cover about fifty miles before stopping at an inn for the night.

They traveled west, following the Seine toward the coast, past wheat fields and villages that looked much as they had for centuries. James wrote about that trip and others that followed in *Harper's Monthly*, conveying his sense of romance and adventure, and his interest in "real" life in France. Sometimes, he wrote, the coach stopped to let a shepherd cross the road "with his flock of sheep nearly hidden in a cloud of dust," or to observe groups he described as "Bohemians"—probably gypsies—the men earnestly engaged in the manufacture of baskets, while the women cooked the chicken and potatoes by the side of the road." The French roads, James said, "had no other aim in life than to make driving a luxury." They were in "perfect" condition, "wide, and usually lined with carefully trimmed trees, which lend beauty to the scene and protection from the rays of the sun."

One of the few photographs of James in his twenties in which he looks relaxed was taken while coaching through France. He is sitting in a field with a friend, wearing a tweed jacket and a flat cap. It would not have been surprising if he had been chewing on a blade of grass. The informal side of his character emerged in his choice of hotels. As he wrote, he avoided the "real smart" ones, and the "medium class . . . which strives to be very smart and is very poor," selecting instead the "small 'dinkey' hotel, where the proprietor-chef does everything and anything for you." He praised the cooking and the kitchens, with their ancient spits and polished brass pots, and observed, "It is in a place of this kind that one learns to know the people and their joie du métier." Readers of *Harper's* in the early 1900s were expected to understand that meant "pleasure in their work."

The first night on the road, the travelers very nearly slept in a French jail. On their way to the tiny village of Pacy-sur-l'Eure, James and his friends noticed a French flag that, as Howlett later explained, was in "a perilous position from a falling staff." Rescuing it before it hit the ground, they attached it to the coach, where it streamed in the wind as they sped along. That evening, Pacy-sur-l'Eure was *en fête*, celebrating outdoors with the local Calvados and beer. The villagers paused to stare at the glamorous coach that filled the narrow streets and bore young men who looked rich, American, and slightly disreputable after a day on the dusty road.

In the courtyard of the Lion d'Or, the sort of local hotel James liked, the innkeeper greeted them effusively. But when James gave the flag a friendly flourish, the host scowled, abruptly walked away, and returned with a small delegation of uniformed gendarmes to arrest them for stealing a French flag. Howlett wrote about the incident some years later, and remembered that his knees were shaking. He and James quickly conferred in English, and Howlett, a native French speaker, explained the misunderstanding. He was jangling some coins in his pocket, and at last withdrew his hand and produced a fifty-franc piece, which he offered the gendarmes "for the poor of the village." After the situation was clarified, James treated the policemen, the onlookers, and the other guests at the hotel to "convivial refreshments." As a protection against future problems, or perhaps as a souvenir, he asked Howlett to obtain a receipt for their donation. On it, James's name was spelled "Hide," which, Howlett remarked, "ruffled his youthful dignity."

When the 1899 trip was over and James was back in New York, he took up coaching in earnest, joined the New York Coaching Club, and began to participate in their races and parades. By 1901, he and Alfred Vanderbilt were coaching companions, and James invited Alfred to join the Equitable board. Bradish Johnson, one of the guests on that first coaching trip, became a director in 1902. James's friends, in their twenties, refreshed the atmosphere in the board-room, where James was barely guided but closely observed.[12]

Chapter Seven

GAGE TARBELL:
NEW YEAR'S EVE, 1899

Gage Tarbell, the Equitable's ambitious vice president in charge of agencies.

Tarbell, in his forties, wanted to be the Equitable's president. James blocked his way to the top, but Tarbell was determined that he should not be a permanent obstacle. *(Courtesy AXA Financial Archives)*

The country was preparing for the last eve of the 1800s—but at the Equitable and New York Life, the date's greater significance was the midnight deadline that would decide a dramatic battle between the two companies. The leader of the Equitable forces was not president Alexander or first vice president Hyde; it was Gage Tarbell, the ambitious second vice president.

Tarbell had started his insurance career by chance. He sold insurance part-time as a young man, to support himself while he studied law, but he found the business unexpectedly exhilarating. "My first act as an agent was to apply for a $1,000 policy on my own life," he wrote in a 1903 article in the popular *Everybody's Magazine*. "As I took the document and read it through again and again it grew momentous, and I said aloud to myself: 'You are a capitalist; if you should die you would leave an estate.'"[1] As he rhapsodized, "When a man hitches his personal ambition to a business of such obvious beneficence, he must be abnormal or degenerate if he is not immensely enthusiastic."[2] He abandoned the law and joined the Equitable full-time in 1884. Five years later, at thirty-three, he was given a one-third interest in the Equitable's northwestern business in nine states and territories. By his account, he then fell prey to gold fever and took off to seek his fortune in the West—although the story about those years that emerged in 1905 was considerably different. When Tarbell returned to the Equitable in 1891 as resident secretary in Chicago, his region contributed $15 to $20 million of business a year, of which he wrote between $1 and $2 million himself. In 1893, Henry Hyde promoted Tarbell to third vice president, overseeing the entire sales force, and moved him and his family to New York.

In the last years of the 1890s, Henry traveled less, James Alexander took over more management responsibilities, and Tarbell became the face of the Equitable around the country. In 1895, over a three-month period, he visited agencies in thirty-five states. Life insurance affected such a large segment of the population that when he came to town, newspapers ran stories with headlines like, EQUITABLE LIFE MEN DINE . . . VICE-PRESIDENT TARBELL PRAISES THE WORK OF MANAGER MCNAMEE.

Tarbell used the Equitable's monthly newsletter to develop his constituency. Often, he wrote about the "hard cases" he had persuaded to buy insurance. One of his favorite stories centered on his attempt to sell a $100,000 policy to Frederick Weyerhauser, whom he referred to as "Mr. W, king lumberman." Weyerhauser had resisted "several brilliant agents . . . sent on from New York," and Tarbell took up the challenge. First he met with "Mr. W's" closest friend, insured him for $75,000, then asked for help in approaching "Mr. W." The friend warned, he "hates the idea [of life insurance] so much that he won't even talk about it," but agreed to write a letter of introduction. Tarbell set off on a three-hundred-mile trip into the lumber region, tracked his quarry to a hotel dining room, stationed himself in the lobby, and waited for him to emerge. When he presented the letter, Weyerhauser agreed to a fifteen-minute appointment the next day. Tarbell brought along the Equitable's local medical examiner, who performed the qualifying examination while Tarbell made his sales pitch. Weyerhauser signed the application to get the paperwork started but said he was unlikely to buy the policy.

After ingratiating himself with Weyerhauser's secretary, Tarbell received a telegram a few weeks later alerting him that his target was due to take a long train trip. Once again, Tarbell traveled north, and "accidentally" encountered Weyerhauser at a railway lunchroom table. When Weyerhauser learned that they were both going to Chippewa Falls, Minnesota, he invited Tarbell to ride with him. That evening, he bought the $100,000 policy, but first, Tarbell said, he asked, "How did you happen to be at the Spooner Junction lunchroom this noon?"

"In order to meet you," Tarbell answered.

"I thought so," the "lumber king" said. In Tarbell's version, Weyerhauser then added, "Let me tell you that in my thirty-five years of business experience your method with me has been the best business I ever saw."[3]

Tarbell had been building his career and reputation for nearly a decade in the spring of 1899 when James Hyde, twenty years his junior, but now a notch above him in rank, accompanied him on one of his trips. The newspapers trumpeted their arrival with headlines like the *Atlanta Constitution*'s EMINENT INSURANCE MEN ARE VISITING ATLANTA, and called James "perhaps the youngest man in America to be a factor in one of the greatest financial institutions of the country." In the second paragraph, the writer offhandedly noted, "Mr. Hyde is here with Mr. Gage E. Tarbell . . . and other officials of the company," quickly returning to James, "a chip off the old block," who, "with energy and thoroughness characteristic of the typical young American . . . went right into the work to learn every phase . . . He was not content to sit in an office and take the credit for what somebody else did, as some sons of wealthy fathers have done . . . but he proposed to know everything . . . about the business which he intended making his life's work . . . like his father he will be president in fact as well as name."[4]

When Tarbell reappeared six paragraphs from the top, it was as "one of the ablest and best known insurance men in America . . . [whose] rise in the insurance world shows what can be accomplished by a man who has brains and push and ability, even if he has to start out with no other capital." It might have been hard for Tarbell to ignore that James was an example of how much could be attributed to accomplishments when a man starts out with plenty of capital.

Whatever the public thought, the sales force recognized their real leader. For Christmas 1899, agents in the United States, Canada, France, and England chipped in to buy Tarbell a gold repeater watch with an Etruscan-style fob and a star ruby clasp, and a heavy gold ring set with a cat's-eye stone. The gifts were presented with a letter in a leather folder, which had been passed from one office to the next until it accumulated five hundred signatures. The package arrived as Tarbell was about to engage in the most exciting maneuver of his career, representing the Equitable in a fight for agents with its principal rival, New York Life. In any company that did not have an heir in place, his success in the first hours of 1900 would have virtually assured him that when the job was open, the presidency would be his.

While Tarbell prepared to take on New York Life, James Alexander was occupied with the year-end accounting, an annual tangle of money-shuffling. Sometimes the purpose was to make the company seem more profitable; at other times it was to shave the bottom line so there would seem to be less surplus to distribute to the policyholders. Advances to agents were recast by fobbing them off as loans by one of the trust companies in which the Equitable owned the controlling interest. On occasion, the Equitable took the opportunity to cover outside deals in which the company and its directors were involved. These transactions placed a strain on JWA, who did not like to be reminded that he was engaging in practices that had to be conducted secretly, so that policyholders and insurance regulators wouldn't learn what was actually going on.

As a consequence, late December was the worst possible time to face off with the top men at New York Life, and Alexander was evidently satisfied to leave Tarbell in charge. The stakes were enormous: New York Life had declared that it would no longer honor an agreement that the two companies would not poach each other's agents, and the Equitable was in a precarious position. On December 1, the Equitable agents had been given thirty days' notice that their contracts would be terminated, and they would be asked to sign the new contracts on January 1. That left a one-month gap, during which they were free to change their affiliation. When the new terms Alexander had announced at the fortieth anniversary celebration went into effect, it was possible that hundreds of Equitable agents would defect.

The president of New York Life was the exceptionally competent John A. McCall, but Tarbell's principal adversary was his opposite number, George Walbridge Perkins, New York Life's canny, ambitious first vice president. Perkins had the eyes of a gunslinger, the mustache of a banker, and the connections of an important industrialist, although he was a second-generation insurance salesman from

Cleveland. His father had started as the warden in a boys' reformatory, but switched careers to run an agency for New York Life, and George left school in his teens to work for him. George was twenty five when his father died, and New York Life promoted him to agency supervisor for the Rocky Mountain territories, then to inspector of agencies west of the Mississippi. In 1892, the company brought him to New York and appointed him to the selection committee for a new president. They enticed John McCall to leave the Equitable, where the top job was blocked by Henry Hyde, and McCall made Perkins vice president in charge of agencies.

Perkins might have preferred to work for Henry. At one time, he wrote Tarbell that he had not been able to "screw my courage up to the point of writing Mr. Hyde," but would be grateful if Tarbell would "intercede" and ask for a large picture of Henry that Perkins could hang in his office, "for myself, to keep always."[5]

When Perkins joined New York Life, it was running third among the top insurers; but as the century turned, the company was jostling with the Equitable for first place. Perkins attributed some of the success to progressive policies he had instituted, providing all three hundred thousand employees with pensions, death benefits, and cash bonuses, based on performance.[6] Quite reasonably, he expected that agents would be loyal to a company that treated them exceptionally well and that was reaching first place. If agents from other insurers had the choice, they, too, might choose to join New York Life.

The conflict between the two racers surfaced in Russia, where New York Life had such an important stake that, according to J. P. Morgan's biographer, Jean Strouse, "Between 1885 and 1914 [it] . . . was the most successful American commercial venture in imperial Russia."[7] Perkins made a deal with the finance minister in mid-1899 to purchase railroad bonds guaranteed by the Russian government. In return, the minister agreed to block the establishment or expansion of other American life insurance companies.[8]

P. J. Popoff, the Equitable's general manager for the Russian Empire, retaliated. On November 23, 1899, he wrote Perkins from the office on Nevsky Prospect that he was discontinuing a long-standing understanding between the two not to "employ or negotiate with" each other's agents. Tarbell had worked out that agreement five years earlier; now Popoff told Perkins that the breach was authorized by the head office.

Perkins let some time elapse while he made plans to raid the Equitable sales force. The day after Christmas, a month after he received the letter from St. Petersburg, he wrote Tarbell, as head of agencies, that as of that day, New York Life "terminates the entire agency agreement existing between our two companies," and instructed New York Life executives to send telegrams to their agents, announcing the termination. They were given a recruiting quota: "Expect you to hire fifteen or twenty new agents within the week."

Tarbell received Perkins's letter on December 27, and arrived at the New York Life office the next morning to meet with Perkins and president John McCall. Nothing was resolved, but Perkins promised to call Tarbell to set a time for them to get together again.

With only three days to convince Equitable agents to join New York Life, Perkins stalled. Tarbell still hadn't heard from him that afternoon at four o'clock, and when he called New York Life, he was told that Perkins had left. He got through to McCall, who advised him that New York Life was not willing to renew the old agreement, but that Perkins would meet with Tarbell the next day and they would work out something on an informal basis.

Perkins did not phone to set up that meeting either. Tarbell telephoned him and McCall, but neither took his calls. In the early afternoon, he slammed his hat on his head, whipped into his overcoat, and walked over to the New York Life offices. Perkins met with him and, as Tarbell reported, told him that "the jig was up." New York Life sent out another telegram, warning, "Confidentially looks now compact with Equitable regarding agents may be restored within twenty-four hours. Any pending negotiations should be closed quick."[8]

On December 30, Perkins and McCall wrote to offer an unacceptable last-minute deal, and Perkins gave Tarbell a deadline of two o'clock that afternoon. James Alexander was not mentioned in any of the correspondence.

At two o'clock, Tarbell was at the Lawyers' Club at 120 Broadway, meeting with Robert Mix, head of New York Life's Manhattan Department. Mix had produced $12 million in 1899, about one-fourteenth of New York Life's total annual business. "I saw that it would perhaps be wise," Tarbell later said, "to let the other people understand that the getting of other companies' agents was a game that two could play at." The next day, New Year's Eve, 1899, at three in the afternoon, Mix arrived with the nine agency managers of the departments he supervised. Six hours later, the meeting adjourned for dinner, then reconvened.

On New Year's Eve, the riotous noise and excitement on the streets reflected Tarbell's mood. The greatest clamor came from lower Broadway, where New Yorkers assembled around Trinity Church, as they had for generations. At midnight, the bells rang out, chiming the favorites, "Old Hundred," "America," "Yankee Doodle Dandy," "Home, Sweet Home," and "Auld Lang Syne," but the noise was so overwhelming that only occasional phrases of music filtered through. As the century turned, steamboats, ferries, and tugboats in the harbor added the hoarse, deep blast of their horns, joined by the steam whistles of factories and locomotives.

At least two women died while observing the change of the year. One was on her knees, praying, in St. Paul's Roman Catholic Church; the other dropped dead on her daughter's doorstep, where she had just arrived to wish her a Happy New Year.[9] William Witt and Anna Waddilove were wed, and declared that theirs was the first New York marriage of 1900. The Associated Cycle Club held a race from Fifty-ninth Street to Yonkers and beyond, to Tarrytown. The Yonkers winner was given a magnum of Champagne; everyone who made it to Tarrytown received cups or medals. Two "sweet-faced old sisters," the Misses Cornwall, who lived together, produced an 1850 newspaper clipping and sent it to the *Times*. One of the sisters, who had been bedridden for seven years, had saved the article when she was twelve, promising herself to look at it again when the century turned. The text began, "Blessed be the young eyes that shall see its future through of fifty years! Blessed be the ears that shall hear the clock strike the century

hour of Nineteen Hundred!" Referring to the Bible, progress, and phi-
lanthropy, the writer also declared "blessed" those who will be able to
"look back over the pathway of humanity to this hour and contemplate its great progress points and the events of happy augury."

Two society leaders, Mrs. Hermann Oelrichs and Mrs. Burke-
Roche, took boxes at the Hungarian Peasant Ball, a charity event for
eight thousand revelers at Madison Square Garden. A mock Hungarian village was set up on the floor of the Garden, with little
houses, a town hall, a jail, a hundred men and women in costume,
and two Hungarian bands.[10]

Men stopped by their clubs for cups of punch, but many were out
of town. At Tuxedo Park, the seven-thousand-acre fenced enclave in
the Ramapo Hills of New York, the club's new indoor court was officially opened, and men in white played on one of the few racquet
courts in the United States. Others skated or tobogganed down a
slide set up opposite the Tuxedo Club onto the ice of Wee Wah Lake.
And on New Year's Eve, a ball was held in the casino adjoining the
clubhouse.

At the Hydes' house in New York, the first Christmas without
Henry was grim. James is likely to have had a number of invitations
for New Year's house parties, and he probably accepted one of them.
What is certain is that neither he nor James Alexander were at the
hotel with Tarbell, negotiating to transfer New York Life's entire
Metropolitan Department to the Equitable.

When the night was over, Tarbell agreed with the *World*
reporter, who wrote enthusiastically, "Another epoch—1900!
. . . the 1800's are gone forever, and brisk, bright, fresh altogether
new 1900 greets everybody. . . . What a celebration it was . . . !"

By five o'clock on Monday morning, the first day of 1900, the
New York Life agents had agreed to submit their resignations to
Perkins and McCall, and sign with the Equitable. They telegraphed
some three hundred other New York Life agents, asking them to
meet them "at their respective homes . . . and before noon," Tarbell
recalled, ". . . two hundred of them and more were carrying Equitable rate books and representing the Equitable Life, and Mr. Mix

was the head of the agency." Tarbell promised Mix a 50 percent commission on policies and renewals, rather than the salaried arrangement he had with New York Life; and a $250,000 advance, an interest-free loan that was 175 percent of his expected first year's premiums.

An early edition of the January 1 *New York Times* published a small, standard announcement of the Equitable's year-end figures: $1.050 billion in insurance; with more than $200 million in new business written in 1899.[11] The Equitable occupied more print in later editions. Reporting on the "Battle for Agents," the *Times* told readers that Perkins and McCall had sent out telegrams convening 600 New York Life agents to stop the leakage. It was rumored that between 250 and 400 agents were joining the Equitable, although Perkins claimed that he had not lost more than four or five men, "with whom we have had differences of a natural kind." He remarked that the Equitable's behavior was based on jealousy, because New York Life "did by far the largest business last year of any company in the world," and he accused Equitable officers of "wining and dining our men right and left of late, and offering all sorts of inducements to them. We have not met these offers and we shall not."[12]

He added, "We presume a stock company like the Equitable can spend its money any way it chooses, but a mutual company like ours, operated for the policyholders' benefit, is, of course, restricted." The implication, meant to mislead, was that New York Life's first priority was its policyholders, while the Equitable profited its shareholders first. That was an arrow aimed not only at the company, but also at James, as the majority shareholder. The Equitable's mutual/stock system was always a point of vulnerability.

James Alexander resurfaced on January 8, when he welcomed the new agents at the annual Metropolitan Department dinner. Everyone knew that Tarbell was responsible for the sweep, yet JWA barely acknowledged him, referring to him only as "an officer of this society."

When the *Insurance Post* reported on the dinner in a story titled, "Trouble Between Two Giants," the writer commented, "President Alexander arose with all the dignity becoming the heir of all reformers," and declared, "We are not in this business to fight. We are in it to try and run it as such a sacred business should be conducted. But when another company forgets its dignity and business honor, it must want war, and it can have it.'" The *Insurance Post* wryly remarked, "Most certainly the sacred interests of the 'sacred business' were not advanced by the pagan raid," and scolded, "There should be no room . . . for those 'undignified methods' of which the Equitable speaks as an eminent authority."[13]

Only eight months after Henry Hyde's death, the new president was absent during one of the biggest fights in the history of the industry; and when the Equitable won, he was ridiculed by a widely read trade journal. The company was showing the first indications that it had been devastated by the loss of its founder.

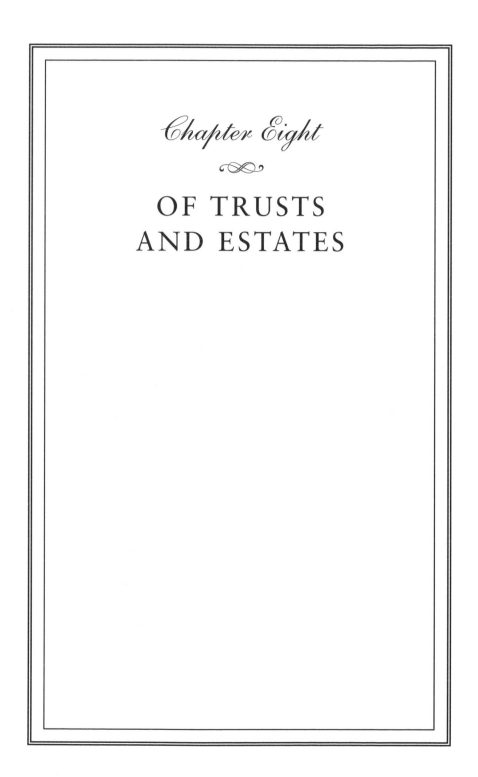

Chapter Eight

OF TRUSTS
AND ESTATES

E. H. Harriman and his daughters, Cornelia and Mary, at the Hyde Ball.

Harriman, one of the most successful railroad investors and executives of his era, had an office at 120 Broadway and took an interest in James Hyde—and in the investment potential of the Equitable. *(Courtesy of the Museum of the City of New York)*

On the afternoon of January 8, 1900, before James Alexander addressed the team of agents Gage Tarbell had delivered, he instructed Equitable treasurer Thomas D. Jordan to draw two checks for a total of $805,000 to the Western National Bank of New York, in which the Equitable had a substantial interest. Alexander was bailing out the Western, which held security for a loan that was so dubious the U.S. Comptroller of the Currency would not accept it. The Equitable took up the assets to keep the bank from losing its charter and to protect its own, and its directors', interests.

The Equitable had been allied with banks and trusts since the 1870s, when the company acquired $1.4 million of the Mercantile Trust Company's $2 million in stock.[1] The two companies were so closely associated that Henry Hyde insisted that the Mercantile, a tenant at 120 Broadway, use an image of the building in its advertising. When the 1873 depression hit, Henry saved the bank by spinning off its unprofitable safe-deposit business, and forming a new company, the Mercantile Safe Deposit Company, to be capitalized with $300,000.

When the Mercantile's books were opened, the safe-deposit issue had no buyers, and Henry took $265,000 of the stock himself. His rationale was that he was protecting the Equitable's investments, but he covered his exposure by borrowing $225,000 from the Equitable at 5 percent. As collateral, he pledged Mercantile Safe Deposit Company stock, an asset no one wanted.

Over the next thirty years, the Equitable continued to support the safe-deposit company, spending nearly half a million dollars to repair and replace its vaults, and charging rents considerably lower than the market. Between 1890 and the end of 1904, the Equitable netted only $3,463 on the MSDC's rent of $483,372.[2] Partly thanks to its special treatment, the safe-deposit company, which Henry owned, flourished.

Henry then turned his attention to the task of strengthening the Mercantile Trust. In 1876, he brought in a new president, Brig. Gen. Louis Fitzgerald, a Princeton graduate and a thrice-wounded Civil War veteran. Fitzgerald became one of Henry's financial intimates, joining the Equitable board in 1878. He served as chairman of the finance committee, and was eventually named one of James's trustees. When Henry borrowed $205,000 from the Mercantile in 1883, the loan was quickly followed by his instruction that the Equitable keep a standing deposit of $1.5 million with the bank. The Equitable earned only 3 percent on its Mercantile deposits, but Henry suggested to Fitzgerald that the bank could make an extra $40,000 by lending out the money at 5 percent.[3]

The Western National Bank of New York entered the picture next. In 1894, the Equitable held nearly eight thousand Western shares, and Equitable directors, including Henry, owned an additional thirteen hundred shares. When a borrower, John W. Young, defaulted on a loan, the Western was left with collateral nominally worth more than $661,000. The U.S. Comptroller of the Currency declared that collateral unsound, too, and threatened to close the bank unless it could recoup the full amount.

Henry persuaded Louis Fitzgerald, who was also a Western shareholder, that the Mercantile should quietly take over the collateral. The transaction was made through Fitzgerald's clerk, George V. Turner, who was paid $15 a week. The Mercantile loaned Turner $661,491 to buy the Young collateral from the Western, and the obligation was then transferred to the Mercantile. This procedure was so common that it had a name, "office boy loans." New York Life "loaned" millions of dollars to George Marshall, a man described as "a Negro messenger, who received a salary of $600 a year and signed whatever dummy notes the directors presented."[4] In one year alone Marshall signed more than $4 million in notes.

Four of the five men who guaranteed the Turner Loan, including

Henry Hyde and Louis Fitzgerald, were associated with the Equitable. The Western was temporarily in the clear, but now the Mercantile, of which the Equitable owned two-thirds, was burdened with the unpromising Young collateral—principally consisting of arid land and unprofitable mineral and timber contracts. Henry formed a committee of the guarantors, plus James Alexander, to explore developing the assets. They hired consultants, who advised them to build an irrigation canal and reservoir, and to sell the land to settlers. To fund the project, the Mercantile advanced more money to George Turner, and the loan was guaranteed by the same five men.

The company, which they called Amity Land and Great Plains Water, built 150 miles of canals with 750 miles of laterals, and a fourteen-thousand-acre reservoir. Its slogan, printed in its tempting sales brochures, was WE AIM TO PUT THE LANDLESS MAN ON THE MANLESS LAND.[5] Virtually the only buyer was the Salvation Army, which had instituted a rural colonization program. The land sales hardly made a dent, and flooding and washouts endangered the infrastructure.

When Henry Hyde died, the guarantors, who now included his estate, were left with a bad investment. Henry had verbally assured them that the Equitable would cover their exposure, but he had never put the agreement in writing. Nine days after his death, in one of James Alexander's first acts as president, he wrote the guarantors in reference to their $2.150 million in loans and advances "to the account of George V. Turner." Alexander confirmed that because the Equitable was the principal owner of the Western, now holding about twelve thousand shares and with $6.6 million in deposits, "and is practically pledged for its protection," the executive committee had authorized the Equitable "to hold the [guarantors] harmless from loss." Subsequent scrutiny of the minutes would not show any such resolution. Less than a year later, JWA went further, and wrote Louis Fitzgerald, promising to pay the guarantors "a fair compensation" on any profits.[6]

The Western board included James Alexander and his son Henry Martyn, Chauncey Depew, Fitzgerald, Gould, James, and other Equitable directors. On January 8, 1900, when JWA moved $805,000 to the Western, to "take up" more of the Western's "doubtful" assets, the money was essentially a loan from the Equitable to itself, and its directors.[7] The problem was finally resolved in 1902, by merging the Western with the National Bank of the United States in New York. The National was controlled by a trust company whose principal shareholder, Thomas Fortune Ryan, was one of the more private Gilded Age tycoons—Ryan's partner, William C. Whitney, described him as "the most adroit, suave and noiseless man he ever met."[8] Ryan was broad-shouldered, blue-eyed, six foot six, and powerfully built. He had the approachable ease of a local politician, but his genial manner was the front for a sharp, tactical mind. He was self-made, estimated at the turn of the century to be worth $50 million, much of it accumulated through developing urban transit systems, with contracts acquired through his relationship with the Tammany Hall political machine.

Ryan was an expert at moving money. (Another bank that he and his partners controlled had made an "office boy loan" to Ryan's $15-a-week clerk, who borrowed $2,060,000.[9]) When the new institution was formed by the merger of the National and Western banks, the Equitable, Mutual, New York Life, and Prudential were represented on its board; JWA and James were appointed to see the consolidation through; and the vice presidents were Richard McCurdy of the Mutual, and J. P. Morgan. The bank merger was the first time James and Ryan did business together, and James did not come away with a good impression of the older man, whom he considered a sharp trader. He would later have occasion to change his opinion, but for the next three years he and Ryan had few contacts.

When the deal was set, Western shareholders were offered $210 per share in a combination of cash and stock.[10] The book value was $260 and the market was buying shares at $600, but the Equitable took the deal at $210.

Despite such transactions the value of the Equitable's stock in eleven banks and trust companies had risen; some of the shares had doubled or tripled, and with a few exceptions the dividends ranged from 8 to 30 percent.[11] That may be why a mysterious account in the Mercantile Trust, alternately known as "the Alexander and Jordan

Account" and "The J.W. Alexander No. 3 Account," was over-looked. On December 30, 1898, the Mercantile Trust wrote JWA checks amounting to $687,273.99, and on January 3, 1899, the Equitable paid the Mercantile the identical amount, for deposit in the JWA No. 3 Account. Those transfers were kept private until they finally broke through the surface in 1905. That year, Charles Evans Hughes, as counsel to the Armstrong Investigation of the insurance industry, deduced,

> It is supposed that it had been the practice of the officers of the [Equitable] society to borrow from the trust company in their individual names moneys required for certain disbursements which it was not desired to enter on the books of the society. . . . The majority of the debit items in the account, since 1898, consist of checks to the order of Messrs. Alexander . . . and others connected with the society. One of the officers . . . would obtain currency from the Cashier, signing a cash ticket which, generally on the same day, would be taken up by a check of the Mercantile Trust Company . . . No record was kept on the books of the society of these loans.[12]

While the trust relationships were principally in JWA's domain, James took over in the investment arena. His brief business career coincided with a period when the U.S. financial markets offered unprecedented opportunity. From the end of the depression in 1897 through 1904, 4,277 firms were consolidated into 257, and 319 railroads merged, requiring $6 billion in capitalization.[13] By the end of 1904, the one hundred largest companies had quadrupled in value, controlling some 40 percent of the industrial capital in the United States.[14] The Equitable, New York Life, and the Mutual's annual premium income amounted to more than 75 percent of the combined gross income of every nationally chartered bank in the United States.[15]

The insurers worked intimately with investment bankers. The Equitable's closest relationship was with Jacob Schiff of Kuhn, Loeb, who was both a director and a member of the finance committee. Schiff sold the Equitable $49,704,408 of stock between 1900 and the end of 1904, 16 percent of its purchases. One vice president of New York Life called such connections "a happy factor." As he explained, "the insurance companies . . . will buy only the best securities. They have a right, in buying, to expect and demand the best price. They will always be in favor of financial transactions that are constructive, never in favor of anything that is destructive. They will always be in favor of peace, never in favor of war. They will be exemplars of the highest type of commercial honor. . . . Their influence on the world of money will be as widespread and benign as it . . . is in the homes of the people."[16]

In 1902 James formed his own syndicate, James Hazen Hyde and Associates, which acted as a middleman between Wall Street firms with issues to sell, and the Equitable, as buyer. He slipped easily into a system in which "the president or vice-president of an insurance company can buy stocks or bonds as an individual (although perhaps with the money of the policy-holders) and then resell them to the insurance company at an advanced price."[17] JWA, who had suggested that the syndicate bear James's name, participated in nearly all of the JHH and Associates deals, and in three instances, he and James were the only partners. In March 1902, alone, James wrote him three times to confirm allotments, which added up to $150,000.[18] JWA and James usually received identical allotments and profits.

In a typical syndicate transaction, JHH and Associates was allotted $1 million of Metropolitan Street Railway bonds at $94 and interest. A little more than a week later, the Equitable executive committee approved buying the bonds from James's syndicate at $97, and James and his partners netted more than $30,000. In another instance, the syndicate bought $1.25 million in Oregon Short Line Railroad bonds, a company of which James was a director, at $96. Five days later, on James's recommendation, the Equitable bought the bonds from the syndicate at $97. JHH and Associates earned more than $25,000, and James and JWA split the profit.

James expanded his offices at 120 Broadway—his clerks and other staff eventually occupied a suite of seven rooms—and he kept another office at home. His secretary, Charles Williamson, moved into the house so he could be available at any time. Williamson explained that he and James began their Equitable work at eight o'clock in the morning and that he "remained with Mr. Hyde on Equitable duty until he retired every night. . . . Mr. Hyde was always at the service of the Equitable and whether he was at his office or whether he was away from his office, if any business that required his attention came up, he always dropped his personal or his social pleasures to attend to that."

James paid Williamson himself for much of this work, and in a replay of Henry's relationship with McIntyre, had him "on call at all hours of the day and night." Sometimes Williamson worked until three or four o'clock in the morning, and occasionally all night—"on Equitable matters, and not personally,"[19] Williams insisted.

With so much coming in so fast, James needed a mentor in business, and JWA had begun to sound like Polonius, with footnotes by Hamlet. The most obvious adviser would have been Chauncey Depew, with his experience in railroads, finance, and politics, and a long-standing knowledge of the Equitable. Henry Hyde had regularly stopped at Depew's house before he went to the office, and again on his way home from work, and they sat and talked in the wood-paneled library, with the Egyptian frieze running around the top of the walls and a stuffed albatross looming from the top of a bookcase. Depew was paid a $20,000-a-year retainer from the Equitable, and, in large part, his services consisted of those informal, but informative conversations. Over time, Depew had developed an avuncular affection for James. On Christmas Day, 1898, during Henry's final illness, he wrote him, using the family nickname, "Caleb, the boy and youth and James the man have been associated with many pleasant hours of speculation and hope, until you have seemed to me for years of my blood relationship. Merry Christmas and Happy New Year my dear boy and lots of 'em, with love to your Father."[20]

By the next Christmas, Henry was dead, and Depew again wrote James, this time referring to "the closest of friendships which was without a shadow for over a quarter of a century,"[21] and gave James a pass for the New York Central lines. A year later, he wrote, "I give you leave to use my name whenever you think it may help along anything in which you are interested." Later, he was to testify,

I had known young Mr. Hyde since he was a boy and had taken a deep interest in his welfare and advancement. I had watched him carefully since he had been connected with the Society and found that . . . he was taking a deep [and intelligent] interest in the affairs of the Society . . . impressing himself upon the members of the Executive Committee . . . and . . . with the financial men downtown as a young man who was getting on very rapidly. . . . He was full of ambition . . . he was rendering valuable service; he was doing a specially excellent service in France—the best evidence of his ability . . . is that he secured from the French Government the decoration of the Legion of Honor—that comes to a great many, and subsequently a promotion in the Legion of Honor, which comes to a very few. It was universally felt that the best asset of the Society was the name of Hyde.[22]

But Henry had not named Depew one of James's trustees, and when James needed him, Depew was a U.S. senator in Washington, while James, the Equitable, and Wall Street were in New York.

Instead James chose his own mentor, the railroad financier Edward Henry Harriman. James and Harriman were an unlikely pair. James stood out wherever he went, but Harriman was the least physically prepossessing of the titans. Henry Clay Frick was only five foot two, but he had a big, handsome head and a solid body. Morgan, who had been a good-looking youth, had developed a disease that made his nose look like boiled strawberries, but he had the stature and carriage of a king. James J. Hill wasn't tall, but he was stocky and strong, and even in late middle age he gave the impression that he could bellow loud enough to blow a train off a trestle. Any of them could have been compared to such members of the animal kingdom as the lion, bull, or bear. But when Harriman's character was described, the creature that came to mind was a small dog with a sharp bite.

At five foot four, he was deceptively mild-looking. His puckish face was framed by ears that stuck out, thick glasses, and an oversized brush mustache. The mustache and the glasses were nearly all that showed when he pressed a broad-brimmed hat over his thinning hair, wrapped his body in a capacious overcoat, and wound a muffler around his throat to protect himself from colds and bronchial ailments. If he wasn't sniffling, he might be spluttering. When he was agitated, he sometimes became speechless and could only bark out "Wow-wow-wow!"

When Harriman wanted something, he sank in his teeth and let go only when he got what he was after. His biographer, Maury Klein, says he "made up in scrappiness what he lacked in size. Where others intimidated through size or strength, Henry did so through sheer force of will."[23] The financier Otto Kahn remarked, "His power of will was nothing short of phenomenal. I have seen him perform veritable miracles in the way of making people do as he wanted."[24] But Kahn also said, "If there was any fighting going on within earshot, however little it might concern him, he was tempted to take a hand in the fray, and the greater the odds against his side, the better." James Stillman of National City Bank was warned that Harriman was "not a safe man to have business with."[25]

Even as a boy, a school acquaintance recalled, Harriman was "the worst little devil in his class, and always at the top of it."[26] He did not stay in school for long; at fourteen he was already a messenger on Wall Street. He made his first fortune as a stockbroker specializing in railroads, which so dominated the economy that in 1885, the New York Stock Exchange listed 125 railroads, while all other sectors accounted for only twenty-six issues.[27] In the early 1890s, he began to acquire great blocks of railroad stock, and in 1893, he joined the board of the Illinois Central. Soon after that, he beat out J. P. Morgan in a fight for control of another road, the Dubuque and Sioux City; and moved to take over the Union Pacific, which had been forced into receivership at the beginning of the 1893 depression. George Gould and Jacob Schiff were spearheading a UP reorganization and were ready to issue $230 million in stocks and bonds. When they kept running into obscure obstacles, Schiff asked Morgan to use his extensive network to investigate, and he reported back that Harriman was behind the disruptions.

Schiff confronted Harriman, who admitted that he was making trouble because he wanted to reorganize the Union Pacific himself.

When Schiff reminded him that his group had the controlling bonds, Harriman replied that he intended to issue $100 million of Illinois Central bonds and use some of the proceeds for the acquisition.

"Well, you will have a good time doing it, Mr. Harriman," Schiff said, "but in the meantime, what is your price?"[28] Harriman did not want to sell; he wanted to be chairman of the Union Pacific executive committee. Schiff, who later described the conversation as "brutal," turned him down. Later, Schiff was forced to go back to Harriman when he couldn't sell enough bonds to finance the reorganization. This time, he agreed to appoint Harriman to the committee. The UP received its new charter, and, a few months later, Harriman was elected chairman.

When James graduated from college, Harriman had already been the driving force behind the reorganization of three railroads.

In September 1900, Harriman made an offer to acquire the Iowa-based Chicago, Burlington and Quincy Railroad, known as the "Q," and combine it with the Union Pacific. His rival for the road was James J. Hill, the founder of the Great Northern Railway.[29] Hill and Morgan were the majority shareholders of another major line, the Northern Pacific. With the Q, they could wrap up an important piece of the northwest traffic.

Harriman and Hill made competing offers that winter. Schiff tried to mediate between them, and persuaded Hill to come to a last-minute meeting with Harriman, hoping to avert another railroad battle. But Hill was skeptical and curt, Harriman lost his temper and threatened him, and Hill, disgusted, walked out.

The Great Northern and Northern Pacific combination made the better suitor for the Iowa-based Q, and while Harriman haggled, its owner agreed to sell to Hill at the asking price of $200 a share.

When Harriman recognized that Hill had outbid him, he embarked on an even more ambitious, strategic—and secret—plan to buy the majority shares of the Northern Pacific. Morgan and Hill believed they firmly controlled the NP, with about one-third of the $155 million in outstanding shares—Schiff had been the lead banker on the deal. Now Harriman engaged Schiff to act for him, and Kuhn, Loeb discreetly began acquiring Northern Pacific stock through agents all over the United States. The purchases went unnoticed for some time, because big investors, known as "plungers," were buying blocks of railroad stock, and the buyers were widely dispersed.

In early May, Harriman owned a $52 million stake in the Northern Pacific, and was almost ready to make a surprise takeover bid. He had two new allies. One was Jacob Schiff, who understood exactly what his role was; the other was James Hyde, who did not.

Chapter Nine

THE UNVEILING,
MAY 1901

Henry Baldwin Hyde, *by John Quincy Adams Ward.*

The bronze statue of Henry Hyde was dedicated in 1901, the same day E. H. Harriman joined the Equitable board and borrowed $2.7 million for the biggest railroad fight in Wall Street history. In 1912, 120 Broadway was ravaged by a fire that interrupted trading on Wall Street, but the statue remained standing in the once-magnificent lobby. *(Courtesy AXA Financial Archives)* wo years after Henry Hyde's death, on May 2, 1901, the directors and officers of the Equitable gathered at 120 Broadway for the unveiling of the founder's statue. The directors met first in the company's Victorian boardroom, with its dark wood wainscoting, brocade wall covering, ornate ceiling, and Oriental rug. Alexander sat in the huge president's chair with an oval back, studded with what looked like enormous industrial rivets. James Hyde settled into one of the six officers' chairs, of similar but lighter design, placed in threes on either side of the president's desk, facing in toward him. Everyone else sat in rows on small, stiff leather-upholstered side chairs.

That morning, at James's recommendation, the directors elected E. H. Harriman to the board, and voted to lend the Union Pacific $2.7 million on collateral of thirty-six thousand UP shares. It was the largest block of stock the Equitable had ever accepted as security. Harriman and Schiff may have been the only directors who realized that the loan would top up the war chest that would allow Harriman and the UP to buy control of the Northern Pacific.

After the board concluded its business, guests joined the directors for luncheon in the private dining room. The luncheon was catered by the Café Savarin, cigars were passed, the men leaned back in their chairs, and the speeches began. James Alexander spoke about the "seed planted" by Henry Hyde growing into a "mighty tree with branches sheltering many thousands of families." Chauncey Depew gave an analysis of the development of ambition in the United States, a 1901 view of American history. The first wave, he said, comprised the "statesmen of creative genius"—Washington, Hamilton, and Jefferson. After them, "ideals changed to men of eloquence at the bar and in the Senate—Webster, Clay, and the Calhouns—[who] could interpret the spirit of our institutions." The Civil War "developed the fighting capacities of our race, and . . . an extraordinary number of soldiers with rare capacity for command." Finally, Depew declared, a postwar "onrush of material prosperity has swept the ingenious youth of the country . . . into the vortex of business activities, speculations, and accumulations, and made a million dollars the mark and more millions the ambition of the boys of our land."

It is likely that every man in the room was urgently considering the status of his own millions. The unexplained activity in the Northern Pacific and Union Pacific had finally stirred investors; rumors spread that one or more of the major rail systems was in play, and the market, driven by uncertainty, had begun to behave erratically. Depew; Harriman; Schiff; Astor; Belmont; former vice president of the United States Levi Morton, head of the bank Morton, Bliss and Company; and railroad presidents A. J. Cassatt of the Pennsylvania, T. Jefferson Coolidge of the Atchison, Topeka and Santa Fe, and Sir William Van Horne of the Canadian Pacific would all be affected if the market continued to react to the mystery.

They would soon learn that a fight was afoot, with stakes far higher than the ownership of a railroad. A biographer of James J. Hill has described the battle for the Northern Pacific as "a contest for supremacy on Wall Street."[1] Harriman and Schiff were in league with the feared combination of the Rockefellers, Standard Oil, and National City Bank, and Equitable director George Gould had joined them.

When the directors adjourned and rode downstairs to the lobby, they found that employees, tenants, and dozens of journalists were crowded around Henry Hyde's statue. Willie McIntyre pulled the cord of the Stars and Stripes and uncovered the dark bronze effigy of Mr. Hyde in a simple frock coat, with a bow tie and spats. John Quincy Adams Ward had made his subject seven feet tall; on a two-foot base, Henry stood nine feet above the crowd.

The reporters were anxious to quiz the inscrutable Mr. Harriman. The day before, the *New York Times* had gone so far as to run a story headlined UNION PACIFIC CONTROL LOST BY E. H. HARRIMAN, asserting, "Chicago and Northwestern interests believed to have secured it." The story reported that the Union Pacific had been bought out from under Harriman, but admitted that no one really knew who was fighting whom. The speculation, "from the porters up,"[2] was that the Vanderbilts had secured control of the Union Pacific. When William K. Vanderbilt returned from Europe that week, his remarks were laconic, but the *Times* took a leap of faith and declared, W. K. VANDERBILT UNDERSTOOD TO BE BACK OF THE BIG DEAL. "Mr. Harriman was caught napping," the reporter wrote—but if Harriman looked sleepy, he was shamming. At the unveiling, he had the self-control to make only one brusque comment: "I have not let go any of my holdings."[3]

James J. Hill was in Seattle when he got wind of the unusual activity in the Northern Pacific. The price of NP common stock had risen from $101 to $117 and climbing, and Hill was certain the steep ascent wasn't an accident of the market. He ordered a special train for the trip across the continent; his ride has been described as a full-speed-ahead dash to avert disaster, but, in fact, he proceeded with deliberation. Hill's office was in the same building as Kuhn, Loeb, 80 Broadway, and on May 3 he arrived to see Schiff.

Kuhn, Loeb had helped finance the acquisition of the Northern Pacific for Hill and Morgan in the late 1890s, when they had acquired about 40 percent of NP stock, and Hill and Schiff had been allies. Now, Schiff told Hill he was representing Harriman to seize control of the same road. One version of his rationale was that he said he was trying to right an imbalance of power. Hill wasn't interested in Schiff's explanation; head down and battle ready, he strode out of the Kuhn, Loeb office and charged over to 23 Wall Street to the Morgan bank, which, appropriately, resembled a Roman temple of Jupiter, the god to whom Wall Street compared the Olympian of bankers. The Morgan partners were more accustomed to obeisance than rage, but when Hill learned that the bank had unwittingly sold some of its own shares of NP as the price rose, he lost his temper. He instructed them to wire Morgan immediately, requesting the banker's approval to buy $15 million of Northern Pacific common at whatever price the market demanded.

Morgan was at the Grand Hôtel in the French spa of Aix-les-Bains, a fixture on the circuit of the rich and the royal. Queen Victoria, King Leopold II of Belgium, George I of Greece, and Empress Elisabeth of Austria[4] had all stayed there. Morgan usually started the day in the thermal baths and on the massage table, but on Saturday morning, he was interrupted by a cable from his office, warning that Harriman had closed in, and that Hill urgently requested that Morgan join him to buy whatever they needed to retain control of Northern Pacific. Morgan, as enraged as Hill, telegraphed his agreement.

At home at Arden that Friday night, Harriman was ill and slept badly. By dawn, he decided that he needed an additional $4 million of stock, more than half of which he could finance with the Equitable loan. Saturday morning, he tried to reach Schiff to place the buy order, but Schiff was at synagogue; a younger Kuhn, Loeb partner went to get his approval for a purchase of that scale, but Schiff sent him away. When the market closed at midday, no one told Harriman that he did not own the additional shares.

The *New York Times* was still publishing theories. Adolph Ochs, the owner and publisher of the *Times*, should have had an inside track; he had been at the luncheon after the board meeting when Harriman was elected a director. Ochs had a long-standing relationship with the Equitable; Henry Hyde had been one of Ochs's investors when he bought the paper, and the insurer still held a mortgage on the *Times* building. Ochs had not learned anything he could use, and the paper looked to the Midwest for clues. On Sunday, the *Times* ran a long front-page article from St. Paul, Minnesota, the headquarters of the Great Northern, titled GIGANTIC RAILROAD DEAL, which speculated on a consolidation of the Hill, Morgan, Gould, and Vanderbilt interests. Harriman might have been amused that he was not mentioned. He was certain that the Northern Pacific was, in the words of the *Times*, his own "gigantic railroad deal."

On Monday, the Morgan-Hill forces sent traders onto the floor with buy orders, and the market went berserk. NP opened at $114; Morgan and Hill kept buying and the stock closed at $133, sparking a rumor that they had lost control of the railroad. Brokers reacted by selling the stock short, betting that the run was over. They sold shares they didn't own, setting a high price for them. They expected that when NP fell, as they were sure it would, they would buy the shares back at a depressed price and make a fortune on the difference. But Morgan and Hill were buying to corner the stock, and they didn't intend to leave any shares lying around for Harriman to pick up. As the price kept going up, the short sellers were forced to go into the market and buy back the stock at increasingly elevated prices as the margin calls began to come in and they had to deliver the stock, and they began to buy whatever they could at any price. It only took two days for Morgan and Hill to own 420,000 shares of NP, and for nearly everyone else to be squeezed out. In desperation, some of the short-sellers bid up NP common as high as $1,000.

The entire market was affected. The volume of trading set a record, as speculators were forced to sell to raise money to cover their NP commitments, driving the prices of other stocks down as the newspapers trumpeted MONEY KINGS IN DEATH STRUGGLE. When it was clear that Hill and Morgan had won, Schiff met with representatives of the Morgan bank; the winners agreed to sell enough shares of NP at 150 to bail out the short sellers, imposing stability and preventing personal and corporate failures. In those days, a few men could reshape the market twice in as many weeks.

Hill didn't like Harriman before the NP threat, and he actively disliked him after it was over. He wrote one of his associates in 1906 that all James Stillman and Harriman "want to make them crooked is an opportunity to cheat someone."[5] Despite that, when Harriman approached Hill in 1902 in James Hyde's behalf and asked him to join the board of the Equitable Life Assurance Society, Hill agreed. He was never an active director, which was unusual: Hill rarely joined a board unless he could give his attention to the company. Perhaps he and Morgan decided that, with Morgan in a position to influence New York Life, it would be useful to have one of them in a position to know what was going on at the Equitable, where Harriman and Schiff were ensconced on the board.

A man with more experience than James would have drawn certain conclusions from these well-known battles. If James misun-

derstood Harriman, it was in part because his father had made sure
he did not understand the way *he* did business, either. Perhaps James
saw Harriman as a man much like Henry: tough; but benign. That
was Harriman's view of himself. As he explained,

> When Mr. Hyde asked me to become a director of the Equitable I
> told him that I had very little time to give to such things and that I
> did not think that the method of management in the Equitable was
> the right one, and he told me that he intended as time went on to
> change it and that his desire was to surround himself with independ-
> ent men that would have no other interest than that of the Equitable,
> to help him in its management; that . . . Mr. Alexander was getting
> old and that his succession to Mr. Alexander was probably not far
> off. I told him if that was his intention that I would become a direc-
> tor . . . [6]
>
> Mr. Hyde . . . was a young man with a great deal of power . . .
> and he was apparently surrounded by people who were catering to
> his particular desires . . . if he were to grow and get experience, he
> would do better by having around him men who were independent
> and had had experience in business affairs, who would sustain him
> and help him. [7]

In Harriman's first years on the Equitable board, he appeared to
be only moderately interested in the company. He did not even own
the five shares that qualified him as a director; they had been signed
over to him to satisfy the letter of the law, and he was a "dummy
director" like many of the others. The Equitable did not seem like a
takeover target for him. A mutual insurance company was not a
negotiable property: it was not traded on the open market; the interest was fixed to the original cost; and its funds could not be dispersed
to the shareholders beyond the 7 percent on the stock's initial value.
The bulk of its assets were earmarked for policyholders. As James
Alexander said before the unveiling of Henry's statue, the
$305,000,000 in the Equitable's treasury when Henry died "might
easily have been the sum left by Mr. Hyde to his children. . . . I know
of no more startling contrast than this $305,000,000 if devised to a
single family with all the possibilities of its use or misuse in the suc-

ceeding generations and that sum held in trust . . . to keep from want 374,000 families, when the breadwinner is gone, and to educate and place in the paths of usefulness hundreds of thousands of orphaned or half-orphaned children." [8]

But as the Morgan bank became more openly connected to New York Life, Harriman's interest in the Equitable accelerated. As the *New York World* noted, he was, "above all, a strategist . . . in [that] respect Morgan is said to be his inferior by capable judges. And he is ambitious . . . to surpass Morgan in the railroad world and . . . jealous of Morgan's great supremacy." [9]

That fall George Perkins, possibly fronting for Morgan, and almost certainly with his knowledge, made the first move to invade the Equitable. For the few who knew about it, the implication was that Morgan wanted to extend his power base by gaining control of all three major players in the insurance field.

Chapter Ten

RIDING HIGH

James Hyde driving one of his famous coaches.

When James Hyde and Alfred Vanderbilt mounted a record-breaking race against time from New York to Philadelphia, thousands of spectators turned out along the route. *(Courtesy Lorna Hyde Graev)*

*G*age Tarbell and George Perkins were the same age, and they had begun their parallel jobs within months of each other, but in 1901, Perkins drew well ahead when he managed the extraordinary feat of joining J. P. Morgan as a partner, while remaining an officer of New York Life. It was the most blatant case of conflicting loyalties in the industry.

Perkins had emerged as a force in the financial world when he was made a director of National City Bank in November 1900. Early the next year, he met J. P. Morgan. The financier had been keeping an eye on Perkins and, at their first meeting, asked him to join his firm, giving him a day to decide. Perkins made some calls—one of the men he asked for advice was President William McKinley—and declined. New York Life rewarded him by more than doubling his salary, from $35,000 to $75,000, which was more than James earned in 1901. A couple of months later, Morgan approached him again; this time, he invited him to become one of his eleven partners, at $250,000 a year, with a share in the firm's profits. Perkins told Morgan that he could accept the job only if he could also continue to serve as a vice president of New York Life, and chairman of its finance committee. Despite the potential for an open clash of interests, Morgan capitulated.[1]

Perkins and Morgan shared a philosophy of "cooperation" in business. As Perkins later explained to James Alexander and President Richard McCurdy of the Mutual, "The entire path of our industrial progress is strewn with the white bones of . . . competition. . . . Co-operation must be the order of the day."[2] To put his theory into practice—and to trump Tarbell after the great agent raid of New Year's Eve 1899—Perkins called a meeting with JWA and McCurdy in early September 1901, soon after he joined the Morgan bank. They met in Paris, where McCurdy took a private suite at the Hôtel du Rhin, where they would be less likely to be discovered by the press. During a three-hour discussion, Perkins outlined his proposal that the insurers merge and be run by an executive committee, which he would head. He warned them that New York Life anticipated such a large increase in business that it would soon leave the others behind, but said he was willing to give up that advantage to achieve a long-term goal. If they amalgamated, they could dash any competition, and their pool of capital would be so large they could sway nations. The plan had "Morgan" written all over it, if only as a reflection of his point of view.

Alexander turned down the idea, then wrote James, expressing his contempt for the "little two-penny scheme." [3] He mentioned offhandedly that Perkins had suggested buying James's stock for "some millions." The terms of James's trust prevented him from selling his shares until he was thirty, without a dispensation from his trustees; but even if he had been free to act independently, he was not disposed to consider offers. Between 1901 and 1905, he twice rejected $10 million from George Haven, a Mutual finance committee member, and an offer for the same amount from the financier Henry Morgenthau, acting on James Stillman's authority.

That fall James was preoccupied by a project that involved spending, not making money. He was preparing for a four-in-hand coaching race from New York to Philadelphia with Morris Howlett and Alfred Vanderbilt. Alfred, a year younger than James, had inherited $42 million the year he graduated from Yale, and was positioned to take the lead at the New York Central Railroad, and in other family investments. Like James, he was convinced that he could combine work and life as a sportsman. Dark, slender, almost handsome, and beautifully groomed, he wore his sleek hair in the center part typical of the period. His winged eyebrows compensated for eyes that were set a bit too close together, and his chin had a becoming dimple. He was an avid horseman and had learned tandem and four-in-hand driving from the family coachman, and from the senior Howlett in Paris.

James and Morris Howlett spent a year organizing the race. They decided to use one of James's coaches, the "Liberty," and sixteen of his horses, along with his harnesses and his stablemen. They hoped Alfred would supply additional horses, and intended to rent the rest. But Alfred, who had initially agreed to join them, seemed to have lost interest. Howlett sent him a blizzard of telegrams, and finally, four days before the race, Alfred replied, apologizing, "My part of the transaction has been a perfect fizzle just from forgetfulness and inexcusably poor judgment. I see it now only too well and regret it with all my heart." He was still "very enthusiastic about the drive," and would match James's commitment of horses, tack, and men to the endeavor.[4]

On the foggy dawn of October 9, 1901, the pudgy-faced "Napoleon" Howlett, as James called him, stood at the Manhattan ferry landing in his Chesterfield coat and broad-brimmed felt hat, and checked the horses lined up to board for the Hudson crossing. Of the seventy-two horses they would need, many had already been sent ahead in a special twelve-car train; each car held three grooms and four to six horses. The railroad cars were left at staging points as temporary stables, and Equitable employees were strategically stationed at each stop.

At the Holland House hotel in Manhattan, James and Alfred, in the top hats and tail coats of the New York Coaching Club, mounted the box. James blew the tallyho horn at 5:55 A.M., and they raced down the early-morning streets, took the Twenty-third Street corner on two wheels, and skidded up to the ferry landing.

Once across the river, they dashed through the countryside, stopping at Newark, Trenton, Princeton, and New Brunswick. The goal was to change the horses in two minutes. To reward speed, James paid the grooms an extra $1 each, with the promise that the fastest crew would be awarded $5 bonuses when the race was over. Excited crowds gathered at each change—two thousand at New Brunswick, and a near-riot of students at Princeton, blowing horns, beating drums, and making the horses bolt. The spectators had been alerted by advance newspaper reports and by James's efficient telegraph system: As the coach left each stop, a telegram was sent to the next relay point, announcing the estimated arrival time. Even the police were enthusiastic; when a horse sprained a tendon near Princeton, a policeman volunteered his mount in its place. He threw his saddle and bridle into the coach, leapt aboard, rode to the next change, then saddled up and went back to work.

In Philadelphia, several thousand cheering people blocked the streets and surrounded the Bellevue Hotel, as the coach drew in at exactly 3:21. DeWitt Cuyler, the Equitable's Pennsylvania counsel and a director since 1876, held the stopwatch. The crowd slowed the change; it took six minutes to switch horses, and then they were off again.

On the return leg, Howlett wrote, "Even between villages there were massed hundreds of eager faces urging us on to victory: it was thrilling!" They were still ahead of the record, but they were losing time. At Trenton, where a crowd of one thousand waited, they were more than an hour late. They grazed a truck on the way to Princeton, and although no one was hurt, they had to stop to be sure the coach hadn't been damaged. By the time they reached New Brunswick, they had fallen two hours behind. It was dark when they entered Newark, and a Western Union messenger guided them through the streets on his bicycle, lighting the way with a headlamp. Out on the open roads again, they used relays of "link boys," who rode ahead on bicycles to warn late-night traffic to get out of their way. A special ferry in Newark "was in motion before the coach wheels had stopped turning," Howlett wrote. "Even the boat caught the fever of breaking the record and did the distance [from New Jersey to Manhattan] in thirteen minutes"[5] instead of the customary twenty-five. The team drew up to the Holland House at 1:34 in the morning. Carriages that had brought friends to celebrate were lined up around the block. The men stood on the sidewalk to cheer James and Alfred, and hug them as they stepped down into the crowd, and inside, as one newspaper wrote, "the corridors were thronged with women."[6] The Hyde team had covered 224 miles in nineteen hours and thirty-five minutes, setting a record.

The next morning, James received an *Evening Journal* reporter at home. The man found him eating breakfast in bed, feeling well, and prepared to clarify a few points. He told the reporter that he and

Alfred had shared the driving, logging about eight hours each, with Howlett filling in, and that an aspect of the race that had escaped notice was that they used the same horses on the return trip as they had coming out. "We could have made faster time if we had used a different set of horses," he said, ". . . but I would not consider that good sport."[7]

Reports of the race were published in newspapers as far removed from the route as Milwaukee, Wisconsin, and Mobile, Alabama, and filled dozens of pages in an oversized album when Charles Williamson cut them out. James was the focus of many flattering stories. The *Philadelphia News* wrote, "Considering that vice-president James Hazen Hyde of the Equitable has only passed five and twenty summers of his life, he is a young man of very considerable versatility . . . a talented *literateur*; a polished writer and essayist, an accomplished linguist, second in command of the Equitable, a director in a score of important companies."[8] Although James was the event's principal organizer and had absorbed nearly all the $2,000 cost, Alfred's name appeared in many of the headlines. Some stories repeated the rumor that Alfred lost a $25,000 bet on the time of the run, a claim James said he believed to be false; others noted that he was called for jury duty the day of the race and, failing to appear, was held in contempt of court, "liable to attachment" of his property. Vanderbilt was an irresistible name, and James gathered the impression that Alfred had intended to steal the credit. James wrote him to express his resentment, but the breach healed and Alfred joined the Equitable board that year.

A month after the race, James offered a $500 prize for the best four-in-hand driving at the National Horse Show, and Howlett won. The next spring, James and his equipage starred in the New York Coaching Club parade. His coach was drawn by four elegant coal-black horses; and his sister, Mary, sat on the box with him. Equitable directors, agents, policyholders, and the competition read about James's increasing visibility in the coaching world, and some began to wonder about the time and money Vice President Hyde was spending on his hobby.

Harriman's reaction to James's notoriety appears to have been to assume that he had a large bank account. The month after the race, he invited James to participate in a financial transaction that would leave them both vulnerable to criticism. Harriman and Schiff had established a syndicate to buy five hundred thousand shares of Union Pacific preferred for $50 million—about half of the UP's capitalization.[9] Their purpose was to anticipate hostile takeovers by picking up shares as they came on the market and keeping the stock locked up in a five-year holding agreement. Harriman proposed that James invest $2.5 million, but James could not afford that kind of outlay, and said he would arrange for the Equitable to buy the shares. Harriman was anxious to maintain secrecy, in part to keep the price from being inflated over the next few years as the syndicate acquired the stock, and he did not want corporations to sign the agreement. James agreed to sign, but the Equitable was committed to pay for the stock. To cover James's liability, JWA wrote him a formal letter, dated January 12, 1903. He assured him that, as the investment was

> for the benefit of the Equitable Life Assurance Society, and that the Society is to receive the profits resulting therefrom, it is understood that the Society, from time to time, will supply such funds as may be necessary . . . and that you personally will be fully indemnified and protected against any personal liability or loss . . . in the course of the carrying out of said agreement.[10]

James did not buy any shares himself, and the stock was not held in his name, but in the name of the issuing bank, Kuhn, Loeb, and "endorsed in blank."[11] Yet, despite Harriman's best efforts, the story would eventually come to light.

In 1902, James was made chairman of the Equitable executive and finance committees; his salary was raised from $30,000 to $75,000; he was paid an additional $25,000 as vice president of two trust companies; and he received fees as a director of forty-six companies, including thirteen railroads, fourteen banks, and four trusts. At a time when most Equitable department heads were paid only $5,000, and factory workers received about $500 a year for ten-hour days and six-day weeks, his income was vast. A great deal of money was coming in, and a lot was going right back out. As an historian of Long Island's South Shore wrote, James transformed The Oaks "from a stately country home to a private casino and country club; on his private siding off the Long Island Railroad would come his private car with 'actresses' and other friends. ... The Oaks, [on] some four hundred acres with all the various improvements . . . became the fourth highest assessed property in the Town of Islip in 1903." William K. Vanderbilt's was first.[12] James built a sixty-foot-wide canal from the bay to accommodate visiting yachts, added a squash court, and enlarged the dining room to seat one hundred, although his dinner parties were not always formal. A writer for *Le Figaro* who visited from Paris reported that there was a fully equipped kitchen in the stables, where James sometimes gave lively suppers. The journalist wrote fondly of an evening when the temperature outside was fifteen degrees, and "The ladies donned old postillion hats or bullfighter bonnets and blew hunting horns while everybody danced the cakewalk."[13] Entertaining at The Oaks was so lavish that some of James's "intimate friends" guessed that he spent $100,000 a year on the estate.[14] Later, when he was trying to make a case to his mother that keeping The Oaks had cost him "a great deal of money," the figure he cited was between $25,000 and $50,000 a year.[15]

The most distinctive aspect of the glamorous life at The Oaks was the museum-quality carriage collection James was assembling. He sought the finest examples, restored them to impeccable condition, and, when he drove them, created a spectacle redolent of a time already passing with the appearance of the automobile. His tack was as gorgeous as jewelry, and even his stable buckets shone. By 1905, he owned "a road coach, mail coach, park drag, pony cart, body break, two skeleton breaks, three opera busses, two hansoms, two broughams, two Victorias, mail and spider phaetons, gigs, jogging, shooting, dog and tandem carts, buggies and runabouts, express wagons, cutters and sleighs."[16] If the Hyde carriage collection had been kept intact, it would have become a significant historical resource.

James was also making a name for himself in New York cultural circles. He was passionately interested in theater and music, and as he acquired the position and financial wherewithal, he became a dedicated patron of the arts, in particular of the Metropolitan Opera, the most prestigious arts institution in New York. The Metropolitan had been founded in 1883 by a group of fifty-two men, many of whom had made their fortunes recently, and were unable to acquire their own boxes in the city's original house, the Academy of Music. The problem was not exclusivity—or at least, not solely—the Academy was too small to accommodate all the new opera lovers: the Vanderbilts alone needed five boxes.

In 1883, the new Metropolitan Opera Company opened with 3,045 seats, nearly one-quarter of them in 122 boxes that seated six and fronted a salon-cum-cloakroom. The opera house was a block-square building between Thirty-ninth and Fortieth Streets, an easy walk from the Hydes'. In 1891, a fire gutted the interior of the house, and a new board of thirty-five members took over. For $30,000 apiece, they bought stock in the Metropolitan Opera and Real Estate Company. Their investment guaranteed each stockholder a box and a one-thirty-fifth interest in the real estate. The boxholders owned the house and controlled its management and repertoire.

That was the Metropolitan's status in 1903, when Heinrich Conreid, an Austrian impresario, appeared on the scene. Henry Morgenthau had agreed to help Conreid lease the house for his Conreid Metropolitan Opera Company, and one of the first backers Morgenthau brought in was James Hyde, who in turn was a source of other sponsors from the city's social families. When the Conreid Company opened on November 23, 1903, with Enrico Caruso making his New York debut in *Rigoletto*,[17] James was seated in the director's box. He became so involved that he did something reminiscent of Henry Hyde at Jekyll Island: He took a strong hand on the board, spearheading a consolidation of its membership, and Morgenthau quit.

Among the sponsors James brought in was the Kuhn, Loeb partner, Otto Kahn. A Kahn biographer, Theresa M. Collins, describes the two men as "like-minded opera enthusiasts and serious art lovers who adored Paris and the theater." Collins explains that they hoped to create a new, more artistic social environment in New York, influenced by the European mélange of the social and the cultural. Kahn, born in Germany, and Hyde, steeped in French culture, understood that their city was "rising to compete, cooperate, and integrate with the economic and artistic life of Europe's capitals."[18]

James was well placed to help engineer that integration. He continued to run the extended Harvard guest lectureship; and when he established exchange scholarships between Columbia University and the Sorbonne, the French government awarded him his second decoration. He became a board member of the new Alliance Français in New York, served as its president in 1902, and was credited with giving it social cachet. Soon after, he founded the Alliance Française des Etats Unis, with chapters in other cities.

Few businessmen in their twenties had accomplished as much in the cultural arena, and when James got final control of the Equitable, he could be expected to throw the power of the company behind his interests. That would have made him one of a new generation of executives who use not just their own fortunes, but also corporate resources to make social and cultural contributions.

His connections with high-placed Frenchmen in the United States extended to the French ambassador to Washington, Jules Cambon. James had been Cambon's host at The Oaks, and had arranged for him to speak at the Alliance. The relationship had important potential for the Equitable: Cambon could advance James's mission to defeat the restrictive regulations that threatened American insurers in France. At the end of 1902, when Cambon announced that he would be returning to Europe, James proposed to Senator Chauncey Dewpew that they jointly host a dinner for the retiring ambassador.

The party was held at Sherry's on November 16, 1902, and 160 guests, all men, attended. Six governors and two cabinet officers, including Secretary of War Elihu Root, attended; along with nine college and university presidents, one of whom was Princeton's Woodrow Wilson; dozens of bank presidents; generals; admirals; an archbishop of the Roman Catholic Church; Jacob Schiff, J. P. Morgan, and James Alexander. President Roosevelt sent a letter of regret.

Guests marched into the lavishly decorated banquet hall as a band played "La Marseillaise." During dinner, they were entertained by a banjo orchestra "concealed from view in the back room," which provided "American music," the sort of unexpected fillip James often added to his parties. Depew gave the principal speech, and James toasted the presidents of France and the United States, and M. Cambon.[19] It might have been politic for him to have invited James Alexander to make one of the toasts, but with the Equitable lobbying in France, it was important to distance the company from the festivities.

The next morning, the *New York Times* declared, "If a history of New York's elaborate dinners were written today, the list would contain few feasts that could surpass the one tendered . . . last night." James paid the bill of nearly $13,000 and the Equitable reimbursed him; the company had much to gain from maintaining a good relationship with M. Cambon.[20]

The Cambon dinner added luster to James's standing in the business world, but his adventures in coaching had a more ambiguous influence—they consumed time when he might reasonably have been expected to be at his office. In the spring of 1903, along with about a dozen other men, including Alfred Vanderbilt, James decided to turn his coach into a public conveyance. He charged $12 a seat, $15 to sit on the box with him, and $100 each way for the entire coach, which accommodated twelve to fourteen passengers. It was hardly a commercial proposition; the income didn't pay for a quarter of the outlay. By one estimate, each equipage ran to $40,000 for a very short season.[21]

James published a flyer announcing that his four-horse "public coach 'Liberty'" would be available from the last day in March "until further notice," for an eighty-two-mile trip from Holland House to the New Jersey resort, Laurel-in-the-Pines. The Liberty would leave New York three days a week at eight-thirty in the morning, travel at seven to ten miles per hour, arrive at six in the evening, and return the following day. James put Morris Howlett, now billed as "the Star Whip of the World,"[22] in charge of the arrangements, and Howlett bought fifty-two horses for the changes.

The "Liberty" was retrofitted from a mail to a road coach; the seats on top were widened and upholstered in scarlet, roller bearings were added to the axles, and the body was repainted chocolate brown, black, and deep vermilion, with the names of the stops and the initial *L* on the body.

For the inaugural trip in April, James hired Jack Allen, who had worked for the president of the Chicago Horse Show Association, as guard, and outfitted him in the gold-braid-trimmed scarlet coat of the old English mail service. He even costumed the grooms at each change; they wore vermilion sweaters with the letter *L* on the breast, and breeches and leggings, instead of the customary workman's shirt and trousers with suspenders. James was soberly but smartly garbed in an old-fashioned coaching costume, a long, loose gray tailcoat, and a gray top hat.

He invited six guests on the first run. Three of them were women, although only one, Greta Pomeroy, was young, pretty, and eligible; she was described in one of the many newspaper accounts as a "clever sportswoman and rider and the only girl in New York society who ever killed a bear." The women wore large hats pinned atop poufed and upswept hair, and heavy coaching cloaks, and they tucked monogrammed blue blankets over their laps against the chill.

Edith Gould sat on the box with James for much of the trip. At each stop, she had to unbuckle the reins while he held them; the pressure was like pulling in a twelve-pound fish. In her forties, Edith was plump and matronly, with a mischievous expression in her eyes and an open smile. She had been an actress before she married George Gould, but she explained that she was "gently raised," and had gone on the stage only because her family lost their money and she had to support her mother. That did not placate George's mother, who tried to block their marriage, and Edith and George were married only after a great deal of family drama.

The senior Mrs. Gould was long dead, and Edith was a popular social leader, but she had to share George's attention with his second family. He had set up a mistress in a big house in Rye, New York, and frequently steamed up the Hudson River to anchor at her dock. He spent enough time there to have three children with her. It is likely that Edith knew about this arrangement—nearly everyone else in New York society did—but George showed no interest in a divorce, and Edith made the best of what she had. On the morning of the inaugural coaching trip, George and two of the Gould sons were at Holland House where they waved Edith off, then left on a tour of their railroads.

The other passengers included H. Rogers Winthrop, whom the newspapers described as a "clubman" and volunteer in an elite New York regiment. Winthrop would soon have a job; James hired him as the Equitable's finance manager, and he turned out to have a good head for figures and a steady working style. Another passenger was the famous amateur driver T. Suffern Tailer, "globe-trotter, keen whip, sportsman and millionaire."[23] Tailer had his own "public" coach and was fond of telling the story of a "Western millionaire" (on the East Coast, "Western" was code for "uncouth") who took over the entire vehicle and seated his daughter on the box with him. At the end of the trip, the girl complained that the "coachman" tried to talk to her, but urged her father to give him a generous tip anyway because he probably didn't know better. One of the attractions of coaching was the association with social figures, but it could take a while to pick up the nuances.

James had arranged for the hospitality at the stops to reflect the style he had learned to like on his French road trips. He transformed a New Jersey inn, the Mansion House, into a French bistro, persuading the hosts to dress as provincial innkeepers, and when he strode up the steps, calling out "Garçon!," they welcomed him and his guests with a few words of French. The luncheon table was set with linen, silver, crystal, and flowers; the walls were hung with Oriental draperies, coaching prints, and whips. The menu has not survived, but the beverage was iced Pol Roger, Cuvée 1889. The trip concluded with a formal dinner, dancing, and cards at the Goulds' palatial Georgian Court in Lakewood, New Jersey. One way by coach was enough; the next day, everyone except Howlett returned to New York on the train.

The Liberty public coach service continued until the summer heat ended the 1903 season. Then James sold the horses and went to Paris.

James's social activities were attracting a great deal of attention. The *Boston Post* reported that he was "New York's new social leader," which was accurate; and said he was the "new business associate of J. P. Morgan," which was not. The story claimed that he "varies the work of taking care of his millions by leading cotillions, driving four-in-hand coaches and in otherwise holding prominent rank as a social leader." *Town & Country* magazine predicted that James would "replace Harry Lehr as leader of society,"[24] and the *Baltimore World* agreed that "James Hazen Hyde . . . has become the successor of the famous Harry Lehr, as the entertainer of the '400.'" The Lehr comparison was barbed. Harry Lehr had followed the social leader Ward McAllister, who invented the "Four Hundred." Both Lehr and McAllister were married, but were understood to be homosexual. James seemed to be untroubled by the press, but James Alexander didn't like it, or any of the rapidly multiplying articles that appeared, chronicling James's robust social life.

JWA wrote James a strong letter from Venice in March 1903 scolding him for his flamboyance and his associations. Sounding like an irate father, he criticized James for "getting thick with all the young Rockefellers, Goulds, Whitneys and other billionaires." The envelope contained newspaper clippings, and JWA wrote, "I think your personal press agency which can accomplish such good things, ought to learn to be as skillful in preventing the bad things. I refer to such as the enclosed. They are of course both injurious to you and the business. I know they must be disagreeable to you." He said he was shocked to hear that "McCarter in Boston" had cited James as "an awful example," and remarked on more bad press in Newark, but praised James for protesting it in a "dignified" letter.[25]

It was hard for James to take JWA's scolding seriously when, only a few days later, JWA wrote again, complimenting James on his "comprehensive" letters, his "intelligent views" and his "wisdom, vigilance and devotion." To top off the praise, JWA referred to a difficult situation James had dealt with, and said he had been "appropriate, dignified and successful."[26]

The conflicting letters were a sign of JWA's concern that James was out of control, and that JWA didn't know what to do about it. It was not good news that James was quoted as saying, "I have brains, beauty and wealth, what more could I need?" That didn't sound like him; the kind of journalists who called him "the richest young man in New York" might have made it up, but even so, it was an indication that James's reputation was jumping the tracks.

JWA was anxious to distance himself from responsibility for James's behavior, and that fall, he tried to resign his trusteeship. He wrote Willie McIntyre, who had replaced Louis Fitzgerald as trustee, a letter marked "Personal," explaining that he had been thinking about his duties and felt he should "do what is necessary" to "clear himself of neglect."

"I haven't the slightest disposition to pry into things and do not want to give anybody any trouble," he wrote, and "if there is any way that I could be relieved from being executor [for James], I think it would be better for all concerned. If I continue however, to be executor, I suppose I ought, from time to time, to exercise such diligence as the law requires." He asked McIntyre to inform him as to how and under whose charge securities were kept, and periodically to show him "the accounts."[27]

JWA sent McIntyre another memo two days before Christmas, asking that either he or James notify Annie Hyde and Mary Ripley of his request to be replaced as a trustee, but nothing came of it. He continued to hold the position until the spring of 1905—even after it was clear that he was James's principal adversary.

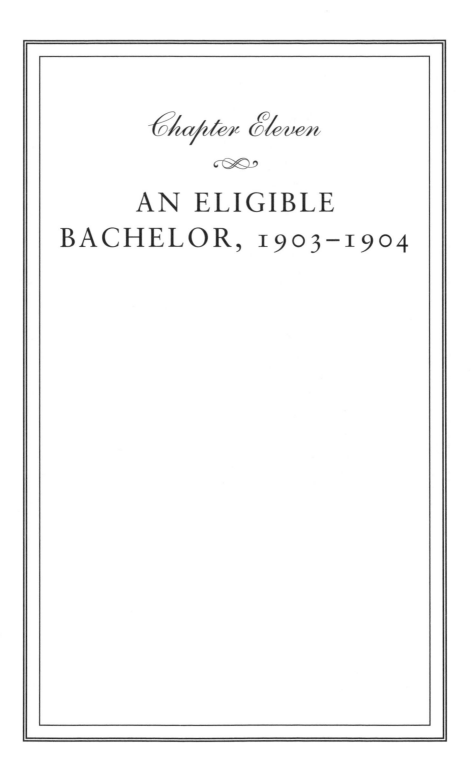

Chapter Eleven

AN ELIGIBLE
BACHELOR, 1903–1904

Alice Roosevelt, photographed as a debutante.

James courted the lively Alice Roosevelt, whose father, Theodore, was President of the United States. One of her nicknames was "Princess Alice" because she was so often rumored to be engaged to a European prince. *(Courtesy of the Library of Congress)*

A man can be considered a prime marriage candidate for just so long before he begins to seem a little stale, and as James closed on thirty, he showed little inclination to choose a bride. Stories circulated that he had liaisons with actresses, shorthand for "mistresses," and his later reputation as a lover suggests that there were women with whom he was intimate. But as one newspaper noted when he was in his late twenties, "Society gossips never have coupled Mr. Hyde's name with that of any marriageable young woman. He has seemed to prefer the company of the young matrons of society. His sister, Mrs. Ripley, and Mrs. George Gould have been seen most often in his company."[1]

Then Alice Roosevelt came along. She was beautiful, peppery, and the daughter of the president of the United States. Her hair was golden, her eyes were a color she called "postman blue," and she tilted up her little pointed chin with an air that could be interpreted as either snooty or curious. Her figure was lovely and lithe, and at five foot seven, she was tall. She could be charming and saucy, and she rarely turned down a dare. She smoked, drove a car, wore makeup, flirted, and told tall tales to the press. She did headstands at a tea for congressional wives, and kept peculiar pets in the White House—a blue macaw that bit, and a pacific snake, "Emily Spinach," which she sometimes slung around her neck. When she did not have enough changes of clothes to please the social reporters, she made up outfits and instructed the White House secretary on how to describe them. She was the subject of two songs, "Alice, Where Art Thou?" and "Alice Blue Gown," which led to the naming of a color, "Alice Blue." A practiced mimic, she could impersonate a monkey or an actress.

Men were attracted to Alice because she was lively, fun, and famous. She was constantly rumored to be engaged; the public was titillated by the reputed suits of princes from Prussia, Russia, and Greece. She was nicknamed "Princess Alice" when Kaiser Wilhelm II's only brother, Prince Henry of Prussia, made an official visit to the United States. The prince invited her to christen the kaiser's new American-built racing schooner, and took her to the Metropolitan Opera, where she sat in a different box for each act.[2]

Like James, Alice liked attention. She was dramatic and self-indulgent: when she did not get her way, she found another way—sometimes to the president's chagrin. In 1903, when her father insisted that she cancel her order for a red four-cylinder touring car, she borrowed a car, also red and open, from her friend, Countess Marguerite Cassini, the daughter of the Russian ambassador. Marguerite was her father's official hostess; it was said that the senior countess posed as her daughter's governess because the czar disapproved of the marriage. At first, Alice and Marguerite drove around with the embassy chauffeur. When Alice learned to drive, she appropriated the vehicle, and the two young women drove from Washington to New York, and on to Newport, much of the way on dirt roads.[3]

The rumors of a romance with James surfaced in October 1903, when the *Sun*'s society pages ran an item headlined "Miss Roosevelt and Mr. Hyde," and predicted that, at a dinner given by the Chauncey Depews, "it is very likely that a card bearing Miss Roosevelt's name will be found at a plate to the right of one bearing this inscription, 'Mr. Hyde.'" The story described James with the usual exaggerations, as "the wealthiest and most eligible bachelor in New York society," adding that he was vice president of "one of the greatest corporations in the country, a patron of the arts, the opera and the smartest society." The *Sun* writer mentioned his membership in "nearly every club in town," his houses in Paris, New York, and Bay Shore, "where he frequently entertains large house parties, including many of the leaders of New York society," and his accomplishments as "one of the foremost coachmen in the country."[4] These were not the sort of credentials the obsessively hearty president was hoping for in a son-in-law; and Francophilia was not a recommendation. Roosevelt once described the expatriate novelist Henry James as "the undersized man of letters, who flees his country because he, with his delicate effeminate sensitiveness, finds the conditions of life on this side of the water crude and raw, in other words because he finds that he cannot play a man's part among men."[5]

A month after the dinner at the Depews', Alice sat with James at the National Horse Show in a box for which he had paid the top price of $650, a figure high enough to merit a headline. Colonel Mann described the opening night scene in the "Saunterings" column in *Town Topics*: "Miss Alice Roosevelt was greeted with great warmness by the throng in the 'clothes walk,'"[6] the promenade from box to box. "The police had to order the crowd to keep moving, so great was the crush in front of the James Hazen Hyde box." He noted that James "was very attentive to Miss Alice Roosevelt, who did not seem to object." The Saunterer added that the spectators also stared at James, but he appeared unflustered by the attention.

Alice wore a pale pink gown with a lace bodice, pearls, and a wide-brimmed lace hat trimmed with pink feathers, and the Saunterer acknowledged, she "dresses in far better taste than formerly, and has so improved in looks that if she plays her cards cleverly we shall soon be hailing her as a beauty. There was no mistaking her popularity at the Horse Show."[7]

Mann's comment about Alice's "improvements" was a reminder that she had worn iron braces from her knees to her ankles until she was thirteen, to protect her brittle bones. Sometimes the braces locked and she fell over, a nightmare of embarrassment, and a severe drawback in Teddy Roosevelt's family; he expected his children to be as hardy as Indian scouts.

Alice returned to Washington, and other eligible women sat in the Hyde box. One evening, two possible rivals were present. Mrs. George Law was a widow who had inherited more than $1.5 million at twenty-two. Now, the Saunterer gleefully warned, "Mrs. Law has just entered her thirty-first year, which, if we are to believe Balzac, is woman's most dangerous period." Her competition was Elizabeth Morton. The Saunterer wrote that if a beauty contest were held that night, Miss Morton would win. Her figure was "perfect," perhaps partly due to her habit of taking long walks. "Her hair is a golden auburn and her complexion is like the coloring of a ripe Crawford peach. Her eyes are a dark brown. There is not even a flaw in her features to detract from the completeness of her beauty, and back of it all is an artistic taste in dress. She clothes herself in brown, one shade darker than her hair. She is certainly beautiful to look upon."[8]

Despite the plethora of beauties, Alice held her lead. James was invited to the White House later that fall, and again in the first week of February 1904. He stayed with the Depews in Washington, although May Depew wrote that their house was small and his valet would have to lodge next door at the Arlington Hotel.

The following December, Alice spent a month in New York. Mary and Sidney Ripley gave a dinner in her honor, and she was a guest at the debutante party Annie Hyde held for her namesake, the Ripleys' daughter Annah, on December 19, 1904. Before the ball, Alice attended the opera, where the Saunterer observed her for "two or three minutes," during which she "had something to say to everybody in the Cutting box [where she was seated], she nodded to someone six boxes up the line, she chewed the lace on her left shoulder, she sent a message to Miss Frederica Webb, she saluted Mrs. John Jacob Astor, who was seated almost a sixteenth of a mile away, she chewed the lace on the other shoulder, she removed a red rose from her corsage and crumpled it in her hands, and she leaned over and whispered to Mrs. Rhinelander Stewart. All the time her eyes and her hands were dancing."[9] Always animated, Alice seemed particularly excited that night. But a few weeks later, a Paris newspaper authoritatively announced that she was engaged to the eldest son of the crown prince of Sweden and Norway.[10] Like all the romantic ideas that she might soon become a real princess, that rumor faded—and so did the speculation about Alice and James.

James had begun to turn his attentions toward Charlotte Warren. One of the mysteries about his life in the turbulence of 1905 is what happened between them.

Charlotte was among the most popular debutantes of the 1903–1904 season. She had a reputation for being "fascinating," perhaps in part because she was so quiet that *Town Topics* once described her as "ghostly." Her beauty had an unearthly quality; she could have been cast as Titania, Queen of the Fairies in *A Midsummer Night's Dream*. She was tall and finely built, soft rather than rangy; her hair was fair, her skin was peachy, and her eyes were large, deep-set, and full-lidded. She had a distinctive small, straight nose, and an appealing slight overbite. With her long neck and lithe carriage, she might have been a ballerina.

She and James shared a happy saturation in French culture. Charlotte's father was the noted architect Whitney Warren, who went to Paris to study at the Ecole des Beaux-Arts when he was twenty, and stayed on for ten years. His Beaux-Arts background combined rigorous training and French eighteenth-century stylistic references, and was reflected in his design for the New York Yacht Club, with its witty, bulbous galleon-shaped windows. His firm, Warren and Wetmore, was among the principal designers of Grand Central Station, a triumph of the Beaux-Arts mixture of grandeur and lightness. Warren was oddly attractive, with a triangular-shaped head; fair, slicked-back hair; and a world-weary expression emphasized by a raised eyebrow. He was just twelve years older than James, and the two men were friends.

Charlotte's mother was also a Francophile. When Charlotte made her debut and Mrs. Warren, who was in mourning for her sister, couldn't give her daughter a ball, she bought out the orchestra and lower boxes of a Broadway theater for a French play, with supper afterward at Sherry's.

Whitney Warren's brother, Lloyd, a bachelor artist, hosted Charlotte's coming-out party in the studio of his house on Fifth Avenue, on January 6, 1904. The theme was the Orient, and the party was considered one of the most exotic of the era. Oriental design was in vogue, a trend that washed over the Victorian period. Victorians posed for portraits wearing Oriental robes; collected genre scenes of Arabs, camels, and tents; and ordered hand-painted wallpaper from Paris featuring Indian maharajas on elephants. The costumes that night were vivid and amusing; guests, from debutantes to dowagers, were decked out as Egyptian nabobs, Turks in turbans and harem dress, Indian princesses, Chinese mandarins, and Japanese geishas. Lloyd Warren wore a plumed and jeweled turban, a striped undercoat, puffed pantaloons, and a scimitar. Charlotte's costume is unrecorded, as is James's, a pity: It would be pleasant to imagine them whirling and flirting that night when their lives still promised untold magic.

Mourning prevented Mrs. Warren from attending the party, so Charlotte's aunt, Mrs. Starr-Miller, was her brother's hostess. A typical Warren, she was described in the *New York Times*'s "Afternoon Tea Chat," as "most picturesque, and she always looks as if she had stepped out of some old pictures. She wears her hair frequently in the mediaeval style and has a penchant for velvet gowns without any elaboration or trimming."[11]

The Oriental debutante dance was the sort of slightly off-center gesture typical of the Warrens. The family was socially impeccable: Mrs. Warren was often mentioned in the society pages; they were annual visitors to Paris; and they summered in Newport, but they were attracted to the artistic. Their circle was wider than most; they knew writers, actors, and musicians—rare enough for Edith Wharton to cite the narrowness of New York society as one of the reasons she decided to live in France. Charlotte would fit well in James's Paris life.

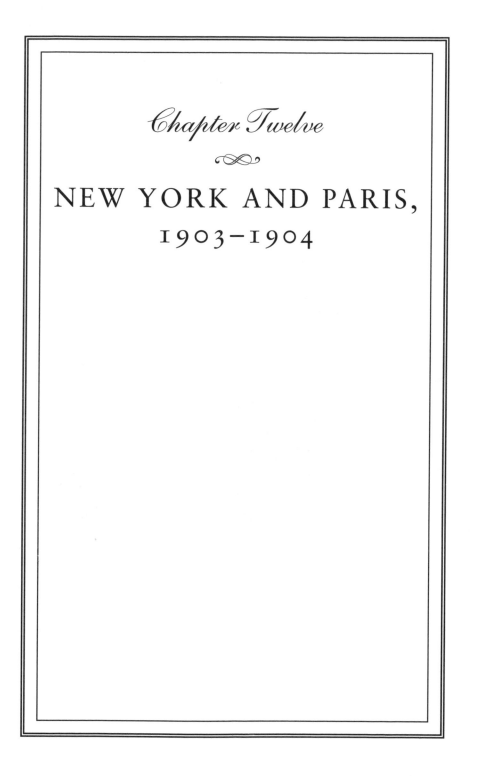

Chapter Twelve

NEW YORK AND PARIS,

1903–1904

Whitney Warren, the Beaux-Arts-trained architect who designed the Hyde Ball.

In the summer of 1904, Whitney Warren, one of the designers of Grand Central Station, was in Paris and helped James Hyde plan his ball. *(Courtesy Museum of the City of New York)*

$\mathcal{I}$n 1903, the Equitable dropped from first to third place among the racers. The competition profited as much from their strengths as from James Alexander's weakness. New York Life's president, the forceful John A. McCall, had been one of Henry's protégés, and was a former superintendent of the New York State Insurance Department. Henry had hired him from the state to serve as the Equitable's comptroller, and he joined the board in 1888. Even Henry treated McCall almost as an equal, with the exception of the demand that he refrain from signing his initials with "seven or eight circles disporting themselves around" them because, within the company, it was Henry's unique prerogative to draw a circle around his initials.[1] With James in the succession, McCall knew he would never become the Equitable's president, and New York Life had lured him away to take over a strong staff, with a particular star in George W. Perkins.

At the Mutual, president Richard McCurdy, nearly seventy, was a lifetime insurance man. He sounded like JWA when he called life insurance "a great beneficent missionary institution,"[2] but he was more autocrat than missionary. He was the head of every department in the company; his son was general manager; his son-in-law had an interest in the New York City general agency; and his brother-in-law was the medical director.

The Alexanders at the Equitable couldn't compare to the McCall or McCurdy teams. JWA's brother, William, the scholarly company secretary, was more interested in history than the future. Their cousin, Charles B. Alexander, was a partner in a successful law firm, but the Equitable was only one of his clients. One of JWA's sons,

Henry Martyn, was starting out as a lawyer in his own firm, and didn't become an Equitable director until 1904; his other son, Frederick, was a stockbroker. The hierarchy prevented a man like George Perkins from emerging; and James believed in his own importance before he had earned it.

As the Equitable's ranking declined, its returns on investments were dragged down by low-yielding deposits in trusts, and too many of its assets were tied up, so the company couldn't move nimbly when an opportunity arose. In July 1903, the cyclical flow of capital out of Wall Street to commodities was particularly pronounced, as crops came in and the agricultural sector needed money to move through the system. That led to a shortage of funds for syndicates, calls on loans, and a slump in stock prices. In midsummer, even the strongest companies were suffering; U.S. Steel common stock was down 50 percent. It was a good opportunity to buy value stocks at low prices, but as JWA wrote James in Paris, "The stock market has gone to pieces and just now when we ought to be averaging up on our holdings of investment stocks we are short of money [with] . . . about $1.5 million of things to pay for [by August] . . . [and] not more than half a million dollars in sight coming in." He philosophized helplessly, "It is the part of prudence to keep out of danger. The true secret of happiness is freedom from care."[3]

A month later, he wrote, "We seemed the other day to be on the brink of disaster," and, while matters had improved, "We would be buying a good many things were it not that we were so strapped for money. We have got between three and four millions to pay in September on the Western National Bank and Bank of Commerce deals . . . very annoying, because if we had five or ten millions to invest now we would make a great deal of money."[4]

The $2.7 million Harriman loan to the Union Pacific had come up for renewal in June 1903. James thought the interest should be higher, and the Equitable's financial manager, George Squire, proposed that the margin be increased. Harriman was about to take a long trip abroad, and the Union Pacific didn't look as strong as it once had. Negotiations with Harriman to change the rate of interest were prolonged and scratchy, and by the time Harriman refinanced elsewhere, JWA was irritated that James had pushed the loan through in 1901.[5]

In the spring of 1904, JWA wrote James suggesting that a way to "cure" the decline in interest on gross assets would be "careful handling of our investments, including purchase and sale of securities at a profit," but his advice to "buy low, sell high" was easier to propose than to implement.

Expenses were also rising. James and JWA had received raises in 1903, and were now each earning $100,000 a year; and James regularly sent unitemized vouchers to the comptroller's office. In March 1904, JWA sent him a testy reminder: "At the risk of tiring you by harping on the same subject, I want to give you a little synopsis of certain very important ends I think we all have to work for. . . . I have already called your attention to most of them, but as I am pressing Tarbell, Wilson, the Secretary, Mr. Jordan, and, indeed, everybody in the office, on the various subjects, it is important that you and I should keep in touch."

Expense accounts and salaries were "growing the wrong way," he wrote, and "I am rallying every officer (Tarbell, Wilson, Jordan, etc.) to crowd down all these things . . . you and I can help by . . . refraining from inaugurating measures that are expensive."[6]

That would be difficult. James was leaving for Paris soon, and he was planning a last-ditch campaign to block the long-pending insurance bill. He had already engaged a former French prime minister, Pierre Waldeck-Rousseau, as part of his lobbying team. On Waldeck-Rousseau's advice, the Equitable bought millions of francs in government bonds to ally itself with influential senators. Now JWA warned that if the legislation were to be passed, it "would knock our basis endwise," by requiring the foreign insurers to put their reserves into French instruments that yielded 9 percent at the most. With $6 million in reserve, which the actuaries estimated would increase at about $500,000 a year, restrictions on the way the Equitable invested its funds would make the French business much less attractive. "A question will come up which may be an awkward one for you personally," JWA wrote, "as well as for us as a company, namely, whether we can afford to stay and do business in France."[7]

That admonition arrived at a time when James had reason to believe he might be able to combine his career at the Equitable with his desire to live in Paris and play a significant role in French-American relations. At dinner some months earlier, Henry Clay Frick had brought up the idea that James might be a suitable candidate as the next U.S. ambassador to France, and he offered to suggest that President Roosevelt appoint him to the job. At first, James said, "I thought it was more or less a pleasant and complimentary remark and paid no more attention to it." Frick mentioned it again, and James recalled, "I thought I might perhaps have the qualifications . . . and . . . he could use his influence and some of his friends to procure [the post] for me." James told Frick, "It was a very serious step for me to take, even if I was able to get it, if it was just said in a pleasant way, it was better to drop it, but if he really meant business I would think it over and let him know, which I did."[8] James told Frick he would be honored to be considered.

In May, James was in Paris, where he planned to spend four months instead of the usual two. He wrote Frick, "Since my arrival here, I have thought a good deal of your kindness . . . in a certain personal matter, and if you are as usual successful I shall be eternally indebted to you, and anyhow I appreciate very much your having thought of me in this most important and complimentary matter."[9]

Frick was not James's only potential sponsor. Two members of the Equitable board had served as ministers to France, and another, Robert Lincoln, President Abraham Lincoln's son, had been ambassador to Great Britain. Harriman and Depew had both assured him that he could count on them in a more general way.

At twenty-eight, James was well established in Paris. He had moved into his own house, 18, rue Adolphe-Yvon, in the fashionable Sixteenth Arrondissement, and spent a good deal of time shopping for furnishings and art. He was a such a regular theatergoer that he knew the actors and managers at the Odéon, and the Comédie Française. Some nights, he dined with Sarah Bernhardt, still a great presence in her sixties. Bernhardt's image as a tragedienne was mingled with the drama of her life, the huge silky wolfhounds that accompanied her like a royal guard, and the satin-lined coffin where she said she sometimes slept, to take the sting out of death.

At the Vaudeville theater (which presented plays, not vaudeville acts), James often stopped by Réjane's dressing room, which was set up as a salon and furnished like the drawing room of a French town house. Réjane was the most famous comic actress in France. She had the exquisite timing of the comic actress, but even in her mid-forties, she was soft and sensual, like a woman in a Renoir painting. On stage, a biographer wrote, she seemed "disconcertingly natural, preferring to choose characters all women could identify with, and with whom all men fell in love."[10]

Artists loved her; a quick, sketchy style seemed to capture her best, and among those who drew her were Henri de Toulouse-Lautrec, Jean Cocteau, Aubrey Beardsley, and the fashionable illustrator SEM. Even her friend Marcel Proust drew a caricature of her. She toured "from Casablanca to Cairo" in North Africa, and throughout Europe. In Germany she performed her most famous role, Catherine in "Madame Sans-Gêne," for Kaiser Wilhelm II, who gave her an eagle-shaped brooch in appreciation. (She said the brooch was unwearable, and he was unbearable.) The King of Portugal gave her a gift she liked far better: a pair of mules to draw her carriage. She dressed them in silver harnesses, with violets nodding over their ears. James borrowed the idea of the violets from her, and at home in New York, the violets in his horses' bridles that matched his boutonniere became his trademark.

Sarah Bernhardt had her own theater in Paris, and Réjane wanted to follow her example, perhaps in New York. She was scheduled for a Broadway run in the fall of 1904, and the timing fit with an idea James had been considering. He wanted to hold a Versailles-themed fancy dress ball that would be a cultural event as well as a lavish party. He invited Réjane to star in a play, as the centerpiece of the evening. She was looking for backers for her theater; James and other Americans she would meet through him were prospects; and the ball in January would cap her New York season. She accepted the invitation, and they began to look for material. They considered short plays written for eighteenth-century court *divertissements*, but none seemed right; they were either too long, too dated, or did not have a good part for her. Instead, James commissioned the playwright Dario Niccodémi to write a one-act play, and ordered the set and costumes to be made in Paris.

He cabled Sherry's to reserve January 31 for his ball—not a Monday, when people came straight from the opera, but a night when the opera was closed so guests could concentrate on getting ready in their costumes, and because he wanted to hire the Metropolitan's orchestra and its conductor, Nathan Franko, to provide the music. Sherry's had been open for only a few years, and the ballrooms were magnificently appointed, but James decided to decorate the hotel to evoke the gardens Le Nôtre designed for Louis XIV at Versailles. When the Whitney Warrens arrived in France, he enlisted Warren to help him design the ball's decor.

Along with the Metropolitan orchestra, he asked the Opera Ballet to perform, and to choreograph a typical eighteenth-century "contra dance" for some of the guests to perform. He would ask Charlotte Warren to be one of the girls in the dance, along with his niece, Annah, who was making her debut that season.

While James was in France, American moguls were lining up behind Theodore Roosevelt's 1904 presidential campaign. Roosevelt barely tolerated tycoons and was the avowed enemy of big business. Yet, as the election loomed, he overcame his distaste and permitted his finance chairman, Cornelius Bliss, to solicit contributions from men whose business practices he had actively opposed. Bliss, a stockbroker in his seventies, who had been an Equitable director since 1884, was an *eminence gris* on Wall Street, and had served as President McKinley's secretary of the interior. A lot of businessmen would not turn him down, even with Roosevelt as the candidate. J. P. Morgan gave $150,000; Frick put in $50,000, and said he would give more if it was needed; George Perkins sent three checks, one from him personally, the others as a representative of New York Life and J. P. Morgan and Company, for a total of $450,000. George Gould donated $500,000, and Chauncey Depew, as chairman of the New York Central, gave $100,000. By one account, nearly three-quarters of the financing for the 1904 presidential campaign was traced to corporate connections.[11]

E. H. Harriman had good reasons to oppose Roosevelt. The president had pressed to quash Northern Securities, the great railroad combination that would have folded in the Great Northern, Northern Pacific, and Union Pacific. Morgan and Hill had talked Harriman into joining them, but after the U.S. Supreme Court ordered Northern Securities' dissolution, Harriman sued Morgan and Hill to separate his interests from theirs, and the case was ongoing in 1904. Harriman had reasons to dislike Roosevelt bitterly, but he was a realist, and he allowed his friend, Governor Benjamin Odell, to persuade him to serve as a delegate to the Republican National Convention. Roosevelt was nominated by acclamation; and after the convention, the president invited Harriman to Washington for a private dinner. Harriman left the White House with the impression that when railroad legislation next came up, Roosevelt would discuss the issues with him, although it didn't turn out that way.

Harriman made a $50,000 contribution to the Republican Party, but said that was his limit, and could not be cajoled into giving more. Roosevelt wrote a friend that Harriman said he "could buy a sufficient number of senators and congressmen or state legislators to protect his interests, and when necessary he could buy the judiciary. These were his exact words. He did not say this under any injunction of secrecy . . . and showed a perfectly cynical spirit of defiance throughout."[12]

The insurance industry had its own political network. The three racers pitched in to share a lobbyist, Andrew Hamilton, an officer of New York Life, to whom they had paid $1,630,803 in the past few years alone for a national initiative to influence "taxation and legislation," which was regulated state by state. The Mutual had its own "lobby house" in Albany, a hospitality center where a man whose official role was as the company's "superintendant of supplies" entertained elected and appointed officials.

Over the summer, James Alexander authorized a $25,000 campaign contribution from an Equitable trust account; the treasurer,

Thomas D. Jordan, managed its unofficial political fund without restraint or board oversight. When James returned from France, he gave Cornelius Bliss another $25,000 for Roosevelt's campaign from the same account. At the same time, James began to gather support for the ambassadorial appointment. Schiff mentioned it to Bliss, and also wrote Roosevelt a letter.

Harriman said he would talk to Roosevelt about James the next time he saw him, but, in October, he had another candidate in mind. He suggested to Roosevelt that he offer France to Chauncey Depew. Harriman's plan was that, in anticipation of the ambassadorship, Depew wouldn't stand for reelection to the Senate, and Odell would be able to run for his seat. Harriman thought Roosevelt had agreed to appoint Depew to Paris, but a couple of weeks later, the president came out in favor of Depew's reelection, indicating that he would not support Odell. Roosevelt later denied having had the conversation with Harriman, and Depew may never have known about it.[13]

James was invited to the White House that fall, but the visit was social, and he never said whether the subject of the ambassadorship was raised.

Gage Tarbell had advised his agents that each of them ask himself, "Am I as much of a success in my business as I ought to be . . . ? If he is unable to answer this question in the affirmative, let him resolve at once to ascertain what stands between him and the success which he covets, and then, having ascertained the barrier, remove it at once."[14] With James back in the office after four months abroad, Tarbell was reminded of the barrier to his own success.

From the early days when they traveled together, Tarbell had understood that, unless he acted in his own behalf before James turned thirty, he was destined to be a distant number two. Even in November 1900, when the young heir was a neophyte and not long after Tarbell had conducted the epic raid on New York Life's agents, the two men were on tour when the *Pittsburgh Gazette* ran a story that put Tarbell in his place. The article was headlined MAN OF AFFAIRS VISITS THIS CITY: JAMES H. HYDE COMES TO PITTSBURGH TO MEET BUSINESS ASSOCIATES. The writer noted offhandedly that James "was accompanied by his secretary and by Gage E. Tarbell, second vice president," then went on to praise James, claiming he was "regarded by men of great affairs as one of the master minds of finance and insurance . . . [and] is probably identified with more important financial and business enterprises than any other man of his years in the country."[15] To make the picture even clearer, Henry Clay Frick, the retired coke and steel magnate and burgeoning art collector, had given a dinner in James's honor at his house, Clayton, while Tarbell was entertained by the head of the Pittsburgh agency—an important man in insurance, but hardly comparable to Frick.

Tarbell understood that James considered him a valuable employee; he had even given Tarbell a raise, bypassing JWA. James would almost certainly make Tarbell first vice president when he became president, but that was not enough: Tarbell wanted the top job himself.

By the fall of 1904, Tarbell was laying the groundwork to undermine his competition. When he met with agents around the country, he was apt to mention James's appearances in the social press, his coaching, and his extravagance, then reassure the agents that James's reputation would not reflect badly on the company. Many of them had hardly heard about these excesses; when James visited their cities, the press usually depicted him as a young genius, a worthy successor to his father. They understood that Tarbell was warning them that there was trouble ahead, and a spirit of unease began to creep through the sales force.

Tarbell was also making progress in his campaign at 120 Broadway. JWA was vulnerable to persuasion; as the Equitable declined under his stewardship, he needed someone to blame. Ironically, in a situation that had been set in motion by Henry Hyde's misjudgment of his own son and the succession, the catalyst for the final break between James and JWA involved a legacy from father to son. Henry Martyn Alexander had recently been elected to the Equitable board, and JWA was pressing for him to be appointed to the executive committee. That brought the next generation of Alexanders into the company; and under other circumstances, Henry Martyn might have been groomed to take over as legal adviser when his uncle, Charles

B. Alexander, retired. But instead of going to work for Alexander & Green, Henry Martyn had started his own firm with a partner, Bainbridge Colby, a Wall Street lawyer and member of the New York Assembly. James didn't like or trust Colby, and he was concerned that he would use Henry Martyn's position to gain access to the inside workings of the Equitable. Exercising his prerogative as a majority shareholder, James vetoed Henry Martyn's appointment in the fall of 1904.

JWA snapped. He called in Alexander and Green, told them he feared that the current system was vulnerable to abuse by a powerful majority shareholder, and asked them to come up with alternatives. They retained the eminent lawyer Charles Evans Hughes as a consultant, and together they studied insurance law, the company's charter, and Henry Hyde's will. It did not take them long to find a way to oust James, or at least to paralyze him.

The solution was written into the charter. Directors could be appointed in one of two ways. Either the majority shareholder could continue to exert control, or another clause could be activated to permit anyone who held a policy worth $5,000 to vote for directors. That system was referred to as "fully mutualizing" the company. The lawyers advised JWA to propose that the board vote for mutualization, arguing that James had misused his power, which proved that an oligarchy was not a safe way to run the business. If they had known about the tangled financial dealings that could seep to the surface during a big fight, they might have advised JWA to leave the system alone.

The change would mean that James would almost certainly be pushed out of management; and if he no longer controlled the board, his stock would lose much of its perceived value. Even though the move would contravene Henry Hyde's carefully drafted intentions, JWA believed it was a better way to preserve his old friend's legacy.

It would, of course, be a windfall for Tarbell. Once the policyholders could vote for directors, the agents in the field could campaign for Tarbell's candidates for the board. With the election of that slate, the new directors could vote James out of office. When Alexander retired, Tarbell would be in line for the presidency.

On January 25, less than a week before the ball, JWA called on James at home. They met in the room where Henry Hyde had often conducted business, and JWA made his case for mutualization. He added that James would probably be called on to sell his stock.

JWA had failed to train James to take over the Equitable, but he now gave him the chance to prove that he was Henry Hyde's son. James firmly told JWA that he had betrayed Henry's trust, and that he would fight for his legacy. When JWA went back out into the January cold after a meeting that was considerably shorter than he had expected, he was even more convinced that James was dangerous.

James was taken by surprise. He had come to discount JWA and, distracted by the ball, had failed to pick up signals in the office. There was very little he could do immediately, without taking the risk that word of the trouble would get out. But the party could give him an advantage when he tried to rally support in the week before the next board meeting, on February 8. If his ball was a success, it would display his stature and connections, and show that he could entertain like an ambassador, or at least like the president of one of the most important companies in the United States. It would have to be a kind of coronation; but, wisely, James did not plan to masquerade as a king. He had the audacity to come to his costume party dressed as himself.

PART THREE

⚜

THE BALL

Parties have no reality until the next day, when they fix the attention of those who were not invited.

Marcel Proust,
as quoted by Jerry E. Patterson in
The First Four Hundred[1]

Chapter Thirteen

THE PARTY ERA,
1883–1905

Mrs. Bradley Martin as Mary, Queen of Scots, and Mr. Bradley Martin in pink satin as a courtier in the time of Louis XVI.

At her 1897 costume ball Cornelia Bradley Martin was bedecked in jewels that had once belonged to Marie Antoinette. Theodore Roosevelt, as commissioner of police, oversaw a force of hundreds who guarded the guests, while his wife danced inside. *(Courtesy Richard Jay Hutto)*

*B*alls preoccupied Gilded Age society, and the Hyde Ball came to be seen as the apotheosis of an era, as well as the centerpiece in the story of a young man's rise and fall. Yet the party was much more than the phenomenon of a particular age. Dancing and feasts are encoded in the memory of the human race: for more than fifty thousand years people have held festive gatherings to display status, invoke good fortune, and forge social and sexual alliances. Socialites who waltzed in ballrooms in New York and Newport costumed as kings and queens were descended from ancestors who leapt around bonfires wearing lion skins to appropriate the essence of power. Twenty-seven thousand generations after dancing figures were first scratched on pottery in the Balkans, virgins still displayed themselves, dancing still pantomimed and lubricated courtship, and people gossiped about the festivities before they took place and long after they were over.

By the time James Hyde gave his ball in 1905, everyone—those who were invited, and those who had never seen a lobster or a silver spoon—instinctively knew that a big party had serious social significance.

Built on a scaffolding of wealth and display, Gilded Age parties mimicked European court entertainments. Footmen, chosen for their height and matched like teams of horses, were dressed in livery, bowed the guests in, announced them, then stood behind each place at dinners that could stretch to ten courses, and were sometimes served on solid gold plates. Some houses were staffed for entertaining on such a grand scale that at least two indefatigable Gilded Age hostesses, Mrs. Ogden Mills and E. H. Harriman's daughter, Mrs. Elbridge Gerry, declared that they could serve one hundred dinner guests without hiring extra help.

Festivity had been paired with nature from the earliest times, and an atavistic instinct led Gilded Age hostesses to festoon their ballrooms with such a profusion of flowers that it was as though summer were the season of the night. Animals added spontaneity to minutely choreographed events, most sensationally at C.K.G. Billings's Horseback Dinner in 1903. Billings, the heir to a Chicago utilities fortune, won a place in the history of entertaining by inviting thirty-six men to celebrate the completion of his rustic stable at the northern tip of Manhattan.[1] The guests arrived at Sherry's in white tie and tails, and were mounted on horses with saddles that were specially fitted with linen-draped trays and Champagne buckets. Dinner was served by waiters dressed as grooms, while real grooms hovered to clean up behind the horses.[2]

Mrs. Stuyvesant Fish gave a party in honor of a visiting "prince," who turned out to be a formally attired monkey, and was seated and served with the other guests. Harry Lehr hosted a "dogs' dinner" for a hundred pets; in preparation for the meal, he had the top of his dining table removed from its legs and propped up at dog height. Birds and fish were usually, but not always, easier to handle. More than one host was dismayed to learn that swans were not docile centerpieces. A Mr. Lukemeyer received a $10,000 tax refund from the U.S. government and decided to spend the windfall on a dinner for seventy-two at Delmonico's. A long oval table set up in the ballroom was landscaped "as one unbroken series of undulations, rising and falling like the billows of the sea, but all clothed and carpeted with every form of blossom. It seemed like the abode of fairies," according to Ward McAllister, the supreme party-giver and -goer of the 1880s. Songbirds trilled from gilt birdcages that hung above the guests, and on a thirty-foot-long "pond" surrounded by a golden wire netting that stretched to the ceiling, four swans from Prospect Park splashed—and fought.[3]

The combative swans were more successful than the ten thousand butterflies that the parents of a Philadelphia debutante imported from Brazil to create a cloud of bright wings at a dramatic moment in their daughter's coming-out party. The butterflies were hung from the ceiling in muslin pouches, but were released too late; they had been asphyxiated, and the guests were pelted with dead insects.

Sand and sea were popular resort themes. One summer night, a sandbox was set in the middle of a dining room table in Newport, and guests were given sterling silver shovels to dig for buried treasure; they took home what they found in silver pails. When Mrs. Hermann Oelrichs gave a "White Ball" at Rosecliff in Newport, her eighty-two-foot-long ballroom was decorated in white, and after the navy declined her request that they sail by to enhance the view, she commissioned a dozen white-hulled faux ships to be "anchored" in the bay. The guests, all dressed in white, could stand on the balconies and look out to sea, and it would appear as though the fleet had deployed an honor guard.

Costume parties were popular, but masks had been illegal in New York since 1829, when the city passed a law against appearing masked in public. The rationale was that face coverings were "of immoral and pernicious tendency, subversive of all just and honorable discrimination of character and calculated to encourage the profligate, seduce the youth of both sexes, and promote licentiousness and disorder."[4] (Nearly two centuries later, New York mayor Rudolph Giuliani used the law to prevent the Ku Klux Klan from marching hooded in the city streets.)[5] Most people had forgotten about the regulation by the 1880s, and occasionally someone would give a "Domino Ball," at which the guests wore small masks over the top of the face, but masks were never as popular in the United States as they were in Europe. Americans were less attracted to mystery and innuendo; they preferred to know who was whispering in their ears.

For much of the Gilded Age, Mrs. Astor's annual ball set the standard for exclusivity. Caroline Schermerhorn Astor considered her position as gatekeeper of New York society to be an inherited prerogative; she was the descendant of a Dutch family that settled in the Hudson River Valley in the 1600s, and her husband, William Backhouse Astor, added his fortune to her lineage. Her calling cards read only "Mrs. Astor," a privilege she usurped from her sister-in-law, who was married to the eldest brother. When she insisted that she be referred to as "*The* Mrs. Astor," her contemporaries and social historians generally acceded. Mrs. Astor's expression was stern, her complexion sallow, and her hair so thin that she wore a rather obvious black wig to fill it out. But her courtier, Ward McAllister, called her the "Mystic Rose," alluding to a character in Dante's *Paradiso,* "the heavenly figure around whom all other figures in Paradise revolve."[6]

Characters like McAllister appear wherever money and snobbery converge. He had been swanning around New York since before the Civil War when he arrived from Savannah. A member of a respected Georgia family, he joined a couple of good men's clubs and positioned himself to make society his career. He soon earned his nickname, the "Autocrat of Drawing Rooms." In the 1880s McAllister became a footnote to history, with Mrs. Astor as a footnote to the footnote, when he remarked that there were no more than "about four hundred" people in New York society. The comment followed him around for years until he finally felt compelled to explain how he came up with the number. He invented an answer; he said it was based on the capacity of Mrs. Astor's ballroom, and "Four Hundred" has been the symbol of social and financial elites ever since. It took him until 1892 to release a list to the New York newspapers; sixteen of them printed it, but they neglected to note that he included only 319 names, representing 169 families.[7]

Mrs. Astor held her party at her large, dowdy brownstone at 350 Fifth Avenue, in a Victorian picture gallery where paintings hung one above the other, stacked four and five high to the ceiling. The house was decorated with thousands of American Beauty roses, the "Mystic Rose's" signature flower, and she was armored and draped in diamonds. She presided from a large red-silk cushioned divan, known as "the throne," on a low dais at one end of the room. The few friends who were invited to sit with her considered it a singular honor.

Most large New York balls followed a formula, and Mrs. Astor's were no different. The parties began at eleven in the evening, usually on Monday, when guests arrived from the opera, having left their boxes in a flurry of capes and furs before the end of the last act. A popular society orchestra played, supper was served at midnight; at about two in the morning, the quadrilles began. These were elaborate, themed, and costumed "figures" danced by small groups. Parties often continued until dawn, when breakfast was served. Guests usually left with favors, which might be custom-made fans, silver objects, and sometimes jewels. Mrs. Astor's balls were features on the social landscape, and, like many predictable events, they were usually rather dull.

Certain Gilded Age parties were cast as turning points in stories of social ascendance or decline. That was the case in March 1883 when thirty-year-old Alva Vanderbilt and her husband, William K. Vanderbilt, held a costume ball to inaugurate their new limestone château designed by Richard Morris Hunt on Fifth Avenue.

Alva Vanderbilt had the temerity to break rules, the stamina to reinvent herself, and the staying power to maintain her position in society. She built the most beautiful houses in Newport and New York; she forced her daughter, Consuelo, to marry a duke; and she, herself, divorced a Vanderbilt and married another social figure, O. H. P. Belmont. Belmont died young, and Alva started again, this time as a leader of the suffrage movement; she then lived the last years of her life in another lovely house, a villa in France. She accomplished all of this without the aid of beauty. She was almost pretty when she was young, but her face was later described as being like a Pekingese, and her principal social rival, Mrs. Stuyvesant (Mamie) Fish, once told her she looked like a toad. Well before Alva's second brilliant marriage, she had grown as plump as a wet nurse.

Shortly after Willie and Alva moved into 660 Fifth Avenue, Mrs. Astor held her annual ball and, as usual, she did not invite the Vanderbilts. Legend insists that Alva gave her great ball that spring principally so that she could *not* invite Mrs. Astor, and, at the same time, could break into the top ranks of society. Although that story has been told for well over a hundred years, the Vanderbilts were already established insiders. It is more likely that Alva wanted to give a party to show off her house, and that showing up Mrs. Astor provided a secondary amusement.

Alva invited twelve hundred guests to a fancy dress ball, which was much anticipated by the press. Mrs. Astor and her daughter,

Carrie, must have noticed that they had not received an invitation; nevertheless, Carrie joined a group of friends to practice a star quadrille for the party. At last, after Ward McAllister insisted that Mrs. Astor face facts, she appeared in her carriage in front of 660 Fifth Avenue and sent a footman wearing the blue Astor livery—designed after the livery at Windsor Castle—to present her card to Mrs. Vanderbilt. The next day Alva had the pleasure of riding downtown and sitting in *her* carriage while her footman in his maroon livery delivered the Astors' invitation.

At eleven o'clock on the evening of March 26, police were holding back the crowds outside the canopied, maroon-carpeted entrance to 660 Fifth. Guests passed through the sixty-foot-long stone foyer and under a vaulted ceiling sixteen feet high, then climbed a magnificent carved Caen stone staircase. Upstairs they found Gobelin tapestries, gilded paneling imported from a French château, signed furniture from the Louvre Palace, a Boucher painting that had been made for Mme. de Pompadour and now reposed in Alva's boudoir, and a bathtub carved from a single block of marble, reputed to have cost $50,000. A huge gymnasium was transformed into a jungle, with palm trees dripping orchids, flowering vines hanging from above, tables set with gold services, and a twenty-five-piece orchestra hidden behind a curtain of smilax under a canopy of roses.

One newspaper announced that Alva would "appear as Cinderella after her marriage with the Prince,"[8] but she looked as though she had been born to the throne. Her yellow brocade gown shaded from butter to sunset orange, with long transparent cloth-of-gold sleeves like dragonfly wings lightly covering her arms. Her rows of pearls had been acquired from the collections of Catherine the Great and Empress Eugénie of France. Willie Vanderbilt was costumed as the sixteenth-century Duc de Guise, who had been stabbed to death by order of King Henry III in the royal chambers at the Château de Blois. Willie copied his costume from a portrait of the duke in his father's collection, and explained that the Château de Blois, which the duke still haunted, was the model for his new house.

Ward McAllister, costumed as Marie de Valois's lover who was guillotined for his transgression, wore white chamois tights; to put them on, he powdered his lower body, then stood on a stepladder while "two sturdy fellows" held the pants. "Descending into them" took an hour, he wrote.[9] A predictable proportion of the guests were dressed as nobles, gods, and goddesses, but the most unusual costumes had animal themes. Worth dressed Mrs. Pierre Lorillard Jr. as a phoenix, in gray silk with crimson borders embroidered with flames. She wore diamonds and rubies, and carried little fluffs of gray down and tinsel that she scattered around her like ashes. One young woman depicted Diana the Huntress and wore a red-satin-lined tiger skin. Another chose smaller felines. Her headdress was a cat's skin; its head drooped over her forehead, and its tail hung down the back of her neck. Her bodice was made of cats' heads; the skirt was of cats' tails. Around her neck, she wore a bell, on which "Puss" was written. All the cats were white and had once been alive, and the ensemble had unsettling overtones of ritual sacrifice. By contrast, it was a relief to see Miss Marion Langdon as a butterfly, with her escort dressed as an entomologist running after her with a net.

The festivities opened with a hobbyhorse quadrille; circus music announced men who pranced about costumed as horses, with ladies in scarlet hunt coats, white satin breeches, and shiny black high boots with gold spurs riding astride on their backs. Some of the hobbyhorses frolicked so wildly that two of the women were thrown. Carrie Astor performed in the star quadrille with the other girls, all of whom wore little electric lights that twinkled in their hair. Four quadrilles later, guests sat down to an eight-course dinner in the tropical forest of the gymnasium, and then everyone danced. At six in the morning Alva led the last guests in a Virginia Reel, as New Yorkers on their way to work picked up newspapers already trumpeting her success. The *New York Times* featured the party in a front-page story. The *New York World* reported that it was AN EVENT NEVER EQUALLED IN THE SOCIAL ANNALS OF THE METROPOLIS, and cost $250,000 (almost certainly an exaggeration); and the *Herald* declared that even the "gayest court of Europe" could not top Alva's party. According to the *New York Sun*, "In lavishness of expenditure and brilliancy of dress it far outdid any ball ever before given in this city."[10]

Balls depended on exclusivity for much of their cachet, but they were so extensively covered by the newspapers that they were a particularly public form of entertainment as well. An important ball could stand as a symbol not only of the status of a family, but of the state of society, and the current attitude toward privilege.

While the description of the Vanderbilt Ball as a tool for social ascent, if only from high to highest, was snide, the party itself was praised for its lavishness. The next great Gilded Age ball, given in 1897, was not as well received. The hosts were Bradley and Cornelia Martin—known as "the Bradley Martins" as though it were a hyphenated name. Their timing was poor: the country had been soured by a four-year depression. The Bradley Martins' extravagance was criticized before the party, and they have been described ever since as having been humiliated by the criticism, having suffered a precipitous drop in prestige, and forced into exile in England. It is true that a fancy dress ball with a French eighteenth-century theme had unmistakable overtones of "Let them eat cake," but the Bradley Martins were not parvenus or social outcasts. They were listed in "The Four Hundred," and both of them were rich; Cornelia Sherman Martin had inherited $7 million from her banker father, and her husband came from an old upstate New York family. They entertained grandly at their houses in Manhattan and London, and on their leased 65,000-acre Scottish estate. Their ties to England were strong well before the ball; their daughter, Cornelia, had married the Earl of Craven when she was sixteen. The earl was land rich but cash poor, a condition the Bradley Martins remedied by settling an amount reported to be some millions of dollars on him.

Mrs. Bradley Martin conceived the idea of her infamous ball in part, she said, to provide employment for purveyors of luxuries, who had suffered during the depression. She sent out the invitations only three weeks in advance so her guests would not have enough time to order costumes from Europe and would have to patronize suppliers in New York.[11] The beneficent angle was played up by the *Times*, but the Reverend Dr. William Rainsford of St. George's Church was not persuaded. J. P. Morgan was the senior warden of St. George's, and members of the congregation had been invited to the party, so when the minister told the *Times* that the ball was "just at this time, ill advised . . . [and] would "stir up widespread discontent . . . now when there is so much suffering and so great a tendency to distinguish between the masses and the classes," he started a public furor. The following Sunday, services at St. George's attracted such a crowd that some had to sit on the chancel steps. In his homily, the Reverend Rainsford criticized "such ostentatious displays of wealth as the [upcoming] Bradley Martin ball."

The *New York Times* "Society Events of the Week" described Rainsford's stance as "what would be called in slang parlance 'a grand-stand play.'"[12] *Town Topics* became fixated on the minister, mocked his enthusiasm for golf and the way his skinny legs looked in knickerbockers, and Colonel Mann put forth a thesis of his own: "The poor are to be very happy in heaven," he wrote. "That being the case, why should Dr. Rainsford, or any other minister plenipotentiary of the court of heaven bother so much about the poor? . . . Why should I pity a person who is unable to pay forty cents for a drink of whisky in the Waldorf cafe, when I know if he hungers and thirsts for righteousness sufficiently he will drink forever of the eternal springs of paradise?"[13]

The Bradley Martins took pains to keep their ball private, so reporters printed whatever they could scrape up. One story addressed the rumor that some guests were said to have asked Tiffany and Company to make rhinestone copies of the family jewels, for security reasons. A spokesman for the jeweler replied briskly, "It is ridiculous to suppose that the quality of people who have these rare and costly gems would ever think of attending such a historic function in sham ornaments. Don't you believe a word of it."[14]

One story tattled that women called in favors from members of "old Southern families," borrowing Colonial-era heirlooms they had managed to hold on to "during the dreadful times of the war."[15] On the night of the party, a man whose jewelry was on loan was quoted as saying, "What bothers me chiefly . . . is my diamonds. I borrowed them from my sister, she being down South, and now I can't seem to keep them on. They are constantly dropping off."[16] Gems were not the only items men borrowed; they begged silk stockings to wear with the knee breeches of their court costumes.

In preparation for the party, the Waldorf was "a theatre of war," according to the *New York Times*. Decorators and florists worked almost around the clock for two days, installing roses and hothouse orchids by the thousands, African asparagus vines, sprays of especially grown white mimosa, and clematis vines gathered by "a great army of poor folks in Alabama." Just before the guests arrived, flowers were to be "hurled en masse against the draperies, and will remain where they catch in the folds."[17]

War metaphors were apt. The hotel was battened down, and the windows on the first and second floors were boarded up so no one could look into the ballroom. Fifty outside workmen were provided with special identifying caps to prevent spies from sneaking in disguised as carpenters.

The Bradley Martins had received so many threats that, as a matter of prudence, New York City police commissioner Theodore Roosevelt stationed himself outside. He said that he knew the guests and would notice anyone who should not be there. Roosevelt deployed a deputy police chief and ten squads, led by sergeants, one of whom had purple-dyed whiskers. It was not easy duty for them, or for the hovering press; the snow fell thickly and the wind slapped against their faces as they watched the guests arrive in their carriages. Inside, plainclothes detectives lounged around the halls in evening clothes, smoking cigars and trying to look nonchalant. The highest guess was that 385 policemen and private detectives were on duty.

Mrs. Bradley Martin was dressed as Mary Queen of Scots, and stood on a dais against a backdrop of her own Beauvais tapestries. Dark-haired, pretty, and fashionably plump, she looked authentically regal in black velvet with a cerise satin lining, a high white ruff, jewels draped across the front of her bosom, and a diamond tiara, which one newspaper exclaimed, "seen by electric light, was a small sheet of fire, emitting iridescent rays."[18]

Her jewelry was historic as well as magnificent. Some of her jewels had been worn by the Empress Marie Louise, others by the

Empress Josephine, and after the fall of the Second Empire, when Marie Antoinette's jewels were sold at auction, Mrs. Bradley Martin sent agents from Tiffany & Company to Paris to buy the best of them. In addition to the tiara, she wore a double dog collar of diamonds and rubies, a diamond pendant that had been part of a royal rosary, a cascade of diamonds in the form of a triple-decker brooch, a four-strand diamond stomacher—a necklace that fell over the breast to the stomach—a lattice overbodice of small diamonds with larger diamond pendants in some of the triangles, and Mme. de Sévigny's diamond starburst brooch, which dated to the court of Louis XIV. For security, much of her jewelry was sewn to her dress.[19]

Mrs. Astor, decked in diamonds, wore the blue velvet dress trimmed with lace and fur in which she had been painted by Carolus-Duran. Alva Vanderbilt, now the distinctly pudgy Mrs. O.H.P. Belmont, was described vaguely as being "exquisitely dressed," costumed as a shepherdess, complete with a diamond corsage and a crook. Her husband clanked around in antique armor that was said to have cost $8,000.

The pageantry was superb, the costumes astonishing. The most dramatic, Richard W. G. Welling, was dressed as an Indian. His headdress was so high, he had to stand up in his carriage on the way to the ball. He wore a necklace of bear claws, deer teeth, shells, and beads, some of which had been part of a trade when his ancestor, John Greene, bought land in Rhode Island from the local chief. (The story was that Greene's holdings were determined by the amount of land he could cover while riding a bull backward.) One young woman, Kate Brice, managed to overcome the short notice and ordered her costume from Paris. She telegraphed Worth to copy the outfit in which Velasquez painted Philip IV's daughter, the Infanta Margarita. The costume was so stiff that it was shipped standing up in a crate; and the Brices took a room at Delmonico's, where Kate was carefully lowered into her costume.

The flaw of the evening was a disappointing turnout. There were more women than men; one sour reporter claimed maliciously (and mendaciously) that the ratio was ten to one. The highlight was the sumptuous supper, but even that worked against the Bradley Martins because many of the younger men hung around the buffet instead of dancing.[20]

The Bradley Martin Ball received some complimentary press. The *New York Sun* remarked, "Once in a generation . . . the rivalry of social ambitions crystallize in an entertainment so stupendous in scope and sumptuous in detail that it makes an epoch in the history of society . . . [and] the fame of the function goes forth to the uttermost parts of civilization," but for the most part, the Bradley Martins were savaged. The *New York World* wrote, "The general verdict . . . at the clubs was that the affair was a magnificent pageant, but stupid . . ."[21] In a further story the *World*'s reporter commented, "The crowd—bewigged, sword at side, or crinolined—was after all, but little different from that which you meet at Coney Island in the Summer."[22] Sketches of society women ran across two pages under the legend THESE SOCIAL LEADERS WERE NOT AT THE BRADLEY MARTIN BALL.

Even New Yorkers who did not care who went to the party didn't like the idea that city police were used to guard a private event, and that streets were closed for the convenience of the Bradley Martins. But the unpleasant press could also be traced to disgruntled reporters who were accustomed to being pandered to by society leaders, and resented being treated like snoops and pariahs.

Society did not ostracize the Bradley Martins. They gave a few smaller dinner parties over the next few weeks, and, on March 11, they sailed for England, where their daughter was about to have her first child.

It is fair to say that if the Bradley Martin Ball had been held a decade earlier, it would have been considered an aesthetic and social success. As usual in the world of events, timing was critical—as James Hyde would discover eight years later.

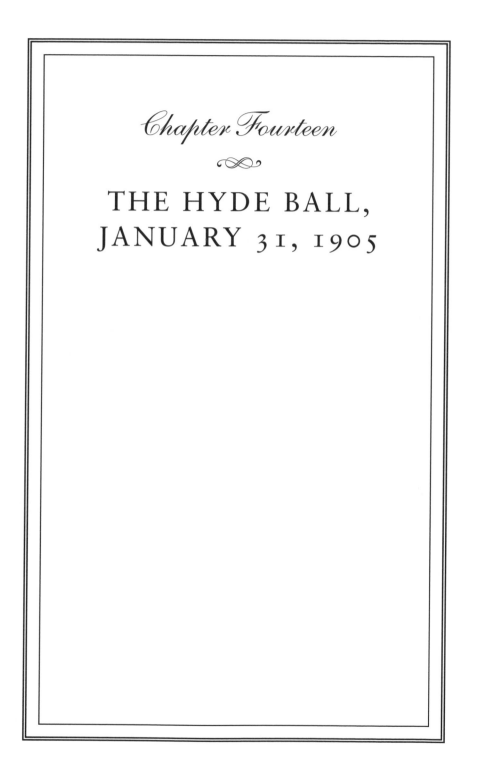

Chapter Fourteen

❦

THE HYDE BALL,
JANUARY 31, 1905

Réjane alighting from her litter at the Hyde Ball.

With Sarah Bernhardt, Réjane was one of the most famous French actresses of her era. She performed at the Hyde Ball in a play written especially for that evening. *(Courtesy Museum of the City of New York)*

*O*n the last night of January 1905, early in a century that was still much like the one before, James Hazen Hyde stood in the ballroom of Sherry's Hotel, on the threshold of the pinnacle of society—from which, as everyone knows, there is nowhere to go but down. He was wearing the formal attire of the New York Coaching Club, a bottle green coat, short in front with long tails behind, and one side of the breast was nearly filled by two crosses of the *Légion d'Honneur*, worn when invitations required decorations. Beneath the coat flashed a red vest; and black breeches and stockings revealed his shapely, slender legs, with ankles slightly turned in over black dancing shoes with grosgrain bows. His starched white shirt front rose to an impeccably tied white tie and stiff collar, which set off his dark beard and mustache, fierce brows, deep-set eyes, and the pronounced widow's peak on his high forehead.

It had not been easy to decide on a costume. The theme was the French eighteenth century, but for Hyde to set himself up as one of the kings lacked subtlety, and he did not want to wear a curled wig like the one that cascaded down over the shoulders of Louis XIV. He considered dressing as Mephistopheles, but as a close observer explained, he decided against that plan because, while "his Satanic Majesty exerted a strong influence over the court society at the . . . time of Louis X . . . he was not in evidence in person."[1]

The invitation offered formal hunting attire as an alternative costume, and his coaching club outfit was a satisfying variation. It would make him easy to find in rooms filled with men in pastel satins and lace, or scarlet hunting coats; and, besides, it was becoming.

Sherry's was a long, rectangular twelve-story building on Fifth Avenue and Forty-fourth Street. Stanford White had designed it in blocky Italianate style for the restaurateur and hotelier Louis Sherry. As soon as the building was completed in 1898, bachelors moved into the apartments upstairs and society gathered at the restaurants and held their balls in ballrooms designed to resemble the reception rooms in a French palace. The ceilings were coffered, the paneling creamy with lush gilt trim, mirrored rondelles, and tall mirrored doors reflected the dancers.

In the days just before his ball, Hyde walked the four blocks from his house to the hotel again and again, overseeing the installation of Whitney Warren's decor. Stanford White stopped by, too, unable to resist making a few suggestions. One supper room was set up under a striped tent; in another, an immense horseshoe-shaped table framed a formal Versailles parterre with real grass underfoot.

The challenge of seating six hundred guests occupied Hyde, his secretary, and his sister for days; even setting out the place cards was a project, and there were important last-minute changes. Just the day before, Alice Roosevelt decided not to come; she stayed in Washington and had a casual dinner with Congressman Nicholas Longworth—they would announce their engagement in March 1906. Alice changed her mind so late that the newspapers reported her as having been present. The Roosevelt family was represented by her cousin Franklin; he would marry another cousin, Eleanor, in the spring, but he went to the ball alone. His costume is unrecorded.

As ten-thirty approached, the actors, dancers, and musicians posed for Byron, the well-known New York photographer James had hired. The Hyde Ball would be the first to be officially photographed on site.[2] Byron and his five assistants set up the recently introduced shadow-free Cooper-Hewitt lights in an anteroom and arranged chairs and pedestals as props. Byron took pictures of Réjane with Hyde, as they waited for the guests to arrive.

The opera's ballet master had coached the debutantes and their partners for the contra dance; a makeup crew was preparing the girls with powder and rouge, and setting little wreaths of rosebuds on their upswept hair. They looked charming in their pink and blue silk taffeta dresses garlanded with pink roses, with full skirts showing their ankles, and pointed satin slippers.

Waiters, made up and bewigged by makeup artists from the Metropolitan Opera, were decked out in vests under red-and-blue-striped jackets trimmed with gold braid and silver lace, and breeches, white silk stockings, and bowed patent leather shoes. From the moment the footmen greeted the guests with the phrase they had practiced, "*Messieurs et mesdames,* this way to the *ascensceurs,*" the cream of the Gilded Age entered a stage set.

After the cold January night, the ballroom had the shockingly fresh scent of another season, with its grassy turf, sweet rosebushes trained on lattice panels, fragrant wisteria, and soft, spicy heather. Against the mostly pink and green gardens, the women in satin and lace might have been promenading in the gardens of Versailles. For that night, they could be courtiers and princes, or kings and queens; more and less themselves, and other people entirely.

Annie Hyde was evidently not there, which was odd, as her name never appeared in any of the newspaper stories about the party, but Mary Hyde Ripley greeted the guests with her brother. Mary's costume was based on Jean-Marc Nattier's portrait of Madame Victoire de France, but she looked awkward in her cerise brocade, with lace sleeves and trim on a low-cut pointed bodice. Her abundant, wavy hair hung over one shoulder in two sausage ringlets and was powdered—"poudrée," as the newspapers wrote. Madame Victoire, a homely Bavarian princess who married Louis XIV's son, Le Grand Dauphin, was not the most likely inspiration. The ambassador whom the Sun King sent to look her over before committing to the alliance was so ominously ambiguous that the king dispatched a portrait painter to Bavaria and ordered him to make a good likeness. The ambassador judged the picture "absurdly flattering," and emphasized that Victoire's nose, as he had already indicated, was fat."[3] All the dauphine's portraits transformed her, so Mary Ripley would not have known what she looked like. Nattier had never seen Madame Victoire either; he was five when she died in 1690.

The showstopper was Mrs. Clarence Mackay, costumed as the eighteenth-century actress Adrienne Lecouvreur playing Phèdre, the Greek tragic queen who fell in love with her stepson and set off a chain of murder, suicide, and resurrection by the gods. Mrs. Mackay's sinuous silvery costume opened over a silver lace skirt, and a long silver train fell from her shoulders. The dress and train were embroidered with turquoises, which were also the stones on her breastplate and were twined in the single braid she wore over one shoulder, falling to her hip. Two children whom the newspapers described as "little negro boys,"[4] wearing pink brocade costumes and sandals, carried her train. The artist John W. Alexander, JWA's son-in-law, had painted her in costume, and the portrait was completed in time to release to the press.

No one at Hyde's party looked as though she were having a better time than Edith Gould. Her white satin dress was embroidered in pearls; the long pale green satin train embroidered with gold and emeralds was lined in ermine and held up by two broad emerald-studded gold straps. Her ruffled lace sleeves were jewel-embroidered, and she was draped and pinned with pearls, diamonds, and more emeralds, even on her jaunty little fluff of a headpiece. Edith knew how to pose; in her photograph she stands with her arms out, showing the dress, smiling naturally, despite the constraint of holding her expression for minutes as the picture was taken.

When everyone had arrived, Hyde took his seat near the stage that was set on a platform at one end of the long ballroom. The stage was canopied and trimmed, but reporters had conflicting impressions; some said the canopy was blue satin, others purple velvet, and it was either embroidered with gold fleurs-de-lis, trimmed with ostrich feathers, or both. It was difficult to make out the details from the lattice-fronted balcony, where older men and women who didn't want to wear costumes, and members of the press could have dinner and enjoy the entertainment.

The guests arranged themselves on groups of chairs, and the Metropolitan Opera orchestra played an overture and introduced the contra dance. Men in their black-and-white Pierrot costumes, with pompoms on their pointed hats, bobbed like puppets, and the girls gathered multicolored ribbons that hung from the ceiling, curtsied, twirled the ribbons around, modestly cast their eyes downward, and held out hands that dipped from the wrists like the necks of feeding swans. Charlotte Warren was the beauty in the group, but Hyde had too much on his mind that night to think more than fleetingly about romance.

The opera ballet performed a gavotte and a minuet, and then Réjane made her sensational entrance. She was seated in a velvet-topped palanquin, borne by four tall footmen wearing tricorn hats. They set the sedan chair down in front of Hyde on the grassy turf that covered the parquet, and she stepped out and onto the stage.

Rose-colored curtains framed scenery painted in Paris to depict two adjoining Renaissance-style rooms. The light plot of the play, titled "Entre Deux Portes," featured a marquis and his marquise, who were meant to be returning from Hyde's ball, and had plotted to arouse each other's jealousy. The marquise, played by Réjane, invited a man to meet her at the house, and her husband invited a young woman; most of the action and dialogue consisted of flirting, stealthily observed by husband and wife through the door between the rooms. Even such a slight private performance by Réjane was an event, and the laughter and applause were genuine.

Accompanied by trumpets, drums, and the march from "Faust," Hyde and Réjane led a parade down the stairs to supper. Hyde was a picky eater, and the food, served with Pol Roger '89 Champagne, was exquisite: "Consommé Voltaire"; lobster ("Escalopes de Homard à la Réjane"); pheasant ("Faisan Piqué Louis XV"); "Salade Madame de Pompadour"; ham ("Jambon à la Gelée Princess"); and for dessert, ice cream, a "Glace à la Reine"; petits fours, bonbons, fruits, and coffee. The music never paused as two orchestras, one stationed at each end of the supper room, took turns playing.

The third-floor ballroom was cleared for dancing and, when only a few of the older guests left after supper, the weary newspapermen outside the hotel realized that the party would go on deep into the early hours. The Hyde Ball finally ended at seven o'clock in the morning, after a second and then a third supper had been served.

It was fortunate that it was a long night. Hyde would attend other, grander balls in Paris in the years to come, but they would all be tarnished by echoes of his party and its aftermath.

Early newspaper reports were reassuring. Admiration was not diluted by the hysteria that accompanied the Vanderbilt and Bradley Martin balls. The *New-York Herald* wrote, SOCIETY ENJOYS A

"LOUIS XVI FETE" IN 1905, MR. JAMES H. HYDE'S SPLENDID EIGHTEENTH CENTURY COSTUME PARTY AT SHERRY'S, and called the party "very charming and novel." The *Herald*'s story went on for pages, and featured an illustration of the ballroom with Réjane alighting from her sedan chair, along with portraits of Hyde, and some of the more celebrated guests. SOCIETY ENTERTAINED AT AN OLD TIME VERSAILLES FETE, the *Herald* announced, BRILLIANT COSTUMES OF MR. HYDE'S GUESTS MAKE PICTURESQUE SCENE . . . NOVEL DECORATIONS TRANSFORM THE PLACE.[5] The *New York Times* agreed: JAMES H. HYDE GIVES SPLENDID COSTUME FETE, SHERRY'S TRANSFORMED INTO EIGHTEENTH CENTURY GARDEN . . . A MOST VARIED AND ORIGINAL ENTERTAINMENT. On Sunday, the *Times* added that the ball was "an artistic creation," and "an event about which the chroniclers of social doings will dilate in future years."[6] *Town Topics*, predictably, wrote that the party "rivaled in splendor all the celebrated fancy dress affairs that have been given in the history of New York society."[7]

The ball impressed people Hyde would never know, and in the next days and weeks odd stories bubbled to the surface. The *World* reported

DAZZLING HYDE BALL TURNED GIRLS' HEADS
After Reading About It Harlem Misses
Run Away to "Shine in Society"

Two young and pretty Harlem girls read with delight the newspaper accounts of James H. Hyde's "eighteenth century" ball at Sherry's and then decided to run away from home, not to return until they had gained a place in society.

The girls are Katy Cogan, eighteen years old . . . and Sophia Peterson, fourteen. . . . The Police Headquarters list of missing describes them as "blue-eyed and decidedly blond."

. . . John R. Maguire, uncle of the Cogan girl, said to a World reporter:

"It is likely that the girls had their heads turned by the accounts of the splendor of Mr. Hyde's affair at Sherry's. They talked about it and said they would some day be great actresses like Mme Réjane, or society women. . . ."[8]

Another story speaks to a condescension that was so acceptable; the *New York Times* published this on page 1 without comment:

"JES' WRIT" TO J.H. HYDE
Then Aged Kansas City Negress Got Money Order for $25
KANSAS CITY, MO. FEB. 14—An old negro woman, Mrs. Mary E. Yancey . . . approached the window of the money order division at the post office yesterday and presented to the clerk an order for $25.

"Who sent you this?" the clerk inquired.

. . . "Some of dose rich folks down in Noo Yoke . . ."

"There must be some mistake," began the clerk.

"No indeedy," she interposed. "Don' you 'member de man dat gib dat swell dinner to all dem rich folks? I see in de papers whar dey done gib dis ball, an I jes' set down an' writ him a letter a-tellin' him dat I war jes a po' nigger woman an' likes a good dinner mahself. An he dun send me dis."

Further inspection of the order showed that it was drawn and signed by James H. Hyde, the New Yorker, who recently was the host at the much talked of fancy costume ball at Sherry's.³

The James Alexanders stayed home, and Gage Tarbell was not invited, but they knew who was at the party; the newspapers ran the full guest list, and it was filled with the prestigious and the powerful. Among them were Equitable directors Astor, Belmont, Depew, Gould, Cassatt, DeWitt Cuyler, Alfonso de Navarro, Louis Fitzgerald, Bradish Johnson, Alvin Krech, William McIntyre, Valentine Snyder, Alfred Vanderbilt, and H. Rogers Winthrop. Jacob Schiff was represented by his son, Mortimer. Harriman was photographed in white tie and tails, sitting on a bench, looking like a pleased mouse against the satin nest of his daughters' dresses. The Charles B. Alexanders gave a dinner before the ball, attended by the Count and Countess de Rougemont, another American heiress married to a titled European. The presence of so many board members indicated that James would have more allies than JWA might have expected.

If the Hyde Ball had been attacked the way the Bradley Martin Ball was, Alexander and Tarbell might have let the party do its own damage, but the reporters had been treated well, invited to watch from inside, rather than having to wait on the street in the January cold, and the Hyde press machine had released information that cast the evening as a cultural event. As a consequence, most of the reports focused on Hyde's elegant taste, rather than depicting him as a society spendthrift. Yet even good reviews can be used against a man who is already in the headlines. Word began to filter out claiming that Réjane was James's mistress; that she stood on a table after dinner, pulled up her skirts, and performed the can-can (she did stand on a chair to recite a poem); and that James's personal style was offensively and effetely French. It did not take long for someone to pass around the fiction that the Equitable was paying bills for the ball amounting to $200,000, and that policyholders were outraged. It is likely that Tarbell was the source of at least some of the stories that emerged.

The newspapers lost track of the details they had recently recounted, and soon gossip was reported as fact. For an entire century, the party continued to mutate. Often the stories concluded with the dramatic "information" that James fled to France after the ball, lived there for the rest of his life, and, as more than one writer erroneously declared, "died without ever seeing his homeland."[10]

More than fifty years later, even the *New York Times* garbled James's obituary. In a two-column story, the *Times* related that the walls were "bedecked" with orchids, and Réjane "read Racine for guests" who dined on "caviar and diamond-backed terrapin." The *Times* claimed that Stanford White had designed the ball, which, of course, was not the case, although White did describe it as "the most gorgeous affair I ever saw."[11] In 2002, a New York magazine published an article about Gilded Age balls, in which a group photograph from the Hyde Ball is captioned as having been taken at "the monkey ball," conflating it with the Newport dinner when the guest of honor was a chimpanzee.

Like the other two most famous parties in Gilded Age New York, the Hyde Ball was misrepresented, but of all the hosts, James Hyde fared the worst.

PART FOUR

AFTER THE BALL

After the ball is over, after the break of morn,
After the dancer's leaving, after the stars are gone;
Many a heart is aching, if you could read them all;
Many the hopes that have vanished, after the ball.

Charles K. Harris, 1892

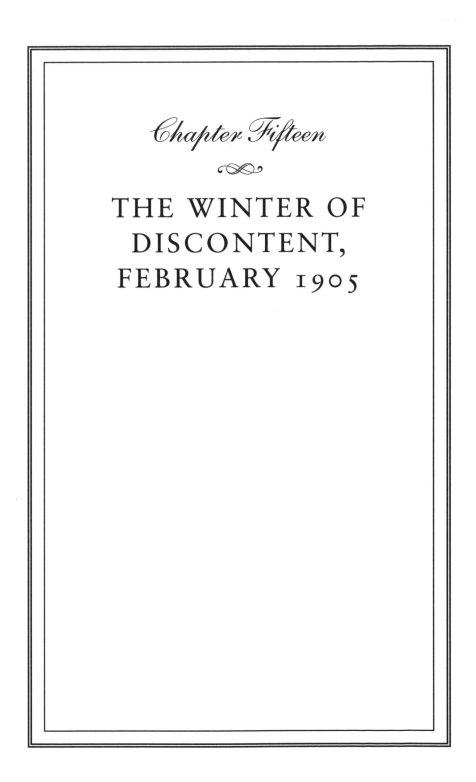

Chapter Fifteen

❧

THE WINTER OF DISCONTENT, FEBRUARY 1905

Headline news!

The Equitable imbroglio merited more than one hundred front-page stories in the *New York Times* alone in 1905, as newspapers competed for details of the fall of the house of Hyde. *(Courtesy AXA Financial Archives)*

*T*he week after the Hyde Ball was crammed with secret meetings, legal conferences, drafts of petitions and discomfiting encounters. Hyde was putting together his legal team, while Alexander and Tarbell continued to organize their assault. They wrote "confidential" and "personal" letters to the directors, asking them to stop by to discuss an important topic on the agenda. Their lawyers drew up a petition for the executives to sign, declaring that they would quit if the society were not mutualized; then they discarded it and wrote another. The second version demanded mutualization, but left out their threatened resignations. It was hand-carried from one executive office to the next, until JWA and Tarbell had gathered thirty-four signatures.

A few executives were difficult to persuade. Henry H. Knowles, the superintendent of agencies and a forty-year veteran of the Equitable, had been trying to bring about a reconciliation between Hyde and Alexander since early winter, and Knowles later revealed that he had opposed the prospective coup. As he would explain—but not until the spring, when events had reached a peak of unpleasantness[1]— Tarbell had stopped by his office one day and mentioned that Hyde and Alexander might be able to "settle their differences," if the company were mutualized.

Knowles asked Tarbell why he would want to damage Hyde's interests; Tarbell replied that Hyde had been "abusive" to him. Knowles reminded Tarbell that he had complained about the way JWA treated him, too; he said he had "knifed" him. "You told me they have said you must be kept out of the financial affairs of the company, as you were not a safe man to handle the finances," Knowles said. "Keep out of this thing. Do not be the tool of anybody. If you try to pull chestnuts out of the fire for other people you will be burned."

Knowles added that he knew Tarbell wanted to become president of the Equitable, and said he would help him in any legitimate way, but, he said, "understand this: You cannot get it by knifing the son of Henry B. Hyde."

When JWA and Tarbell began to circulate the petitions to be submitted to the board, Knowles didn't want to add his name, but Tarbell told him, "Mr. Hyde had been guilty of misappropriating funds of the company, that he had been accused of malfeasance in office, and of the usurpation of the president's powers . . . [and had] worked an injury to the society which might be irreparable." Knowles asked for proofs, and Tarbell told him they would be presented at the board meeting, and that a majority of the directors favored Hyde's resignation.

Tarbell assured Knowles that Hyde would be certain to resign immediately, sell his stock, and move to France. Knowles retorted, "He did not know the blood if he thought James H. Hyde would not defend himself . . . [he] had everything to lose and nothing to gain [by not fighting]. . . . I told him the thing he proposed was to degrade this young man, take his property away and practically throw him into the street. I advised him that Mr. Hyde would struggle for his rights to the last ditch." Tarbell prevailed in the end: Knowles signed both petitions, as did the twenty-four department heads and men under them. Most of them earned no more than $5,000 a year, and could not afford to risk their jobs by offending their bosses. The only Equitable executives whose names were missing were James Hazen Hyde and William T. McIntyre.

Salient portions of the text read:

The number of [Equitable] policy-holders and beneficiaries now exceeds 500,000, and the accumulations held by the society for their benefit and the protection of their families now amount to over $410,000,000. The investment and conservation of this vast fund is obviously a trust of the highest character . . . and enjoin the utmost conservatism. . . .

We have become convinced that [the Equitable's] continued welfare and progress and the due administration and protection of the
trust funds in its charge render a change necessary, and that it is
incompatible with present public opinion, as well as with the interests of the society and its beneficiaries that the policy-holders, as the
real parties in interest, should continue to be without any voice in the
administration of these funds, but that the entire power of selecting
directors should be vested in and exercised solely by the holder for
the time being of a majority of the society's nominal capital stock.

We, therefore, earnestly recommend that the Board of Directors
take the necessary action so as to provide that each policy-holder,
insured in not less than $5,000, shall be entitled to one vote at the
annual election of directors, and that the necessary legal steps be
taken to secure power to further provide for the extension of this
voting right to all classes of beneficiaries.[2]

On February 3, five days before the board was to meet, JWA
walked into Hyde's office and laid the document on his desk. He had
kept the petition secret until, as Hyde said, "the trap was ready to be
sprung." Hyde was outraged, but he was certain that JWA was playing a weak hand: The charter could be changed only if thirty-nine of
the fifty-two board members agreed. It was unlikely that so many
directors would attend the meeting, and only the most remote chance
that they would vote unanimously.

When JWA realized that Hyde would not back down, he circulated another petition:

We also deem it proper to add that in our opinion, after the most
careful and anxious consideration of the subject, the re-election of
Mr. Hyde as Vice-President and acting President in the absence of the
President, with all the powers he has exercised, would be most prej-
udicial to the welfare and progress of the society and the conserva-
tion of the trust funds held for the benefit of our policy-holders.

Mr. Hyde's prominence in various ways and his acts as Vice-President are such as tend to provoke criticism of the society, to create
misgivings as to the conservatism of its management and to injure its
business as an institution. . . . [3]

As word of the impending rift ripped through the board, Harriman kept his own counsel until he had a better sense of whether the Alexander feint would draw blood. Two other directors reacted immediately. The first was George Gould, who offered Hyde between $4 and $5 million for his stock, two days before the February 8 board meeting. As they were about to walk into the boardroom, Frick offered Hyde $5 million in cash for his entire holdings, or $2.5 million for half. The attempted coup had the smell of the steel strikes Frick had broken in the 1890s, with employees turning against owners. Whatever else Frick was thinking when he proposed to buy James's stock, he was an implacable opponent of employee revolts. James turned down both the Frick and the Gould offers, and later that month declined $7 million from George W. Young, the head of the United States Mortgage and Trust Company, a subsidiary of the Mutual.

JWA opened the meeting and passed around the two petitions, and the room was silent while everyone read. Harriman coughed—he was sick so often that he sometimes cleared his throat out of habit. Depew, Schiff, and Cornelius Bliss, all experienced negotiators, maintained neutral expressions, put their papers down, and waited for the next move. The most excited men in the room were Alexander, overflowing with righteousness, and Tarbell, bursting with ambition.

That first meeting was so rancorous that the board decided to cut the discussion short. They appointed a Committee of Twelve to consider the issues, and agreed to meet the next afternoon at two o'clock. Alexander, who was frustrated that his plan had not received wider support, went back to his office, closed the door, and dictated an eighteen-page memorandum.

Harriman summoned Hyde to his office upstairs, where he was meeting with former governor Benjamin Odell, now chairman of the New York State Republican Committee. Although Odell was about to leave for Europe, he said he would cancel his trip if they needed him. Odell had recently profited from his association with the Equitable. Harriman had put him into a syndicate that involved the Mercantile Trust Company and went bad; and, at Harriman's instigation, Hyde arranged for the Mercantile to pay Odell $75,000 of the money he had lost. Hyde later testified that Harriman had warned him that a bill was pending in the legislature to repeal the Mercantile's charter. The Equitable, which owned the majority shares in the Mercantile and was a large depositor, had the most to lose from a Mercantile disaster, and was indirectly the source of much of the Odell payoff. Odell made sure the bill never surfaced, and the day the Mercantile drew the check, announced that he was supporting Chauncey Depew for reelection to the Senate. As a further indication of gratitude, according to Harriman, Odell "wrote a letter either to the President or to the Secretary of State, advocating the appointment of Mr. Hyde as French Ambassador."[4]

On the afternoon of February 8, in Harriman's office, Odell assured Hyde that he "could have the Legislature pro and con," and that he could make sure any proposed bill to require that the Equitable be mutualized would be killed in the Insurance Committee. Harriman made it clear that he intended to lead the fight, and, according to Hyde, he said, "we are in control—" meaning matters appertaining to the Equitable; and "[we] don't take young men's advice" meaning Hyde.[5]

Harriman's decision to take over the Hyde faction was one he would later deeply regret. As Otto Kahn said, "Mr. Harriman had nothing whatever to do with the original trouble. There was no earthly reason why he should have been drawn into the fierce and bitter contest . . . but in he jumped with both feet and laid about with such vigor that in the end he became almost the principal and probably the most attacked figure of the conflict, both the warring factions pausing in their fight against each other to pour their fire of abuse and innuendo upon him."[6]

When Harriman joined the fray, the situation seemed far less complex than others he had taken on, particularly as the principals were not nearly as powerful as his prior adversaries. Harriman clearly saw that, despite their petitions and bluster, Alexander and Tarbell would have a difficult time unseating Hyde. They might be able to push him out as an executive, but as long as he owned the stock, he would remain on the board and could direct its decisions. Alexander's plan to change the Equitable to a purely mutual company could take a long time, if he ever succeeded, and Tarbell would still have to gather the votes to stack the board. If Tarbell were eventually elected president, Harriman would not have gained anything by siding with him. Tarbell was a salesman, he had no track record in the investment world, and there was no reason to assume that he would favor Harriman in future dealings. Hyde, by contrast, had already shown himself eager to work with Harriman; Hyde was malleable, and Hyde held the cards. If Harriman backed him, he could increase his own influence and get rid of Alexander and Tarbell. Harriman had already told Hyde that one of the reasons he agreed to join the Equitable board was that the company was not being run properly.

As for Hyde's acceptance of Harriman as his advocate, he needed a powerful ally, and no one else volunteered. Hyde had learned that Alexander's "sacred trust" was decidedly secular, and that fancy locutions were no substitute for practical power.

The board-appointed Committee of Twelve met the next afternoon, the second day of the crisis. Five of its members were company officers: JWA, Hyde, Tarbell, McIntyre, and George Wilson. The others were directors, of whom four, Harriman, Frick, Schiff, and Gould, were rumored to have formed a pool some months earlier to buy Hyde's stock. Hyde prepared himself for the meeting with typed notes covering nine points, most significantly, "4. Be in a receptive frame of mind. 5. Get subject matter before Commmittee right. 6. If mutualization has to come protect all interests and equities. Alternative: Counsel give proper advice as to trust deed for five years might be best for all interests concerned. 7. Value Stock."[7]

JWA opened the meeting by asking the committee to confine itself to mutualization and avoid discussing personalities. Then everyone started to speak at once. Harriman said the company was running well under the present system; Belmont warned that it would be dangerous to give the agents control through the policyholders. Tarbell insisted that the agents felt mutualization was urgent, and that James's "powers as Vice-President must be curtailed." He valued the stock at $750 a share; Cuyler retorted that the number was absurdly low (at that price Hyde's 502 shares would have been worth

$414,000). Tarbell countered by offering Hyde $1 million for the lot, but did not reveal who would be putting up the money. Hyde said he was not unequivocally against mutualization, however, if the board decided to take that course, the change should be managed by a proxy committee so they would not exchange "one domination for another."[8]

When JWA couldn't get the meeting to settle down, he read his eighteen-page memorandum aloud. He began by remarking that since some of the members "make no claim to extensive or accurate knowledge of the business of insurance," he would educate them on the mutual system and the company's history.

Nine pages into the document, after copious quotations from authoritative sources—including the Insurance Commissioners of Wisconsin and Massachusetts—Alexander launched a blistering attack on Hyde. He accused him of "open, aggressive and misguided" misuse of his stock control, which, he said, he had used to force his way onto boards of directors. He complained that Hyde overrode, bypassed, and ignored him, and "undermines the Presidents [*sic*] authority behind his back and admonishes officers and subordinates and notifies people dealing with the Society to have their transactions with himself, stating that the Presidents [*sic*] wishes, action and judgment in any matter may be ignored."

Hyde, he said, had established "a personal proprietary regime," made possible by a "fundamental weakness" in the charter. While Henry had operated the same way, his autocracy was "covered and palliated by [his] able administration. But now pride seeks to parade what discretion concealed. Personal ambition has sought to assert a power which a wise man was content to possess."[9]

Saying he found it "distasteful" to speak of such matters, JWA nonetheless detailed what he called the "evil condition" caused by Hyde's "strong personal ambition and an inordinate and unsafe love of prominence, a quick responsiveness to flattery, a pliancy in the hands of persons whose interests are not necessarily parallel to those of the policyholders of the Society."

Hyde, he said, had acquired an "unpleasant notoriety by reason of his recreations and enjoyments of a more or less public nature, which is exceedingly harmful to the company. . . . Such notoriety . . . cannot be said to be a misfortune that has overtaken Mr. Hyde, because he has cultivated it, striven for it and even used the instrumentalities that he commands in the Society to achieve it." Finally, JWA made a claim that Hyde would easily disprove, that Hyde was "absent from his post at least half of every year, spending his time chiefly in Paris."

From that first week through the end of the battle, JWA would reiterate these charges. He had been bottling up his resentment, and his anger had grown out of all proportion to the situation. His tone gave him away; as the fight became tougher, victory more elusive, and exposure more probable, the pitch of his indignation rose.

> Public coaches, special trains, elaborate banquets, costly and ostentatious entertainments, accompanied, as they are, by continuous notoriety of a flippant, trivial, cheap description, are not only damaging to the influence of Mr. Hyde as an officer of the Society but are directly hurtful to the Society. They suggest a lack of serious attitude and feeling towards his duties . . . a deflection of his time and energies into channels and pursuits from which the Society can gain no advantage and from which, on the contrary, it may suffer. They suggest by their obvious expensiveness the possibilities of enrichment in the service of the Society, which should not exist and are impossible to explain . . . these pursuits are matters of notoriety and prove a serious obstacle to the success of the work of the Society's agents. Some of his personal clerks, who are carried on the Society's payrolls, are chiefly occupied in the collection and dissemination of news concerning him.[10]

To overcome the difficulty of assembling the necessary three-quarters quorum of the board, JWA declared, his "five eminent counsel," who included Charles Evans Hughes, recommended that the directors ask the legislature to amend the charter so that a simple majority could prevail on such issues as mutualization. Alexander's lecture about the basics of insurance; his diatribe, and his threat to meddle in politics, were more than Harriman's temper could stand. Harriman shook his fist at him and cried, "We will put you out of the window."[11] One member of the committee described the meeting as "a living hell."[12]

Directors took sides, and within a week, the *World* counted twenty-four for mutualization, and twenty for Hyde. Of those the *World* believed to be allied with Alexander, the most important were Cornelius Bliss and, unexpectedly, Chauncey Depew. Five were Equitable executives, and a sixth was JWA's son, Henry Martyn. The Hyde faction appeared to include DeWitt Cuyler, Frick, Valentine Snyder, Schiff, Harriman, Belmont, Gould, Melville Ingalls, and Charles Alexander; as well as Hyde's friends Alfred Vanderbilt, Brad Johnson, and H. R. Winthrop; and his brother-in-law, Sidney Ripley. The *World* assessed three directors as "doubtful"; one was A. J. Cassatt of the Pennsylvania, John Jacob Astor was another.

None of the alliances were firm, and Gage Tarbell was chief among those who could jump sides at any time. On February 12, Tarbell, who had appeared to be firmly in JWA's camp, met with Hyde at the Union League Club and offered to pay him "a fair price for his stock." If Hyde agreed, Tarbell said, "his name would be glorious,"[13] and, Tarbell added, he would be well taken care of in the company, but if not, his "name would be mud." James was polite to the point of apologizing for thinking Tarbell was behind the fight, but he didn't trust him, and he was receiving warnings that corroborated his instincts. One correspondent, writing in a handsome flowing script on stationery from the Hotel Rexford in Boston, wrote:

> The sooner you quietly, though effectively sidetrack G. E. Tarbell the better it will be for all concerned. He is vain, pompous, inordinately ambitious, selfish, self-centered, hated by the agency force of the Society and in a word a menace in all respects. . . . I knew and observed him for years—from the time he "blew out" of Wisconsin (1890) (because a lot of indignant people whom he had induced to buy Gogetic iron stocks threatened to take his scalp) until his picturesque career in Chicago terminated. When your father was practically forced to bring him to New York where his undoubted energy could be utilized—and curbed—as to expenses. Since the death of your father Tarbell has had his eye on the presidency. Yesterday's [February 16] proceedings were part of the plan. Mr. Alexander must

in the nature of things soon retire from active business life. "Help me throw Hyde overboard" says A "and I'll help you to the throne."[14]

The second page of the letter is missing, along with the signature, but some of the allegations would be proven out a few months later when the story of Tarbell and the Gogetic iron stocks became public.

Such personal attacks were rife. One of the most colorful originated in Denver, where George J. Kindel, a mattress manufacturer who was disappointed in the profits on his Equitable policy, circulated a flyer titled "Kindel's Gallery of Dead Characters." On it were pictures of three "outlaws": Jesse James, Henry Hyde, and a man named Jefferson "Soapy" Smith. It accused Henry of having "consorted with outlaws and confidence men."[15] In mid-March, the Equitable's local inspector had Kindel arrested for defamation of character and Hyde brought suit against him, but later dropped it; one crank seemed petty by comparison to his other concerns.

Hyde would have liked to have made peace with JWA, and around February 15, he dictated a letter in which he appealed to his former mentor's honor and loyalty. He wrote that Henry had trusted Alexander to assure "that the control [of the Equitable] be kept intact, in selected hands, as long as possible," and asked JWA to consider: "Have you used your best endeavors to this end? Are you willing to ignore this personal trust placed in you by my father? This stock control has selected you for your present position. Do you not on this account also owe its owners a duty? . . . In spite of the personal nature of the attacks which have been made upon the present regime," he added, "I decline to treat them here as personal, and am ready to unite with you and our co-trustee [Willie McIntyre] and the other directors . . . in carrying out my father's wishes." He reminded JWA that Henry's opinion about whether policyholders would "elect a better Board or would contribute to stability and consistency of management" was not "a matter of doubt. His oral and written opinion and instructions to you and to me on this point are clear."[16] Hyde never sent the letter.

The legal team Hyde had assembled consisted of five brilliant and distinguished men: Elihu Root; Samuel Untermyer; Frick's Philadelphia lawyer, John G. Johnson; Charles B. Alexander, who chose to support Hyde instead of his cousin; and William Gulliver, Hyde's personal counsel.

Root, with his deceptively countrified fringe of short brown bangs and rough brush mustache, was one of President Roosevelt's wise men. Roosevelt called him "the brutal friend to whom I pay the most attention,"[17] and said he was the only member of his cabinet who "had the qualities to succeed him as President."[18] Root had just served as secretary of war, and would soon be called back to Washington as secretary of state. Between government appointments, while he was practicing law, the president asked Root to run for governor of New York. He wrote that if Root were elected governor, he would "become . . . the man likely to be nominated by the Republicans for the Presidency in 1908," but Root declined. He had a lucrative private practice, and he was scheduled to defend J. P. Morgan against Harriman before the U.S. Supreme Court, over issues of stock ownership that developed after the Supreme Court ruled against the Northern Securities railroad combination. Root believed that the Equitable situation was so "disastrous" that he asked the Supreme Court to postpone the argument while he worked on the Equitable's problems, and the justices agreed. That gave Harriman another incentive to wind up the Equitable situation; he had tens of millions of dollars on the line in the Northern Securities suit.

Samuel Untermyer, a trial and corporate lawyer, also had an auxiliary career in public service. Six years after the Equitable crisis, he was appointed counsel to a U.S. House of Representatives investigative committee, which led to the creation of the Federal Reserve and Clayton Antitrust Acts. John G. Johnson, a famous Pennsylvania lawyer, had represented Frick when he sued his former partner, Andrew Carnegie, for fraud and malice—and Carnegie settled. According to one report, Johnson declined to take a fee for the Equitable job because he thought the affair was so scandalous.

The lawyers understood that even if the fight never reached the courts, their client would be tried in the press, and it would be impossible to dam the torrent of inside information that was printed daily. On February 15 alone, the *World*, the *Herald*, and the *New*

York Times all ran major articles about the power struggle, most of which appeared on their front pages. The *World* printed a box in the center of page 1 with the verbatim text of JWA's February 8 petition, and succinctly summed up what was going on in a story titled ALEXANDER IN OPEN WAR ON JAMES H. HYDE.[19]

The newspapers waged their own battle over the Equitable situation, competing for the inside track. Dozens of reporters covered the events as they unfolded, and the papers became more important than any single participant or faction. The chief rivals were the *Times* and Pulitzer's *World*. Adolph Ochs of the *Times* was forced to scramble to refinance his loan from the Equitable before a Pulitzer reporter found out about it and could claim that the *Times* was biased in Hyde's favor.

Hyde expanded his press department, which the *World* called "the most wonderful thing of its kind that has ever been seen in the financial district. Those who have come in contact with the Hyde press bureau have dubbed it the 'sewer grapevine' because of its subterranean and devious methods. It has its starting point in the Equitable offices, then it runs into the offices of Alexander & Green, then into August Belmont's office [at 120 Broadway], then through an unknown party up to the City Hall, and its agent there sends the news by an assistant down to the financial district."[20]

Tarbell had his own system for disseminating information. He and Charles Chapin, the city editor of the *Evening World*, had once lived in the same hotel, and one evening Tarbell approached the reporter at the Majestic Hotel. According to Chapin, Tarbell said, "I will furnish your paper with full particulars of the greatest business scandal this country has ever known and what I will give you will tear hitherto unblemished reputations and smear many men with the mud of their own iniquity. But mark what I now tell you: When the exposure that is bound to come is sifted to the bottom, Gage Tarbell is going to come out of it with character unstained and with a clean bill of health."

Chapin, not surprisingly, was hooked. The next day he introduced Tarbell to one of the *World*'s investigative reporters, to whom

Tarbell turned over "proofs" of his allegations. After that, the *World* assigned a reporter named Ferguson to the story. According to one source, Ferguson "went to the Equitable Home Office so often that he became personally popular there. . . . 'It is a nuisance going all the way to Park Row; why can't I write these stories in this office?' Somebody said he could, and the strange spectacle was observed of the *Evening World* sensationalist writing the blasts of the society on its own typewriting machines."[21]

The Equitable directors were so concerned about leaks that a week after the first board meeting, the executive committee passed a resolution condemning the "unauthorized discussion in the public press of the internal affairs of the Society and . . . the unauthorized publication of written communications recently submitted to the Board of Directors and still under consideration by them," and resolved to go to law if necessary to "quash further discussion in the public press."[22] The board also instructed James Alexander to find out who was talking, and take action. Those resolutions were leaked as well. According to the *World*, both sides had hired detectives, "and on certain days additional detectives are hired to shadow the detectives on the other side to find out whom they are shadowing."[23]

Among the published rumors with the most potential for causing trouble were those that involved Jacob Schiff. One of Hyde's counsels met with Schiff to discuss how to deal with the persistent perception that Schiff had offered to buy Hyde out, acting for a syndicate headed by Harriman. Kuhn, Loeb released a statement that Schiff had not even learned of the "trouble which was brewing" until early February, "when he was called upon by counsel for Mr. Alexander, who advised him of Mr. Alexander's determination to oust Mr. Hyde from the control of the company. . . . Mr. Schiff from the outset declared himself as unqualifiedly in favor of participation by the policy holders . . . [but it] should be brought about in a dignified, orderly, and just manner. . . . The gist of the entire controversy is this: Mr. Alexander and his associates desire to secure control of the company and elect [their own] board of trustees.[24]

A second full board meeting was held on February 16, one week after the first. A near-record forty-five directors attended; Depew, who took a special train to New York from Washington, had to make his way through a throng of the curious, who jammed the great lobby of the Equitable Building. The building was always busy; the Equitable alone had some seven hundred clerks on the main floor. Now, a phalanx of least fifty reporters jostled to get near the directors as they came through, and "every banking and brokerage house of importance in the financial district had a man present to try and get the first news."[25]

The most sensational rumor was that Harriman would replace Alexander as president. The *World* claimed that the Hyde faction was determined to elect Harriman, and that James was being considered for an ambassadorial appointment (the article correctly reported that he had hoped to be given Paris, then wandered off into speculations about offers to serve in Spain or Venezuela).[26] The story took on a more sinister tone when the *World* suggested that if Hyde was sent out of the country, Harriman would become his surrogate at the Equitable. The story sounded as though it had made its way to the newspapers through Harriman; perhaps he was trying out the idea that he might be the right man to step into the leadership of the Equitable.

The board meeting began at two o'clock on the 16th, but some of the directors became so overwrought that they almost immediately agreed to adjourn. They chose a Committee of Two (also known as the Committee of Conciliation)—Schiff represented Hyde, and Tarbell was meant to speak for JWA, and Schiff and Tarbell were sent out of the room to meet privately. They returned in less than an hour with the proposal that the company should be mutualized, and that "the position of president remain unfilled."[27]

JWA's self-control unraveled, and he leapt to his feet. In a voice shaking with anger, he accused Tarbell of "throwing the company president over,"[28] and called the idea an insult and an accusation. One director described the Schiff/Tarbell recommendations as "monstrous,"[29] while Hyde's supporters loudly called for order in "anything but parliamentary language."[30] Harriman and Schiff spoke against JWA's reelection as president, called the question, and when they were outvoted forty to two; the room erupted again. Depew managed to impose quiet on the "scene of wild disorder," and told the directors that they must come to an agreement before they left the room.

For the next twenty minutes, Hyde held the floor, speaking from his own notes, seven points, typed on pink paper. Cautioning that the raging publicity would damage the company, he asked the board to find a solution promptly. He then submitted a written offer, prepared by Elihu Root, proposing to place his shares in trust for five years, to be voted according to the wishes of the majority of the directors, and agreed that he would consider mutualization or an internal buyout of his shares during that period. It was a prompt and conciliatory response to the crisis, but JWA rejected the idea, claiming that it was a power play to put off the change of control, while Hyde stacked the board with his friends.

At last, when everyone had vented, the board reelected all the officers, starting with JWA and Hyde, and reappointed Hyde chairman of the Executive and Finance Committees. The vote would have been unanimous, but Harriman dissented, although it was unclear why. The board agreed to one momentous change, resolving that policyholders should be given the right to vote for directors—but not immediately.

They then appointed another subcommittee, the Committee of Seven, and instructed its members to come up with a plan by April 12. These committees would proliferate all winter, as each tried to solve the problems, failed, and was replaced.

Hyde and Alexander were members of the Committee of Seven; despite the obvious conflict, among their mandates was to negotiate with Hyde about his stock, and consider whether the Equitable should buy in all outstanding shares, retire them, and make the company a pure mutual. The most obvious source of the money for a buy-in was the Equitable's $80 million surplus, but, in principle, it was owed to the policyholders, so its disposition presented ethical, political, and legal hurdles.

The question of the stock's value was highlighted by Thomas W. Lawson, a Boston stockbroker said to be worth $50 million, much of it made in a deal that involved Standard Oil and Amalgamated Copper. Lawson telegraphed Hyde with an offer to buy his shares for $20,000 each, a total of $10.2 million. The proposition was "conditioned upon Mr. Hyde's supplying to him 'evidence of any fraudulent transactions which may have been committed by the company.'" Lawson promised to pay a $1 million deposit immediately, and forwarded a copy of the telegram to the New York newspapers.

Lawson was the author of a series of sensational articles, entitled "Frenzied Finance," which *Everybody's Magazine* published in 1904. He attacked business transgressions, focusing particularly on Amalgamated Copper. In one segment, he recounted how "a hundred million had been lost, thirty suicides committed, and a plunder conspiracy started which if allowed to continue would precipitate a fratricidal war and destroy the nation." "Frenzied Finance" was hugely successful. Within a year, *Everybody's* circulation increased from 150,000 to 750,000, Lawson was given much of the credit for the fantastic jump, and the catchy expression "frenzied finance" entered the popular jargon. With his $10 million offer to Hyde, he was fishing for information on illegal dealings in the insurance industry, which would give him the scoop of the decade. Hyde instructed his secretary to tell reporters that he "did not consider [the] telegram worth his attention."[31]

The talk about the value of Hyde's stock and his salary were threads that ran through the year. That winter, the U.S. Senate had debated whether to give the president a raise to $75,000 and decided to leave his salary at $50,000. It did not escape notice that Hyde was paid double what the president of the United States earned. One newspaper reckoned that, as a director of fifty corporations, which was only a slight exaggeration, if Hyde received the standard fee of $20 (often paid in two $10 gold pieces) plus expenses, for each meeting he attended, he would average $1,500 per company, or an annual total of $75,000. The writer did not include the calculation that he would have to attend six hundred monthly board meetings a year to earn that much.

Hyde and Alexander had a sudden, brief, and uneasy reconciliation, evidently initiated by JWA. He was angry at Tarbell and was looking for an ally; and was sensitive to the opprobrium of directors who blamed him for plotting against Hyde without consulting them, and for betraying Henry Hyde's trust. Men who might not otherwise have taken James's side were offended by "the personal nature of the attack made . . . by a man of Mr. Alexander's years and experience, a friend of . . . Mr. Hyde's father, a trustee of his estate, who should have assumed the position of father or advisor rather than a critic or enemy."

Colonel Mann wrote a long article in *Town Topics* that favored mutualization, but defended James and criticized Alexander.

> Young men of the present day, inheriting much wealth, undoubtedly indulge in the foibles and frolics that their fathers would have regarded with amazement. I am not aware that Mr. Hyde is any more given to those fribbles than most of the young men of the day. On the contrary, I have thought, from the interest he took in French literature . . . the many enterprises in which he is a director . . . and from his sports of the outdoor class—coaching, riding . . . that he is more serious and more devoted to the important features of life than the majority of men his age. . . . If the follies of young men have sometimes attracted him, it would have been better for those whose importance was the creation of his father to extend kindly counsel and friendly solicitude to the son. . . . If departed spirits are in touch with affairs on this sphere, the late Henry B. Hyde must have had some sad moments lately in reflecting upon the ungratefulness of certain people.[32]

On February 17, newspapers reported that JWA and Hyde had reached an "armed truce," and claimed "harmony restored." The Hyde camp issued a statement that "Mr. Hyde and Mr. Alexander are now on more friendly terms than they have been at any time since the death of Henry B. Hyde," and blamed Tarbell for setting up the fight. Alexander's supporters decried Tarbell's behavior, using words like "treachery," and "bitter recrimination." The statements were so destabilizing, especially to the sales force, that JWA, Hyde, and Tarbell quickly found it prudent to issue a joint announcement that they were in agreement after all, and that Tarbell was not a "traitor." JWA sent a telegram to the Equitable's general agents to reassure them that, "Statements in the papers to the effect that differences exist between Mr. Tarbell and myself, or that he has been lacking in loyalty, are false and malicious. I think it proper that you should know immediately that he has been at all times the loyal friend and supporter of the movement for the recognition of the policy holders, and enjoys my fullest confidence."[33]

At the next Committee of Seven meeting, "harmony" was again said to have been achieved, but the effort required was prodigious. A reporter followed an exhausted Hyde to his office, where he admitted that had slept for only a few hours in the last two days. The reporter noted, "By his side was a bottle of claret."

Wine and youth revived him. That night, Hyde attended the opera, sitting in the front row of the directors' box, where most of the audience could see him. When he nodded to an acquaintance across the theater, Colonel Mann noted that he seemed to be bowing to the house. During the intermission, Hyde stood onstage with Otto Kahn, Willie McIntyre, and another man; presented a watch to Hans Conreid; and made "a neat little speech."[34] It was either courageous or arrogant to appear before an audience that knew he was fighting for his financial life.

The ball, which had begun to seem as though it had taken place years earlier, rather than just a few weeks before, was resuscitated in a *Herald* article headlined MR. HYDE TO BUILD RÉJANE THEATRE, based on an interview Réjane gave in her "cabin deluxe" just before she sailed for France. Reporters were often invited aboard when a celebrated passenger was willing to give an interview, and Réjane delighted the journalists by wearing a leopard skin coat, yellow shoes, and "the usual rose-colored veil over her hat." She also called their attention to James's bon voyage gifts: three large bunches of fragrant camellias, a box of long-stemmed roses, and a basket of hothouse fruit. Réjane told the group that she was considering starting a theater in New York (she changed her mind and opened one in Paris instead), but the headline exaggerated her claims about Hyde's commitment. Réjane had only said that, along with "other patrons of French art and literature," he was "interested." Describing him as "a cultured, refined young gentleman," she assured the reporters that he certainly had not discussed the Equitable situation with her. "I know nothing about the insurance business," she said, before returning to the subject of her proposed theater.[35]

The Hyde family was notably missing from the Equitable battle. Annie was chagrined and worried, but she did not understand business, or her son. Mary Ripley supported her brother and defended him to her friends, including Equitable directors and hostesses whose backing carried some weight. But her husband, Sidney Dillon Ripley, who officially maintained his positions as the Equitable's treasurer and director and had an office at 120 Broadway, did not attend the February board meetings, serve on any of the committees, or advise his brother-in-law behind the scenes.

Sidney's lack of interest could be attributed, at least partly, to his long-time estrangement from Henry and James Hyde. He had somehow offended them, and they openly disliked him. Perhaps one reason was that he didn't work very hard; as his obituary would remark, he "held largely aloof from business as well as from public affairs."[36] The Hydes found Sidney arrogant and took opportunities to deflate him, at least between themselves. When James was at Harvard, his father wrote him scornfully, "Sidney told great stories about his hunter last night, but I notice by this morning's papers that on Thanksgiving day he followed the hounds by going on the main road!"[37] That was the easy route—no fences. In another letter James remarked to his father that Sidney (who was in fact quite handsome) had a "brutal" face. Henry's penultimate pronouncement on the subject of Sidney was conveyed through Willie McIntyre in 1898; McIntyre wrote James to report, "Mr. Hyde sent a message to Mr. Ripley toady that he did not wish him ever to go to [the Hyde's house on] L.I. for anything."[38] Henry's ultimate judgment was conveyed in his will, which stipulated that the income from Mary's portion of the trust should be "free from the influence of any husband she may have."

Nevertheless, in the first week of February, when the Equitable was about to explode, Sidney warned his brother-in-law that the crisis was imminent. Under pressure from another executive, Tarbell had telephoned Sidney to tell him what was brewing. The same day Alexander had called Hyde and said that he urgently needed to see him, but it was Friday, Hyde was already in Bay Shore, and he said he would meet with him at the office on Monday. But when Sidney called and repeated Tarbell's warning, Hyde took the train to New York, where JWA presented him with the first petition that he planned to submit to the board. After that, Sidney retreated into his customary lack of interest.

And then something happened that would affect Hyde's peace of mind, although it would have no impact on the fate of the Equitable: In the last week in February, Sidney's appendix burst. On a Tuesday morning he told Mary he was having severe stomach pains, but when she proposed to call the doctor, he said he was sure he would feel better soon. Hours later, he was in agony. The doctor came, diagnosed his condition, and operated immediately, but it was too late to save him.

Sidney deteriorated so rapidly that his three sons couldn't get home from college in time to say goodbye. Only two days later, Mary and her daughter, Annah, along with James, Sidney's brother, and the doctor, assembled for a last vigil. Annie Hyde appears not to have been there; the newspapers dutifully reported on who attended the deathbed and her name was not mentioned.

Hyde was badly shaken; he felt responsible for his sister, and had counted on her; now it was he who would have to offer her emotional support. The evening of Sidney's death he rode down from the Ripleys' house to attend a meeting of the Committee of Seven at the Metropolitan Club. The grand limestone building that J.P. Morgan had built on Fifth Avenue across from the southern end of Central Park loomed white in the winter dark, as Hyde's carriage drew into the paved courtyard. He had once made a famous bet that he could turn his road coach around in that tight space, and won, a feat documented in a picture that still hangs in the club. Now that phase of his life had passed. Hyde sat quietly at the meeting, and for the most part, Jacob Schiff spoke on his behalf.

The issues on which the Equitable fight had initially been based, mutualization and leadership, were rapidly overshadowed by a growing understanding of the connections between Wall Street and the insurer. In that regard, Schiff continued to be the focus of attention. It seemed clear that he had broken the New York State insurance law forbidding any life insurance director to profit from selling securities to a company on whose board he sat.[39] Kuhn, Loeb issued a denial that "Mr. Schiff, as a director of the society, had taken part in the purchase by the latter of a large amount of securities from the firm of Kuhn, Loeb and Co.," adding, "whatever dealings his firm has had with the Equitable Society have been most advantageous to the latter. If his firm has sold high class investment bonds to the Equitable it has sold of the same bonds many more millions during the same period to other insurance companies in which Mr. Schiff is not a director."[40] According to reliable sources, in 1904 alone, Kuhn, Loeb sold the Equitable $22 million in bonds, netting $500,000 in commissions.

The same law applied to George W. Perkins, as a New York Life director. Since Perkins had become a partner in J. P. Morgan, New York Life had bought some $39 million in securities through the Morgan bank. Hyde tried to deflect some of the criticism of the Equitable's practices by accusing Perkins of being the real instigator of the Equitable row, and New York Life promptly issued a statement calling the charges "too silly to warrant denial,"[41] but denied them anyway. The *Herald* commented, "The relations of [the insurance companies with] prominent banking houses, members of which were active in the directorates of the big insurance companies . . . form a subject of discussion which is constantly irritating and agitating Wall street [*sic*]."[42] Thomas Lawson was praised on the financial pages of the *World* on Sunday, February 19, in a story headlined EQUITABLE FIGHT MAY BE OF SERVICE TO WALL STREET, GRAVE DANGERS TO THE FINANCIAL WORLD EXIST IN THE PRESENT METHODS—PRIVATE INTERESTS HAVE PROFITED BY USE OF INSURANCE FUNDS . . . THE PRACTICE IS A VIOLATION OF THE SPIRIT OF THE LAW.

Lawson wrote a lengthy article in the *World*, HOW THE INSURANCE "COMBINE" JUGGLES WITH ITS BILLIONS OF RESOURCES, describing how "the insurance tree branches intertwine with all the foliage of Wall street. [*sic*] There are three great life-insurance corporations in New York that are steadily drawing closer together in their financial affairs to form 'The Family Tree of Billions,'" he claimed.

> These companies—the Mutual, Equitable and New York [*sic*] already have combined resources of more than a billion dollars and their branches spread out into other financial corporations controlled or influenced by them, until another billion is involved.
>
> . . . The financiers who form the boards of trustees of these three companies are the controlling spirits in many other great corporations which aggregate a third billion of dollars.
>
> This great tree of billions sinks its roots deep into the pockets of the masses, drawing from hundreds of thousands of policy-holders their small contributions in annual premiums. The sap of gold is sucked up . . . and then shot out into the branches supplying the financial life of trusts, railroads and even governments. . . .
>
> It is a safe estimate that these three insurance companies have a hundred million dollars to put out each year.
>
> No other corporation, no individual, no syndicate, has near any such sum at its disposal. The power of that amount to affect the affairs of mankind . . . is very great. . . . [43]

Lawson, who had not mentioned his $10 million offer for Hyde's shares again once he had gotten the press's attention, explained, "Half a dozen of the 'System's' most active and avaricious votaries were to make a few millions on the side in steering Hyde's stock through the whirls and eddies to its final resting place, and here the apple-cart turned over. . . . The young society head of the Equitable happened to light on some of the side millions that were passing, and with a pugnacious activity which has, thank goodness, not as yet been blunted by too severe contact with the many queer transactions which weekly slide through the locks and sluices of the system's canals, attempted to intervene and to criticise [*sic*]. . . ."

Lawson speculated that this purported attempt to interfere set JWA and other members of the "System" against Hyde. The threat to the branches and trunks, mazes, streams, and sluices was "a man who had never participated in the plundering of the past; a man absolutely uncontrolled; a man in such a queer position as to be absolutely immune to the terrors of the 'System's' threats of cajoleries—James H. Hyde." Although Hyde "had shown no desire to interfere with conditions in the Equitable as he found them . . . he could if he wanted to, and, being young, only twenty-nine [*sic*; he was 28], educated, widely experienced in the world of don't-care-a-figness for recognized rules of dollar-getting precedents, an athlete, a 'sport,' a rich man by inheritance, a free man by environment, a man, in fact, who recognized no law but his own will, he might, if he chose, suddenly upset all calculations and stir up incalculable trouble."

Lawson's analysis of how the "few millions" would be made as Hyde's stock changed hands was vague, but his perspective reflected a growing sense that, even as Hyde was being attacked and ridiculed, he was not an entirely unsympathetic character. He had profited, but he had been used, and while he had gone along, now he was fighting back.

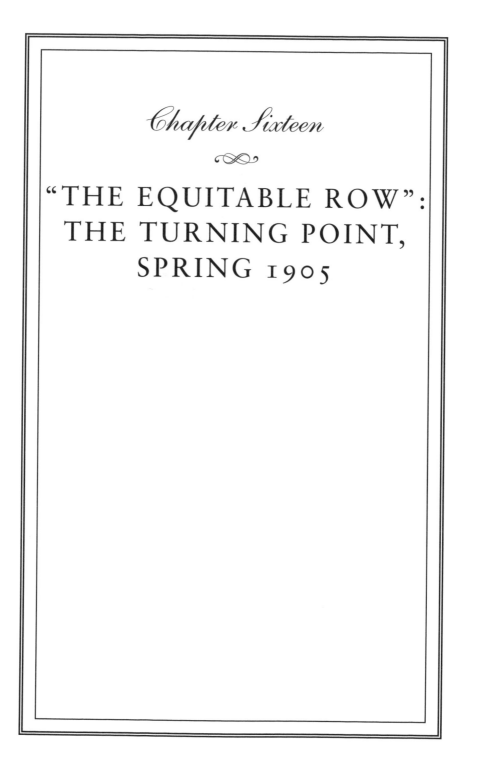

Chapter Sixteen

"THE EQUITABLE ROW": THE TURNING POINT, SPRING 1905

"HE WAS YOUNG AND INEXPERIENCED."

—From the testimony of E. H. Harriman at the Insurance Investigation.

Newspaper cartoon of James as a plucked peacock, with Wall Street and political "fat cats" marching off with his feathers.

The cartoonists made a feast of lampooning James; he was by no means the worst character in the debacle, but he was the easiest for an artist to draw. *(Courtesy AXA Financial Archives)*

*T*he winter of 1905 was the second coldest on record, with 53.3 inches of snow.[1] Like rain at a funeral, the damp winds off the Hudson and East Rivers, and the slush mixed with horse manure on the city streets were an appropriate background for the mood on Wall Street. Bankers and brokers at most of the major houses were waiting to see how fallout from the Equitable's problems would affect them.

March began with the appearance of a new outside faction, the self-appointed Policy Holders' Protection Committee. The committee was headed by John D. Crimmins, whose construction firm built the Croton Aqueduct, providing much of New York City's water supply. Crimmins was politically well connected; he had been a member of the state Charter Revision Commission and president of the Board of Commissioners of Public Parks. He was cultivated—he had a famous collection of some five thousand maps and pictures of New York—and he was devout: he had built the lovely Chapel of St. Anne at St. Patrick's Cathedral in memory of his late wife.[2] None of this meant that he was a disinterested party, although if he had a personal interest, it was not apparent. The Crimmins Committee's lawyer, Frank H. Platt, was another matter; he was the son of Thomas C. Platt, who had served in the U.S. Senate since the 1880s and was the New York State Republican boss. Platt's son had an inside track in Albany and Washington.

The Crimmins Committee's stated purpose was to create a voice for the policyholders, by introducing legislation requiring all life insurance companies chartered to do business in New York State to operate solely as mutuals. But when the committee demanded that the Equitable provide a complete list of its customers, the suspicion arose that a rival company was behind Crimmins and his associates. The Equitable refused to hand over the list, but the committee managed to acquire the names of New York State policyholders anyway, and wrote asking them to support the mutualization plan. The response was immediate: By the end of the first week in March, Crimmins told the press, five thousand letters a day were coming in favoring mutualization, and his committee had made up its own list of thirty thousand names from the letters.

There was political profit to be made from the publicity attendant on the pursuit of the Equitable, and it started at the top: President Roosevelt was concerned that the fray could kick off a financial breakdown, but he was also satisfied to find another example of the business malfeasance that was a feature of his March 4 Inaugural Address. "Dangers from abroad," he said, were "trivial in comparison with our dangers at home!" These included "the menace of corporation control of American political institutions . . . [and] the system of organized greed and cunning."[3]

New York State Assembly members took advantage of the opening to propose bills recommending mutualization, and modifications in the general corporation law to prohibit any officer of a life insurance, trust company, or savings bank to do business with the company.[4] Reform required a more comprehensive approach, and new legislation would not pass in 1905, but government interest added another layer of uneasiness in the business community. That was exacerbated on March 13, when New York state senator Edgar T. Brackett filed a suit on behalf of Mary S. Young, a constituent in Saratoga County, who held one share of Equitable stock. Representing herself and six other policyholders, Mrs. Young sued the Equitable and James Hyde in the state Supreme Court, demanding that Hyde return the $200,000 salary he had earned in the past two years. The suit also alleged that the board was packed with "dummy" directors, who did not actually own the five shares of stock listed in each of their names that qualified them to sit on the board. Mrs. Young claimed that thirty-eight of the fifty-two directors held stock that really belonged to James. Among the men she accused were Harriman, Frick, Schiff, Vanderbilt, Astor, Gould, and Belmont. All of them could easily have afforded to buy five shares of the stock, but it would turn out that most of them were, indeed, owners in name only.

A process server for the Young case traveled to New York from Saratoga on March 14, and caught up with Hyde as he was about to get into his carriage in front of 120 Broadway. Hyde's friend H. Rogers Winthrop had given him an eight-pound walking stick with a round silver head that was described as "the size of a baseball," and Hyde raised the stick and shook it at the process server. "Get away from me," he snapped. "Don't you dare touch me or I shall strike you." Then he swung himself up into the cab of the carriage, slammed the door, and ordered his coachman to drive on. The process server tossed the papers in through the window, and although Hyde threw them back out onto the street, once he had touched them, he had officially been served. It was one of the rare occasions when he lost his temper in public.

Brackett had identified himself with a cause that would keep him in the public eye, and gave him a chance to compliment his constituents. At one point, he declared, "What the Equitable needs is a good deal less Wall street [*sic*] and more common country sense on its Board of Directors," then mentioned three locally important men in his own district as candidates.[5]

Harriman was hard at work trying to keep the politicians in check, and told the Equitable board that he had "with considerable pains succeeded in preventing an investigation of the society in the legislature."[6] The newspapers regularly referred to Harriman's political machinations, but he didn't blink, even when the *World* wrote,

Mr. Harriman is a warm friend of Benjamin B. Odell, Jr., the Republican boss of New York. His friendship with Mr. Odell gives him much influence with the State government, but—

Can Gov. Higgins afford to encourage the suspicion that he is being influenced in the private interests of E. H. Harriman?

Can Attorney General Mayer afford to encourage the suspicion that he is being influenced for the benefit of E. H. Harriman?

Can the State Legislature afford to encourage the suspicion that it is being influenced for the protection of E. H. Harriman?

If Mr. Harriman believes it to be to his advantage to prevent a

real investigation into the affairs of the Equitable, can the government of New York afford to go on record as believing that the interests of E. H. Harriman in this matter are paramount to the interests
of 600,000 policy-holders?

The editorial closed by warning the Equitable board that it was
playing into the hands of "the hordes of Socialism and Anarchism"
by "smother[ing] the scandal."

Sensation followed sensation. A new "report" revealed that Hyde
proposed to shut down the Equitable, and disperse the $80-some
million surplus among the stockholders. Under that rumored plan,
the Equitable's policies, and its $418 million reserve fund would be
turned over to New York Life and the Mutual. Hyde immediately
denied that he had ever had any such idea.

Counsel for the Alexander and Hyde factions convened in urgent
meetings to discuss mutualization, fearing that the crisis would set
off a panic. Hyde's representatives offered the concession that half
the fifty-two directors could be elected by policyholders; JWA's
lawyers rejected it.

The Equitable's Committee of Seven was still meeting. On Wednesday, March 15, they sat together all afternoon and into the evening
and, when they emerged at last, announced that JWA, Hyde, Tarbell,
Snyder, Bliss, Cuyler, and Depew had unanimously agreed to recommend that policyholders select a majority of the directors, twenty-eight
of the fifty-two. Hyde's stock would not be retired, although it would
lose some of its perceived value when he had less control. After the
ceaseless furor, it was almost a letdown to learn that the only point of
difference was how long it should take for the board to turn over the
twenty-eight slots. Tarbell was making progress toward the goal of
being able to influence the composition of the board, but, meanwhile,
it was said that he had been approached with an open offer from the
president of a rival company.

Senator Brackett had no intention of letting the Equitable solve its
problems internally, and said he would continue to prosecute the

Young case. The night before the third full board meeting in a month, with the political pressure mounting, Harriman held a council of war at his house at 1 East Fifty-fifth Street. His goal was to press for a solution so the situation could be resolved before the legislature took action.

Thirty-four directors attended the meeting. Sidney Ripley had died only a week earlier, and Hyde was noted to be more soberly dressed than usual, in a black cutaway suit, waistcoat, and white shirt, with a cravat tied in a bow. Schiff and Harriman dominated the meeting, which was over in an hour. The board voted to adopt the twenty-eight/fifty-two version of mutualization, with a four-year phase-in. Hyde seemed to have made enough concessions to protect his interests and those of the Equitable, and reporters who saw him leaving the meeting wrote that he looked jubilant. Sketches in one of the papers showed him bending over paternally to talk with uniformed employees, a contrast to the usual illustrations of him as a coachman, a party host, or in the company of "great men." The new images gave the impression that by fighting for the company, Hyde had made it more his own.

The directors' plan came too late: Six weeks of ceaseless publicity had placed the insurer on the public agenda. Superintendent of Insurance Francis Hendricks added a section about the Equitable to his 1904 fire insurance report, saying that mutualization's "justice and wisdom are beyond question."[8] One source told the press that Hendricks had been given new information which, if revealed, "would tear the roof off of the Equitable Company and explode like a carload of dynamite."[9] If that happened, the superintendent would be on the line, too; the obvious question would be why the insurance department hadn't known that the dynamite was being stockpiled and done something to stop it.

By the end of March, Senator Brackett had petitioned the state attorney general to remove Hyde as vice president and director. For the first time, the accusation that Hyde had charged the ball to the Equitable—at an alleged cost of $100,000—was floated publicly. The subhead of one story read, SENATOR BRACKETT DECLARES EXPENSE

OF "COSTUME BALL" WAS BORNE BY SOCIETY.[10] The language in the Brackett petition was suspiciously similar to the "confidential" charges JWA had made in his eighteen-page address in February.

Brackett also asked that the attorney general force Schiff off the board and bar him from serving as a director of any other insurance company licensed in New York State. Pointing out that Schiff had sold millions of dollars in securities to the Equitable while serving as a director, and received a share of the commissions as a partner in Kuhn, Loeb, Brackett demanded that he and his company return their profits.

Brackett's clerk delivered a copy of the petition to JWA, and asked if he "would swear that the facts alleged . . . are not true?" JWA said that he wouldn't swear to anything and would seek advice on the matter.

Depew defended the Equitable's investment policies, explaining that nearly every banking house in the city submitted a list of securities and their prices to the insurers. They bought and sold through the bankers, Depew said, because if they made the transactions on the open market they would drive the prices up. Schiff invited a *World* reporter to his house and gave him a lecture about why insurance companies benefited from their connections with bankers.

On March 29, after a day with his lawyers, Hyde issued a statement denying the Brackett and Alexander accusations. He pointed out that he could not have charged bills of the magnitude of the ball to the Equitable, even if they were considerably less than $100,000, without JWA's knowledge. That evening, carrying on at least a simulacrum of social life, he returned home by five, dressed for dinner, had friends in for drinks, went to the theater, and then stopped at the Knickerbocker Club, all the while followed by a reporter to whom he politely refused to comment.

Alexander did not openly allege that Hyde had charged the ball to the company; instead, he took up the issue of the Cambon dinner, which was easier to "prove" because the Equitable had, in fact, reimbursed Hyde for its cost. JWA claimed that the Equitable had paid for the dinner "without my knowledge and without the knowledge of the Executive Committee."

Mr. Hyde . . . stated that the dinner had been given for the purpose of advertising the Society. No other officer or person connected with the Society was aware that it was being advertised by this dinner, and I accepted an invitation to attend the same as Mr. Hyde's guest in entire ignorance of the fact that I was participating in the advertisement of the Company of which I was President. Mr. Hyde's real purpose in giving this entertainment, and in making this very liberal use of the funds of the Society, was kept secret from me until two years and a half had elapsed since the date of the dinner.

The name of the Equitable Life Assurance Society was not mentioned at the dinner, nor was anything said or done in connection therewith from which any clue could have been derived as to the advertising purpose of the dinner. . . . It would have been a most improper and injurious method of advertising the Equitable if its name had ever been connected with it.[11]

The allegations hurt Alexander as much as they did Hyde, indicating that he was either irresponsible, oblivious, or a liar.

In a sudden about-face, Crimmins defended Hyde. He said, "I do not believe for a minute that he used the money of the society for the expense of the fancy dress ball . . . [and] in regard to the Cambon dinner . . . certain expenditures of that sort on behalf of the society are perfectly legitimate if the society benefits from it." He added that he would do the same if he thought it would help his business.[12] The Crimmins Committee's lawyer, Frank Platt, obtained a copy of a letter Hyde wrote to Alexander, directing that the Equitable pay for the dinner, and Platt brought the letter to Albany to show Superintendent Hendricks. Hyde chose not to press the point. Before the end of the month he had sent the Equitable a check for more than $13,000, repaying the costs of the dinner.

Now that some form of mutualization seemed inevitable, Crimmins was ready to let the Equitable settle its own troubles, but most of his committee members wanted to stay in the game. They met three times during the last two days in March, debating until ten-thirty at night at Crimmins's house. The members became increasingly estranged, and while they remained part of the process, they were overshadowed by Senator Brackett's relentless offensives.

The elements of the story had settled into certain grooves. Hyde's character was the most titillating; the possibility that famous directors had enriched themselves at the policyholders' expense was the most sensational; and mutualization was kept alive as the structural issue that provided access to the more exciting aspects of the scandal. As excess, greed, and financial chicanery oozed out, it became evident that the saga was driven by huge sums of money. The stakes were getting higher all the time, and it seemed that reputations would be ruined, legal actions taken, and the sight of the mighty being led off to prison might give the drama an explosive last act.

Even after two months of public acrimony, the Equitable crisis could have been resolved. Early in the morning on March 31, insurance superintendent Hendricks took the train from Albany to New York. When he arrived at his office at 11 Broadway, he telephoned the principal antagonists and asked them to come to a meeting immediately.

When Hyde drove up in his hansom cab, it was noted that, as usual, his horses wore violets in their harnesses, that the coachman sported a large bunch of violets in the buttonhole of his livery, and that Hyde was wearing a large, floppy purple tie. A reporter got close enough to determine that the horses' violets were artificial, but could not decide if the coachman's boutonniere was real. Hyde was met at Hendricks's office by Gulliver, Root, and Bliss. JWA was already there, with one of his lawyers; the Policy Holders' Committee was represented by Crimmins, Frank Platt, and Henry Morgenthau, Hyde's former fellow opera-board member. Harriman had no official role, but he was there, too.

With Hendricks running the meeting, they reached a rational, realistic compromise: policyholders would be permitted to elect fourteen directors in 1905, and another fourteen in 1906; and Crimmins could approve the choice of the men to fill the two current vacancies left by deaths. They disbanded before lunch.

As Alexander was leaving, reporters asked him what had happened, but his lawyer told them the proceedings were "sacred." Everyone else declined to comment, although Hyde politely stopped, and explained, "I should like to tell what is going on, but really I have nothing to say. You must excuse me."[13]

Hendricks, ignoring the appearance of inappropriate influence, went to lunch with Platt at Delmonico's. When a reporter approached them outside the restaurant, Platt interrupted with a curt, "The Superintendent has nothing to say," and threatened to call the police if the reporter did not leave.

Hyde, Harriman, and Root returned to the Equitable Building and shut themselves in Harriman's office for the next hour.

The next day, Hyde issued a public request that Hendricks conduct a thorough examination of the Equitable, in part so Hyde could clear himself of Alexander's charges. He added yet another concession: He offered to give up control of the Executive Committee and agreed that, of the committee's twelve members, Hendricks should approve four new men, two of them chosen by Bliss, and two by the policyholders.

Mutualization seemed to be a fait accompli, until Alexander backed off again. He said he would not agree to any plan unless James resigned.

The participants in the struggle for control had begun by believing they had much to gain, but they had arranged matters so badly that they now had even more to lose.

JWA could have announced that, with partial mutualization agreed upon, he had accomplished his goal; and he could have retired with honor at the end of the year. But pride and Gage Tarbell kept him from backing down. He tried to maintain his high moral ground, yet he was standing on a mudslide. Sometimes, he seemed to understand that he was losing traction, but then he would catch himself and regain his footing. At a board meeting on April 5, after Hyde made a moving speech in his own defense, one observer said, "With tears streaming down his cheeks Mr. Alexander . . . left his chair and walked toward Mr. Hyde, with his hand extended, and before the assembled directors apologized for his part in the attack." Later, JWA firmly denied that he had wept.[14]

Tarbell might have gotten what he wanted if he had been more patient. The trend was toward mutualization and over the next few years, there was a good chance that he could gain control of enough of the board to persuade the directors to name him chief executive officer, with Hyde as chairman. But Tarbell was left out of most of the unofficial meetings, and he prepared to influence the outcome by calling up his own regiment.

It was hard to know what more Hyde could have done. Insiders who talked about the way directors behaved at meetings noted that he stood up for himself with dignity, was well prepared, and that his concessions would bring policyholders into the decision-making process. His legal team was superb, and Harriman was handling the political aspects of his strategy. His attitude toward the press was pleasant and frank; reporters mentioned his unhurried courtesy and apparent openness. Even when he had "no comment," he was willing to pause and look them in the eye. About the only option he did not take was to tone down his wardrobe, but his distinctive style was one of the few aspects of his life he could still control.

Finally, with no resolution in sight, the state and the Equitable board both initiated investigations. Hendricks opened an official inquiry into the Equitable's business in mid-April, inspiring some cynical commentary. One cartoon showed Hyde dressed in dancing pumps with bows, wearing tights and a tailcoat, sprawled across Hendricks's knee, about to be spanked, as little money bags labeled "Cambon Dinner," "Paris Expenses," and "Syndicate Profits" fell out of his pockets. Hendricks would not release his findings until early summer, but the other investigation had a tighter schedule. The Equitable board had appointed yet another committee. It would be chaired by Henry Clay Frick, and it was directed to examine the management of the company.

The third event in April, planned to create another kind of momentum to jerk the process out of its stall, was a hastily convened agents' convention arranged by JWA and Tarbell. Sales had held up in March, but agents around the country reported that customers were getting nervous. Tarbell had offered a four-dollar-per-thousand bonus to agents as an incentive to sales, but prospective policy-holders had begun to hold off and the other racers were taking advantage of the Equitable's troubles. It was said that they had instructed their agents to bring back $2 million in business in the next three months. The story about an Equitable agent in Chicago who committed suicide by shooting himself in the head in his boardinghouse went the rounds, and Equitable representatives understood that he had been in despair over the loss of business and fearful that the company would dissolve.

The conference opened on Tuesday, April 18, and the day before, 220 Equitable agent managers began arriving at the Savoy Hotel, where they and their wives would be guests of the company. They were welcomed with white carnations to wear in their buttonholes, which some interpreted as "emblematic of the purity which the working force believed the only salvation of the society."[15] As they circulated through the halls and lobbies, JWA and Tarbell greeted them and held informal conferences. Hyde stayed away.

That evening, Tarbell arranged a "secret" caucus to present his case prior to the official meetings, at the Hotel Netherland, across the street from the Savoy. The 180 agents who attended were carefully screened at the door for identification and credentials. Tarbell hoped the security would foil the omnipresent journalists, but secrecy would never be an element of the Equitable story: By morning, the papers published the account that the caucus had passed a resolution to "uphold the personal integrity of James W. Alexander," but had not gone so far as to endorse his management of the society.

At eleven o'clock on Tuesday, Hyde waited alone in an anteroom next to the Savoy ballroom. He had prepared himself with handwritten notes on "Hyde Problems," in the list form he preferred. The notes, which did not mention JWA, indicated that Hyde understood Tarbell to be his most dangerous enemy:

Problem No. 1
    Tarbell's opportunity to make trouble should be minimized so far as possible at once.
    First, by curbing his official power . . . without destroying his cooperation.

Second, by removing the element of fear of Tarbell from the men . . . by backing up your carefully selected and trusted lieutenants in any proper assurance they may give the men.

Third, enlarge the powers of Western Superintendent, also the scope of his duties, so that he may do personal work among the men in *your* behalf . . .

Fourth, by gradually, with as little friction as possible, eliminating all disturbing elements in departments and fields.

Problem No. 2

You should get into closer touch with the men, and become better understood by them. . . .

Fifth. Follow up with a series of monthly letters, attractively printed, to the men, which shall at once instruct and inspire, and which shall gradually stamp your personality on the men and secure from them a recognition of your strength, determination, business ability and high ideals.

Problem No. 3

Any unjust estimate of yourself in the public mind should be skillfully and systematically removed by inaugurating a campaign of publicity, through which diplomatically worded character sketches may be sent out to the country papers throughout the States. . . .[16]

JWA and Tarbell were already seated on the dais when Hyde entered the ballroom. His arrival caused a predictable stir but no demonstrations, either of enthusiasm or disapproval, and he took his seat on one side of JWA, with Tarbell on the other. George Wilson, Tarbell's chief rival within the company, had been asked not to attend the meeting; the preceding week he had been a guest at a luncheon Hyde gave at the Lawyers' Club for members of the board and had spoken up against personal attacks. The "Tarbell faction thought from his tone that Mr. Wilson had better be denied an opportunity to make a similar speech to the agents."[17]

JWA stood, to general applause, praised the agents, and introduced Hyde. Before Hyde began to speak, in the only unpleasant incident of the day, Julius Bohm of New York sprang up and hissed. As some reported, Hyde responded, "This is indeed a compliment."

In another version, he said, "That's all right . . . you may hiss. You owe $50,000 to Mr. Tarbell [a reference to Bohm's unusually high advances against commissions]. Only two animals hiss, a goose and a snake."[18] Bohm was subdued by another agent, and no one followed his lead.

The room fell silent as Hyde spoke of his loyalty to the company his father had built, and summarized his concessions toward mutualization. In a pointed allusion to Tarbell, he added, "I hope that all the agents here who have the future of the society at heart will not follow the example of one officer of the society who sold out his future interest."[19]

He was referring to an incident that he had brought to the attention of the press just before the agents' convention. On February 8, the day of the board meeting at which JWA presented the initial petitions, JWA had arranged for the Equitable to pay Tarbell a lump sum of $135,000, "in lieu of any future premiums." The payment was not approved by the Executive Committee, and violated the terms of the agreement Tarbell made when he became an executive of the Equitable. Hyde told the press that it was "evidence that Mr. Tarbell was 'putting his house in order' with the aid of Mr. Alexander on the eve of the campaign for the control of the company."[20] Hyde's friends added that Tarbell "understood [the fight] would injure the company, and . . . was so careful of his own interests that he wanted to get them all out before the campaign began."[21] Unfortunately for Hyde, he made better copy than Tarbell, and the newspapers garbled the issue. The *World* published a page 1 box titled GIVE UP AND GET OUT, accusing Hyde of returning "$135,000 of graft."[22]

Tarbell followed Hyde on the podium and began in a temper. "I want to tell you one thing," he declared, "and that is that I will never have to pay back to the Equitable one penny that I ever received from it."[23]

He was taking advantage of two of Hyde's attempts to show good faith; Hyde had not only reimbursed the company for the Cambon dinner, he had just presented the cashier with an escrow check of $61,446, representing his profits from the James Hazen Hyde and

Associates syndicate transactions involving the Equitable. His intention was that the treasurer would hold the money until the board determined whether he was entitled to keep it.

When Alexander, Hyde, and Tarbell had finished speaking, they said they would withdraw, so the agents could talk without restraint. Hyde left the hotel, but JWA and Tarbell installed themselves in an anteroom, screened behind heavy portieres, within earshot of the ballroom.

The results of the sessions that followed were inconclusive and didn't give the press much to write about, but that afternoon, Henry H. Knowles, the Equitable's former manager of agents, emerged from behind the scenes with a story that could turn the convention upside down, and reverse Tarbell's rising fortunes.

Shortly before the convention opened, Knowles, who had been a reluctant ally from the start, tangled with Tarbell and Alexander. Alexander fired him for "insubordination" on the Saturday before the agents arrived, and Knowles finally resolved to make public what he knew about the genesis of the fight for the Equitable. He announced that he had a story to tell, and convened a contingent of reporters after the first day's meeting adjourned, to recount his disturbing and credible version of events.[24] Knowles, who was a few years younger than JWA, had started work at the Equitable at about the same time. It had taken a great deal to turn this loyal old fireside dog into a harrier. He looked like a solid burgher who enjoyed every meal; his round face was fleshy, his nose was shaped like a potato, and his eyes were creased in fat, but his mustache turned up at the ends as though it were smiling, and his expression was benign and friendly.

Knowles had been skeptical about the proposed coup from the inception. When the first board meeting in February was not the clean sweep Tarbell had promised, Knowles questioned him, and Tarbell "showed his hand. He [Tarbell] said he had an agreement with Mr. Alexander. . . . The president was growing old and wanted to get rid of all the hard work he could; he said it was his intention to retire from the presidency in a year or two, and if Tarbell would keep to his agreement with him, he would make him president of the company on his retirement." Knowles began to suspect that Tarbell was setting up both Hyde and Alexander, but still hoping, as he put it, to "pour oil on troubled waters," he suggested that Tarbell speak to Hyde. Tarbell stopped in Knowles's office to tell him that he had offered James $2,000 a share for his stock, and had put together a syndicate to raise $1.5 million. Knowles wanted to know where Tarbell would get his hands on that kind of money, and why anyone "would pay so much for stock which he [Tarbell] had said had no value." Tarbell's answer was vague, but, in any case, he said, James would not sell. Knowles accused Tarbell of tarnishing the Equitable's reputation. Tarbell retorted that he could have the entire company placed in the hands of a receiver, if he chose.

Profoundly disturbed by that prospect, Knowles talked to James's lawyer, William Gulliver, and Gulliver met with Tarbell, who said he would not back down unless he was assured that he would be made president when JWA retired.

In early March, Knowles continued, Tarbell took the fight to the agency managers, sending them a letter asking them to notify him of any problems they were having with policyholders. He promised to "help them" if they would send along the information. When Knowles confronted Tarbell about the letter, accusing him of trying to damage Hyde and the society, a "warm scene" followed. "So you're looking for trouble, are you?" Tarbell asked. If Knowles didn't like the way Tarbell and JWA were handling the situation, Tarbell said, perhaps he should resign.

"That is a cheerful suggestion to come from you to a man who has been forty years in the service of this society, and because he has manhood and courage enough to express his opinion," Knowles recalled saying.

Tarbell told Knowles that *he* was prepared to resign, if that was what it took to win, and that "he was worth more than half a million dollars . . . and . . . he would spend every cent to get Hyde out and make the company a proxy mutual." Tarbell did seem to have amassed a small fortune; he now had his own four-in-hand coach and prize-winning horses, and had hired Hyde's own "star whip of the world," Morris Howlett, to teach him to drive.

Finally, Knowles said he would have to cut their conversation off because he "did not like to remain in an atmosphere of doubt and suspicion," and walked out of Tarbell's office. At that point, there was less than a week before the agents' convention, and it was decidedly inconvenient to have the manager of agents, who worked directly under Tarbell, as a potential troublemaker.

The next day, JWA sent Knowles a note at home, asking that he come in to see him. The Equitable's Alabama manager had died, and JWA proposed that Knowles go to Alabama immediately to take over and look for a new manager. When Knowles replied that "was just a trick of Tarbell's to get me out of the city," JWA accused him of insubordination.

Knowles told JWA he was being used as a "tool." "Tarbell has told me that he has an agreement with you," Knowles said, "and if your plans were successful he would be president of the company in one or two years. Tarbell has said to me that what he most feared in this fight which he had undertaken with you was your backbone. He said he had to stiffen it almost daily. Mr. Tarbell said that the reason the charges of malfeasance in office were not pressed against Mr. Hyde was that he found you were as deep in the mire as Hyde was in the mud."

Alexander was visibly shaken, but returned to the subject of Knowles's leaving for Alabama, and Knowles agreed to let him know that evening. JWA was too nervous to wait; at midday, he rode up to the Lawyers' Club where Knowles was lunching, and asked to speak to him privately. JWA complained that he hadn't gotten his answer about Alabama, and Knowles pleaded with him to get together with James. Tarbell, Knowles said, had lost credibility with the agents, which would be reinforced when they learned that he had been paid $135,000 in lieu of future commissions. "Take away from Mr. Tarbell the right to punish the managers and agents who disagree with him, and he will not have a corporate guard left," Knowles promised. But JWA didn't want to stand alone. "I cannot swap horses in the middle of the stream," he said.

Knowles had taken over JWA's self-appointed role as the conscience of the company, and, on Saturday, April 16, JWA fired him.

The reporters listened to Knowles's presentation, took it down, and published it verbatim. Tarbell read the news the next morning at the Savoy Hotel and lost control. Surrounded by agents, he "fairly shook with anger, and 'It is false,' he cried. 'I deny it all.'"[25] He shouted so loudly that people left their tables in the dining room to see what was going on. Nearly a hundred people crowded around him as he ranted. Suddenly he changed course and embarked on a lavish endorsement of JWA: "There has never been any question of Mr. Alexander resigning in my favor. He is the last man in the world to desert his post. He is the one man in this country who is fitted to hold the position and the suggestion that he resign is preposterous. He will hold the presidency of the Equitable until he dies. He is the soul of honor and integrity and would make any personal sacrifice for the welfare of the society," he declared. He delivered this encomium with such excitation and thrashing that he gathered an even larger audience. Picking up volume, he called out, "I want to tell everybody within the sound of my voice that the society's interests will be protected. . . . Men may talk and make all manner of accusations, but the institution will stand, and the men who have safeguarded it will remain in office."

At a pitch of hysteria, Tarbell shouted, "Who is this Knowles anyway?"

Someone in the crowd called back, "He was one of your most intimate lieutenants. . . . You ought to know him."

Other agents chanted in Tarbell's support, "Who is this Knowles?"

An outraged bystander shouted, "Half of you agents got your appointments through Knowles, and now you ask who he is!"

The Knowles incident seemed like an unexpected piece of good luck for James. As one of his press agents wrote,

> My information is that the agents have done all they have been brought on here to do. They wonder now what you will do and some are getting weak kneed [sic]. They have used themselves up.
>
> May I make one suggestion—Either keep the [agents'] Committee on the run or don't see them—This will put them to a great disadvantage. In the mean time [sic] they will be fed through the newspa-

pers with suggestions to the effect that it is only a matter of a short time when the Alexander-Tarbell faction will fall and they will read their fate. They will desert Tarbell over night [*sic*]. Believe me, no action on your part is the best. Try the policy of "masterly inactivity."

I am getting in a lot of paragraphs of value [to the newspapers] and keeping things shaped up.

The *World* is impossible, the *Times* doubtful, but the *Sun* I will bring around.

P.S. I wish Mr Knowles would come to my office.[26]

That Thursday night, Henry Knowles and his wife and daughter were asleep at their apartment in the Martinique hotel near Herald Square. Knowles had locked the front door, but around midnight, Mrs. Knowles was awakened by a strong draft. She woke up her husband, who promptly got up and turned on the lights. When he looked around, he found no one there; and nothing in the apartment had been disturbed or taken, although Knowles later told the police that a burglar could easily have found $50,000 worth of valuables, including jewelry. The Knowleses' apartment was on the seventh floor; the entrances to the hotel were guarded around the clock; and the guards said they had not seen anyone come in or out, but the front door was indisputably open, and the cold air from the hall was blowing in. It looked like an act of mischief, or a warning.[27]

The newspapers weren't finished with Tarbell. Reporters and detectives, some on James's payroll, traveled to upstate New York and Wisconsin to look into his past, and returned with information about disastrous business dealings earlier in his career. Tarbell had started life as the son of a subsistence farmer near a tiny hamlet, fifteen miles from the nearest town—and even that only had a population of about one thousand. "A dashing, magnetic boy," according to a local man, Tarbell got an education and was practicing as a country lawyer and Equitable insurance agent when he met his wife, the daughter of a well-off family.

One of her relatives was interested in iron mines in Wisconsin's

Gogetic district, and Tarbell joined him in buying mines and selling their stock. They established an office in Milwaukee, and Tarbell soon started a firm, Gage E. Tarbell and Company, with two Wisconsin offices and a wholesale iron mine brokerage in New York, on Wall Street.

Some of his deals were legitimate; others were not. In one case, when the Anvil Iron Mining Company planned to take out a $100,000 mortgage to cover its debts, he asked shareholders to subscribe for more stock. Anvil continued to flounder, and Tarbell told the shareholders that the directors were selling the mine for $100,000 to a new entity with a nearly identical name, The Anvil Mining Company. It would be capitalized at $200,000 to cover debts and provide working capital. Shareholders were invited to turn in their old stock for new. Many did, but few of them noticed that the terms had changed. The original stock was "non-assessable," while shareholders in the new Anvil were liable for assessments. One man, tired of paying a series of dollar-a-share assessments, sent Tarbell his stock to sell. He received a letter telling him that it had been sold for a total of two dollars, and he owed an additional $18 in assessments.

Some shareholders sued, claiming misrepresentation.[28] Tarbell was indicted, but not convicted. According to one of James's informants, "His [own] father gave testimony 'that he could not be believed on oath and that he had not a straight hair in his head.'"

In 1887, the iron business slumped, the mines "petered out," and Tarbell returned to the insurance business. A former partner who ran into him at a Milwaukee bank heard him "pleading for the renewal of a note for $1,400," and helped him start over. He bought a large insurance policy from him and gave him letters to friends, including Frederick Weyerhauser, "the lumber king" whom Tarbell had so diligently pursued.

Following the emergence of this history, in late April, the newspapers uncovered another vulnerability. Tarbell's secretary, Anna Amendt, who earned $12,000 a year, was one of a very small number of powerful women in insurance, with considerably more influence than the title "secretary" implied. As one article remarked, "Her work

opens up an entirely new life to a woman. She is absolutely independent. Best of all, she knows that she is making money. . . . She lifts herself out of the rut of women's occupations in general. In life insurance
a woman has the most broadening experiences. She meets all classes of
people, she commands respect wherever she goes. In a short time she
develops entirely new faculties." Miss Amendt worked in an office
with gilded moldings, a mahogany cornice and a parquet floor; she
wore three rings, one of which was a circle of large diamonds, and
lived in "an artistic and tastefully decorated" apartment at 71 Central
Park West, where she entertained "like any woman in fashion." She
shared an interest in horses with Tarbell's wife, Ella, who was
described as "an intimate friend." Miss Amendt's saddle horse, Dark
Secret, won a second-place ribbon in the National Horse Show at
Madison Square Garden.[29]

The article fed the rumor that she had more than one dark secret,
and *Town Topics* picked up the story:

> No little amusement has been afforded passengers on certain Sixth
> Avenue elevated trains of late by the public exhibitions given almost
> daily of the fond affection which evidently exists between Vice-Pres-
> ident Gage E. Tarbell, of the Equitable, and his private secretary,
> Miss Amendt. The pair ride uptown together each afternoon, and
> their mutually tender sentiments are apparent to the most casual
> observer. Miss Amendt and Mr. Tarbell have been associated very
> closely for the last thirteen or fourteen years . . . she became his ste-
> nographer in Chicago, and when he removed to New York he
> brought her with him, and eventually elevated her to the position she
> now holds. The public exhibitions, however, are apt to be misunder-
> stood, and in the present condition of affairs, when questions of
> morality play such a conspicuous part in a business controversy, are
> certainly most ill-timed and unseemly. Mr. Tarbell may regard this as
> his own personal affair, but for an officer of a great financial corpo-
> ration to make sentimental displays in public is hardly becoming, to
> say the least.[30]

Colonel Mann was notorious for his promiscuous allegations
about sexual alliances and dalliances, and readers could be amused

without necessarily believing the story. But the combination of the Knowles revelations, the Gogetic story, and the allegedly too-private secretary should have inflicted enough damage that, as one reporter said, it seemed virtually inevitable that "upon Mr. Tarbell is to be made a demand that he sever all and every connection with the Equitable society."[31]

Instead, Tarbell maintained his momentum. On the second day of the agents' convention Hyde was in his office with his lawyers when he got a call notifying him that the agents had passed a resolution requesting that he resign as vice president, and that a delegation would like to meet with him at five that afternoon. His lawyers waited with him as five o'clock passed, and then five-thirty, until they finally decided to leave. Downstairs, as Hyde got into his automobile, he managed to convey the impression that he was not worried. Photographers took his pictures, he laughed, and he rode home to change for a night out. He was spotted that evening at the Empire Theater in a box with George Gould.

The next morning, five agents called on Hyde at home. They were late again; the appointment had been set for nine, and they arrived at nine-thirty. Agent Joseph Bowes of Baltimore, who had represented the Equitable for many years, handed James the petition, which asked him "to voluntarily retire from the Vice Presidency." Bowes explained to Hyde that he had agreed to be the spokesman because it would be less unpleasant if someone sympathetic to him headed the delegation, and that the agents had deliberated for nearly five hours before making their decision. He added that the petition was considerably toned down from "harsher" versions, and that the vote in favor of resignation was an overwhelming 176 to 13.

Hyde stood firm. He said it would be "cowardly and disgraceful to the memory of my father" to retire, and told the agents they were acting on incomplete information. He suggested that they wait for the Frick Committee's report before recommending any action. The meeting was over in twelve minutes.

After Hyde refused to resign, the agents asked him to address them again. He declined, but sent them a letter. "While I resent, and

I am justified in resenting, your mistaken action toward me," he wrote, "I am by no means indifferent to your good will or callous to your hostility, and I trust that in the future of the society's affairs I shall be able to gain for my own part in their administration the support and approval of the men who have now so intemperately misjudged me."[32]

With all the furor, James Alexander was often treated as a secondary character, but Samuel Untermyer brought him back into the foreground shortly after the agents went home. The issue of JWA's participation in the James Hazen Hyde syndicate had been building momentum, largely because JWA so insistently denied knowing anything about its dealings. Now Untermyer reminded the public that JWA had started the fight, and was lying about his financial affairs.

> There is . . . something sad and almost grotesque in the belated effort of Mr. Alexander after participating with Mr. Hyde for many years, to find in innocent transactions to which he was a party and by which he equally lost or benefited, a ground for attacking Mr. Hyde, and at the same time trying by profuse eleventh hour letter writing to extricate himself. . . .
>
> If the assertion of Mr. Alexander that he did not during all these years that he has been president know the source with which his private bank account was being replenished by these large checks, is to be taken seriously, his absence of curiosity on the subject is at least remarkable. It would be interesting to know whether in the instance in which Mr. Alexander lost money in the syndicate, he ascertained on what particular transaction the losses were made before paying them. . . .

JWA had kept his profits, from the syndicate's inception in 1902 until January 1905, when he turned his two most recent syndicate checks over to the Equitable. If he hoped no one would look further back and discover that he had deposited five previous checks, Untermyer set him straight:

In the light of subsequent events one can, perhaps, understand why Mr. Alexander, on January 11 and 23, took these checks from Mr. Hyde as syndicate manager, deposited them in his bank to his private credit, and as we are now told, subsequently quietly turned over the amount of these checks (without accounting for previous ones received in like manner) to the cashier of the society, without a word or suggestion or remonstrance to his associates.

Apropos of Mr. Alexander's pathetic story of how ignorant he was of the sources of all these moneys, which his wicked partner was pouring into his (Alexander's) coffers from syndicate operations during all these years, by what chance did he learn that he ought not to retain the checks he received while the plot to ruin Mr. Hyde was under way? If he did not know what the checks represented, why did he return them. And why did he not return the others. . . .

It is unfortunate for Mr. Hyde that this huge conspiracy against his reputation and his property is to be dragged into the searchlight of publicity. It started by masquerading in the sham form of "mutualization," but its real purpose is at last apparent, and its hideousness may be seen of all men. Stripped of all cant, it is nothing more than a sordid attempt to destroy the property of the young man.[33]

In just a few days, JWA had been described in the press as a tool, as lacking backbone, and as grotesque, pathetic, sordid, and a liar. The word that he would soon be replaced gained credibility. FRICK TO TAKE HELM OF THE EQUITABLE LIFE, the *Herald* confided.

Despite the revelations about Tarbell and Alexander, Hyde continued to be the saga's central character. The newspapers printed JWA's claims that the Equitable paid his personal servants $16,000 a year, that his unitemized travel expenses amounted to $12,000, and that he had made $1 million by selling bonds to the company. One night, when he took a box at the theater for a musical comedy, *The Rollicking Girl,* and invited a party of friends to join him, he was regaled with a song "about a young man who tried to fill his father's shoes and stood in danger of being wiped off the insurance map." The audience gaped at him when the play was over, and the newspapers reported that, too.[34]

Hyde's reactions were well hidden, and journalists rarely commented on his demeanor. But the parodies were taking as much of a toll as the fight to hold on to his position. Hyde had courted publicity and he had built up a professional press department. He cared about what was said and written about him, more perhaps, than most men. He had turned the spotlight on himself, and now he couldn't turn it off.

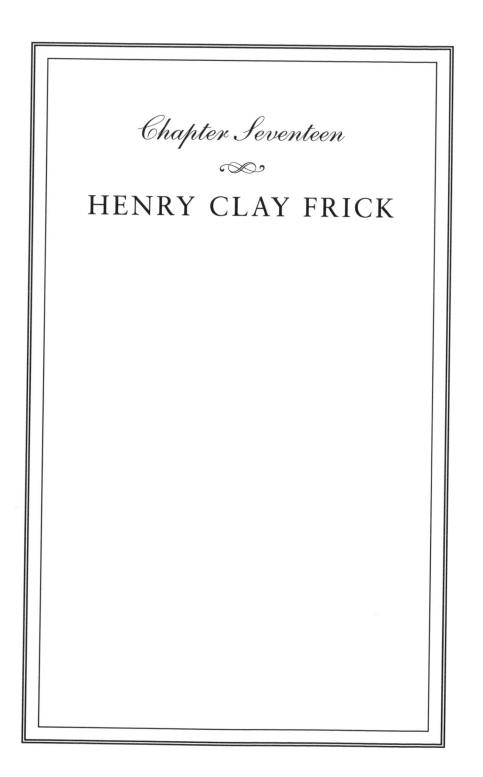

Chapter Seventeen

HENRY CLAY FRICK

Henry Clay Frick.

Equitable director Frick entered the fray as a savior, but the politics of Wall Street and the insurers were too much for even him. *(Courtesy Martha Frick Symington Sanger)*

The steel and coke magnate Henry Clay Frick had not been engaged in a mortal fight for a few years, but if anyone should have been able to find a way to settle the Equitable crisis, Frick, at fifty-six, was the man. Indomitable, incorruptible, self-made, and hugely rich, he had been chairman of the Carnegie enterprises, which produced half as much steel as all of Great Britain, and his H.C. Frick Coke Company had the exclusive contract to supply the fuel for the Carnegie mills. In the past, Frick had printed his own money when the government ran low, mustered his own army to fight armed mobs of strikers by the thousands, survived an assassination attempt, and sued Carnegie, receiving some $30 million in stocks and bonds. In 1902, Frick and his family moved from Pittsburgh to New York, where they rented William Henry Vanderbilt's house at 640 Fifth Avenue.[1]

Frick could be an awesome ally or foe. He had been sickly since childhood, and regular attacks of inflammatory rheumatism sometimes felled him for as long as a year; but like the young Theodore Roosevelt, he considered illness a goad, and he had the grit and genius to turn obstacles into opportunities. During the 1873 panic, as a young man who had just started his coke business, and was living in a shack near the works, he hitched mine mules to his wagon, and set off as early as two in the morning, to look for land with coal potential that he could pick up cheaply. By dawn he was back to oversee his coke works, and at seven, took the train to Pittsburgh, where he went on foot to see his customers and take orders before returning to the mill in the midafternoon. Frick had a childhood goal of being worth $1 million by the time he turned thirty, and he was right on schedule.

Frick was a fierce opponent of the strikes that rocked the coal region and hired his own police force, who had shoot-to-kill orders. The most famous of the strikes took place in the summer of 1892 at Carnegie's $6 million Homestead mill. Frick ordered three hundred Pinkerton detectives to be on call, then locked out four thousand men. On Independence Day, the workers organized their own army, and Frick sent in the Pinkertons, who arrived by barge at three in the morning. When the strikers spotted them, they blew the factory whistle, and men, women, and children rushed to the riverside with weapons, from guns to hoes.

After ten men had died and sixty were wounded, the governor sent in ninety-five train coaches carrying thousands of Pennsylvania National Guardsmen, and declared that, if necessary, he would use the entire $6 million in the state treasury to keep the guard in place "until law and order are restored."[2]

Frick disdained to hire a bodyguard, and the *New York Times* noted, "He can be seen at his desk from the public hall of the building, and anybody can reach the hall by going up in the elevator."[3] It was not difficult for Alexander Berkman, a Lithuanian-born anarchist, to get an appointment with Frick, claiming to represent an employment agency that could help fill jobs left open by the strike. Berkman went to Frick's office on a mid-July Saturday afternoon, slammed open the door, and stood there holding a pistol. When Frick heard the noise, he rose and turned; Berkman shot him in the neck.[4]

The Carnegie vice president, John Leishman, a man who would, much later, become James Hyde's father-in-law, was sitting at the other end of Frick's long office table. He leaped on Berkman and grabbed his gun hand, but not until Berkman had shot Frick in the neck a second time; a third shot went wild. Despite Frick's wounds, and his size—five foot two, although he weighed a solid 160 pounds—he jumped into the fight, and he and Leishman wrestled Berkman to the floor. A carpenter who heard the commotion rushed into the room and hit Berkman on the head with his hammer, but Berkman, still conscious, pulled out a homemade stiletto and stabbed Frick in the hip and leg. A deputy sheriff finally subdued Berkman, but Frick noticed that his jaws were moving. When they forced his mouth open, they found that he was trying to bite down on a capsule of fulminate of mercury: a minute later and the building might have exploded.

When the doctor arrived to treat him, Frick insisted that he not give him an anesthetic so he would be conscious and could help him locate the bullets. Frick stayed in the office to finish some work, but was finally brought home in an ambulance and carried into the house on a stretcher.

Thirteen days later, Frick went back to work, on the public street-car. When he was asked what precautions he was taking for his safety, he said, "If an honest American cannot live in his own home without being surrounded by a bodyguard, it is time to quit."[5]

Under the circumstances, Frick's letter to Carnegie that September is confounding. He wrote of "how kindly we do feel towards those who are in our service; [and] . . . are just as anxious for their welfare as we are for our own."[6] Carnegie later defended Frick's actions, and called the post-union Homestead the "church of true faith."[7] The workers settled in mid-November, with the winter coming on, money running out, and families facing starvation.

In 1895, Frick was demoted to chairman of Carnegie Steel's board of managers and John Leishman was promoted to president. Leishman didn't last long, and Frick resigned in 1899, at Carnegie's insistence. Frick sued Carnegie, and they settled in 1900, after Frick received $30 million in stock and bonds. In 1901, J. P. Morgan bought out Carnegie for $480 million in the merger that created the mammoth U.S. Steel, which controlled 60 percent of the American steel industry. Frick's net worth went up to $65 million. He sold much of his U.S. Steel stock to invest in railroads, which he declared were "the Rembrandts of investment."[8] (In 1905, he enriched his art collection by buying a Van Dyck, a Titian, and El Greco's *St. Jerome*.)

When the Equitable crisis got under way, Frick had just moved to New York. He was a director of four railroads, including Harriman's Union Pacific, and as a director of the Atchison, Topeka and Santa Fe, he and Harriman were working together on an agreement of cooperation between the roads. At one point, Frick would have more than $40 million invested in seven railroad companies.

Frick had been on the Equitable board since 1901, had joined the Mercantile and Equitable Trust boards, and had invited James to become a director of his Union Trust Company. But it appears that the first time he attended an Equitable board meeting was on February 8, 1905, when he was alerted that a fight was brewing. His offer to buy James out just before that meeting may have been connected to his railroad investments; control of the Equitable's capital pool would be a useful asset. But Frick was also annoyed with himself because he hadn't paid enough attention to the company to realize that its management was falling apart.

Initially, Frick seemed to be in Hyde's corner. He had set in motion the possibility of the French ambassadorship—now, of course, out of the question—and early in the fight, he met with Hyde downtown and offered to help him. According to Hyde's notes, Frick said that the mutual system at New York Life and the Mutual only hid the underlying autocracy; everyone knew that very few policyholders even bothered to send in proxies. By contrast, at least the Equitable's stock control system made it clear who held the power. Frick advised Hyde to "clear out all the traitors," make a public announcement that the Equitable was financially sound, and promise to release an annual accounting to the policyholders so they would know where they stood. If he did that, Frick said, Hyde would be "the greatest man in the insurance world."[9] Despite his show of interest, Frick took a distant second place to Harriman in his actual involvement in the fight, until the Frick Committee was formed.

Hyde thought he could count on at least two other members of the Frick Committee to favor his position. One was Harriman; the other, the midwestern industrialist Melville Ingalls, had aligned himself with Hyde early. Cornelius Bliss, who also served on the committee, had declared himself in favor of mutualization, but that didn't mean he was a supporter of JWA's. Only the fifth member, Brayton Ives, seemed tricky. Decades earlier, he had tried to buy the majority shares in the Equitable and had only been turned away when Henry Hyde bought them himself. Ives was an Alexander supporter.

Frick had asked James J. Hill to serve on the committee, and Hill briefly considered accepting. His condition was that he would have to bring in his own accountants, which would have cost him considerable time and money, but he understood that the situation required a close reading of the numbers by a team that had nothing to gain or lose. That would also mean that Hill would be de facto in control of the investigation, and he preferred not to become involved at all. In the event, Frick and Harriman didn't want to turn over their power to Hill, and he declined to join the committee. He remained on the board, but not for long; he would resign later that spring.

The Frick Committee opened its investigation on April 6 by requiring that Alexander and Hyde supply information dating back to January 1900. Frick asked for data about salaries, and other compensations; employees' relationship to directors and executives, and loans to any employee or director. To explore the allegations that Tarbell was behind large unsecured loans to agents, Frick asked for the contracts and terms of employment of leading agents worldwide. Dealings with banks and trusts were covered by a request for statements of the Equitable's holdings, including amounts, dates, who authorized the purchase, from whom the holdings were bought, and what they cost. On the investment front, Frick requested a complete accounting of brokerage houses and individuals through whom the Equitable had bought stocks, bonds, or securities; who authorized the purchase; "what became of the property"; and any benefits officers, directors, or employees of the Equitable received from the transaction.

So much money was unaccounted for that Frick insisted that he be provided with a monthly statement of the Equitable's cash balances starting in 1900, where they were deposited, and on what terms. He also asked for a detailed explanation of two items that appeared in the December 31, 1904, statement: one listed more than $7 million for "commissions, advertising, postage and exchange"; the other, also for just over $7 million, was for "other disbursements."

Frick's aversion to publicity was legendary, and he was insistent that the actions of his committee should remain private. (One story told about his attitude toward journalists claims that when he and

James Stillman of National City Bank were meeting to discuss a bear market, "a financial writer whom both respected persisted in seeking their opinion of the situation and, after waiting an hour, he received this card: 'The U.S.A. is a great and growing country. (Signed) James Stillman, Henry C. Frick. This is confidential and not for publication unless names are omitted.'")

Frick instructed Hyde and Alexander not to talk to the press, but by mid-April, JWA had leaked so many criticisms of Hyde's syndicate transactions that Frick agreed that Hyde could release a letter to the newspapers. It was published on April 19, and in it, Hyde explained the $61,446 escrow account representing the profits from his syndicate's dealings with the Equitable. He wrote, "This money was deposited to be disposed of as the propriety of these transactions might be finally determined. I made no restitution. I admitted no wrong-doing. I admit none now. . . . My concessions have been deliberately misconstrued, my silence has been misrepresented . . . [by] the self-seeking persons who have prepared the present trouble, and who, masking as friends of the policy-holders, are striving to deprive me of my property and to secure for themselves continued control of the society." He also released proof that JWA had been a syndicate participant.

His letter made matters worse. The *World's* headline read, JAMES H. HYDE . . . CONFESSES WORLD'S CHARGES ARE TRUE . . . MAKES REMARKABLE ADMISSIONS AND ASSERTS PRESIDENT ALEXANDER IS AS DEEP IN THE MIRE AS HE IS IN THE MUD.[10]

Hyde wrote Alexander suggesting that he, too, put his profits from James Hazen Hyde and Associates in escrow, but JWA continued to insist that he had never invested with Hyde at all. In response, "men in sympathy with Mr. Hyde" confirmed that JWA had been a syndicate partner, and provided information in response to Frick's queries about nepotism. By one count, Alexander family members were earning $196,000 a year from the company. JWA received $100,000; his brother William, the company secretary, $30,000; Henry Martyn was on a $25,000-a-year retainer; Frederick D. Alexander, JWA's other son, as a partner in a brokerage firm, earned about the same amount in commissions on sales to the Equitable. Dr. Arthur Pell, the brother of JWA's wife, Elizabeth, earned $10,000 as medical director; and a nephew was head of the securities department and was paid $6,000. The list did not include fees paid to Henry Martyn's law firm, to one of Elizabeth Alexander's nephews, or to JWA's son-in-law, the artist John Alexander, who had painted the portrait of Henry Hyde in the boardroom.

JWA stonewalled, sending Frick letters filled with recriminations but few answers. On April 25, the committee was driven to make a formal resolution, viewing "with surprise and regret" that JWA had failed to provide the information they had asked for on April 8, and gave Alexander a deadline of April 28 to provide the material. Alexander sent two more stalling letters, and Frick replied sternly, but JWA continued to offer excuses and withhold information.

Hyde had been providing Frick with information; it came in more slowly than Frick might have liked, but it was thorough. Eager to cooperate with the committee, Hyde wrote Frick regularly and in the interest of "cleaning house," as Frick had suggested, gave him a list of questions to ask JWA, and an eleven-page memorandum with queries for Tarbell. At the end of April, Hyde submitted an accounting of the transactions made by his syndicate and other facts the committee wanted.

At last, JWA submitted a twelve-page letter. In it, he repeated his charges against James, dwelling on his habit of ignoring JWA's authority and complaining that Willie McIntyre carried out transactions without consulting him, and when asked if JWA needed to approve them, dismissed the suggestion. He listed the boards on which Hyde sat, and the stocks owned by the Equitable and carried in Hyde's name, and again took aim at his social celebrity, extended stays in Paris, the Cambon dinner, his unattributed expenses, and alleged that his reputation was not only hurting the Equitable, but also aiding the competition. Criticizing the JHH and Associates investments as speculative, Alexander again denied that he had participated.

The committee had heard it all before. Frick testily reminded JWA that Hyde had documented his syndicate participation and demanded that JWA explain why, as president, he had not intervened sooner. JWA's answer was again unsatisfactory.

Hyde sent the committee a thirty-page letter on May 18, with photographs of JWA's canceled checks for syndicate profits. In regard to the attacks on his lifestyle, he wrote,

> If it is an offense to drive a coach, or to give entertainments out of my private means, it is one that is committed by many men of means and by officers identified with the Society. I have learned to realize that undue publicity attaching to the doings of officers of an insurance company is hurtful to the Society, and I very much regret that the older officers, who now claim that injury has resulted from this cause did not see fit to call my attention to the fact which they now make the subject of complaint. . . . I would not have resented, but would have appreciated such action. . . . So far, however, from assuming that attitude towards me the President permitted me to gather my experience and to make my mistakes without guidance or hindrance from him."[11]

That was not quite true, but JWA's criticisms of Hyde's social life had been occasional, and he had not pursued them strenuously. As for the reports that "occurrences of a scandalous and indecent nature took place" at his ball, Hyde added, they were "inspired from the same sources that are now attacking me."[12]

JWA made another attempt to distance himself from Hyde. His son, Henry Martyn, wrote a formal letter to Hyde and McIntyre stating that, as of May 3rd, 1905, JWA had resigned as one of Hyde's trustees. Hyde refused to accept the resignation and persuaded his mother, Mary, and Willie to join him in suing JWA. Their suit mentioned the "wicked fabrications" about the ball,[13] but its legal center was the charge that JWA was guilty of a breach of trust when he proposed mutualization, which would depreciate the stock's value.

As the fight dragged on, the directors were getting restless. Jacob Schiff, concerned about the continuing criticism of his firm, arranged an unofficial meeting attended by twenty-three board members to discuss what action to take to save the company. The large attendance indicated that the directors were losing faith in Frick's ability to bring in his report before everyone associated with the Equitable was damaged.

Harriman advised patience and said the report would be in by the end of May. Ingalls remarked that all the principals were at fault and that the accusations against Hyde were hurting the Equitable, even if they weren't true. Ingalls said that Hyde, Alexander, and Tarbell were all weak and that no sensible businessman would want to work with them, or, in Tarbell's case, be a member of any board on which he sat.

Schiff agreed, but blamed JWA, whose behavior, he said, was unforgivable. He praised Hyde's manly behavior, expressing the greatest respect for him.

The directors concluded that Alexander, Hyde, and Tarbell should resign, and that they should seek a new president of unimpeachable national reputation.

Harriman watched each step of the march toward disaster; he went to nearly every meeting, held councils of war at his house, and became more openly agitated. After one stormy board meeting, a reporter asked him if he had burst out in the famous, tongue-tied "Wow, wow" that was sometimes all he could utter when he was too angry to speak, and he answered with asperity, "Well, if I didn't I ought to have."

It was not necessarily in Harriman's interest for the situation to be resolved. As conditions within the Equitable disintegrated, he might end up running the company, or buying the majority shares at an attractive discount. Meanwhile, he thought he was protected from the kind of accusations Schiff was facing. He had not invested in the James Hazen Hyde and Associates syndicates; he claimed that neither he nor any of the railroads in which he was a principal had ever borrowed money from the Equitable; he disclaimed the $2.7 loan to the Union Pacific in 1901, and he said that none of his railroad interests had sold securities to the Equitable. This provoked such a roar of incredulity that he backed down and allowed that he had perhaps forgotten a loan of some $2 million because it had been repaid. He had been thinking ahead when he insisted that the 1903 commitment to purchase $2.5 million of Union Pacific stock be held in Hyde's name, even though the money came from the Equitable.

The *World* contested Harriman's assertion that he had not been profiting from his directorship. According to the paper's estimate, the Equitable bought $17,883,000 of Harriman railroad securities in 1903 alone. The *World* also speculated that Harriman was using Hyde to help him create a giant insurance trust, combining the Equitable, New York Life, the Mutual, and Prudential. The theory was that he was in cahoots with Standard Oil, the most unpopular of the giant corporations, to take "control of pretty nearly all the available money in the country."[14]

Harriman was under fire for using political influence, but other forces, possibly representing major insurers, were also at work in the state capital. When Harriman met privately with insurance commissioner Hendricks during the state investigation, no secretary was present and no notes were taken. After the meeting, Harriman wrote Odell that he was shocked by their conversation. He left with the impression that Crimmins and Frank Platt were on the Alexander side. As for Hendricks, he remarked, "This is the first time I have been so far below the strata into indecency in my life, and I have a feeling that it will take a long time to get rid of the filth."[15]

He redoubled his lobbying efforts, and the *Evening Sun* editorialized, "It is impossible, we say, that public opinion will tolerate a Harriman in the control of such a public institution as the Equitable Life! We admit that this man controls the legislature, as he boasts that he does. . . . He is a powerful and most baleful figure in the depraved politics of our unhappy State, and . . . the fountains of justice and the law are poisoned by him at its source."[16]

Through all of this, Hyde continued to confide in Harriman, who later confirmed, "I had been befriending Mr. Hyde during the attacks that were being made upon him, and the attempts to oust him out of the Equitable. . . ."[17] Hyde told Harriman that he was getting offers for his stock, and Harriman encouraged him to hold on; when Frick asked Harriman if he had heard about the offers, Harriman said he had, and told Frick to insist that Hyde not sell, and to keep him informed about his plans. Around that time, as Hyde later revealed, Harriman proposed to buy his shares—Hyde recalled that the number floated was the same that Frick had offered on February 8: $5 million for all the shares, or $2.5 million for half—but the idea seems to have been put forth more as a fishing expedition than a firm offer.

At the end of May, when the Frick Report was about to be presented to the board, Harriman met with Hyde's personal lawyer, William Gulliver. Harriman later testified that he had strongly advised Gulliver to tell Hyde to favor adoption of the report. If he did, Harriman said, "I would stand by him through thick and thin."

Harriman told Gulliver that Hyde could explain to the board that he had only been following the existing practices. If Hyde apologized, Harriman said, the board might give him a second chance because of his youth.

Gulliver said that would not be the advice he would give his client, but he would pass it along.

The day before the Frick Report was to be issued, Hyde went upstairs to consult with Harriman. In Hyde's copy of the Armstrong hearings, which were published in 1906, he made marginal notes in blue pencil on certain pages. He scrawled a large question mark next to the following testimony by Harriman:

> When Mr. Hyde came to my office and I made the same suggestion to him that I had to Mr. Gulliver about his course as to the Frick report, and I told him then that this might be something which he would not feel courage enough to stand up under and it might jeopardize the value of his stock, but that I did not think that anybody but the Equitable ought to own that stock other than himself, and that if he had any fears on that subject that I would subscribe half a million dollars to a fund to help him hold it, and if we thought it desirable, to turn it over absolutely to the ownership of the Equitable without any compensation [to Harriman and the other investors] and that I thought others could be induced to do the same thing."[18]

James later angrily recalled, "He led me to believe, through a mutual friend, that the report of that committee would be very friendly to me, and did everything he could to dissuade me from sell-

ing my stock, at the same time doing everything on that Committee
to knife me and destroy the value of the stock."[19]

On May 31, four months to the day after the Hyde Ball, thirty-
eight members of the Equitable board, including Hyde and
Alexander, met to consider the Frick Report.[20] The committee's conclusions were unflinching, if incomplete. The report criticized inappropriate participation in syndicates, mingling of trust and Equitable
business, the irresponsibility of the president and vice president, and
high advances to agents. Notably missing were James's defense
against JWA's most damaging accusations, and any mention of Harriman's dealings with the Equitable.

The matters of syndicates and trust company dealings had the
longest reach and were the most problematic, extending beyond the
behavior of individuals into the culture of corporations. The committee determined that even if it were legal for directors to profit
from syndicate transactions, "Unqualified fidelity of an officer to his
trust is required; and to secure this the law will not permit him to
occupy a situation in which he *may* be tempted by his private interest
to sacrifice his principle." Six of the nine members of the Executive
Committee were members of the Hyde and Associates syndicate, and
participated in transactions in which the syndicate profited from selling securities to the Equitable.

The Frick Report concluded that members of the Executive Committee who participated in the profits from the JHH and Associates
sales to the Equitable were "justly indebted to the Society for the
amount of said profits." If the board agreed with the report, James
would forfeit the $61,000 he had placed in escrow.

Dealings with trust companies crossed the same lines of propriety,
and although Frick was a director of at least two of the trusts in
which the Equitable had a substantial position, the committee criticized the intermingling of trust and insurance interests, and the use
of trusts to adjust the company's cash balances for year-end reports.
In 1904, for example, the Equitable's average monthly balance in
trust companies and banks was $36 million, but on December 31, it
dropped precipitously to $20.8 million. The funds were parked in

collateral loans, so it would not appear that the Equitable was depositing too much money in the banks and trust companies in which its directors were stockholders. In early January, the funds reappeared in the Equitable's trust company accounts.

The committee described this practice as "injudicious intermingling of two essentially different lines of finance." Just how injudicious was indicated by the interest rate the Equitable received on its deposits, sometimes as low as 2 percent. Between 1899 and 1903, the committee learned, "the Equitable Society realized next to the lowest average rate of interest on its invested assets of the thirty companies tabulated by the Insurance Year Book . . . in the year 1903, it stood absolutely the lowest on the list."

The "advances" to agents, actually interest-free loans from the Equitable, were tied to the trust company relationships. The system of advances had been severely criticized in 1894, when the Equitable's outstanding advances to agents were $2.8 million. The insurance commissioners in New York, Massachusetts, and other states "refused to admit these loans as assets," and Henry Hyde began to use the trusts to get around the injunction by selling the loans to banks and trusts, pledging the agents' future commissions as security. The accepted, safe ratio for advances was five times annual renewal interest, yet as an inducement to leave New York Life, Tarbell agreed to give Robert Mix advances adding up to nearly $300,000, equal to about fifteen annual renewals; Julius Bohm, the man who hissed at Hyde during the agents' convention, had been advanced nearly $432,000—eleven annual renewals.

The trust companies became the standard hiding places for these liabilities. By the end of 1904, the Equitable's annual report indicated that the company had $1.5 million in outstanding loans; but another $5.8 million was carried by the trust companies, making the actual indebtedness $7.3 million. The system accomplished its purpose; the insurance commissioners remained oblivious to the accounting procedures, which made the Equitable seem to have less financial exposure then it really did.

When the report addressed personalities, Hyde at last understood what a serious mistake he had made in trusting Harriman, who knew that the committee was planning to flay him when he proposed that Hyde move to accept the report. The Frick Report's commentary on JWA's allegations against Hyde was devastating:

> These charges constitute a serious arraignment of Mr. Hyde. They involve his personal and official integrity and they allege a condition of affairs in the management of the Society that is in utter defiance of all the safeguards provided by . . . the general rules of law, and sound business practices. So open, flagrant, obvious, persistent, and dangerous are the practices of which Mr. Hyde is accused, that the establishment of their truth convicts of equal guilt all who were cognizant of their existence and failed promptly to set about their correction.
>
> If Mr. Hyde . . . is guilty of one-half of what is charged against him [by] Mr. Alexander . . . he has shown his entire disqualification for the important and responsible office which he occupies.

That said, the committee turned to James Alexander:

> Anyone holding a position of trust in the Society who had knowledge of any one or all of these practices is culpable in neglecting or failing promptly to disclose his knowledge thereof to the Board of Directors. . . . Mr. Alexander was culpably negligent in acquiescing in them for so long a period . . . [he] concealed from the directors the irregularities of Mr. Hyde, of which he was cognizant and of which he now complains, but Mr. Alexander openly encouraged them . . . so far as Mr. Alexander's charge against Mr. Hyde is true, namely, "that he has displayed a strong personal ambition and an inordinate and unsafe love of prominence, a great responsiveness to flattery, a pliancy in the hands of persons whose interests are not necessarily parallel to those of the policy-holders of the Society," that Mr. Alexander is largely responsible.

The committee accused JWA of having "encouraged and participated in" many of the irregularities of which he accused James, and confirmed that the evidence that he had been an active syndicate partner was irrefutable. In regard to the alliance between JWA and Tarbell, the report added, "The attack made by the officers upon Mr. Hyde was designed to further their plan to mutualize the Society."

In sum, the committee commented, these conditions

> had their origin in one fundamental error, and that is the departure from the true principles and ethics of life insurance . . . by subordinating economy to rapidity of growth. . . . The ambition for bigness naturally extends to the investment of funds. There is chafing under the laws which govern the investments of a life insurance company. Alliances are made with other institutions with the idea of yielding to the Society results which are not possible under the operations permitted to insurance companies. . . . The general policy of the Society having been diverted from its true course . . . there is found throughout its official personnel a sort of moral obliqueness—a condition where personal gain seems to be at times the paramount idea . . . the Society's transactions with outside concerns have so systematically been placed so that profits fall into the hands of those closely connected with the Society's officers; and it is this which has led the officers . . . to say with undoubted sincerity that they saw no wrong in accepting profits from syndicate transactions in which the Society played an important part."

The committee concluded that the evidence against James was convincing; that JWA had not done his duty and had acted hypocritically and for his own ends; and that Tarbell had paid favored agents outrageously high advances.

In an unequivocal finale, the report declared that all three men were derelict in their duties and should be replaced.

Hyde was temporarily blinded by the disastrous conclusions of the report. But like a man who was hit so hard he couldn't see through the blood on his face, something kept him on course, and he fought with everything he had left. He was on his feet as soon as the report was read, reeling off detailed replies to five of the findings against him and protesting that the explanations he had submitted had been left out of the report. Towering over the room, he accused Frick and Harriman of treachery and claimed that Harriman was trying to take over the company. On that note, the board put off voting on whether to accept the Frick Report's recommendations, and adjourned.

They reconvened at eleven in the morning on June 3, and did not leave again until five that afternoon. Melville Ingalls later described the meeting as "a cat and dog fight."[21] A disgusted director "from a Western state" remarked that this was the sort of behavior that caused people in his part of the country to have "an idea that any Wall Street man was a hopeful candidate for warmer regions," and that the business would be "doomed" if policyholders believed the Equitable was inextricable from Wall Street.

JWA defended himself on the basis that the company was successful, financially solid, and well managed. For the most part, that was true, but if customers were losing faith, Alexander was the immediate cause, not the Hyde Ball or the Cambon dinner. Alexander indignantly protested that he was being punished for taking a courageous stand against Hyde's irregular behavior. Once again, he emphasized the lie he refused to give up, that he hadn't "knowingly participated" in inappropriate syndicate transactions. His remarks only confirmed that he was out of touch with reality and was becoming a smaller and smaller feature of the company's landscape.

Hyde acknowledged "that he recognized this to be the crisis of his life," and said that while he had tried to conduct himself with patience and dignity, he would defend his reputation from "plots and counterplots." He addressed the criticisms one by one, arguing his case, but it was much too late.

Schiff had abruptly changed sides in a move reminiscent of his switch from Hill to Harriman in the Northern Pacific battle. At the meeting he called a few weeks earlier, he had praised Hyde and excoriated Tarbell. Now Schiff insisted that Hyde and Alexander should both be fired, and took up Tarbell's defense. He claimed that Tarbell had been unfairly treated in the report, that none of the charges were strong enough to justify his being asked to resign, and that he was loyal and discreet and had avoided the temptation to make statements to the press. It is unlikely that anyone was convinced, but the message was that someone who knew the business had to stay in management, at least during the proposed transition, and that Tarbell's sense of self-preservation would make him malleable enough to serve the purpose.

Schiff moved that the board create the office of chairman, and establish a committee to find a man of the highest national repute to fill it. When the motion was passed, he proposed another, requiring Hyde to divest himself of his stock within three months, on terms approved by the board.

Hyde leaped up again from the vice president's chair and turned his wrath on Melville Ingalls—perhaps Ingalls was the first person who caught his eye. Hyde accused him of having leaked the Frick Report to the newspapers, and added that Ingalls had accepted a rebate on his own life insurance policy. Ingalls now jumped to his feet, shaking his finger and shouting, "Young man, whom the gods would destroy they first make mad!" Hyde went on to accuse Frick, Harriman, and Schiff of pretending to be his friends and advisers, and then betraying him, and revealed that Harriman had recently offered to put together a syndicate to buy his stock. He continued to rail until Frick stood and snarled, "I will no longer sit on the same board with that young man."

The scene froze as they faced each other across the room, Hyde as long and lean as a shadow, and Frick, short, solid, and implacable, with his tailored white beard and sharp blue eyes. In Frick's rise to prominence, he had shed blood and sacrificed lives, but this vicious infighting was more like his detested personal battles with Carnegie. In the matter of the Equitable, he was like a brilliant general who is undermined by the kind of politicians whose principal goal is self-advancement, rather than a perception of the common good. Frick took a moment to look around at the other directors, and then he announced his resignation and left. On a furious impulse, Harriman declared that he was resigning, too, and strode out behind him.

In a burst of relief, Hyde declared, "By the resignation of these gentlemen this board stands more truly unified than if I had gone out of it. Now I am willing to offer the control of my stock on such terms as may be deemed wise. I have said that I would never get out under compulsion. Now I do so voluntarily." He was wrong about unity; Bliss resigned next and walked out of the room. The day was only half over, and four of the five members of the Frick Committee had quit. Only Brayton Ives was left.

At nearly five that afternoon, six hours after the meeting convened, Schiff's resolutions were passed: the board agreed that the new position of chairman should be established, and that Hyde must divest himself of stock control in the next three months. But when the meeting was over, JWA was still president, James was still first vice president, and the Frick Report had been rejected.

Tarbell and Schiff left together, and a reporter asked Tarbell why he looked so happy. "Well, it's enough to make a fellow smile to have Mr. Schiff stand by me the way he did this afternoon," Tarbell declared, and added, "He said there wasn't a spot or a blemish of any character on my work in the society."

That night Frick dined at Sherry's, where reporters wanted to know "whether he thought it likely that a railroad fight between E. H. Harriman and George J. Gould was responsible for the rejection of the report." Frick said he had no idea, but doubted it. How about the Standard Oil interests? he was asked. "I don't know or care," he said.[22] A couple of days later, he sent a telegram, which he released to the press, stating that he would not serve on any board with Hyde. It was understood that he also expected Hyde to resign from his directorship in the Pittsburgh Union Trust Company.

Back in Cincinnati, Melville Ingalls told a reporter that Hyde was "a hot-headed young fellow," that Ingalls had rather enjoyed all the commotion, and remarked that Hyde "wears lovely clothes."[23] Ingalls sent in his resignation on June 7.

Brayton Ives, the fifth member of the Frick Committee, and a board member since 1893, told a reporter, "I am going away on my yacht and try to forget it."[24] He, too, resigned his directorship later that year.

Harriman did not pretend to be indifferent. He let it be known that if James did not retire from the company and sell his stock, he would press for a legislative investigation. Within a few days, newspapers were reporting that Governor Frank Higgins, who had maintained a neutral position, had "seen the light," and that Harriman "intended to assert his influence to have a special session of the legislature called to open up his fight on the Equitable." Harriman was said to be so determined on revenge that he would no longer offer the Equitable securities in his railroads; a counter rumor was floated that the Equitable was planning to unload the Harriman railroad stocks, but that was unlikely, as it was unclear who would be making investment decisions.

The "unblemished" Tarbell pressed on, in the tone of a man who, having been excluded from a club, watches the clubhouse burn and expects to be able to acquire the real estate at a good price. Tarbell released his remarks from the last directors' meeting:

> I plead guilty to the claim made that I was not totally unselfish in refusing to join in the dangerous game of making personal statements [that] were likely to be preserved as evidence and used against the society. . . . So grave is the situation that I cannot longer remain quiet, but must acquaint you with these serious conditions and do everything in my power to right them and see that justice is meted out to our policy-holders and agents.
>
> Up to the time that I was sent for by Mr. Alexander and acquainted with the step he proposed to take to bring about mutualization of the Equitable, I was it might be said, entirely ignorant of everything that was going on in connection with the financial end of our business. . . . I was astounded. . . . I had never assumed for instance that the President of the society received a salary of more than $25,000 per annum [a disingenuous claim, considering that Tarbell was paid $60,000. On the subject of Hyde's salary, he said,] "the least he could have possibly done would have been to take an active interest in our business, to try to learn something of it and to stay in this country and devote his time to it. . . .
>
> This is no kindergarten, no school for reform, no place for men who have once been found wanting to be tried again to see if they can do better. The Equitable is no place to help a friend or to punish a foe. . . .
>
> I shall say Amen to a reorganization which relieves the society from a one-man control and establishes a government upon the basis of taxation and representation. . . . [25]

Tarbell's moment in the sun of Schiff's approbation was brief. Superintendent Hendricks was considering a recommendation that the attorney general begin proceedings to have Schiff removed from the board, but Schiff preempted him by resigning. Schiff blamed JWA and wrote, excoriating him for failing to rebut the criticisms of the relationship between Kuhn, Loeb and the Equitable, and perhaps even encouraging the agents to keep the stories in circulation.

The considerably depleted board met again on June 6. Most of the strongest members had resigned, and James and JWA, in a last struggle to survive, united to forestall a movement to force them out. The board did vote to reconstitute the Executive Committee: James and JWA would still be members, but Tarbell, George Wilson, and Willie McIntyre would be dropped and replaced by the comptroller and four directors. The board passed other reform measures, reducing executive salaries and advances to agents, placing a ceiling on the amount that could be deposited in banks and trust companies, and appointing a nominating committee to seek a chairman. The Equitable was in such disarray that it was hard to imagine who would take the job.

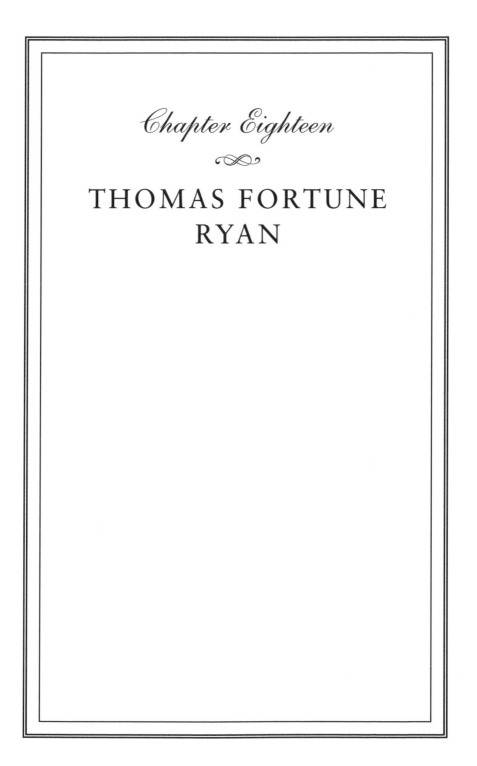

Chapter Eighteen

THOMAS FORTUNE
RYAN

Thomas Fortune Ryan.

One of the most powerful financiers of his time, Ryan avoided publicity until he stepped in to save the Equitable. *(Courtesy AXA Financial Archives)*

$\mathcal{J}$ ames Hyde turned twenty-nine on June 6, 1905, the date of the last Equitable board meeting he would ever attend. He had believed that exactly one year later the directors would be meeting to elect him president of a thriving company. Instead, he had been instructed to sell his shares, and the Equitable was in a parlous state, at risk of sliding into receivership. President Roosevelt was considering federal intervention; Harriman was pressing for a government investigation; and Thomas Lawson was talking about creating a policyholders' organization to buy out all three racers. Yet the Equitable's investment fund remained a hugely valuable asset. George Gould, who had been interested in acquiring Hyde's stock for some time, formed a syndicate with William Rockefeller to offer between $4 and $5 million for James's shares. The price reflected the underlying stability of the company, and the validity of the rumor that the Rockefellers' Standard Oil was interested in the insurer. On the night of June 8, Gould and Hyde representatives negotiated until one in the morning, working toward a deal. Hyde was still reluctant to turn over control to a single man or syndicate, yet the longer he waited, the less his stock would be worth.

The next morning, Thomas Fortune Ryan appeared as the Equitable's unexpected savior. Ryan had the reputation of a privateer—or, as a more laconic observer remarked, "an opportunist." He had not been involved in the Equitable row or served on its board, but he was a major investor in the Bank of Commerce, which was threatened by an Equitable collapse. In a magazine article titled "Why I Bought the Equitable," he claimed that he was motivated to intervene by the belief that "a man's success in this country was to be judged mainly by what he did, and the more I thought of it the more

I was convinced that this was something worth doing. . . . It occurred to me that I might even make this [saving the Equitable] the culminating point of my active career."[1] That would appear to have been as strong a motivation as his plan to avert a banking crisis.

Ryan was a politically connected, canny, mysterious, and hugely successful financier; at fifty-four, he had amassed an estimated $50 million. In middle age, he was imposing, with straight shoulders, a distinguished profile, gray hair, a neat mustache, and one brow set slightly higher than the other. He had a soft southern accent, which made him seem deceptively gentle, but when he was angry and dropped his voice to a whisper, he sounded as fierce as Harriman on a rampage.

Like many Gilded Age financial geniuses, Ryan had grown up poor enough that his childhood had provided ample impetus to ambition. Stories about his family vary; it is a fact that Ryans had lived in Virginia since the late seventeenth century. His father may have been a farmer, or a tailor, but when Thomas was fourteen, the question was moot: He was an orphan. His grandparents, the Fortunes from whom he got his middle name, took him in until 1868, when, at seventeen, he left to seek his future. After the Civil War ambitious southerners were moving west, and sometimes north, and Maryland was a popular destination. Ryan made his way to Baltimore and knocked on doors until John D. Barry, the owner of a dry-goods business, hired him. Even as a teenager, Ryan looked competent and composed, and he was impressively large, although he had not reached his full height of six foot six.

Two years later, he went to New York to clerk at a brokerage house, and when he was twenty-two, converted to Catholicism and married John Barry's daughter, Ida. With his father-in-law's help, he bought a seat on the New York Stock Exchange, and became associated with Tammany Hall, New York City's mostly Irish political machine. But when he found a partner, it was William C. Whitney, whose background was so different from Ryan's that they did not seem to have much more in common than their love for horses. Ryan had established a superb horse-breeding facility on his farm in Virginia, and Whitney bred the finest racing stock; one of his thoroughbreds won the English Derby; and he was a bulwark of the racing season in Saratoga. A Yale graduate and lawyer, he lived at 2 East Fifty-seventh Street, across from the Cornelius Vanderbilts.

Ryan and Whitney quietly established a diversified empire, founded on an urban transportation monopoly they snatched from bidders with an inside track at Tammany Hall. Ryan recognized that electricity was the coming thing, and he and Whitney built electric trams and elevated trains. Their network included the tracks on and above the streets and underground: their construction company, capitalized with $100 million in stock, nailed down the valuable subway contract for the city of New York.

Whitney swam in social waters and had the kind of reputation that led Grover Cleveland to ask him to serve as his secretary of the navy, a job that was apt to go to gentlemen whose naval experience had largely been acquired on yachts. When Ryan and Whitney's transit monopoly was described as "a model of crooked public-utility manipulation,"[2] much of the onus attached itself to Ryan. According to one source, their Third Avenue System's "stock was hiked by artificially maintained dividends to $269 a share." The company went bankrupt, and $35 million raised by a bond issue disappeared. The receiver "succeeded in tracing twenty million to political graft and padded construction contracts but never was able to get on the track of the remaining fifteen million."[3]

Bankruptcy in one company didn't stop Ryan. He had established the American Tobacco Company and melded it with English interests into the British American Tobacco Company; anyone who chewed Bull Durham added to his bank account. He was a partner of King Leopold of the Belgians, whose Société Internationale Forestière et Minière du Congo pillaged the Congo's mineral and rubber resources on 9 million acres in "concessions." Ryan had a piece of that, and with his interests in banking, railroads, oil, electricity, public transport, and tobacco, "the enterprises he controlled were estimated to be worth around $1,500,000,000."[4]

Ryan would die with nearly double the fortune of J. P. Morgan, the benchmark of the era; being richer than Morgan was analogous to being "richer than Croesus." In 1928, Ryan's estate would be valued at $141,824,497—but for most of his career he was hardly known outside of business, the Catholic Church, and politics. He had backed Grover Cleveland since 1884, and counted him as a friend; and he contributed $450,000 to the Democratic campaign fund when Judge Alton Parker ran against Roosevelt in 1904.

The Ryans and their five sons lived in a big house at 858 Fifth Avenue, which adjoined another house that Ryan bought to be used as an art gallery, where he displayed five busts of himself, three of them by Rodin.[5] The Ryans' country place in Westchester was luxurious, and their farm in Virginia was glorious.

Their personal priest celebrated daily mass in the sanctified chapels in the Fifth Avenue house and in Westchester, and the church was the beneficiary of much of the family's prodigious charity. Ida Ryan's generosity, estimated at $20 million, included building a church and a hospital, and founding a seminary; she was rewarded by Pope Pius X, who made her a Countess of the Holy Roman Empire. Ryan showed his own gratitude for God's beneficence by building the elegant Church of St. Jean Baptiste on Lexington Avenue and Seventy-eighth Street in New York.

William Whitney died in February 1904, and in the spring of the next year, Ryan said, he had begun to think of winding down. "I had reached a time of life and a position in the business world which led me to contemplate retirement from its grinding activities," he explained. "I had long had in mind many things that I wanted to do, and not one of them had borne any relation to a desire to make more money or to add to the fortune I had already accumulated."[6]

Ryan's only involvement with the Equitable had been when the Western National Bank merged with the Bank of Commerce, but as the insurance scandal assumed catastrophic proportions, he was moved to act. He freely admitted that he would benefit from a resolution, "as would anyone whose interests would be affected by any disturbance of the financial situation or by the lack of confidence in the fiduciary institutions of New York. . . . To avert [a receivership of the Equitable] and to prevent the frightful losses that would occur by the breaking up of such an organization, involving, as it perhaps would, a like fate for other companies . . . it seemed that someone ought to devise a method for meeting the peril that threatened," he wrote.[7]

In May, before the Frick Committee had completed its investigations, Ryan began to develop a plan. He went to Kentucky to look at some horses, and there, "remote from the scenes of activity and struggle, away from news and financial gossip, free from all interruption and yet cognizant of all the underlying conditions in the problem," he wrote, "I could look over the whole situation much more critically than if I were on the ground." After he returned to New York, the Frick Committee submitted its report, the board was rocked by resignations, and Ryan retired to his Virginia farm to think some more. "The matter was too delicate to be discussed," he explained, and besides, "it did not concern any one else. It seemed to be my task."

On June 9, Ryan asked Hyde to come by his office. Only hours after the Gould and Hyde lawyers concluded their negotiating session for the night, Hyde and Samuel Untermyer strode past a phalanx of guards and office boys at 82 Nassau Street to meet with Ryan and his lawyer, Paul Cravath. In a large inner office, which one reporter described as "a baronial stronghold," Ryan pushed back his large leather chair and stood to greet them; he was one of the few men tall enough for Hyde to look directly in the eye.

It is not certain what Hyde expected Ryan to propose, but it must have been a relief to be dealing with someone reminiscent of Henry Hyde: decisive, straightforward, and seemingly acting in the interests of the Equitable. Ryan did not waste words; he presented his plan and made it clear that there was little room for negotiation. He offered to buy Hyde's stock for $2.5 million, only about half Gould's price, but the other part of his offer was more appealing: He proposed to place the stock in a blind trust, supervised by trustees of unimpeachable reputation. He would have no control over the way the stock was voted, the appointment of directors, or the company's management or investment decisions. It was apparent that he intended to cauterize the Equitable's wounds in such a way that he would not be in a position to profit directly, and Hyde, too, would be expected to make a sacrifice by accepting a smaller amount for his shares.

Ryan had had lined up three illustrious custodians. Grover Cleveland, the former U.S. president, who would be chairman; and Judge

Morgan J. O'Brien, presiding justice of the Appellate Division of the New York Supreme Court; and George Westinghouse of the Pittsburgh-based Westinghouse Electric and Manufacturing Company.

Cleveland was living in straitened circumstances in Princeton, New Jersey, where Ryan noted "with sorrow, that he was hampered by lack of means to maintain the dignity of a man who had twice filled with such distinction the Presidency of the United States." To date, the only moneymaking offers Cleveland had received would have eroded the stature of the presidency—he was even asked to consider managing a winter resort hotel.

Ryan wrote Cleveland that as the Equitable's chief custodian he could "do some public service really worthy of his position and character," and earn enough to live on respectably. When the former president agreed to take the post, Ryan wrote him privately, "No permanent success is possible if we forget moral obligations or duties."

The other two trustees were somewhat flawed. It was questionable for Judge O'Brien to take a corporate appointment while he was on the bench; and George Westinghouse had been a friend of Henry Hyde's, and James had inherited his father's position as a Westinghouse director. There were also questions about Paul Morton, whom Ryan chose as chairman of the board and chief operating officer. Morton had been secretary of the navy but had just retired under fire when he was accused of rebating—a widespread, but improper form of price-cutting—in his prior job as second vice president of the Atchison, Topeka and Santa Fe Railroad. One beneficiary of the reduced rates was the Colorado Fuel and Iron Company, where Morton had been vice president before he joined the Atchison. On his watch, Colorado Fuel and Iron was charged $1.10 a ton for freight, rather than the standard price of $2.25. Morton's defense was that "everybody did just as we did and they had to, or go out of business." One of the commissioners on the Interstate Commerce Commission remarked in response, "In all my experience with the railroad operation I never saw such barefaced disregard of the law."[8] Yet Morton was otherwise considered an honorable man, from a family with a tradition of public service; his parents founded Arbor

Day, and his father, J. Sterling Morton, was Cleveland's secretary of agriculture.

Hyde and Ryan agreed on their terms that morning, and the sale was announced in the late editions of the newspapers, providing yet another round of headlines. The *Herald* predicted RYAN'S COUP MAY SAVE THE EQUITABLE, over a story that opened, "Wall street [*sic*] breathed a sigh of relief. . . ."[9] The *World* weighed in with EQUITABLE GOOSE LAYS NO MORE GOLDEN EGGS AND WALL STREET IS VERY SAD,[10] and stretched the animal kingdom analogies in a huge page 1 cartoon that depicted Ryan as a wolf, crawling on all fours out of a cave labeled "Equitable." The ground was littered with bones, labeled to indicate some of his companies: Metropolitan Traction, 3d Avenue R.R., Seaboard Air Line. In the foreground, lambs wearing collars labeled "policy holder" shrank together as Ryan prowled toward them, his fangs sharp and dripping. The caption read, "The Wolf and the Lambs."

The *Times* editorialized that Hyde had done the right thing: "To say that his action is creditable is praise of which the insufficiency will be well understood by many a strong man in this city who feels in his heart that he would not himself have risen to that height of renunciation. Mr. Hyde's sacrifice will command the admiration of the community and its gratitude as well, for he was the one man who could end the controversy . . . and he has chosen the one effective way to end it."[11] The *Times* took a month to make up its mind about Ryan, but when it did, the editorial was friendly: "Mr Ryan's experience with the Equitable has been the occasion for manifestations of pure human nature that are amusing, if not edifying. So far as appears, not only from his professions but from his acts, he did a service of great value to the public and to the policy holders of the Equitable. The situation was dangerous. He made it, if not positively safe, at least vastly safer. . . . Whereupon pretty much everybody fell upon Mr. Ryan, accusing him of grasping at the Equitable millions and of doing many other wicked things. If he imagined himself a philanthropist he must presently have concluded that he was at heart a designing monster."[12]

Few reporters had been exposed to Ryan's charm, and those who were now granted interviews were quickly won over. A *Times* profile that took up most of page 1 began, "Unlike most good things, Thomas Fortune Ryan was easy to reach." Even the *World*'s cynical reporter described him as though he were a favorite uncle: "His gray eyes have a kindly twinkle, his manner is mild and affable and there is a genial and wholesome magnetism about him that puts you at your ease at once. If he is losing a million for every minute of your stay he has a way of making you think your company is cheap at the price, and on leaving you square your shoulders and throw up your chin and feel almost convinced that it is so." Toward the end of the story, the writer apologized, "If this interview reads more like a press notice than a roast it is not my fault; my intentions were all right, but what could I do . . . I crumbled my list of clever questions in my pocket . . . and set a new course."[13]

Harriman's reaction was like that of a wolf just outside the borders of the *World*'s cartoon who watched a bigger wolf take down the flock he had been stalking: He was ferocious, and dangerous. The night of Thursday, June 8, Harriman was at Arden, his country estate, and the next morning he took the Erie Ferry to New York. He heard about the agreement between the time he disembarked from the ferry and his arrival at his office. As soon as he reached the Equitable Building, he telephoned Ryan and told him, "It was rather staggering to anybody that [he] wanted to control the Equitable."[14] Ryan suggested that he come by to talk about it, and Harriman was at 82 Nassau Street fifteen minutes later.

Once again, Harriman found himself facing off with an adversary who, like Hyde, was more than a foot taller—and in Ryan's case, burly as well. Ryan told him that his motive in buying the Hyde stock was to provide a public service, and Harriman retorted that he doubted it. If Ryan wanted to prove his sincerity, Harriman said, he would have to share the control, preferably with him.

When Ryan stood firm, Harriman improvised. He proposed that Ryan increase the number of Equitable trustees to five, and permit Harriman, or some other "disinterested" party, to choose the additional two. As a negotiating tactic, he told Ryan he would use his influence to get Paul Morton approved by the directors. Later that day, Ryan called to thank him and, according to Harriman, said "he would do nothing further without conferring with me and getting my consent—that is a very strong statement—and wanted to know where he could reach me that evening." Harriman had planned to go back to Arden, but he agreed to stay in town. He told Ryan he would wait for his call at the Metropolitan Club.

He was still waiting at eleven o'clock that night when Paul Cravath arrived and told him that the appointment of Ryan's three trustees would be announced the following day. Cravath conveyed Ryan's apologies, but explained that Ryan had not had time to consult with Harriman before he released the news.

Harriman said, "I told him that Mr. Ryan had a telephone on his desk and there was a telephone in the Metropolitan Club, and there would not have been five minutes lost by its announcement to me. . . . I resented such treatment, and told Mr. Cravath that I was not in the habit of being trifled with in that way, being deprived of going to my home and staying in town in such a way, and that I considered that an act of bad faith, and an evidence of Mr. Ryan's intentions. . . . I believe I turned my back on Cravath and walked away."

Monday afternoon, Harriman went to see Ryan and found Paul Cravath and Elihu Root already there. "You want my cooperation?" Harriman asked. "I tell you what I will do. I will take half your stock. I don't know what it cost [you] and do not care—provided you will agree to the appointment of two additional trustees who will be absolutely independent." Ryan refused again, and, as Harriman later recalled, "I became practically satisfied that his intentions were not what he stated they were." Harriman took a late train that evening in case Ryan might reconsider, but Ryan called and told him he had not changed his mind.

Later, under pressure from the Armstrong Committee, Ryan reluctantly testified, "Mr. E. H. Harriman desired to share the purchase with me, and I refused." He "would have taken any part of [the stock] that he could get."[15] Ryan said that Harriman told him "as he had devoted a large amount of time and work to the Equitable situation, I should not have come into the situation without consulting him and as I had bought Mr. Hyde's stock he demanded that I should . . . let him share in the purchase and have an equal voice in the management. . . . He also said that he did not think that I could carry out my plans without his aid. . . . He said his entire influence, whether political, financial or otherwise, would be against me . . . [and] that the Legislature would probably take action."

In June, when it was clear that Ryan would succeed in keeping Harriman out, Paul Morton wrote his wife, "Harriman is so mad— he got terribly left in the shuffle and is horribly broken up about it. He shook the tree for months and months and Ryan walked off with the plums."[16]

The Hendricks Report was released on June 22. Its findings did not substantially differ from those in the Frick Report, but because it was a matter of public record, it was released to the press. President Roosevelt wrote Paul Morton that the "'crooked and objectionable practices [that] have hitherto prevailed' in the Equitable . . . [have] furnished another argument for Federal supervision of insurance."[17]

Chapter Nineteen

❧

SUMMER 1905

Charlotte Warren dressed for the quadrille at the Hyde Ball.

In the summer of 1905, when Hyde had sold his stock and resigned as vice president and director of the Equitable, he spent much of his time in Newport, often in the company of Charlotte Warren. The rumors of their engagement remain one of the mysteries of Hyde's life. *(Courtesy Museum of the City of New York)*

$\mathcal{J}$ ames Alexander was the biggest loser in the Equitable crisis; he was hit hard financially; but the worst damage was emotional. In mid-June, he sent the Equitable a check for $20,053.23, the balance of his profits from seven James Hazen Hyde and Associates syndicates. He had already repaid $40,000 from other syndicate profits on February 1, in anticipation of the fight. One of Paul Morton's conditions for accepting the chairmanship was that JWA resign, along with Hyde, Tarbell, Wilson, McIntyre, and any director serving on an Equitable committee. Soon after JWA submitted his resignation, he was felled by a nervous collapse. The doctors warned his family not to let him see the newspapers, so he did not learn that Morton had accepted his resignation, that he had been censured in the Hendricks Report, or that Morton was keeping Tarbell on as second vice president in charge of agencies. JWA was staying with his daughter and son-in-law, the John W. Alexanders, on East Sixty-fifth Street, and was so ill he could not join his wife, Elizabeth, at their summer house at Oneonta Park in upstate New York.

The family let reporters know that JWA was exhausted by the nervous strain of the last six months. In mid-July, the *Herald* ran a page 1 headline, ALEXANDER ON DEATHBED, and revealed that he had been moved to Unkeway Farms, a "strictly private and very expensive sanitarium" near Bay Shore, Long Island. Unkeway occupied a house described as a "mansion," on beautifully manicured grounds with old trees and deep green lawns, but JWA was in no condition to enjoy the scenery. He arrived with a doctor and nurse, promptly had a stroke ("apoplexy," as it was called), and three more nurses were brought in so he could be attended twenty-four hours a day. Elizabeth Alexander was notified of his condition but told to stay in Oneonta, while the Alexander children went to Unkeway to see their father and talk to his doctors. The heat caused JWA to suffer a set-back, but his doctors reported that he "was not in any danger of death."[1] His mental breakdown was a consequence of the fight, but it is also possible that the first sign that he was unbalanced was the ill-conceived and highly emotional attack he mounted on Hyde.

After five weeks at Unkeway, JWA and his nurse were spotted at the Babylon train station, where he looked as though he were "in the best of health." He stepped on the station's weighing machine, "seemed pleased when the dial showed 158 pounds," boarded the train, and changed in New York for the trip north. At Tannersville, he was met by members of his family, who did not wish to discuss how long he planned to stay at Oneonta. That was the last anyone would hear of him for a long time. The doctors ordered him to remain incommunicado; and according to Wall Street scuttlebutt, he would take a long trip to Europe when he was well enough. As one editorial remarked, "The physical inability of Mr. Alexander to afford the District Attorney certain information to assist in his prob-ing into Equitable matters would . . . considerably handicap the department of justice. His absence in Europe would entail a like embarrassment."[2]

Over the summer, the papers pursued a mystery that linked JWA and the Mercantile Trust. The Mercantile had carried a special account in the names of James W. Alexander and comptroller Thomas Jordan since 1899. That account currently consisted of an outstanding loan of $685,000. Responding to the furor about the insurance-trust company interrelations, on June 14, the state super-intendent of banks ordered that the loan be taken up by the signers.

That was the trust account Henry Hyde had originally set up in his own name in the early 1890's to acquire enough shares to establish majority ownership of the Equitable. The account was too useful to leave idle, and when it had served its initial purpose, it became one of the slush funds for such transactions as loans to agents and officers, quiet settlements to avert litigation, and political contributions. Alexander had instructed James Hyde to write a letter to the Mercan-tile in 1903, in which, as vice president, Hyde indemnified the Equi-table from liability for the account. At the time Hyde had not understood that the Mercantile regarded that letter as his personal guarantee.

In June 1905, when the banking department intervened and insisted that the Equitable repay the money, Paul Morton ordered an investigation and found that the $685,000 was missing from the books. He asked Thomas Jordan to explain, and when Jordan refused, Morton fired him, and held him, JWA, and Hyde responsible for repayment. Within a week, Jordan hand-delivered a check to the Mercantile for the full amount. The mystery of who had signed the check was illustrated in a *World* cartoon that showed a laundry basket labeled "Mercantile Trust Company." A hand reached out of a window labeled "Equitable Corruption," and dropped a wrapped bundle of $685,000 into the basket. The caption read, "Whose Hand?"[3] Of the three, Hyde was the only one in a position to raise that kind of money. A reporter went to Bay Shore to try to find out more, but Hyde "sent word through his butler that he had nothing to say."[4] JWA was out of reach of the newspapers, and Jordan had disappeared.

The same week, the New York legislature announced that it would hold an investigation of all the insurance companies licensed to do business in the state. The committee, headed by state senator William W. Armstrong, would have the power to investigate, but not to prosecute, and would report back to the legislature. Its members were state senators and assemblymen, most of whom had been publicly neutral about the scandal. If any action needed to be taken after the hearings were held, the attorney general might call a grand jury to determine if there was sufficient evidence to prosecute an individual or company.

The investigation was a predictable next step, but it was still unsettling to the other insurers and financiers, especially those who had not yet been dragged into the scandal. The Hendricks' Report concentrated on the Equitable; now the net was spread to pull in the entire industry, Wall Street, banking, and assorted businessmen. The only certain way to escape being exposed on the witness stand would be to leave town and stay out of the legislature's jurisdiction.

Harriman's response to the announcement of the Armstrong Committee's formation came through Odell and was duly published:

The *World* printed his statement on the front page under the head-line LET EQUITABLE CRIMINALS GO TO JAIL—ODELL. The subhead assured readers that the former governor DOESN'T BELIEVE CHARGES AGAINST HARRIMAN.[5]

The chief counsel for the committee would face formidable witnesses, and Senator Armstrong embarked on a search for a man who could withstand pressure and bullying. One of the most promising candidates was Charles Evans Hughes, who had enhanced his reputation as a litigator by his deft conduct of the New York Legislature's Stevens Investigation into the gas and electrical industry that spring. Hughes was so brilliant that he had graduated from high school at the age of eleven and was tutored at home by his father, a Baptist minister, until he was old enough to go to college. At nineteen, he graduated from Brown University, ranking first in his class in English literature. From there he went to Columbia University Law School; after he passed the bar, he practiced law, became the litigating partner in his father-in-law's firm, and taught at Cornell University Law School.

At forty-three, Hughes was handsome and precisely groomed. His hair was combed straight back off his forehead, with a gray streak in the black at one temple; he had a straight nose, fine eyes under strong eyebrows, high cheekbones, and an old-fashioned, long beard. He could be prissy on occasion; Teddy Roosevelt called him the "Bearded Lady."[6]

Hughes would have been unassailable if he had not been advising James Alexander on mutualization from December 1904 until March 1905, when he resigned to become counsel to the Gas and Electric Light Investigation Committee. But he had also demonstrated how effective he could be in conducting a legislative investigation, and because of his Equitable experience, he understood the insurance business. The Armstrong Committee weighed the risks, and publicly floated the names of other candidates. Finally the chairman, Senator Armstrong, telegraphed Hughes, who was on vacation in Europe with his wife and their three children, to offer him the job.

The Hughes family had spent the day enjoying the high country—Hughes's hobby was mountain climbing—and, after hiking across the Grossglockner Glacier, they returned to their inn, where they found the telegram, which had been brought from Munich by courier. Hughes's first reaction was regret; he badly wanted to accept, but, as he later wrote, "On account of my connection with President Alexander of the Equitable . . . I did not feel at liberty to act." Early the next morning, he drove to Munich to use the telegraph facilities. He was so preoccupied that he barely looked at the scenery; as he explained to his wife, "My dear, you don't know what the investigation would mean. It would be the most tremendous job in the United States."[7]

From Munich, he telegraphed Armstrong, mentioning the appearance of conflict of interest, and asked the senator to consult with lawyers representing JWA, James, and Ryan. When he was assured in a return telegram that none of them would object, he booked passage home. He had barely a month to prepare for the "tremendous job."

After Hyde resigned as vice president, he filled his time much as he had in 1899, when he went to Paris after Henry's death. On June 29, he was in Cambridge for a festive Harvard Class Day, attended by many of the prettiest girls in New York. His social standing was undiminished; if anything, the scandal added to his allure. In Newport, where he spent most of the summer, one newspaper called him "the most popular visitor Newport has had in decades." He was given guest privileges at the clubs,[8] and when he stayed with his coaching companion, T. Suffern Tailer, his dressing-room table was littered with invitations. On the last Saturday in July, he and Paul Morton were both guests at a dinner dance at Mrs. Stuyvesant Fish's Crossways.

With his tether to the Equitable cut, Hyde was free to think about marriage. Many of his friends were married or engaged—Alfred Vanderbilt, Brad Johnson, and Henry Clews had all been married for a couple of years, and H. Rogers Winthrop became engaged that summer. A rumored romance that entertained "the colony," as Newport liked to call itself, was Hyde's "engagement" to one of the Deacon sisters, although it wasn't clear which one. The story began because he was staying at Snug Harbor as a guest of Mrs. Charles Baldwin, Gladys and Edith Deacon's grandmother. But Gladys, the elder and more likely fiancée, was in Rome with her mother and had never met Hyde. Her younger sister, Edith, had just completed her education at a convent school in Paris and was scheduled to make her debut the next winter, but she had led such a sheltered life that her grandmother was considering waiting another year before taking her to New York, which was "too fast."⁹ Edith was not very grown up; her favorite companions were teenage twins, Frank and Maurice Roche, who lived at Elm Court. One day, she went into town, bought ties for the boys, and told the salesgirl to address one of them to "Mr. Cock Roche"—the salesgirl had to turn her down; she said it would get her in trouble. Neither Deacon girl was currently a prospect for Hyde, but the family felt it necessary to issue an official statement denying that he and Gladys were engaged. She would later become the Duke of Marlborough's second rich American wife, but in 1905, the duke was still married to Consuelo Vanderbilt. As for Edith, her family didn't even mention the possibility that she and James might be involved.

Hardly anyone remarked on how much time Hyde was spending with Charlotte Warren. He was a close friend of the Warren family, and when he and Charlotte were together, her parents were often there, too. But Charlotte might not have found it easy to laugh off the story about the Deacons. She and Hyde saw each other nearly everywhere they went, and she looked prettier by the week. She was tilting her head under a white "chip hat" trimmed in tulle and pink velvet, wearing a becomingly simple dress of embroidered white linen at the tennis matches at the Casino; she was playing a winning hand of bridge; and she was dancing in costume at the party on Bellevue Avenue. If imitation is a form of flattery, that evening was an homage to Hyde. Eleven pretty girls, including Charlotte, wore costumes similar to those at the Hyde Ball for "an ancient dance"; U.S. senator George Peabody Wetmore's daughter, Edith, read a poem in French; and two social Newporters starred in an amateur performance of a play, Le Baiser, "The Kiss," also in French.

Hyde was back on Long Island the first week in August for the Bay Shore Horse Show, which he had helped found in 1901. The show specialized in carriage driving, and that year, Alfred Vanderbilt won the James Hazen Hyde Cup, holding his horses to a steady pace of twelve miles per hour over a seven-mile course. The second-place team was driven by J. Campbell Thompson, who was so reckless that his coach seemed about to turn over at the finish line. Thompson owed his new avocation of driving to an unpleasant situation over an inheritance. His stepson, a young lawyer named Charlie Greenough, had contested Thompson's claims to part of his mother's estate—Thompson was her third and last husband. They settled out of court, and, just that spring, Thompson had bought eighteen horses and a coach. Charlie Greenough would not be on Long Island to watch Mr. Thompson driving, but he might be in Newport while James was in Bay Shore. He, too, was interested in Charlotte Warren.

That summer, the *New York Times* ran a feature entitled "The 'Gentleman Farmer' Fad: Well-Known Young Bachelors in New York Society Who Have Gone in for Rural Delights," which described The Oaks as "one of the most extensive properties on Long Island." By the time the story was published, Hyde had already decided to sell. It didn't take long to find a buyer: Lewis Bossert, a prosperous Brooklyn lumber merchant, and his friend, a former Brooklyn sheriff, drove out to Bay Shore for the horse show. When they passed The Oaks, Bossert was enchanted; he heard it was for sale and made an offer. The deal was transacted almost immediately; Bossert returned on August 18 with his wife and son, to work out the details with Charles Williamson while Hyde was in Boston. Bossert paid between $400,000 and $500,000 in cash, although the property was said to be valued at $750,000. By September 1, he would own the house, the four-hundred-acre property, including nearly a mile of waterfront on the Great South Bay; herds of cattle and elk; lakes and the swans that lived on them; an indoor aviary filled with rare birds; farm horses and wagons; an $80,000 carriage house and a figure-eight-shaped carriage drive that was two miles long; and a $30,000 sewage and drainage plant. Hyde would keep the horses, carriages, furniture, and art, to sell separately.

A week later, on August 24, Hyde sold his private railroad car, the

Bay Shore, to a railroad man named Edwin Hawley, who planned to change its name but keep most of the fittings. The $50,000 car included a dining room, observation room, smoking room, kitchen, and bedrooms. At about the same time, Hyde quietly disposed of his harness and saddle horses at a country sale. He could have gotten more for them, but he didn't have the heart to see his horses used as another circus event for the press and society.

He had listed his house at 9 East Fortieth Street for sale, and had persuaded his mother to sell number 11 with it, at $250,000 for the pair. When an offer of $225,000 came in, Annie changed her mind. The prospective buyer offered Hyde $125,000 for number 9 alone, but he turned him down; and to please his mother, withdrew his house from the market, although he did not intend to live there.

It seemed that he was planning to change his life. Gossip about an engagement accelerated, along with speculation that he was in the market for a Newport "cottage." Alva and Willie Vanderbilt's Marble House had been vacant since their divorce; a Newport realtor let it be known that Hyde was negotiating to purchase it for his bride-to-be, although that was probably a ploy to ride on the coattails of Hyde's notoriety. The realtor said he did not know the name of the fortunate young lady, but others thought they did. At the end of the season, *Town Topics*, a reliable Hyde mouthpiece, published the following notice:

> In Newport . . . a little bird flew down . . . and this is what it whispered: "James Hazen Hyde has won the heart and hand of Miss Charlotte Warren . . . and they are to be married in New York next winter." I have good grounds for believing that the bird's whisper will, in a very short time, be followed by the formal announcement of this engagement. It will come as a great surprise to everybody except the young woman's most intimate friends. For a year or more Mr. Hyde has been exceedingly attentive to Miss Warren. . . . [She] was introduced to society a year ago last December at one of the grandest entertainments New York society has ever known, an Oriental dinner-dance given by her wealthy uncle, Lloyd Warren. She was the most popular debutante of the season.[10]

The Warrens did not issue a denial. Charlotte and her mother returned to New York and sailed for Europe on the *Kaiser Wilhelm II* on September 14. Whitney Warren and his brother, Lloyd, were already there. So were Mary Ripley and her daughter, Annah, who had rented their New York house for the winter and were planning to stay abroad for some months. The day after Charlotte left, the *World* thought rumors of her engagement to Hyde were credible enough to publish the story on page 1, with large photographs of the couple. It appeared that Charlotte was planning to buy her trousseau in Paris, and that she and Hyde might be married there to avoid publicity.

When the Armstrong Investigation opened the first week in September, Hyde was still out of town, and people wondered if he would return to testify. It seemed more likely that he would be following the Warrens to Paris.

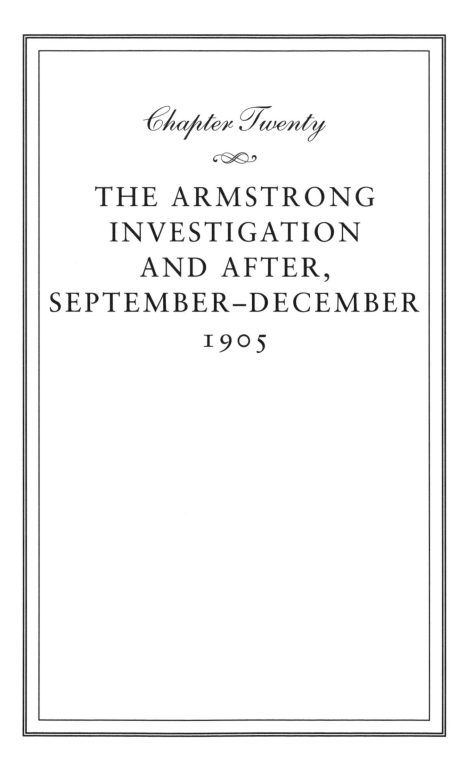

Chapter Twenty

THE ARMSTRONG
INVESTIGATION
AND AFTER,
SEPTEMBER–DECEMBER
1905

*Aldermanic Chamber during hearings of
the Armstrong Investigation.*

The government investigation held in the impressive
mahogany-paneled Aldermanic Chamber at City Hall attracted a large audience; when James testified, there were an
unusual number of women in attendance. *(Courtesy AXA
Financial Archives)*

*E*ven after seven months of relentless coverage, the newspapers and the public were still showing an avid interest in the Equitable affair. The sensational rollout of revelations in the winter and spring, James's surprise sale to Ryan, Harriman's fury, and JWA's breakdown kept the story alive. With Harriman in the mix; Morgan rumored to be involved behind the scenes; Roosevelt commenting from the White House; and a former president, Cleveland, pulled in as part of the cleanup crew, the situation had international significance.

The hearings began on September 6, concluded on December 22, and generated enough material to fill 6,483 pages in nine thick volumes. Each day, the committee, reporters, witnesses, and as many members of the public as could squeeze in assembled in the large, mahogany-paneled Aldermanic Chamber in City Hall. The room was usually overflowing; there was a lot at stake. As the *New York Times* commented, "Many insurance secrets are also Wall Street secrets, and Wall Street secrets are deeply buried and bear no headstones announcing names and dates."[1] Even so, the days were long, and, especially after lunch, people yawned, dozed, or turned aside to snap open a newspaper, perhaps to read about the proceedings of the previous day.

When the weather was still hot, striped awnings shaded the windows, and warm air drifted up toward the high ceiling. Men sat at long tables with their straw boaters in front of them, or in uncomfortable wooden chairs with their hats on their laps. Eight legislators and their aides were positioned in front of a large fireplace, flanked by fluted, carved Ionic columns. The chairman presided at a desk with two microphones; on either side, other committee members were seated in wooden swivel chairs. In front of them, Hughes's team was placed behind a curved desk, facing a temporary, unvarnished wooden platform about four feet wide and twice as long, furnished with a single chair. Witnesses sat with their profiles to the chairman, and Hughes was apt to put a foot up on a chair and lean his elbow on his knee, so sometimes the man on the stand and his interrogator looked as though they were engaged in a private conversation.

Hughes was well prepared, but even he was surprised by what he called "the sensational disclosures,"[2] as financiers and executives at all three major insurers took the stand, and reported, with a near-universal absence of contrition, that they had overpaid themselves, engaged in conflict-of-interest transactions, made a mockery of company accounts, and funneled large sums to politicians.

As J. P. Morgan had feared, the incestuous relationship between the House of Morgan and New York Life set both up for ridicule. George Perkins took the stand three times, indulging in what one newspaper called his "stump speeches,"[3] arranging his own stage set by moving the heavy witness chair so that he could pace back and forth on the tiny platform. Hughes tried to present a neutral attitude, but the Perkins/New York Life/Morgan connection was an irresistible target; some of the maneuvers were so blatant that it was startling that Perkins had carried them out at all. The year-end sales to fix the books offered particularly juicy examples of the money maze. In one instance, at the end of 1903, to take a bad investment off the record, New York Life rigged a fake sale to J. P. Morgan & Company and "sold" $800,000 in bonds to satisfy a call on a troubled issue known both as the Navigation Syndicate and the Mercantile Marine. The bonds had dropped in value, and, by making a real sale at that time, New York Life would have lost as much as $175,000. Perkins sold to Morgan at the price New York Life had paid when it bought the stock from the Morgan Bank. That allowed New York Life to avoid listing the bonds in its statement at a loss. Then, Perkins explained, with an utter absence of embarrassment, he bought the bonds back "after the first of the year for exactly the same figure at which we had sold . . . and entered [them] in our assets again as a further purchase, and went on trying to sell . . . again." The move paid off: Perkins held the bonds until he could sell at a better price, halving New York Life's loss.[4]

Hughes hammered home the point that, as the *New York Times* explained, "Mr. Perkins of the life insurance company sold to Mr. Perkins of the banking firm of J. P. Morgan & Co. $800,000 securities and a few days later . . . the same gentleman in his 'dual' capacity bought back from himself the same securities, with the net result that the securities did not figure in the report to the Insurance Department."[5]

Hughes commented, "Now that all might have been done while you were sitting at the desk in five minutes, and when in that five minutes . . . did you cease acting as a New York Life officer and began acting as a partner of Morgan & Company?"[6]

Perkins equivocated, and Hughes pressed on: "When, in your judgment, are you acting for New York Life?"

"All the time," Perkins said.

And when was he acting for J. P. Morgan & Company? "It depends on what the actual case is," Perkins said.

In another 1903 year-end accounting screen, New York Life's books showed that the company had bought shares in four railroads from J. P. Morgan. That, too, was not a legitimate sale, but a device to fill a temporary gap. Perkins had committed to buy $4 million in St. Louis Terminal bonds for New York Life, but in December, Morgan wasn't ready to issue the bonds. Perkins had to demonstrate that he had bought something for $4 million by the end of the year, so Morgan provided a stand-in. When the St. Louis bonds were delivered on February 16, 1904, New York Life "sold" the railroad securities back to Morgan at the price it had paid for them.

Hughes asked Perkins if any other representatives of the insurance company were involved in that purchase.

"I bargained for the bonds and finally bought about $4,000,000 at par, which was one per cent, or $40,000 better than my instructions," Perkins said.

The counsel retorted, "When you bargained for the bonds did you bargain with any other person than yourself?"

Perkins replied, "I cannot recollect, but I think I . . . probably did it myself." Hughes noted that since the agreement with J. P. Morgan was between Perkins and Perkins, and there was no written record of it, New York Life would not have proof of the terms if Perkins suddenly died. Perkins's explanations were rooted in the concept of honor among gentlemen, but they sounded more like "honor among thieves."

When Hughes produced a newspaper clipping that stated that since Perkins had joined the bank in 1901, New York Life had bought $132 million in securities floated by Morgan, Perkins compared the allegation to other tabloid stories. "I see that statement on one side [of the newspaper] and I see on the other side, 'Slowly Tortured to Death,' and 'A Woman Tells a Startling Story,'" he said. He claimed that the actual figure was just over $39 million, and remarked that, in any case, he was only a junior Morgan partner and received a smaller percentage than some others.

Morgan was not called to appear before the committee, but speculation abounded that he was waiting backstage to buy the Equitable shares so he could merge the company with New York Life to form another giant combination like U.S. Steel. Unflattering articles and cartoons featured Morgan as a master of intrigue. The *World's* cartoonist depicted him as Charles Dickens's thief, Bill Sykes, in *Oliver Twist*. Perkins was shrunk to the size of one of the gang of boy thieves, and Morgan was pushing him through a New York Life window to steal the "policy holders dough."[7]

When it was their turn to testify, Mutual executives provided similar examples of abuse. Members of a small subcommittee of the Mutual Finance Committee "acted as middlemen between the Mutual and such interests as wanted to borrow of the Mutual, and when they had placed the loan they got their rake-off."[8] The company also had its own trust company, the Mutual Guarantee Trust, of which the Mutual's president, Richard McCurdy, and his son, Robert, the general manager, were shareholders.

There was a surfeit of McCurdys at the Mutual, and they were well paid. Richard McCurdy earned $150,000 a year, the highest salary in the business; Robert's base salary was $30,000, but he had organized the foreign department and received a commission on all foreign sales; some years he earned as much as $137,000. He was also a partner in Raymond and Company, which acted as general agent for the New York Metropolitan district, and he took a percentage of Raymond's profits. In 1893, president McCurdy's son-in-law, Dr. Louis A. Thebault, joined Raymond and Company, where he built up to a three-fourths share, earning $147,000. Nepotism was a Mutual tradition: Richard McCurdy's brother-in-law was medical director, and other officers had relatives at the company—a nephew here, a brother there. Most of them received preferential treatment in regard to expense allowances and commissions. The newspapers added the income of the two McCurdys and Thebault, starting in 1885, and came up with more than $4.6 million. That averaged out to just under $77,000 a year each, over twenty years, but the grand total made a better headline.

Unfortunately for the McCurdys, Robert was unprepared to answer questions about aspects of the business that a general manager might be expected to know, such as salaries, expenses, and past and current assets. In defense of the executives' pay, he testified that the company had done $26 million in new business in 1904; Hughes informed him that the correct figure was $16 million. The senior McCurdy, at seventy, was a better witness. He noted that the company had been treading water when he took over in 1885; under his presidency it had increased its policies from $40 million in 1884 to more than $231 million in 1904. Its assets were now "larger than the Bank of France, the Bank of England, and the Bank of Germany combined," he said.[9] By the time that was brought out, his accomplishments were considered somewhat beside the point, by comparison to the corporate transgressions. In late November, the McCurdys resigned en masse.

Political influence-buying was easier for the public to follow than finance. New York Life president John McCall testified that the company's lobbyist, Andrew Hamilton, was paid $1,167,697 over a ten-year period; in 1905 alone, he received nearly half of the $1 million the company spent for "law expenses." Hamilton was unavailable to confirm or deny; he was touring southern France by automobile, and sent word that he was too ill to return to the United States.

New York Life had made nearly the same contribution to the Republican Party for the 1904 election as the Equitable, but it gave the money more indirectly: New York Life made out a check for just under $49,000 to J. P. Morgan & Co., which transferred the funds to Perkins, who, in turn, gave them to Cornelius Bliss, Roosevelt's finance chairman. When that information was revealed, the attorney general said he would consider bringing a civil suit for wrongful use of the policyholders' funds, citing three years of donations to the Republican Party, totaling $150,000. If the suit succeeded, McCall and Perkins might be forced to repay the money to New York Life from their own pockets.

The Mutual's political contributions were so murky that exact numbers never surfaced, but it seemed virtually certain that the company had made donations as large as $25,000 to the Republican Party. As such contributions were illegal, Colonel Mann commented wryly, "The impossibility of securing campaign contributions from the life insurance companies this year seems to be paralyzing the Republican machine."[10]

The connections between politicians, financiers, and insurers was dramatically illustrated one month after the hearings began. In early October, the New York State Republican Party revealed that it was considering Charles Evans Hughes as its candidate for mayor of New York City. Campaigns were brief in those days, so the short timing was not unusual, but the choice of Hughes was suspect. On Saturday, October 7, Hughes went to Long Island to play golf. Late that afternoon, reporters were waiting outside his apartment house on West End Avenue. He told them he had just played the worst round in his life, but refused to comment on the nomination, which, he pointed out, had not yet been officially offered. His wife was less reticent. " 'I do not think Mr. Hughes wants it and I do not think it at all desirable,' she said."[11]

Hughes declined to run, resisting what a magazine profile described as "an offer splendid enough to shake most men's sense of proportion and of duty—particularly when presented as a duty."[12] The Times speculated that Odell had set the plot in motion in "an attempt to 'queer' the investigation," just as Hughes was making headway. The *Times* wrote,

> The Republican machine, under the guidance of ex-Gov. Odell, proposed to him [Hughes] a nomination which, if he accepted it, would practically reduce to ridicule his position as an investigator. . . . The scheme of the machine was at once cynical and insulting. . . . It demanded of him that he should sacrifice the honorable reputation he has arduously and patiently attained . . . in the hope of transferring to his party some of the prestige he has gained. And the sacrifice would be absolutely futile. He could not transfer his prestige; he would simply lose it. His work as counsel, if he went on with it, would be fatally discredited. If he abandoned it, his candidacy equally would be discredited . . . the State Republican machine . . . are trying to reduce the investigation to relative uselessness by withdrawing or by discrediting the counsel . . . the fact that they have undertaken this odious job shows how widespread is the evil of which the investigation has disclosed but a part.[13]

The "evil" was so damning that important witnesses stayed out of the jurisdiction of the New York State Legislature. Willie McIntyre was somewhere in New England—when Hyde was asked about his whereabouts, he said the last time he had communicated with him was some five months earlier, when he had heard he was in Boston. The Equitable's treasurer, Thomas Jordan, disappeared so effectively that his son testified that he didn't know if his parents were dead or alive. JWA was still declared too ill to testify. And the Equitable's financial manager, George Squire, really was sick; he testified under oath at his home in Manhattan.

Early in the investigation, it appeared that Hyde would remain in Newport to avoid being subpoenaed, but that was another false rumor. He was in Newport when the hearings opened, then returned to the city and prepared to testify in November.

Two weeks before Hyde was to take the stand, the ocean liner carrying Charlotte Warren and her mother docked in New York. *Town Topics* noted Charlotte's return, accompanied by trunks filled with what seemed like a bridal wardrobe:

The seizure by the Customs officials last week of what was called the
trousseau of Miss Charlotte Warren, and the compelling [of] the
young woman to pay $1,800 in duties to secure its release, has set the
gossips talking. Of course the old story of Miss Warren's reported
engagement to James Hazen Hyde was revived by this . . . incident. . . .

It is said that both mother and daughter only declared dutiable
articles to the amount of $240, and that the eyes of the inspector
opened very widely when he came to inspect the daughter's trunks on
the dock.

Mrs. and Miss Warren went to Paris in September, after the close
of the Newport season, during which Mr. Hyde's attention to the latter had been marked. From the moment they arrived in Paris they
haunted the milliners' and dressmakers' establishments, and are credited with having made a special trip to Cluny to buy laces. It is probable that this unusual activity and the large purchasing on the part of
Mrs. and Miss Warren attracted the attention of the Government
agents . . . from the special search that was made of Miss Warren's
trunks on her arrival here. . . . [14]

That item was the last time Charlotte Warren and James were mentioned as a couple. Whatever understanding they may have had toppled
onto the pile of losses that began with his stock and his position, and
mounted as he sold The Oaks. On the mid-November morning when
he was to appear before the Armstrong Committee, newspaper readers learned that another symbol of Hyde's ebullient youth was about
to fall. One week later, Van Tassell and Kearney's auctioneers would
sell his carriage collection, valued at hundreds of thousands of dollars.
Everything would go: hundreds of blankets, lap robes, and exquisite
fittings[15]—he was even selling the stable buckets. The star item was the
Liberty, but no single coach was as important as the range, quality, and
meticulous maintenance of the collection as a whole.

When Hyde sold his saddle horses in early September, he had held
back his favorite, Lexington, a large bay gelding who won a blue ribbon at the 1904 National Horse Show. Now he would be auctioned
off, too. In a rare expression of sympathy, Colonel Mann commented, "There was something rather pathetic" about the idea of
seeing Lexington on the block.[16]

The Oaks and the carriages would bring in well over half a million dollars, but Hyde did not need the money as much as he needed a fresh start.

On November 14, Hyde appeared at City Hall to face Charles Evans Hughes and an audience of friends, enemies, and the neutrally curious. The gallery was full, with a larger than usual complement of women, and Hyde did not disappoint them; his demeanor was grave, but his shirt was ruffled. That day and the next were the most exciting of the hearings: much of the material Hughes brought out had already been aired in the papers, and had been included in the Hendricks Report; but this was the first time the public heard Hyde's explanations in his own words.[17]

When he explained his relationship with his father's company, Hyde sounded as though he were speaking of the custodial responsibility of an heir to a family estate. "I had always been brought up to consider my legitimate life work to succeed my father in the Equitable," he said simply. "I expected to make it my life work."

For the most part, he conveyed an air of dignified bewilderment; when he testified that he didn't know or couldn't recall, it was hard to discern whether he was naive and trusting, careless, or disingenuous. He conceded that when JWA asked him to give the George H. Squire Trustee account a large participation in an issue floated by J. P. Morgan, he did not know what Squire was trustee of, and hadn't inquired. "The fact that he [Alexander] asked me probably I considered sufficient reason for doing it," he said.

Hyde had asked JWA how the account was used, and Alexander told him its purposes were: "First, to settle suits which might tie up the affairs of the Society in a long litigation and generally interfere with the business and cause great complications and make a great deal of loss of time, and bother. Second . . . purchase of [Equitable] stock, as this stock from old stockholders had been bid up by speculative interests to a fictitious value. . . . It was hurting our agents in the field, being used as an argument against them." The third use was for political contributions. When Hughes asked Hyde whether he had considered it his "duty as an officer of the Equitable" to look further into those donations, Hyde answered ruefully, "That is a very good illustration of the fact that I unfortunately relied upon other people doing right."

As vice president of the Equitable Trust and the Mercantile Trust, he said, he was a "most active director" and visited both trust companies and spoke to their presidents nearly every day. "It was my business as Chairman of the Finance Comittee [of the Equitable] to be in a great many boards and influence a great deal of business toward [the trust companies] which . . . increased one of the valuable assets of the Equitable," he explained.

But when Hughes probed particular transactions, Hyde did not always remember the train of events; nor did he recognize letters that had been sent out over his signature. When Hughes produced evidence that shares were bought and sold in his name by the firm in which George Squire's son was a partner, Hyde was surprised. The transactions, which seemed to be fake paper exchanges that were meant to look like purchases or sales, had usually taken place when he was out of town. He explained that his secretary routinely signed his letters, and that when he was away JWA "directed and managed" any syndicate matters that required decisions. Hyde, who documented his personal life through meticulously filed letters and clippings, had allowed his secretaries to stuff the records of his James Hazen Hyde and Associates syndicate into envelopes. In this fiscal nonchalance, he was very similar to his father.

Sometimes Hyde and Hughes stubbornly sparred over semantics. Hughes asked if Hyde "knew" that a venture would be profitable before committing the Equitable to it, and Hyde answered that there was no way to know. "On the whole of my syndicate I have lost," he said. "If I had as valuable a mathematical forecast of the future as I now have of the past I would be a good deal better off."

"Did you or did you not believe it would be a profitable venture?" Hughes pressed.

"I did not know," Hyde said.

"Please answer yes or no," Hughes insisted.

"I did not know," Hyde repeated.

"Did you believe at the time . . . that this would be a profitable venture?" Hughes persisted.

"I hoped so but there is always a danger of a loss," Hyde said. "A man does not go into a transaction expecting a loss. He expects to make a profit."

As the audience shifted uneasily in their chairs, Hughes repeated, "Did you believe it would be?"

Untermyer interrupted, "Is it a proper question, Mr. Hughes?"

"I have answered all I can answer," Hyde put in.

"No, you have not answered," Hughes said. "You can say yes or no to that question, whether you believed it would be a profitable venture."

"I hoped it would be."

"That is not an answer. Did you believe it would be?"

"I hoped it would."

Hughes appealed to Senator Armstrong, as chairman, to "direct the witness to answer."

"I am trying to answer," Hyde said. "I had the hope it would be, that is all. By belief do you mean did I know it to be a fact or did anybody come and tell me and guarantee it?"

"No, I am asking in regard to your belief, your confidence, your expectation, as distinguished from the mere hope."

"I believed and hoped it would be a good thing," Hyde said.

"You have answered the question," Hughes at last conceded.

The point Hughes was making was that if Hyde believed an investment to which he had committed the Equitable would be successful, he could not argue that he was spreading the risk by sharing the position with his fellow board members. In that case, Hughes could assert that, rather than protecting the Equitable, Hyde was giving the directors something for nothing. All Hyde could say in his own defense was that the system "existed before I came downtown."

Harriman entered the picture when Hughes delved into the Equitable's participation in the Union Pacific Preferred syndicate. Hyde told Hughes he would be "very glad" to clarify his role in the Union Pacific situation, "because I have been very much misrepresented. . . .

Mr. Harriman first talked to me about the matter at his office," he said, ". . . and asked me, on behalf of the Society, to go into this syndicate, that is, he asked me to suggest it as an investment. I said I would have to take it up with the president of the Society, which I did . . . and he, I believe, had some conversation with Mr. Harriman on the subject."

Why, Hughes wondered, did Harriman want the signatories to be individuals, rather than corporations?

"I presume he had a good business reason," Hyde said.

"Was it because it was more convenient to deal with individual signatures or with individuals than with corporations?"

"Well, he is very fond of convenient things, Mr. Harriman," Hyde said. The audience laughed and had to be reprimanded by the chairman.

Examples of the Equitable's intricate investment entanglements proliferated, until the room grew stale with the same questions asked in slightly different ways. Whenever Harriman's name came up, the atmosphere was enlivened. Hughes explored Harriman's role as procurer of the Mercantile's $75,000 settlement to Benjamin Odell, and Hyde told him that Harriman was behind it and had warned Hyde that there was a move afoot to repeal the Mercantile Trust Company charter, and that Odell might retaliate if he were not recompensed for his loss. He brought up the issue "in just that naked form," Hyde declared.

When the embarrassing subject of Hyde's proposed ambassador-ship was raised, Hughes asked whether, in connection with the Odell payment, "or otherwise, was there anything said to you about obtaining an appointment as ambassador?"

James reviewed the discussions of the French post that began with Frick, and when Hughes asked about the involvement of other Equitable directors, he said that some of them had discussed it with him "considerably later. I think their reasons for taking this extraordinary interest in my absence from this country became rather obvious since then. . . . I think they thought they would acquit themselves of their friendly stewardship with great profit and pleasure to themselves."

"To whom do you refer?"

"Mr. Frick."

"Anybody else?"

"I think Mr. Harriman would not have looked on it with great regret," Hyde said, and when the audience laughed again, he added, "I say that seriously, although it seems to provoke a great deal of mirth."

When Hyde talked about the Frick Committee, he revealed the depth of his sense of betrayal. "I do not think their investigation was fair, nor do I think it complete," he said. "I think they had decided to seize the control of the Society."

"Through the purchase of your stock?"

"Yes, after having battered me up and having done everything they could to destroy the market value of the stock," Hyde said, adding that Frick had endeavored "to absolutely dominate the Society and inaugurate a reign of terror such as I have never seen."

When the hearings reconvened the next morning, Hughes agreed to Hyde's request that he make a statement defending his father's role in the Mercantile Safe Deposit Company. "I think it but just to the memory of my dead father, Mr. Hughes," Hyde said.

One of the issues that had arisen over the preceding months was the accusation that the exceptionally favorable safe-deposit company leases were "devised by my father for the purpose of personal gain," Hyde said. But, he claimed, it was "precisely the contrary. These leases were entered into . . . at a great personal pecuniary risk . . . to avert a serious loss to the Society." Hyde reviewed the situation that followed the panic of 1873, when the Mercantile, in which the Equitable held the controlling interest, was in jeopardy, and the directors voted to spin off the safe-deposit business. When the directors of the Mercantile and the Equitable declined to subscribe to the stock in the spinoff company, Henry personally invested $200,000. That money was used to buy out the Mercantile's lease at 120 Broadway and turn it over to the new safe-deposit company.

Hyde explained that his father had offered his safe-deposit stock to the Equitable at his cost, but the directors refused to take it. With the "sole object" of increasing "the funds of the Mercantile Trust

Company," he said, Henry Hyde had stepped "into the gap and furnish[ed] the necessary funds for the purchase of the stock at higher prices than the stock was then considered worth." He subsequently bought two more safe-deposit companies to strengthen the business, at a cost of some $600,000. If Henry had not intervened, the Equitable might have lost its $1 million investment in the Mercantile. Instead, stock of the Mercantile held by the Equitable was worth over $11 million.

Hyde had instructed his lawyers to reconstruct the facts of the Mercantile transaction so he could read a statement into the record that exonerated his father. It was a convincing corroboration of his claim that he had sold his shares to Ryan and accepted a steep discount because he believed he would save the company and restore his father's legacy.

The man Hyde once trusted as a business adviser and leader of his fight for the Equitable took the stand at two-thirty in the afternoon of November 15, while Hyde sat in the chamber and listened. Hughes opened his interrogation of Harriman by tracing his connection with the Equitable, but Harriman claimed that his memory was cloudy. He indicated dismissively that as far as he could recall, James Hyde had suggested that he become an Equitable director, and he had agreed only because the young man needed guidance. Harriman acknowledged that Hyde had qualified him with the necessary stock, implying that since he hadn't bothered to buy shares himself, it should be evident that he had little personal interest in the company. As for the $2.7 million he borrowed from the Equitable in 1901 for the Northern Pacific takeover bid, he said that it was coincidental that the loan was made the day he joined the board.

Hughes questioned him persistently about the 1903 UP syndicate and Harriman said vaguely, "I do not think any of us would want to go into an agreement with a corporation . . . there might be many complications which you cannot tell." Conveying a sense of hurried condescension, he tried to take control. "Now, just one minute, Mr. Hughes—" he interrupted. "May I stop you for a minute. I may save you some time and myself," but Hughes continued to probe. Harriman's responses to the questions were often that he could not remember. "I have had something else to think about beside Equitable matters, as you probably realize," he said.

Harriman's memory was entirely deficient on the subject of the Mercantile Trust's $75,000 payment to Odell. He could not recall when, or if, a meeting had taken place; and he claimed that Hyde had come to see him about settling with Odell, rather than the other way around, and that only then did he talk to the former governor about accepting. He said he had never heard of a threatened movement to repeal the Mercantile's charter, or mentioned it to Hyde. Even after Hughes read Hyde's testimony aloud, Harriman denied that he had suggested that the charter might be revoked if Odell weren't pacified.

Hyde was sitting only a few feet away when Hughes asked Harriman about the ambassadorship.

"Mr. Hyde came to me and asked me to use my influence in trying to have him appointed . . . [and] I told him that when I saw the President I would speak to him about it," Harriman said.

"Did you do so?" Hughes asked

"Yes, sir."

"Did you recommend him?"

"No, sir," Harriman said curtly.

None of the newspapers noted whether Hyde showed any reaction to Harriman's recital of betrayal.

When Hughes moved on to Harriman's conversation with Hyde prior to the release of the Frick Report, Harriman said he had not given Hyde any indication about the contents, or, as Hughes remarked, "suggested to him that it would in effect recommend his removal," but had said he would "stick with him through thick and thin" if he admitted his mistakes and asked for a second chance.

"Did you ask Mr. Hyde to move the adoption of the report of the contents of which he had no knowledge?" Hughes asked.

"I told Mr. Hyde that no matter what the report might be, no matter how much it might be against him personally or otherwise . . . no matter how stringent the report might be, that if I were in his place that I would favor its adoption and go to the extent of moving its adoption," Harriman said.

It was at that point in Hyde's copy of the published hearings that he penciled a long blue line next to that testimony, and wrote, "Ha, ha!" He also marked the place where Hughes asked, "Was it regarded by you as an advisable thing for Mr. Hyde to move the adoption of a report which in fact provided for his removal for misconduct?"

"I had been acting as a friend of Mr. Hyde in trying to protect him against the apparent attacks of people who had been his associates and were trying to oust him out of his position in the Equitable, and as a friend, I still advised him, with my knowledge of what the Frick report was, of what he should do," Harriman said.

"Didn't you know if the Frick report was true it would disgrace him?" Hughes asked. "Was it after the adoption of the Frick report that you stated you would subscribe $500,000 for Hyde's stock?"

"It was never adopted," Harriman said.

"After its submission?"

"I don't remember," Harriman said.

Harriman became impatient, snapped at Hughes, interrupted, said, "I would like to have your attention," and burst out, "I want you and this committee, and everybody else, to understand that I have something else to do besides devoting my time to life insurance. . . . My affairs were much more important than the Equitable in magnitude . . . when a man has some sixteen thousand miles of railroad and thirty-five or forty steamships . . . he has not much time to think about life insurance."

As busy as he was, Hughes made sure Harriman understood that he wasn't finished, and, a few days later, called him back to the stand.

Thomas Fortune Ryan's testimony provided a contrast in tone. He took the stand on December 8 and again on December 12 to answer questions about his motives in buying Hyde's stock and his arrangements to protect the company. As he had all along, he said that his intention was to perform a public service, while protecting his own interests, which would have been influenced by a general loss of confidence. He was reluctant to repeat his private conversations with Harriman, but when instructed to do so by the chairman and his lawyers, Ryan told the committee about Harriman's desire to buy a portion of the stock, and his threat to make trouble if Ryan refused to let him participate.

When Harriman was recalled, Hughes asked him what Ryan had told him "about his desire to make a name for himself."[18]

"That he had plenty of money, that he never had done anything conspicuous and that now he thought there was an opportunity for him to do something. . . . I rather questioned the motives," Harriman said. "There is no sacrifice to a man—he makes no sacrifice to put up two or three millions of dollars with the prospect of getting it back again after he has got control of the society."

Harriman's own interest, he said, was solely that "I had been instrumental in trying to straighten out the tangled affairs of the Equitable, and in protecting it against the attempt on the part of one faction to obtain control of it over another, and had been instrumental in bringing about the Frick report; and I felt, as I think other trustees who had resigned from the Equitable felt, that they were somewhat responsible, and were willing to go a long way toward getting it finally and properly disposed of. Other than that I had no interest except that of one who had been inveigled into getting himself into a false position."

"Did you tell him that you did not propose to have anybody else own that stock without your participation?"

"I have no recollection of saying anything of that kind."

"Will you say that you did not say that?"

"Well, I had no intention of saying anything of that kind, so whatever I may have said they can put an improper interpretation upon. . . . It was absolutely no demand for the stock, it was a demand that he should satisfy me that . . . he was acting from an unselfish motive."

"And that he could do by giving you half of the stock?" Hughes asked, rhetorically, and then continued, "And then you told him your influence would be thrown against him?"

"I do not want this twisted around, Mr. Hughes," Harriman said crankily, although he could not help adding, "I have been against some people, and . . . I will use any effort I can to defeat an unworthy object."

"Did you take any steps to thwart his plans?"

"Not yet," Harriman said.

"Did you have any political influence?"

"I think I have. . . . If I had been in [Ryan's] place . . . I would have taken it for granted that I would use every effort that I had in my power, whether it was political or otherwise."

"It has been charged that through your relations with Mr. Odell you have political influence."

"Well, I should think that Mr. Odell had political influence because of his relations to me," Harriman said.

Hughes tried to dismiss Harriman, but he was not ready to step down. Addressing the chairman, he said, "I would like to get through with this so I will have no possibility of being called again, and if I can encroach on your time a little I would like to do so, to clear up a few things." The request was granted, but clarification was not forthcoming; instead, he and Hughes engaged in another verbal joust, until Harriman, exasperated, said, "Well, you know that most of the people read headlines and do not read the testimony through, and they get their impressions through the headlines, and there are headline manufacturers in connection with the Press. May I be excused."

Hughes agreed that he was finished with his questioning, and Harriman stepped down; but his business with the Equitable was not over. It is almost certain that at some time in the next three years he persuaded Ryan to sell him half his Equitable shares. The source of the information was another secretive financier: In 1909, J. P. Morgan bought the Ryan shares for $3 million. When Morgan testified before the U.S. Senate's Pujo Committee on Banking and Currency in 1913, Samuel Untermyer was counsel for the committee. Morgan told Untermyer that he had bought the stock from Ryan, who was consolidating his interests, because, as Morgan said, "I thought it was best to have that stock where there was no danger of its being divided up into small lots. Mr. Ryan had already sold half of it. . . . Mr. Harriman died [in 1909] a few months afterwards, and if that had gone into his estate you could not tell how it would have been divided."[19]

The Armstrong Investigation ended on December 30. The next step would be the release of the findings some time in 1906, but Hyde did not intend to wait. He would be in Paris by then. His valet packed his trunks, and Charles Williamson tried to put his papers in order so they could be shipped abroad, to be sorted out over the next months.

Before he left, Hyde gave one more party.

Sarah Bernhardt arrived half an hour late, and in an irritable mood, for the dinner in her honor at 9 East Fortieth Street. Her coachman had taken her to the wrong address, and she had to wait outside a men's club where the members were playing poker until he got the right directions. She reached Hyde's house at eight-thirty, swept into the vestibule, and hissed at her manager not to step on her gold-embroidered white satin dress. Dinner for twelve was served in Annie Hyde's dining room, but Bernhardt was the only woman.

Twenty years earlier, the absence of ladies at a dinner for an actress would have meant something. Another notable New York host gave a reception for Bernhardt after a performance in the 1880s, and the invitations caused a social stir because some of the men were not sure their wives should meet her. Too many of them had heard what she said to the Bishop of Gloucester's wife, when she met Bernhardt's little boy, Maurice. The bishop's wife asked, "Ah, madame is married?" to which Bernhardt answered, "I'm not that much of a fool." ("*Pas si bête, Madame.*")[22] Even the most charitable and churchly Victorian lady could not be expected to resist repeating that remark.

James's dinner for Bernhardt was respectable and unexceptionable, although many years later, a newspaper story about his alleged extravagance made the claim that the party for twelve cost him $30,000, a number that must have been at least ten times the actual outlay.

For the last time, James spent Christmas with his mother. Then, on December 28, he sailed to France. Sailings were announced in the newspapers as a matter of course, and when a ship was due to sail, names of prominent passengers were published. Reporters hovering at the gangplank of the ship were looking out for Hyde, hoping to scavenge one more sensational tidbit. But Hyde had not said very much to the press directly during the Equitable scandal, and that day, he asked them to indulge his desire for privacy after a difficult year, and declined to comment.

When Hyde was troubled, Paris was the place he wanted to be; that was where he went after Henry died. Now, with The Oaks gone, and the houses on Fortieth Street feeling more like his mother's than his own, the Paris house was his only home. He was wounded and needed a refuge, and time to think. For all his frivolity, Hyde had been serious about finance and culture. He had no desire to be an unemployed dandy in New York; instead, he would be a man of letters in Paris until the trouble died down, the unresolved issues were settled, and he could find a way to make his life worthwhile. There was, too, the fact that an American financial scandal would not be of particular interest in Paris, as long as Hyde still had the money to live well. He would not be the first foreigner to find that Europeans could be forgiving, as long as the scandal only involved Americans.

Hyde had already announced that he would be taking a long trip to restore his health and well-being. He never imagined how long he would be away.

CAIRO, WINTER 1907 OR 1908

Egypt was much in favor as a winter destination for wealthy Gilded Age Americans. They sailed from New York harbor on such ships as the White Star *Adriatic,* stopped in Mediterranean ports, then crossed to the North African coast. After 1906, James Alexander was in Egypt twice, as part of an extended round-the-world trip. He had left New York in April of that year with a friend, a Mr. H. B. Davies. His wife, Elizabeth, was not with him, and he had no timetable for his return—he stayed away for two years. As he explained in a newspaper interview when he finally resurfaced in 1908, "I began to move from place to place under medical advice in order to obtain health through change of air and scene and the diversions of travel."[20]

The first time Alexander was in Egypt he sailed up the Nile to see "the wonderful ancient remains and monuments," then sailed to India. He traveled through the Subcontinent, and continued on to Burma. The faraway places he visited sound exotic still, and were more so then: Mandalay, Rangoon, Ceylon, and "up the Yangtzee-Kiang to Han-Kow . . . on a French steamer." From Japan, he took ship to Vladivostok, and crossed Russia on the eleven-day trip on the Trans-Siberian Railway. He returned to spend the winter of 1908 in Egypt.

That year, Harvard University and the Museum of Fine Arts, Boston inaugurated the Joint Egyptian Expedition at Giza, which would spend three decades excavating the Sphinx and three great pyramids of Fourth Dynasty kings. The expedition leader was the archaeologist George Reisner, who had been a celebrity since 1905, when he felicitously acquired a historic papyrus[21] from a local villager, who presented it tied up in his head cloth. It had been tightly rolled for thousands of years, and as Reisner carefully unscrolled it, a spill of ancient dust and the brittle shells of insects dead since the early second millennium B.C. dropped out. When Reisner translated the hieroglyphics, he found they were medical prescriptions for ailments, including "bites by human beings . . . and pigs and hippopotami."[22] Reisner's new expedition had quickened the interest of American travelers.

James Hyde, based in Paris, traveled quite a bit in those early years of his self-imposed exile, trying to restore his equilibrium. Hyde was in Egypt at the same time as JWA. He was accompanied by a party of friends, his valet, and copious baggage—he brought along his own china, silver, and crystal as a precaution against germs. His Harvard connections would have made him welcome at the Reisner site at the Pyramids; and JWA's former position as a trustee of Princeton University qualified him to visit the excavation as well.

One morning, while the desert was still cool, Hyde descended the stairs of his hotel and settled into a closed two-horse victoria for the ride to Giza. Around the same time, James Alexander set out from his lodgings, and both men headed for the Pyramids. They arrived before the midday heat, when the sky was still pale blue where it met the desert. The air was cool enough so Hyde was comfortable in his travelers' tweeds and solar topi—earlier travelers had been apt to get themselves up in the robes of the desert tribes; it was just as well that fad had passed.

Hyde and Alexander did not see each other at first; they had sep-arate guides and their camel handlers were set up some distance apart. The camels folded their knees on command, and turned their heads back to watch the tourists mount the smoke-and-dung-smelling saddles. Perhaps Hyde noticed an older man across the sand, wavering between the ground and the camel's hump, and saw the spindly driver put two hands beneath his well-upholstered bot-tom to shove him into place. Hyde mounted his own camel grace-fully, pulling his shoulders back with the straight posture that was still a mark of caste. Then both groups started off, the riders bump-ing along, trying settle into the camels' swaying gait.

James Hyde and James Alexander recognized each other when they were a few feet apart. They might have spoken, but they did not even acknowledge each other; there was nothing left to say.[23]

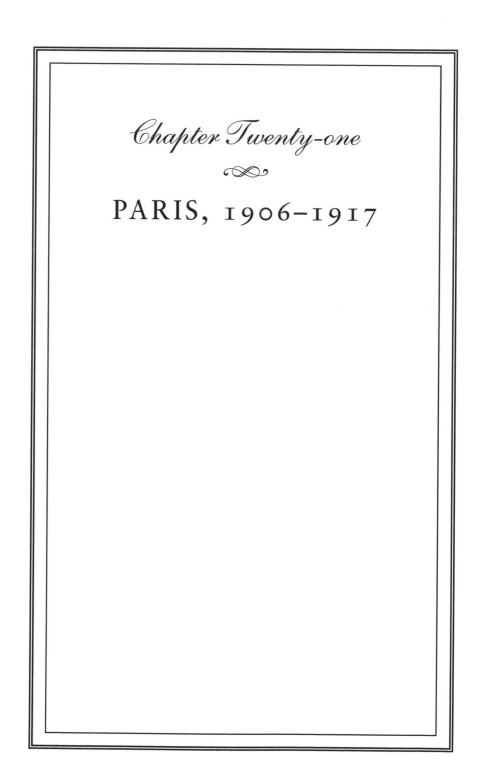

Chapter Twenty-one

PARIS, 1906–1917

*Marthe Leishman, Countess Gontaut-Biron, married
James Hyde in 1913 in Paris.*

Martha was an American heiress who had a disastrous
arranged first marriage. Her life with James was more glamorous but not much happier. *(Courtesy Lorna Hyde Graev)*

$\mathcal{I}$n the aftermath of 1905, Hyde was like a man who has suffered a severe illness, and no matter how healthy he looks, or how long he lives, is never entirely well again. Obvious manifestations of his nervous malady were an obsession with his health and diet, a flowering as a promiscuous ladies' man, and an irritable resentment that he was not as rich as he might have been.

To keep his balance, he developed a fanatically fastidious regime. His bedroom walls were covered in cork to absorb outside sounds. His diet became ever more refined; he drank wine but never hard liquor, and rarely ate meat. He was so particular that he had cards engraved, reading, "*M. Hyde ne mange que . . .*" (Mr. Hyde only eats . . .") with a list of the foods he found digestible. After he accepted a dinner invitation, his butler routinely left one of the cards at his hostess's house.

Despite Hyde's seductive social persona, he was as isolated from intimacy as he had been at Harvard. He had learned that no man could stand in for Henry, and he turned toward his mother for sympathy. Annie had never been maternal—or, at least, if she had wished to be, she was so thoroughly usurped by Henry that she hadn't had the chance to learn the technique, Now, with an ocean between them, she and her son began to express their resentments of each other. Hyde was angry because she didn't seem to care about him, she hadn't attended his ball, and she hadn't supported him through the Equitable crisis. He measured her solicitude by her willingness to release money from the Hyde Trust and from her own income to make his life more comfortable. Annie was distressed because she feared her son had jeopardized her financial position by mishandling his legacy. Their correspondence reveals the ways in which they used money to play out their disappointment.

Annie was nearly sixty, a rich enough widow, but with only a life interest in much of the property Henry had left her. In Henry's will he specified that she was to receive "all my silver and silver plate, clothing, jewelry, books, pictures, objects of art, china, glass, household furniture, horses, carriages and farming utensils." He assured that she would have a companion, and left four hundred dollars a year to their housekeeper, Camille Everard, as long as she continued to work for Mrs. Hyde (she was still with her twenty-three years later). Income from rents and investments supported Annie (Henry's largest positions were nearly $1 million in the Coney Island and Brooklyn Railroad; more than $100,000 in the Mercantile Trust Company, which had appreciated 447 percent from par; and more than $335,000 in cash). But most of his property was held in trust, to be passed on to James and Mary on their mother's death.[1]

From the time James arrived in Paris at the beginning of 1906, he and his mother wrote to each other weekly. Their letters usually began with lists of people with whom they had dined, and James often reported with enthusiasm on such excursions as his private tour of Malmaison, where Napoleon and Josephine had lived. When he went to lectures, he sometimes sent her the papers; and he proudly told her that he had been asked to serve as vice president of the Amis de Fontainebleau, to help the French government repair and maintain the château. He had dinner with the *Figaro* drama critic, went to the opera, and attended Réjane's dress rehearsals (he noted unsympathetically that her plays were not as successful as they had been because, like "many other artists she made a fatal error when she became director of a theatre").[2] And then, abruptly, the tone of his letters was apt to switch to petulance, self-pity, and resentment.

Annie's responses reflected the same feelings. When he wrote that her lack of generosity made him physically ill, she responded she was sure he wished she were dead so he could have it all.[3]

Neither was sure what they might lose when the courts were finished with them. Hyde had more than $3 million in capital from the sales of his shares in the Equitable, The Oaks, and his carriage collection; he owned his house in Paris, and he received an allowance from his mother. But the lawsuits dragged on, and legal fees increased. It was possible that he would be forced to repay funds that policyholders claimed he owed them; it seemed unlikely that the Equitable would return his escrow account containing the profits from his syndicate; and probable that the company would keep the money he had paid back when Paul Morton refused to honor the Mercantile loan that JWA had directed him to endorse. Hyde's lawyers advised him to stay in Europe until everything was settled.

Annie was a defendant in some of the suits. Feeling vulnerable about her financial status, she decided to reduce her son's allowance. As he admitted to her, he wanted the money, but he didn't really need it. His letters make it clear that what he really needed was to feel that she was eager to help him. In late October 1908, Annie wrote him, her pen scrawling thinly over paper that was still banded with a black mourning border after nine years of widowhood:

> Last Summer you sent word by Henry [Mary Ripley's son] that you felt hurt I had cut down your allowance. . . . I wrote you a long letter while you were in India, saying that B. Coney [Brooklyn and Coney Island Railroad], Westinghouse, Bank of North America did not pay anything. Perhaps you did not get the letter. Did not wish to embarras [sic] you on your arrival in Paris where I heard you had built a library, so raised the allowance, paying $4,000 besides. I now feel in view of Equitable settlement coming on soon your Father's Estate only paying me $28,000 yearly (and if you remember owing me $100,000 which I skimmed myself to lend) I can only give you $1000 a month. Mary has never had anything but her $5000 a year, and I know you can live on what you have. Hope you will not wish me dead, but please never again ask Henry to speak to me about such matters.[4]

Hyde had been trying to persuade Annie to sell her house and stable on Fortieth Street so that he could sell number 9. On November 5, Annie's sixty-third birthday, he telegraphed a response to her October letter:

> BEST WISHES HAPPY RETURNS DAY PLEASE ARRANGE ALL REAL ESTATE MATTERS AS I WANT THUS REMOVING ALL FUTURE BUSINESS DISCUSSIONS

THEN NO MORE OPEN QUESTIONS NOR CALLS ON YOU WHICH WE BOTH
WANT. I CAN GET COUNTRY PLACE YOU WILL BE HAPPIER AND HEALTHIER
ELSEWHERE AND SPEND NO MORE THAN NOW. NO HURRY STABLE. YOUR
FAVORABLE DECISION WILL BE MUCH APPRECIATED. ANSWER. CAN I COME
NEW YORK LATER OR SEND WILLIAMSON HELP YOU FIX UP NEW RESI-
DENCE.[5]

He elaborated in a letter, which he wrote the same day:

Why say that you [sic] would not wish you dead; such a thought is as
far remote from me as the North Pole is far from the South Pole. All
I want you to do is please not be unreasonable. . . .
    I think, and Mary agrees with me, that you are very fond of petty
uses of authority; the matter is neither big nor very fine: I am under
heavy expenses with my lecturers in America and here; I have had to
pay very big bills for the repair of my house here, repairs which had
to be done; I am paying a great deal of attention to the expense of my
house and wasting no money. . . . This allowance you can certainly
afford to give me and I will consider it very unfriendly if you do not.[6]

A few days later, he added:

I do not want you to think that I am selfish or grasping . . . but you
must remember that I have had somewhat through my fault and
somewhat through others, a hard time; I was also, and this is not my
fault, very much spoiled; I have cut down a good many things out of
life and the few things which I have left I am very keenly interested
in; I do not want to wait until I am too old to have to enjoy life and
to do useful things. . . . Write or telegraph me a good "Yes." . . . I am
sometimes pretty lonely and I think you are not as cordial as you
might be, so that makes me feel unhappy."[7]

When Annie cabled her "good 'Yes,'" he wrote back to thank her,
but added that he had been "violently ill" after dinner earlier that
week, because worries "about my affairs [affected] . . . my digestion."
    Hyde had not been back to the United States for nearly three
years, and now he wrote, "When this settlement [with the Equitable]
goes through I hope that then there will not pass as long a time . . .

before we see each other, either by the mountain going to Mohammed or Mohammed going to the mountain."[8] He wrote her the following July, in a letter marked, "CONFIDENTIAL. *Please destroy!*" that a friend had invited him to sail to America on his yacht. He had been tempted to accept "so as to have the pleasure of seeing you again," but his lawyers thought he should stay away a little longer so he would not "upset this settlement which means too much to us all."[9]

Instead, in the summer of 1908 he went to Smyrna on another private yacht, the *Emerald*, where he received letters announcing that his niece, Annah Ripley, would marry the Comte de Vielcastel in the fall, and that she hoped James would come to the United States to give her away. That, too, would prove impossible; he had chartered a yacht and invited guests and could not could arrive in New York before late October, "as I am not feeling very strong and my doctor in Paris and the doctor on board the Emerald both advise me to take a few days rest between this cruise and my departure to America."[10] He told Mary not to hold the wedding off on his account, sent Annah a check, and stayed in Europe. When Annah's wedding was reported in the newspapers, many of the most prominent guests were listed. Among them were dozens of couples who had been at the Hyde Ball, including the recently married William Greenough and his new wife, Charlotte Warren. James appeared in the subhead of the story, MISS RIPLEY TAKES COUNT AS HUSBAND, followed by SPECIAL TRAIN FROM NEW YORK FOR WEDDING OF JAMES HAZEN HYDE'S NIECE.[11]

That fall saw another eruption of money letters between Hyde and Annie. He wrote that his health continued to be poor, and that he was suffering from a serious ear infection. "The slightest change of air gives me buzzing in the ear, particularly when my head is on the pillow . . . disagreeable and annoying, especially that I am partly deaf from one ear, and besides this, as I am looking well everybody seems to laugh at me." Annie had just turned down a good offer for the stable on Fortieth Street, and he had hoped to use the money to

buy a small country place here. My long travels are now over; my doctors advise me very strongly to have a place where I could go and rest, not an expensive place like Bay Shore. . . . With the results of the sale of your stable I could have bought such a place without touching to [sic] my capital, and besides this sale would have resulted in an economy for you and less trouble than having horses. . . . [I hope that you will] think the matter over [and] perhaps you may still find your way to help me.[12]

Hyde bought an estate—not small—in Versailles, even though Annie's stable hadn't been sold.

Annie's will was another sore subject. James wanted to know what she planned to leave him, so he could gauge what he could afford to spend, and he was asserting himself about the way the capital was invested. He wrote her,

> You must remember that when you came into the Hyde family, you brought nothing but your good looks, which, I am told, were great. At various times, certain properties were put in your hands: you know why . . . it should have been proper & friendly to have said that you divide your property between myself and my sister. . . . I think this is what my father would have wanted you to have done. . . . But this, apparently, is indifferent to you, as he was not very long dead before you at once, publicly, resumed certain relations which you know he positively objected to. [This might refer to Sidney Ripley.]
>
> I fear one of the reasons of your annoyance with me is the fact that I am independent of you.
>
> If this is of any interest to you, your strange attitude in this matter has made me ill . . . if you desire to make me feel comfortable, and come to America to see you, which I had intended to do next summer, but as this seems to my deep regret, for I am a lonely person, to be of no interest to you. . . . [13]

Annie responded that she was lonely, too, and Hyde answered sadly, "I had expected to see you almost daily all my life . . . do not demoralize me any more or I will think what is the use of anything."

He wrote that he hoped his last letter had "cleared the atmosphere," and that he might come over to see her in the summer, if they had settled the money matters between them.

Speculating about the root of their "differences," he wrote, "Perhaps I was hurt by what appeared to me your withdrawal of confidence in me, as evidenced by the fact of my being no longer familiar with all of your affairs."

He was most concerned that, if she did not name him an executor of her will, it would imply that she had no faith in his financial acumen:

> I think you can not have appreciated the full public as well as private, personal, sentimental import and effect . . . of my being named an executor of your will. Rightly or wrongly, I have been . . . subject to a great deal of hostile criticism, and from a moral point of view, I consider that if you do not name me as an executor of your will, it will appear as though you had joined the ranks of my detractors and had dealt me the hardest blow of all. . . . [W]hat I want you to do is to name me an executor, and to tell me now what provisions you count upon making for me in your will. . . .
>
> [D]o not talk any more about being dead, or about anybody wishing you dead. . . . It is too bad for you to be so lonely, and too bad to have disagreements and quarrels at this time.[14]

At last, in 1912 Hyde and his mother sold the two houses. The contentiousness between them settled down after that, but so did the hope that they would establish a closer rapport. It was not until Hyde met Marthe Leishman, Countess Gontaut-Biron, that his melancholy lifted.

The hypochondria and depression that shadowed the early years of Hyde's exile did not affect his appearance. He was more handsome every year. He shaved his beard and mustache, and a little gray began to flicker in his dark hair. His eyes, which were often described as deep-set and brooding, brightened when he was engaged in an animated discussion of art or literature, and twinkled when he was flirting. He used his beautiful long hands the way the French did, as part of his vocabulary. His elegance still set him apart, but in Europe, a distinctive style was an asset, not a curiosity. By 1910, he had made a place for himself in cultured French circles. A *New York Times* reporter who visited Paris in September of that year and spent time with him filed a story titled JAMES HAZEN HYDE ESCHEWS GAYETY [*sic*] FOR LITERATURE. The subhead reported that James was writing a book ON THE INFLUENCE OF FRENCH AND AMERICAN MEN OF LETTERS. The reporter described Hyde as "immersed in his researches in French and English literature, spending most of his time in the magnificent library in his fine house in the most fashionable quarter of the city." Hyde never wrote the book, but, the reporter noted, he did continue to associate principally "with men of distinction in the arts." The reporter confided, "The James Hazen Hyde of the tally-ho parties and the violet bouquets on his horses' bridles has changed to James Hazen Hyde, bookworm. He keeps no horse, he has no carriages. One modest automobile is the extent of his vehicular possessions in Paris."⁵

While other wealthy American expatriates ran their horses on the French racetracks and spent their nights at Maxim's, the Dead Rat, and the Abbaye, "The American bars know him not, the gay resorts he does not frequent." But the "bookworm" saw such American friends as the Bradley Martins, the George Goulds, and Ambassador Bacon; and "constantly" gave dinners and receptions attended by literati whose names meant little to most readers of the *Times*, but whose credentials they could recognize: the curators of Versailles and the Louvre and the conservator of Fontainebleau; cabinet ministers; authors; scholars; and artists, one of whom, Auguste Rodin, had made the portrait sculptures of Thomas Fortune Ryan. Sorbonne professors were such intimates of Hyde's house at 18, rue Adolph-Yvon, that "they call informally at all times." Hyde's particular mentor was the "the greatest living French writer," Anatole France, "with whom, despite the disparity in their ages, the warmest personal friendship" existed.

Hyde was pleased to invite the *Times* reporter to look in on his life, but refused to discuss the Equitable, except to say that he has "never discussed these matters at any time for publication, even when they were crucial, and that he was at all times grossly misrepresented and misquoted in the New York newspapers."

Hyde's popularity in Paris transcended the intellectual and artistic worlds; if he was depressed and hypochondriacal, he kept it to himself. In public, his magnetism was intense, and he made a string of romantic conquests, earning his reputation as a *"couche partôut."* There was a pause in his flirtations when, at thirty-seven, nearly a decade after he left New York, he married Marthe Leishman, Countess Gontaut-Biron, the American widow of a French count.

Marthe was the elder daughter of John G. A. Leishman, the Carnegie Steel executive who subdued Frick's would-be assassin, and was promoted to president of Carnegie Steel a few years later. That job didn't last long: one of Carnegie's biographers, Joseph Wall, describes him as "weak and ineffective," if "genial" and "easygoing," and adds that Carnegie "lashed [him] unmercifully." [16] Wall reported that Carnegie scolded Leishman about his personal financial practices, in particular his speculation in ore,

> which you bought when already in debt, simply because you thought it would rise in value and pay you more than the interest upon the loan. The stock has been of less value than your debt upon it. . . . The gamble didn't win.
>
> Now there may be other complications in your private affairs. *You conceal*, keep silent. . . . Our President should have reputation, hence influence and financial strength, if not from capital, yet from *character*. The Carnegie Steel Co. is daily compromised by its President owing private debts. I am told of an instance where you borrowed from a subordinate. This is madness . . . every financial step in your private affairs has serious consequences [for the reputation of the company]. It was for this reason I put you out of debt, as I thought, but you *concealed from me again your true position*. . . .[17]

Inevitably, Carnegie fired Leishman, which would eventually lead to Marthe's appearing in Paris, where she and Hyde met. In February 1897, Leishman announced that he was resigning from Carnegie Steel due to poor health, sold his stock, netted $800,000, and began a new career in which geniality was more useful. President McKinley appointed him minister to Switzerland, and he went on to become American ambassador to Turkey, Italy, and Germany.

The three Leishman children, Marthe, John, and Nancy, were brought up in a thoroughly international world. When Marthe was old enough to marry, the family was in Turkey; Istanbul was not the ideal place to meet a titled European, so her father hired an attorney in Paris, a Mr. O. E. Bodington, to make a match for her. She was piquant, chic, and cultivated, and had an attractive dowry, and Bodington arranged a marriage with Count Louis de Gontaut-Biron. The *New York Times* described the June 1904 wedding as "a notable event in American and French social circles." Marthe was attended by the American ambassador and a general in the United States Army. The Sultan of Turkey gave her the diamond, ruby, and emerald-studded Grand Cordon of the Nicarn-i-Chefakaf, the only Turkish order women were permitted to receive; and the pope sent a signed medallion. Hyde was in Paris, but while "many officials, diplomats, and members of the French nobility,"[18] were at the wedding, there is no indication that he was among the guests.

The marriage foundered, and three years later, in 1907, the count saved Marthe the trouble of completing their pending divorce when he died, apparently of syphilis. The attorney who arranged the marriage sued John Leishman for his $5,000 fee, but as the groom was dead, he was unable to collect.[19]

Leishman was stationed in Berlin in 1911, when his younger daughter, Nancy, a famous beauty, attracted the interest of the German Duc de Croy. The duke was enormously rich, and his titles were ancient; Kaiser Wilhelm II was said to have wanted him as a son-in-law himself. The year after Nancy became a duchess, her father resigned as ambassador to Germany. His departure coincided with the stirrings of war, but also with a lawsuit a New York brokerage firm won against him. The court fined him $75,000 for making investments based on privileged information he gained as a diplomat.[20]

Marthe stayed on in Paris after the count died, and as a niece recalled, she was "a much liked young widow, witty, funny, elegant, not pretty but very charming."[21] She was part of a clever, raffish, and talented group. Her friends were Cole and Linda Porter, the Italian jewelry designer Fulco de Verdura, the London style-stetter Daisy

Fellowes, the society decorator Elsie de Wolfe, and the dancer and choreographer Diaghilev. Hyde liked intelligent women, and Marthe was quick and witty. It was natural that she and Hyde would cross paths, although hardly automatic that they would fall in love. Many years later, when their only son was asked why his parents married, he said he had always understood that Hyde would lose his inheritance if he did not have a child before he was forty. Marthe must have told him that, but it wasn't true: Henry Hyde's[22] will did not contain any such stipulation; on the contrary, the 1896 codicil specified, "I authorize my said son, should he die leaving no issue him surviving, to appoint the shares held in trust for him to and among such persons or corporations as he may deem advisable."[23]

Nevertheless, Hyde did want a child, and it was possible that Marthe had been infected by her late husband's venereal disease and was either a carrier or was sterile. Hyde insisted that she be examined by a doctor. The examination should have been done in any case, but Marthe was humiliated. She and Hyde were married in November 1913, in a civil ceremony at the *mairie*, the City Hall, of the Sixteenth Arrondissement; Marthe's witnesses were her brother-in-law, the Duc de Croy, and the New York social arbiter Harry Lehr. Hyde was represented by Myron Herrick, the American ambassador, and Henry Clews, who had become a sculptor and lived with his wife at their Château la Napoule near Cannes. At the religious service, held at the American Church of the Holy Trinity, the Duc de Croy gave Marthe away; Princesse Guy de Faucigny Lucinge, known as "Baba," one of the chicest women in Paris, was her attendant. Ambassador Herrick was Hyde's best man.[24]

Annie did not come to Europe for the wedding. The letter she wrote to congratulate her son reads, in its entirety:

> My dear Caleb:
>
> As you know my aversion to writing I am sure you will not mind my dictating a letter to tell you how pleased I am over your marriage and to thank you for your various letters and cables.
>
> I am sure from all that I hear that my new daughter must be most charming, and I only wish I could have been present at your wed-

ding. However, I was with you all day in spirit and we all drank to your future health and happiness.

With love to you and Martha [*sic*] and the wish that the future may hold much joy in store for you, believe me,

Affectionately,

[signed] Annie F. Hyde[25]

James and Annie never saw each other again, although she lived for nine more years.

Marthe and James resided on the rue Adolph-Yvon; and between June and September, they were in Versailles at the house Hyde had described to his mother as a "simple country place," at 7, rue de l'Ermitage. A French visitor described it as "a magnificent property, where the gardens, following the taste of Le Nôtre, echoed those of the Sun King [Louis XIV]."[26] Hyde was a good golfer; his team had won the club championship on Long Island, and he built a nine-hole course on the grounds, which were large enough to accommodate a main house and a series of satellite buildings. The villa's library was filled with a superb collection of art books, and in the principal rooms Hyde displayed the art, furniture, and objects he was collecting with the theme of the Four Continents.[27]

In October 1915, the Hydes' son, Henry B. Hyde, was born in Paris in the midst of a war in which James was much engaged. A year earlier, he had loaned l'Ermitage to the French Red Cross as an auxiliary hospital for wounded soldiers; and he became a member of the Executive Committee of the American Relief Clearing House, until the United States finally joined the Allies and the American Red Cross took over. When the issue of command between the French and American armed forces arose, Hyde helped to persuade the French prime minister that the American forces should operate independently, under the command of Gen. John ("Black Jack") Pershing, rather than serving under the French. From 1917 until 1919, Hyde was a member of the Red Cross, received "the assimilated rank of captain," wore a uniform, and served as an aide to the American

Red Cross commissioners stationed in Paris. He was a member of the American Committee on Public Information in France, visited the front, and wrote articles and gave speeches about what he saw. He was so proud of one of his articles, *"Impressions du Front, La Vaillante Armée des Vosges"* ("Impressions of the Front, the Valiant Army of the Vosges") that he had it bound in multiples in hardcover.

The war gave Hyde a sense of purpose and pride, and it seemed that the disgrace he referred to in his letters to his mother was a smaller matter by comparison to the great, shared cause. When peace came, he received a new decoration, the Medal of French Gratitude, for his relief efforts.

On the marital front, the war created its own fatal skirmishes. Hyde and Marthe had violent political disagreements. According to the *New York Times*, Marthe was fond of Germany because she had lived there as a young woman, and her sister was there still; while "Mr. Hyde, who has been a resident of Paris for many years, is ardently pro-French and frequently was embarrased [*sic*] by the remarks of his wife concerning the people of Germany." They were so badly at odds that in the middle of the war Marthe took Henry to Biarritz, and, while she was there, she and James agreed to separate. Five years after they were married, their divorce decree was reported on page 1 of the *Times,* which emphasized that their "incompatibility" was attributed to "feeling over the war." The *Times* added that "there is no other man or woman involved," and that Hyde had given his wife $20,000 and set aside a trust, which would produce $30,000 a year in income.[28] Politics aside, the marriage did not have a great chance of success; Hyde never could sustain an intimate relationship for long. Perhaps that was true of Marthe, too. She had a full social life, but never married again. Because James and Marthe shared a child, they had to stay in contact, and their estrangement escalated to deep dislike. When Hyde wrote the secretary of his class at Harvard about his listing in the twenty-fifth anniversary notes, he said, "The lady I married, I fortunately lost by divorce some time ago. Under the circumstances, you will do what you judge tactful concerning the records."[29]

Hyde was alone again, but now that he had a son, he had the chance to try to reconstruct the kind of relationship he had with his father. He still worshiped Henry B. Hyde, and his own son would later recall that he mentioned him every day of his life. But he did not have the talent to inspire a child's love and admiration.

Afterword

"THE AUGUST MOON": HENRY HYDE

James Hazen Hyde and his son, Henry (foreground).

James brought up his only son to be trilingual and bicultural, skills that would serve young Henry Hyde well when he became a World War II spymaster in the OSS. *(Courtesy Isabel Hyde Jasinowski)*

*H*enry Hyde's childhood was defined by the inescapable fact that his parents loathed each other. He was never sure who had official custody; he thought it was his father, but he lived principally with Marthe. She had married two impossible men, she did not need another husband, and Henry did not have to share her attention. He was petted by his mother's amusing friends in the fashionable apartment she leased from Mme. Jeanne Lanvin of the couture house, and later at the flat she bought at 1-3, rue Beethoven. On the walls, she hung the chic pastel-toned oil portrait of herself by Marie Laurençin, another Laurençin portrait of little Henry, and a Vuillard drawing of Henry in aquarelle and pencil. The apartment featured a fabulous Coromandel screen, much like the one that decorated the apartment of Marthe's friend Coco Chanel at the Hôtel Ritz. (Chanel was Marthe's favored dressmaker, and Henry often accompanied her to fittings, where he sat on a pretty little chair and watched, even as she was fitted for underwear.)

Henry was the agent of his parents' animosity, but he tried not to be its emissary. Marthe and James were rivals in the Parisian worlds where pedigree, money, and culture mixed, and Henry afforded them another field for competition. Hyde invited his son to leave his mother and move in with him, but Henry was dismayed, and said he would prefer to stay with Marthe. Hyde was angry and hurt; Marthe told Henry that he was just trying to set him up so he could call him a "mamma's boy." Hyde tried to make l'Ermitage a little boy's paradise, giving him gifts like a pony and cart and a custom-made miniature Rolls-Royce; but when Marthe heard about the lavish presents, she told Henry that his father was spending all his money and there would be none left for him. Yet even Marthe could not entirely strip the Versailles house of its glamour. For one thing, everyone there was impressively tall, especially from the perspective of a small boy. And, as Henry was well aware, even the footmen were wonderfully courageous. Two of the criteria for working for Hyde were height, and bravery in combat. James required his staff to wear their World War I medals on their livery, and the story was often repeated that a French general who came to dinner remarked that the only time he had been in the company of so many heroes was on the battlefield.

The first Henry Hyde had been too close to his son; but James Hyde was unusually remote. He and his little boy didn't even sleep in the same house at l'Ermitage. Hyde lived in the main villa, Le Pavillion, with two white Pomeranians, which bounced along, yipping and scrambling on the waxed parquet floors; Henry and his nurse were housed in their own cottage. Although Hyde was stiff and unapproachable, he was deeply interested in his child, and most particularly in his education. He hired tutors and governesses to teach Henry at home; and sent him to a French boarding school, Collège de Normandie, when he was eight. Marthe complained that her former husband was punishing her by taking her child away.

After four years at Normandie, Henry's English was so flawed that Hyde sent him to Chillon College in Switzerland to make the language transition before he went on to Charterhouse, the British public school. Charterhouse, founded in 1611 on the side of a monastery built for the monks who produced the liqueur Chartreuse, was then one of the half-dozen best schools in England. Henry was a good student and athlete, but he was singularly unhappy there. Hyde withdrew him in December 1932, in the middle of the school year, not because he was miserable, but because it was time for him to improve his German, and sent him to board with an art history professor in Bonn. Marthe might have approved.

While Henry was in school, Hyde married twice again. His second wife, another American heiress whose marriage to a titled European had failed, was Helena (Ella) Walker, Countess Matuschka. Ella, born in Detroit, was the granddaughter of the hugely wealthy owner of Hiram Walker Distilling Company, which made Canadian Club whiskey. At twenty-two, in 1897, she married the German count Manfred Matuschka, Baron von Toppolczan and Apaaetgen, an officer in the emperor's own Bodyguard Regiment, and the owner of an important estate in Silesia. He and Ella were part of the kaiser's inner circle, and of the group around the Prince of Wales, later King Edward VII. The life was glamorous, but the marriage unpleasant. The Matuschkas were divorced in 1925, and the union was annulled. Ella and Hyde were married five years later.

Ella was a year older than Hyde, small and pretty. Her hair was reddish brown, her complexion was delicate and fair, and her eyes were a vivid blue. She had an intelligence and elegance Hyde appreciated, but she was warmer and less brittle than Marthe. In their wedding picture, the satanic look of Hyde's youth was replaced with a twinkling, blissful expression. That didn't last: the marriage was over within eighteen months. Neither Hyde nor Ella was forthcoming about the reasons, but there were rumors: Some said that Ella returned from a trip and found her trunks packed; others that she discovered her husband in bed with another woman. People still told those kinds of stories about James Hyde.

They were divorced in May 1932, and both remarried within the year. Ella's third husband was Prince Alexander von Thurn und Taxis, first Prince della Torre e Tasso, and first Duca di Castel Duino. Hyde's third and last wife was Marthe Dervaux Thom, a pretty French widow with a contagious smile and an active interest in public service; she established a school for Catholic scouts in the park of her estate near Paris.[2]

Between his marriages, and probably during them, Hyde continued his liaisons. The library at l'Ermitage was a favorite spot for seductions, and sometimes Hyde called Henry in for a chat while he and a mistress were in postcoital dishabille. Henry's confidence was undermined by his father's success with women, and his magical appearance. When they walked together on the streets of Paris, people turned around to stare, and Henry, who was tall and attractive, felt small and chubby by comparison. Later, when Henry introduced his father to the women he dated, Hyde charmed them, while his son slipped resentfully into the background.

Henry began to enjoy himself when he entered Trinity College,

Cambridge in the fall of 1933. A university friend, John Roper, recalled that in those days, life "went on gaily enough. You played your squash and tennis (were you not one of the young French amateurs to whom Lacoste himself gave the first shirts with the famous crocodile?). And, when we met in the mornings, Lord! How bright-eyed and bushy-tailed you were! And parties and girls and so on. We were all very young."[3]

Hyde had been thinking about Henry's future, but Henry admitted that he had no real plans; although after his experience in Bonn, he had been considering becoming an art historian. Hyde had centered his life around culture, but that was partly because he had lost the chance to do anything else. He wanted Henry to have a career, and he did not intend to support a gentleman of leisure; he insisted on enrolling Henry in Harvard Law School. As Henry later recalled in an unpublished memoir, his father "stressed . . . [that law school] would be a good intellectual discipline . . . and might also result in [my] becoming interested in being an international lawyer, which . . . [my] European background would well suit [me] . . . for." Hyde added that three years at Harvard would also give his son the chance to "make up his mind whether he wanted to make his life in Paris or in the U.S.A."[4]

Henry received his degree from Cambridge in modern history and economics, and a month later, he steamed across the Atlantic. He arrived in the United States for the first time when he was twenty, unprepared for what he feared would be a "radical transformation."[5] He was brilliantly educated and socially polished, but emotionally under-developed, and his adjustment, he recalled, was "most arduous." He had no more than "a handful of acquaintances, [while] both of his parents continued to reside in France, and his only relatives in the United States were older first cousins [Mary's children] whom he had never met before." He had always been an outsider: in France he was too American; in England, too French, but he seemed particularly foreign in the United States. Even Americans who affected a blasé air tended to be optimistic and open, while Henry was secretive, subtle, and skeptical.

One observer described Henry's mind as "Cartesian,"[6] referring to René Descartes, the French seventeenth-century philosopher whose dictum was *"cogito ergo sum"*—"I think, therefore, I am." For Déscartes, nothing could be absolutely proven, so "very little remains, only the simple fact of doubting itself, and the inescapable inference that something exists doubting, namely Déscartes himself."[7] For the most part, Henry "existed doubting."

Neither of Henry's parents attended his graduation from Harvard Law School, and, in the summer of 1939, he returned to Europe and took off to travel around Europe with a group of friends. They were in Corsica in late August when it became clear that war was about to break out, and they rushed back to Paris. Henry's French friends joined the army, and he went to Versailles to tell his father that he, too, planned to enlist; he said he "felt it was his duty and all of his friends were already or were about to be mobilized."

Hyde's reaction was "violent,"[8] Henry wrote. He predicted that the war would swamp France, and insisted that Henry return to the United States to take the bar examination while his studies were still fresh in his mind. When his father threatened to stop his allowance, Henry "reluctantly" and "regretfully" sailed back to New York in September 1939. He found an apartment and a job with a law firm; he studied for the bar, and passed the exam the following January.

Marthe Hyde was in New York, too. She had returned from France, via Lisbon, in 1939, and was living at 521 Park Avenue, while her sister, Nancy, stayed in her apartment in Paris. Nancy was divorced from the Duc de Croy, and she and her second husband, a Danish diplomat, Andreas d'Oldenbourg, planned to remain in France throughout the war. To protect herself from the Nazis, Nancy established her Aryan ancestry: An American aunt provided a notarized document tracing their family back four generations, including information about where each family member was baptized, worshiped, and in what Christian cemeteries they were buried. The aunt testified that she knew Nancy was an Episcopalian because she was her godmother and had been at the christening. With these bona fides established, the d'Oldenbourgs placed the Danish consular seal on the door of Marthe's apartment and hunkered down.

Henry met Marie Emilie (Mimi) de la Grange in New York soon after the French entered the war. Mimi and her brother, Henry Louis, were both accomplished concert pianists and had come to the United States together so that Henry Louis could pursue his musical interests. Their father, Baron Amaury de la Grange, was an important French senator, and deputy secretary in the Ministry of Commerce in the war; their mother was American. The baron insisted that it was too dangerous for their children to return to France, and instructed them to stay in the United States.

One autumn weekend at Tuxedo Park, Mimi and Henry were in the same house party. They were both homesick for France, and as they talked together in French, they discovered that their baby nurses had wheeled their carriages side by side in the park in Paris. After a short courtship, they decided to marry.

The wedding of James Hyde's only son finally set him on course for New York.

Hyde had stayed in France as long as possible, but, in 1941, it was too dangerous for an American to live in Paris. He made certain that his art books would be preserved by donating his library to the city of Versailles; and turned over the title of the house on rue Adolph-Yvon to his wife, to protect it from being looted or confiscated by the Germans. The second Marthe planned to remain in France; she and Hyde had managed to stay married for a decade, but their relationship was strained. For the first time in thirty-five years, Hyde prepared to sail across the Atlantic. He made his way to Lisbon and booked passage to New York for himself and his valet on the American Export Line *Excalibur*.

As much as New York had changed, one tradition remained: reporters still met the ocean liners at the docks. When Hyde landed on Saturday, March 10, 1941, the newspapers ran banner stories about his return. He was already giving interviews the next day, in the apartment where he would live for the rest of his life, on the twenty-sixth floor of the Savoy Plaza Hotel between Fifty-eight and Fifty-ninth Streets overlooking Central Park. The articles that appeared about him were steeped in nostalgia for an elegant era, rather than laced with barbed remarks about a lost empire. A *Sun* reporter noted that Hyde was "as courtly and exquisite at 64 as he was that chill December day in 1905 when he drove his own hansom

down to a French Line pier and bade good-by to the United States."
Now, the reporter mentioned, he had a trace of a French accent.

When Henry Hyde and Mimi de la Grange were married at the
George D. Wideners' house at 5 East Seventieth Street in April 1941,
James and Marthe were both there.

That month, a society page reporter for the *World* interviewed
Hyde in a story titled ELEGANT INTELLECTUAL.⁹ The *World* had harried
him relentlessly when he was young, but this writer was enchanted.
She described Hyde as "elegant and elongated, with the head of a
thinker and the dress of a dandy . . . a gentleman from another century." He wore a "pale gray suit [that] was longer than average, with
a flap back, accentuating his height. His stiff white collar looked the
more old fashioned for his wide, loosely knotted blue silk bow tie . . .
famous for his wardrobe since Harvard days . . . there is a legend that
as a youth he wore black silk pajamas to match the black silk sheets in
his bedroom and his ebony breakfast china . . . [and] had his valet
change the laces in his shoes every time they were worn."

Hyde's philosophy had adapted as times changed. His motto, he
said, was, "Simplicity and moderation in all things," adding, "The
luxurious style of living we knew before the war will never return."
As an example, he mentioned that, at the opera, "a sack-suit in a box
would have been a scandal years ago," but "today it demonstrates
the democratic evolution of American society. It is very interesting—
the opera as a public institution and New York shooting up because
it can no longer spread out." Glaring out from beetling brows, he
said, "'The trouble with this world is too much materialism!'"

The reporter noted, "[Hyde's] train of thought moves gently,
pausing for contemplation. His conversation is amplified with anecdotes, bon mots and philosophical observations." Even the French
admired his intellect, and had elected him an associate in the prestigious Academy of Moral and Political Sciences, to fill a seat vacated
on the death of Dr. Thomas Masaryk, the former president of
Czechoslovakia. James was one of only three living Americans to be
chosen by the academy. The others were Columbia University president Nicholas Murray Butler and Gen. John J. Pershing.¹⁰ The
World's photograph showed Hyde in profile, with his hand on the

standing globe by the fireplace, next to his "book-littered desk."

A few less respectable publications replayed stories of his youth. Those that did, like the *American Weekly*, which ran a piece titled "Tragedies of Society," were apt to get the facts wrong. The *American* called him "heir to a fortune of more than 20 million dollars," said his nickname was "wonderful Jimmy," and declared that he used to give "nightly dinner parties."[11]

In his sixties, Hyde's eccentricities seemed more quaint than shocking. He still wore spats and a cape, and he sometimes traveled around town by horse and carriage—a favorite conveyance was a converted hearse. He was a vegetarian, and when he went out to dinner, he was accompanied by his valet, who brought his special foods into the kitchen, and served him at the table. Most people put up with this little drama; it made for good gossip, and he was a sophisticated, entertaining dinner partner.

Henry was practicing law, but he was determined to be part of the war effort. He volunteered for the United States Naval Intelligence Service, and was "declared unfit on account of his eyes and feet,"[12] he wrote, but explained privately that his German connections made the navy nervous. He had studied in Bonn; his father often traveled to Beyreuth to hear Wagner operas; his grandfather had been ambassador to Germany; Leishman sounded like a German name; and his aunt had been married to a German aristocrat. The articles about Marthe's German sympathies in the last war exacerbated the concern that her son's allegiance was unreliable.

His international background looked more interesting to the recruiters for William ("Wild Bill") Donovan's new espionage service, the Office of Strategic Services (OSS.) Donovan was a World War I Congressional Medal of Honor winner, a confidant of President Franklin Roosevelt, and a successful New York lawyer of sixty. He recruited so many OSS operatives with credentials like Henry's— European travel, German governesses, French ladies' maids, and elite educations—that the organization was nicknamed "Oh, So Social." As Henry later explained, "It could most effectively be staffed with civilians with considerable foreign backgrounds and connections like the British Intelligence Service." The agents Donovan attracted were "the most brilliant yet motley group of peacocks ever assembled in a Washington agency," but the service was not solely social. The radio propaganda department was headed by the Pulitzer Prize-winning playwright Robert Sherwood; agent recruiters included President Roosevelt's son, James; Supreme Court Justice Felix Frankfurter's daughter, Estelle; and John Ford, who had recently produced the movie *The Grapes of Wrath*.

Henry went to work at the OSS French Section in Washington, underwent a three-week intensive training, and was sent abroad. He was twenty-eight, only a few years older than his grandfather had been when he founded the Equitable, and the same age James was when he fought to hold on to the company and lost. It was his turn to embark upon his own great adventure.

The troopship S.S. *Santa Lucia* slid into Algiers harbor on a sunny February day, after passing without incident through waters once dominated by the pirates of the Barbary Coast, and now infested with German submarines and warships. Henry, crammed at the rail with soldiers and war correspondents, leaned toward the land, and absorbed the sunlit colors and pungent smells of the early North African spring. He was traveling under loose cover as a journalist, wearing a U.S. Army uniform without insignia, but Algiers was seeded with spies and there was no hope of keeping his OSS connection secret.

In the unpublished memoir he wrote thirteen years later about his experiences in the OSS, he recalled that the casbah looked "like the movies," and that the city rose steeply to the foothills of the Tell Atlas Mountains, where white-walled villas set in mounds of purple bougainvillea were backdropped by stands of black-green cypress.

Members of the OSS lived and worked in an eighteenth-century Arab villa in the hills, built around a fountained, mosaic-tiled courtyard. As Henry arrived with his baggage, principally a duffel bag of dirty laundry, the truck navigated a *boules* court in the driveway, and he could see tents bristling in the backyard, where drivers, guards, secretaries, and enlisted personnel were billeted. The villa looked glamorous and exotic, a place where luncheons with fruity Algerian wine might be followed by long siestas, but it was a round-the-clock center of critical operations. It was normal to go for days with only a few hours of sleep, to be bone-cold in the marble rooms during the winter, and to eat unpalatable food because the cook's principal qualification was her "inability to understand any European language," as Henry wrote.

Henry joined a tight, brilliant group, who had been given the chance to use their skills, energy, and nerve to help win the war. The team included two labor lawyers, a Harvard anthropologist who was fluent in Arabic, a "kindly" stockbroker who "for some unknown reason, found himself temporarily in charge of creating sabotage and guerilla warfare in France," a German-American English professor who was the chief radio instructor, and a staff of women, mostly secretaries. They were all volunteers, for whom the work, as Henry explained, was "a privileged opportunity." They felt "obliged to perform above our usual standards. . . . A trifle pompously, perhaps, we started talking among ourselves about being potentially unique repositories of valuable techniques which could be of use . . . to our Government." Henry wrote that one of the academicians, who "went a little too far . . . compared us to the monks in the Irish monasteries who carried on the classical tradition through the dark days of the barbarians from the East."

Henry's memoir of his time in Algiers began:

> This is the story of a very successful military intelligence operation in the southern half of France in World War II. It was carried out by two Frenchmen in their twenties who worked with O.S.S. Jacques, the chief, was aided by Mario, his radio operator . . . until he was arrest [sic] by the Germans, built up and ran in a twelve months period one of the most effective Allied networks anywhere in France. Right up to the U.S. southern French landings in August 1944, its three hundred agents located and covered the nine German divisions in the southern half of France and sent in much other air and naval data. Their reports . . . were officially described by the British G-2 in

the Mediterranean Theatre as phenonally [*sic*] accurate. The information. . . contributed more than all the rest of our O.S.S. sources combined.

Henry was a natural intelligence officer; he found the work "as fascinating an intellectual exercise as trying a lawsuit or playing chess, as intimately human as is the relationship between a doctor and a patient in crisis, or that of a man and woman in love. . . . The organizer's mistake can lead to his agents' torture, and to a fatherless home. Most staid bankers, successful accountants and full professors who have tasted its blood would drop their established lives in an instant for a chance to get back to it."

The OSS was divided into divisions with different functions. The brief of Special Operations (SO) was sabotage; Henry was in Secret Intelligence (SI), which trained and sent in undercover operatives to develop networks, gather information, and transmit it by short-wave radio. One of the OSS's highest priorities was to infiltrate "Fortress Europe" through southern France, in preparation for Allied invasions from the Mediterranean and Atlantic.

Henry's mandate was to gather military information in a region that stretched from the Spanish to the Italian borders, and as far north as Vichy. When he arrived, in February 1943, he did not have a single agent or radio operator, or any means to insert them into southern France by air, ship, or submarine. With the pressure to establish networks to report on German troop movements before the Normandy invasion, the OSS was missing another crucial ingredient for success: cooperation from the Allied espionage services, which were not disposed to work with each other.

It was in these delicate negotiations that James Hyde's expatriate life and passion for education paid off: He had raised his son to be trilingual, bicultural, and well established in the realms of society that fed the European intelligence services, which were dominated by men whose last names were hyphenated, or began with a "de." As Henry said, "I had not lived in France for twenty years and married a good French girl for nothing," and he used his contacts and background to develop relationships in the British and French services. As one historian of the OSS remarked, "Like most *boulevardiers,* [Henry] seemed to know everyone who counted, and everyone who counted seemed to know him."[13] Soon he and one of his top British spy contacts were listening to the Edith Piaf records Henry had brought over, gossiping about French ballad singers and house parties before the war, and drinking each other's health with the Englishman's precious cache of wine and brandy. "The fact that I had happened to go to school and college in England, during a youth spent in France," Henry wrote, "helped a great deal to establish a common ground of understanding and mutual confidence with [the] English officers." And, as his British friend acknowledged, "when working with Frenchmen of standing, living well established a bond and good wines warmed the cockles of their hearts, and . . . these and other intangibles gave an intelligence service the last vital touch of class and weight in their eyes."

It was well into the spring, after pursuing a series of dead-end leads, that Henry finally met his first agent, Jacques de Rocquefort. Henry recognized in Jacques "the quick graceful manner of moving that made me see that he was a product of la Vieille France with a possible touch of the swagger of a one-time cavalry officer." Yet Jacques was physically a kind of "Everyman," who would blend in easily. It was one of Henry's talents to recognize the nuances that would make a good spy; another was his ability to inspire trust in men he was sending into danger. He and Jacques found each other sympathetic, and over drinks and dinner, they talked about the philosophy of André Gide, and the adventures of Saint Exupéry, the pioneer aviator and author of *The Little Prince.* Jacques lived with his wife and children in the Algiers suburbs; he had helped the Allies prepare for the North African landing and was eager to work as a spy. He was a native of Lyon, a hub of Henry's territory, where his contacts with important industrialist families and the political establishment—his wife's great-uncle, Edouard Herriot, had been the premier of France—would be important in setting up a network. Jacques also had a significant contact in a Jesuit priest who ran a private school that he had attended. A core group of alumni treated the school as a kind of club, dropping in for dinner, and to play bridge and billiards. When Jacques was last in Lyon, the priest had given him a copy of a Resistance pamphlet, which he reprinted and distributed in Algiers. There were also three doctors in Jacques's wife's family who had cars and fuel, and could be helpful if someone had to be treated secretly.

Jacques was ready to sign on, but Henry needed to find him a radio operator, and it was even more difficult to find qualified radiomen. When Henry met Mario Clement, Mario's conditions for working for the OSS were that Henry would introduce him to American radio manufacturers after the war so he could represent them in the store he wanted to buy in Toulon; and that his pay go to his mistress in Algiers.

Algiers was not a battleground, but it was a theater of war; and when Henry made his way home from the hectic, informal parties that went on night after night, he watched the searchlights and red and white tracer bullets, and listened to the antiaircraft guns in the hills, and the German planes coming in. One night, as he stood on his balcony, an explosion resounded from the harbor and he heard a tremendous crash. His house shook, the windows shattered, and he dropped to the floor until the bombardment was over. But the greatest peril in Henry's mission was not that he might be wounded, captured, or killed; it was that he would send others to their deaths. Talking to operatives who had been in the field, he began to understand "the relentless loneliness of an agent's life and his constant fear of apprehension and torture, even when things are going well." One man "told me of his horror at remembering suddenly in the middle of the night that it was his duty to try and kill himself if he were caught, lest he be beaten into giving the others away, and his doubts about bringing himself to do so." Henry already understood loneliness; his boarding school experiences had prepared him for what he called the cardinal rule of espionage: "Security is symbolized by the figure '1' and no one needs to know any more than is required to do his own particular job."

Romance was a natural by-product of the charged atmosphere of wartime Algiers, and by some accounts, Henry and Ann Willets, one of the OSS secretaries, fell in love. Ann was an American socialite, a graduate of Miss Porter's School in Farmington, Connecticut, who had studied at the University of Florence and Columbia University. After the war, she became a novelist; her second book, *Sting of Glory*, published in 1954, takes place at the Algiers station, and her characters are modeled on the OSS team. Henry appears as the spymaster Bion Hargreaves, whom she introduces when her character, a young woman named Harrison Carter, is lying on a cot at the OSS villa, trying to nap. Bion comes in from the rain, tosses his damp raincoat over her, and takes hold of one of her ankles. He sits in a chair and tells her that one of his agents has just committed suicide by shooting himself after a practice parachute jump. As she describes Bion,

> He has a big pale face and . . . his eyes have no color and are always weary unless he's excited over one of his missions, his acts of creation. Then they are filled with a glistening nervous light. . . . He lives with some Frenchwoman in town but he hasn't warmth for anything but the work. That's all he thinks about, talks about and expects everyone else to feel the same way. He'd sell his grandmother for a good agent, good intelligence. He can be charming when he wants to be; most of the times he doesn't want to. Most of the time he's malicious and takes joy in it.[14]

Bion puts his hands over his eyes and asks Harrison why the agent didn't talk to him about his terror.

> "He was afraid of shame. . . . You make it sound like some sort of glory—a glory for aristocrats and gentlemen. He felt caught between the shame and the fear." . . .
> "How do you know so much, Harrison?" he asks.
> "I've watched you for a long time, now," she says. As she turns to look at him, he says sadly, "Ah, pretty, pretty. So much wasted prettiness."[15]

Ann and Henry worked in the closest proximity in Algiers. In one photograph taken at the villa, she can be glimpsed, brown-haired and pretty, peering curiously around a partition next to her desk. Henry sits at a table a few feet away. He has crossed one leg jauntily over the other, an ankle on his knee. His jacket is part of a pinstriped suit; his rumpled trousers do not match the jacket; his shirt is dark, probably blue, and buttoned at the neck, without a tie. His eyes are bright and lively, and he looks big, strong, and cocky. He half smiles, with a cigarette dangling out of one corner of his mouth, and a bottle of whiskey or wine and a couple of paper cups on the table in front of him. For all James Hyde's elegance, he probably never looked as relaxed or happy as his son did in that photograph.

Ann Willets indicated that Henry fantasized about being undercover. "You realize, don't you," her character said, "that secretly Bion is living in a cellar sending radio messages out to the joes [operatives] while the bombs drop overhead? . . . That's the dream he hugs to himself when he goes to bed at night."[16]

Later in the book, her character confides to one of the agents, "He gets himself all stirred up so that he feels creative but afterwards he won't be satisfied with anything he has done. . . . He thinks he has to live irregularly and think irregularly in order to fit into an irregular business. He's afraid of being normal. . . . He's in love with a way of life."[17]

Henry's first agents, Jacques and Mario, completed their twelve-week training and were prepared to leave to launch Henry's Operation Penny Farthing, but the OSS did not have its own aircraft for an airdrop; the U.S. Army wouldn't let him use one of their planes; and the British aircraft were committed. Henry had arranged for the French to give the men a berth on a French submarine, but the vessel was otherwise engaged.[18] Once again, he used his charm and his contacts.

One of the British intelligence services in Algiers was headed by Col. A. Douglas Dodds-Parker, a graduate of an English public school and the University of Oxford, and an officer in the elite Grenadier Guards. He was the sort of Englishman Henry had been to school with, and he even had an American wife. While Dodds-Parker was sympathetic with Henry's dilemma, all his planes were scheduled for other missions. Instead, he overrode regulations, and arranged priority air travel on an American transport plane headed for Prestwick, Scotland, supplying Henry and the agents with British uniforms and papers that described them as "British secret personnel returning to England on urgent business." Henry, Jacques, and Mario began their trip on June 28, 1943. Their goal was to reach England in time for "the July moon," the brief window for agent landings, when there was enough light to see the ground. If the weather was not favorable, the agents would have to wait a month.

Henry brought along his American passport so that one of them would have legitimate papers; he doubted that they would be able to pass themselves off as British soldiers at Scottish airport security. They were detained in Scotland for three days. Henry played golf and the British and Americans sorted out their diplomatic breach. Then they were flown to London, their status unclear. Henry was enjoying his secret mission; one night he turned up at the Berkeley Hotel "wearing a trench-coat and claiming to be an officer in the U.S. Marine Corps in London for a few hours," according to a Cambridge friend who recalled, "After an unsuccessful but alas *not* inaudible invitation to me to 'dump the dame so we can have a good talk,' you vanished again."

Henry talked his way out of trouble when he was bustled over to the headquarters of the Special Intelligence Services near the Houses of Parliament, and instructed to forget where he had been. He was interviewed by SIS deputy chief Sir Claude Dansey. The session had the chilly precision of university dons quizzing a doctoral candidate, but Dansey warmed up when Henry mentioned his friend, Ted Ryan, also serving in the OSS in North Africa. Dansey had once worked for Thomas Fortune Ryan in British West Africa, and admired him. Henry did not mention that Ryan had bought his father's Equitable shares, and evidently Henry and Ted never discussed their fathers' business dealings. Charles Evans Hughes's grandson, Stuart Hughes, was also in the OSS in Algiers with Henry. They, too, were friends, who avoided the subject of the unhappy connection between Hughes's triumph and James Hyde's disgrace.[19]

At last Dansey agreed that the agents could be dropped into France from a British plane. On July 16, they left London for an estate in the country that was on loan to the government. Along with some thirty other agents who were to be dropped behind enemy lines that night, they ate a farewell steak dinner. The colonel in charge made a short speech, a young French agent stood to sing *La Marseillaise*, and everyone in the dining room pushed back their chairs and joined in. Henry wrote that was "as moving as anything else that evening because it was so badly sung and brought tears to all the French eyes."

In the last hour after dinner, Henry checked his agents' clothes and removed an overlooked sixpence and a pack of English matches that could have given them away if they were caught and interrogated. "From then on," he wrote, "it was agreed that I and later on the dispatcher would dole out and light cigarettes for them." Out at the airfield, the planes were lined up in the gathering dark, and just before nine, the men suited up and boarded the plane. Henry waved them off from the blacked-out field.

They were back at dawn. As they flew in low over the place the French resistance had designated for the drop, the pilot saw the signal lights on the ground abruptly go out. The Germans had arrived in time to arrest the reception committee, but they missed the OSS agents, who never landed. Henry's first team did not make it into France until the next month, during the August moon.

By the time the Allies landed in southern France a year later, Henry had established "one of the most effective Allied networks anywhere in France," as he would later write. A map in *The Overseas Targets War Report of the OSS*,[20] classified as top secret until 1975, shows that as of August 15, 1944, OSS Special Intelligence, Algiers had set up seventeen radio stations in chains from the Spanish border on the west to Italy on the east, and as far north as Clermont-Ferrand, only miles from Vichy.

At the end of *Sting of Glory*, Ann Willets writes that five days after southern France was liberated, Harrison and Bion met at another villa, in Marseilles, a city "wrecked and wild [with] . . . a burned-out beauty of late summer." Bion's best operative had been tortured and killed, and he had lost others, and despite his success, he was exhausted and sick with guilt. In the garden of the villa, he and Harrison sat at a glassed-in bar, and he laid his head on his folded arms. She looked at him and thought that he would "never again be as eager or as hopeful with his enthusiasms."

The fictional Harrison was right about that, but Algiers was a turning point for Henry in other ways as well. More than fifty years later, when both men were eighty years old, Henry's Cambridge friend, John Colville, who had been one of the brilliant team on Churchill's wartime staff, wrote him, "for all your anxieties about your agents, the hours and nights of waiting for their radio contacts, I believe it was those months which, perhaps for the first time relieved you of any conceivable concern about whether you belonged in the United States or in France. You were the right man in the right place—bang in the middle."[21]

After the war, Henry was named a delegate to the Nuremberg Trials, and his wife, Mimi, joined him in Berne. She became pregnant there with the first of their two daughters, and they moved back to New York, where Henry formed his own law firm, specializing in international law. Henry and Mimi were divorced when their daughters were young. As a lawyer, Henry kept his OSS ties. Among his clients were many of his wartime comrades, among them the authors Irwin Shaw, Peter Viertel, and James Jones, whose novel *From Here to Eternity* was a touchstone of the passions of war.

All his life, Henry Hyde looked back with pride and nostalgia on an experience that nothing could ever approach for its glory; perhaps that was the sting Ann Willets wrote about. After the war, he was awarded the Bronze Star with oak leaf cluster by the U.S. government; and the French presented him with the *Croix de Guerre* with *Etoile d'Argent*. When he became an *Officier de la Légion d'Honneur*, he followed the example his father had set and had the little red ribbon sewn into the buttonhole of his suits so he could wear it every day. The father who disappointed him, and whose extravagance made him angry whenever he spoke of him, had trained Henry well. James Hyde had flawlessly prepared his son for the role of the international gentleman spy, an outsider with the knowledge and style of the born insider.

Denouements

James Hyde, undated photograph.

James never lost his dramatic flair or his extraordinary good looks. In the 1950s, he still kept a carriage in New York. *(Courtesy Lorna Hyde Graev)*

Consequences

After the Armstrong Investigation, a few people were sued, although mostly to insignificant effect—lawsuits involving James Hyde were among the reasons he did not return to the United States in the first few years. Yet, despite the embarrassment and inconvenience of the Equitable crisis, there were no dramatic displays of high-ranking executives being led off in handcuffs, no show trials, none of the companies involved was fined—and no one went to jail. Even those who broke the New York State law against selling stocks to companies on whose boards they sat, including Jacob Schiff, James Hyde and Geroge Perkins, or those who suborned government officials, most notably E. H. Harriman, were not prosecuted. The top insurance executives fared the worst. By the end of the Armstrong Investigation, the presidents of the Equitable, New York Life, and the Mutual had all been replaced, while others lost jobs, money, face, and health. As for the financiers and railroad men involved in the scandal, all of them went on to become richer and more powerful.

Equitable Officers

JAMES HAZEN HYDE lived in the Savoy-Plaza Hotel on Fifth Avenue for the rest of his life. He never retrieved the Paris house he had put in his last wife's name; and, much against his son Henry's wishes, he sold l'Ermitage in 1950.

After the war, he traveled again, but mostly in the United States, visiting local chapters of the Fédération de l'Alliance Française, the offshoot of the Alliance Française he founded in 1902. He was often in Cambridge after Harvard appointed him a member of the Romance Languages and Literatures Visiting Committee. One of his granddaughters, Isabel Hyde Jasinowski, recalls that when she and her sister, Lorna, went to see their grandfather, their mother reminded them that if he asked the little girls where they planned to go to college, they should be sure to say "Radcliffe." In the summer of 1959, when Hyde was eighty-three, he went to Saratoga Springs, the summer resort his parents favored, and there he fell dangerously ill. His son, Henry, came up to be with him, conferring with doctors who said they expected he would last hours, or days, at the most. But Hyde held on for a week, until July 26, 1959. He died as the Equitable was celebrating the one-hundredth anniversary of its founding. Henry believed that his father stayed alive that extra week through sheer force of will. James Hyde had always liked the grand gesture.

JAMES W. ALEXANDER returned from his long round-the-world voyage in the spring of 1909, and moved in with his son, Henry Martyn. The *New York Times* considered his arrival enough of an event to publish an interview, in which JWA spouted an enthusiastic travelogue. He said he had "no immediate business plans," but that he spent two hours a day, from eleven in the morning until one, at Henry Martyn's office "superintending his personal estate." In December 1909, Alexander sold his large limestone house at 4 East Sixty-fourth Street; the price was published as $400,000. It took him a while to return to his clubs—he was a past president of the Princeton and University Clubs, and a member of the Metropolitan and Century Clubs—as he was afraid he might be snubbed by his old friends, but when he did stop by, he was welcomed. He and his wife Elizabeth were estranged, and JWA was at Henry Martyn's house in Tuxedo Park when he died, on September 21, 1915. He left an estate of $243,042, of which $121,370 was in the form of life insurance.[1] After his death, Elizabeth Alexander unsuccessfully sued the Equitable for the pension she had been promised, as part of the same flawed transaction Henry had made for Annie. Elizabeth was described during that episode by an Equitable director as "that harridan." He added that "her husband loathed her," and that she "persecuted" him.[2]

GAGE TARBELL left the Equitable in 1907 to join a real estate development company. His farewell dinner was held at the Hotel Knickerbocker on March 2, 1907. In his speech to the agents, he compared his new career to the old one: "Heretofore I have been teaching you as best I could how to provide for the home after the head of it had been taken away. I presume it is likely that I shall be bending at least some of my energies in the future in trying to show people the necessity of their providing a suitable home for their families while they are still living . . . the good work is already started and moving on, I am glad to tell you that they report sales of 31 lots to-day." In parting, he said that the "worthy and true" friendships he had formed among the agents, "will remain not for a day but for all time," echoing the Equitable's motto. Tarbell remained an Equitable director until 1936.

THOMAS JORDAN, the former Equitable treasurer who disappeared during the Armstrong Investigation and was unavailable to explain the $685,000 account that became known as "the yellow dog fund," dropped dead on a subway platform on July 11, 1909. According to an account in the *New York Times*, in 1905, Jordan had "fled from the state, and officially was not known to be alive or dead until nearly two years later." He turned up in Little Rock, Arkansas; moved on to Atlanta; and was understood to be in New Jersey for the next two years, during which time he sometimes came to New York "under cover." At last, he voluntarily presented himself to the attorney general, was indicted by a grand jury on nineteen counts involving "perjury and forgery in connection with the Equitable's affairs," and pled not guilty. The most serious charges involved "loans" falsely entered on the Equitable books as having been made to employees of Kuhn, Loeb, which were meant to adjust the books "with a view to reducing the Equitable's actual bank balance in order to conceal the amount of policyholders' money lying idle in bank at a small rate of interest."[3] Jordan was scheduled for trial in criminal court in the fall of 1909, but his secrets died with him.

WILLIAM T. MCINTYRE was rarely mentioned in the correspondence between Annie and James after James moved to Paris, and when he was, it was in the past tense.

THE WOMEN

ANNIE HYDE did not meet her daughter-in-law, Marthe, or her grandson, Henry B. Hyde, who was born in 1915. She died in 1922. Her housekeeper, Camille Everard, was with her until the end.

MARTHE HYDE and James never overcame their dislike of each other. She died of cancer in New York in 1944. Their son, Henry, was allowed to leave his post in Algiers for the dangerous trip across the wartime Atlantic to say good-bye to his mother.

MARTHE DERVAUX THOM HYDE was living in New York in 1948 when she, too, died of cancer.

ELLA WALKER MATUSCHKA HYDE, PRINCESS DELLA TORRE E TASSO, had the most interesting life of Hyde's three wives. During World War II, the Nazis requisitioned her Villa Serbelloni in Italy, and she was rowed across Lake Bellagio, where smugglers led her across mountainous terrain to the Swiss border. Her "shoes were worn to threads" when she arrived and, exhausted, was taken to a clinic. There, she lived in a single room for the rest of the war, sharing the income from her trust in the United States with members of her husband's family in Italy. She had adopted her first husband's niece when the girl's parents died, and one of her stepgrandchildren, Princess Diane de Bourbon Parme, lived with her for much of the princess's childhood. Princess Della Torre e Tasso studied ancient Greek and European art, and her collection included paintings by Tiepolo, Guardi, and Cranach, a bust attributed to Leonardo da Vinci, and four Fragonard panels. She and Hyde died the same year, 1959. She left an estate of $10 million: $2 million and her Italian villa went to the Rockefeller Foundation, and the balance to her adopted niece.

MARY HYDE RIPLEY remarried after Sidney died. Her second husband, Charles Scott, was a Hong Kong–based British banker, whom she met on a cruise. According to family lore, her mother, Annie, who had become more snobbish as she grew older, remarked, "Imagine marrying a Hong Kong bank clerk and changing your name to Scott when it has been Ripley." Mary was not a warm mother. She was too busy with her social schedule to attend either of her sons' weddings, and was often in France and England, where she was presented at court.

ANNAH RIPLEY, COUNTESS DE VIELCASTEL, attended the scholarly Brearley School for girls in New York. She wanted to go on to college, but her mother, Mary, was eager for her to make a European marriage, and she married Pierre Count de Vielcastel, and they had three children. During World War II, the Germans took over their house in Normandy and moved Annah into the servants' quarters. Her French was so flawless that they did not suspect she was American, or a spy. When she took baskets of eggs into the nearby town to sell, she hid notes among the eggs, containing information on what she had gathered from eavesdropping on the Germans who occupied her house.

ALICE ROOSEVELT LONGWORTH lived to be the doyenne of Washington and died in her nineties.

CHARLOTTE WARREN married the New York lawyer William Greenough, and they continued to spend their summers in Newport, where Charlotte was a director of the Redwood Library. She devoted herself to finding and returning books that had been brought from England in 1747 for the library's first collection. Her own interest was in French books and manuscripts, and she built one of the most extensive collections in the United States. The Greenoughs had one child, a daughter, Beatrice, in whom the Warren tendency toward eccentricity was pronounced. When she was married to her third or fourth husband, Charlotte became the legal guardian of Beatrice's only child, Gabrielle Ladd. A Wellesley College classmate described Gabrielle as

> tall, and thin, with wheat-colored hair and eyes like deep water. Her shoulders shook when she laughed, and she'd run her fingers through her . . . hair. Her mind darted, like a firefly, making its own light. She loved air, and space, oceans, ledges, boats, plants, trees, skies, horses, the Rocky Mountains, all the moving, living parts of the world. And people. There was nothing public about her. She wrote poetry, and she painted and in her poetry and her art there was no excess; only the clear words and colors mattered . . . Music always filled her rooms. . . . When she graduated in 1958, she was awarded the Wing Memorial Prize for Lyric Poetry. Three months after graduation she was married.[4]

Charlotte did not live to attend her granddaughter's wedding to Strafford Morss, a lieutenant in the navy, and the son of the president of the American Simplex Wire and Cable Company. Strafford was stationed at Norfolk, Virginia, when Gabrielle, twenty-three, went to visit her mother, who was ill in California. On January 18, 1960, the Capital Airlines plane on which she was returning from Los Angeles crashed in Virginia, and Gabrielle was killed. No one now living knows the story of her grandmother and James Hyde.

INSURANCE, WALL STREET, AND POLITICS

CHAUNCEY DEPEW wrote the official version of his life, *My Memories of Eighty Years*, in 1922, when he was eighty-eight. Most of the "memories" are of his encounters with great men and important events. Although Depew was active on the Equitable board for twenty-eight years, from 1877 until 1905, earned hundreds of thousands of dollars through his association with the company, and had been voluble about his close friendship with Henry Hyde, neither Henry nor James—nor the Equitable Life Assurance Society—appear in the book.

E. H. HARRIMAN died in 1909, after having, at last, persuaded Thomas Fortune Ryan to sell him a portion of the Equitable stock. The *New-York Herald* Paris edition estimated that he was worth $400 to $500 million, but soon adjusted the number down to $75 to $100 million. Harriman would never know that he probably accomplished one of his ambitions: beating J. P. Morgan, whose estate was worth some $80 million when he died in 1913.

CHARLES EVANS HUGHES was elected governor of New York in 1906, based on his strong showing as counsel to the Armstrong Investigation. He was appointed to the U.S. Supreme Court in 1910, and became the Republican nominee for president in 1916. He was nominated at the Republican National Convention by New York governor Charles Whitman (whose granddaughter-in-law, Christie Whitman, was the first woman governor of New Jersey). A distinctive element in Hughes's presidential campaign was that while he still served on the court, he refused to make any policy statements, so Whitman was forced to invent a platform for him. After Hughes was nominated, he resigned from the court, but lost the election to Woodrow Wilson. Hughes was appointed secretary of state in 1921, and later returned to the Supreme Court. He served as chief justice from 1930 to 1941, and was known for his efforts to blunt President Franklin Delano Roosevelt's New Deal programs.

JOHN A. McCALL, president of New York Life, was one of the Armstrong Investigation's victims. He was fifty-six, a vigorous witness, "large and dynamic, charming and self-assured." Yet, on February 18, 1906, he suddenly died. Before his death, he paid New York Life $235,000, funds the company had advanced to the agent/lobbyist Andrew Hamilton, who claimed to be too ill to return from Europe to testify at the investigation. McCall did not engage in transactions for his own benefit, as his estate indicated: he left $40,385.[5] New York Life is one of the few large insurance companies to remain a mutual.

RICHARD A. MCCURDY, president of the Mutual, and his son, Robert, both resigned in November 1905. McCurdy cited ill health as the reason he could no longer work. The Mutual was sued for $6 million in claims for improper use of policyholders' funds, and the officers were accused of self-enrichment. The suits were settled by 1909; the Mutual was required to pay $750,000, of which McCurdy personally repaid $250,000.⁶ McCurdy, who was seventy at the time of the Armstrong Investigation, lived until 1916. The Mutual Life, now Mutual of New York, is no longer one of the top three insurance companies in the nation. It is now not a mutual, but a public company, owned by its stockholders.

GEORGE W. PERKINS remained avid and ambitious, as a December 1909 cable to J. P. Morgan's son, Jack, indicated. It was in "top secret" code, and some of the highlights included: "We have concluded purchase of Guaranty Trust Co. . . . We have sold all the Steel Common of the Paris syndicate and closed the account . . . profits . . . average something over 90. Newspapers have commented most favorably on Senior's [J.P. Morgan's] purchase of Equitable stock. . . ." Jack Morgan's answer read, "Unless you feel it very desirable hope you will not buy the earth." Morgan appointed Perkins to the new voting trust of the Equitable in May 1910, and it is likely that he favored him to become the Equitable's president, but not strongly enough to return from Europe when the board voted—and chose another candidate. Perkins was no longer a partner of J. P. Morgan in 1911.⁷ After he left Morgan, Perkins became involved in Reform politics, where he was a cranky gadfly, but was never elected to public office.

THE INSTITUTIONS

THE ARMSTRONG LAWS were passed in 1906 by New York State. Under the tightened regulations, life insurance companies were forbidden to own common stock or make advances to agents, and were required to distribute surplus above 10 percent of assets to policyholders. The legislature also required that life insurers be mutualized, and that their directors be held accountable for such aspects of the business as salaries and investments. Certain products were banned, cutting deeply into the Equitable's profits; among the most stringent regulations was the cap applied to insurers who had more than $1 billion in insurance in force. Henceforth, they could only do $150 million of new business a year—the Equitable had sold three times that amount in 1904. The new regulations had such dramatically devastating potential that the insurance department extended the time for insurers to comply for many years.[8]

THE EQUITABLE LIFE ASSURANCE SOCIETY had sales of $307 million in 1904, bottomed out after the scandal at $73 million in 1907, when the sales force dropped from 10,000 to 2,800; then began to climb again. In 1909, 5,000 agents sold $100 million in policies. Mutualization was not yet in place in 1909, when Thomas Fortune Ryan finally conceded to E. H. Harriman's importuning and sold him a portion of his Equitable shares. J. P. Morgan, alarmed, persuaded Ryan, who was ill, to sell him the balance of his Equitable holdings. On Harriman's death in 1909, Morgan bought his shares as well, attaining the control of the Equitable many believed he had wanted all along.[9]

Until 1910, when the regulations were finally enforced, the Equitable continued to hold substantial National Bank of Commerce shares, which impacted one of Morgan's important positions: Along with James Stillman and George F. Baker, he controlled the bank. According to Equitable historian John Rousmaniere, "The trio and their banks [had] control over almost two-thirds of the bankers' balances on deposit in New York."[10]

Morgan agreed to fully mutualize the Equitable in 1910, and appointed George Perkins as one of the three trustees. The Equitable's mutualization became law in 1911, but it still had not been implemented in 1913. J. P. Morgan died that year, and when the majority shares came up for sale again Coleman du Pont bought them for $4.4 million. It was du Pont who had purchased the property at 120 Broadway after it was devastated by fire in 1912, and erected an office building as proportionally grand as Henry Hyde's original structure. (The building, only one block from the World Trade Center, was so well built that it survived the catastrophic events of September 11, 2001.) Du Pont made approximately $400,000 on his purchase of Morgan's stock in 1914, when the Equitable was mutualized, and he and the other shareholders were bought out.

A half century later, in the 1970s and 1980s, the reversal of the stringent regulations that prevented life insurance companies from engaging in certain kinds of financial activities was well under way. The Equitable's executives determined to reenter the investment business to a degree hardly imagined by pre–World War I financial leaders. In 1985 the Equitable bought Donaldson, Lufkin & Jenrette (DLJ), the first Wall Street money management and brokerage firm to go public; and two of its associated firms, one of which, Alliance Capital, managed $20 billion in assets. Under the existing laws, however, DLJ could not sell equities to the Equitable Life Assurance Society.

Two years after the DLJ acquisition, in October 1987, the stock market crashed. In 1988, commercial real estate, in which the Equitable was heavily invested, plunged. And in 1989 a situation comparable to the Equitable crisis of 1905 brought down the junk bond market when, in a widely publicized scandal, Michael Milken of Drexel Burnham Lambert was convicted of insider trading and served a prison sentence. The Equitable, overweighted with commercial real estate and junk bond commitments, found itself in trouble, and scrambled to fill its depleted coffers. Among the solutions under consideration were a merger with another major mutual life insurance company, and the sale of DLJ and Alliance Capital. The situation was so severe that the directors removed the company's president and CEO, and elected Richard H. Jenrette, one of the founders of DLJ, as chairman, president, and chief executive.

To raise the necessary funds, Jenrette set a demutualization process in motion, returning the company to stockholder ownership. The French insurance company, Groupe AXA, loaned the Equitable $1 billion, while Equitable worked out the terms of its public offering. Some 2.2 million policyholders were sent a 336-page demutualization plan; 900,000 voted and 92.3 percent of them approved the change. Certain classes of policyholders were issued shares in the Equitable and, on July 15, 1992, an additional 50 million shares were publicly offered in a new issue on the New York Stock Exchange. AXA's $1 billion loan was converted into 49 percent equity. Five years later, AXA bought in the remaining public shares and took the Equitable private again. To raise funds for the purchase, AXA sold its controlling interest in DLJ to Credit Suisse First Boston, a subsidiary of Credit Suisse Group in Switzerland.

KUHN, LOEB has been absorbed into the maw of Wall Street, merging with Lehman Brothers, which then joined with E.F. Hutton. American Express acquired the combined company, along with Shearson Hamill, and created a new entity, Shearson, Lehman. Eventually, Lehman was spun off and is again an independent firm.

J. P. MORGAN & COMPANY was required to separate its commercial and retail banking from its underwriting, bond and stock functions after the passage of the Glass-Steagall Banking Reform Act in 1933. Morgan Stanley & Co. was established in 1935 as the investment banking and securities arm, while J.P. Morgan & Co. retained the banking functions. Morgan merged with Guaranty Trust to form Morgan Guaranty, and then Morgan Guaranty Trust, which later became a subsidiary of J.P. Morgan and Company. Morgan Stanley and the brokerage firm Dean Witter, founded in 1924 in San Francisco, joined forces in 1997. With the repeal of Glass-Steagall, and diminished restrictions on crossovers between retail, commercial, and investment banking, J.P. Morgan and Chase Bank merged on January 1, 2001, and created a new entity, J.P. Morgan Chase.

THE TWENTY-FIRST CENTURY

The cycle of growth and restraint inexorably continues. Huge prosperity begets a "Wild West" mentality, leading to excess and abuse. Inevitably, a few overreachers emerge, and their blatantly unrestrained violations of basic morality elicit outrage. The perpetrators

are exposed to public censure, often punished, and the system is regulated—a version of closing the barn door after the cows have gotten
out to trample the garden. Usually, by the time new laws are in place,
the system has peaked and is on the way down, and the stiffer regulations are apt to accelerate the decline. That, of course, is exactly
what happened to the major insurers after 1906.

A new cycle begins, as business scrambles to restore its profitabil-
ity. Eventually, it becomes clear that the system needs a boost. One
approach is to relax the enforcement of the rules, as the New York
State insurance department did during the transition period immediately following the passage of the Armstrong Laws of 1906. A more
drastic solution is to repeal the laws that were passed when the system was over-ebullient. The repeal of Glass-Steagall was just such a
case.

It is tempting to believe that if James Hazen Hyde were asked to
comment on the events of the past hundred years as they affected the
Equitable and Wall Street, he would remark, *"Plus ça change, plus
c'est la même chose."*

I first heard about James Hyde after I met his son, Henry B. Hyde, in 1969. I was on my honeymoon—we were coming back from a trip around the world—and a blizzard in New York rerouted our plane, bizarrely, to Niagara Falls. Henry was a successful international lawyer, en route to New York from London, where he had been been meeting with one of his film clients, the director John Huston. Henry recognized that we were in for a long layover, introduced himself as we were boarding a bus from the airport to a motel, and the three of us joined forces. We took the time to visit the Falls—I wish I still had that photograph—then spent three arduous but amusing days together making our way back to New York. Through Henry we met his daughters, Lorna and Isabel, who were about our age, and who also became our friends. Although Henry was the generation of our parents, we asked him to stand as godfather to our son, Alex, when he was christened in the little beach community where we spent the summers.

We often visited Henry and his second wife, Liza, in their apartment in New York. Each time we passed through the foyer, we walked by a set of charming watercolors of coaching scenes, set against the dark green walls. But the foyer was softly lit and was just a passage to the living room. I never stopped to look at the pictures, and no one mentioned that the man on the box was Henry's father. Henry did not talk about James much. When he did, he made it clear that James had lived in dauphin-like splendor in a château in France, where—to Henry's dismay—*he spent everything*! That was not quite accurate, but the dissipated fortune was a fixation of Henry's, and it is true that James was a profligate spender and a difficult parent. What Henry did not say was that his father was one of the handsomest men of his era, among the most cultivated, and, for one battering year, the most controversial. I never once heard him mention the Hyde Ball.

Forty years after James Hyde's death, after Henry, too, had died, Henry's daughter, Lorna Graev, was moving, and unearthed some of her grandfather's memorabilia. I was taken by a pencil drawing of James and the scrapbooks she was having rebound, and I became increasingly curious about the young dandy who got himself in such trouble for giving a ball. One day, the title *After the Ball* popped into my mind, and something fell into place that sounded like a book. That was two years before the first financial scandals of the twenty-first century began to make headlines that were astonishingly like the stories I was reading in the 1905 newspapers.

The answers to the legal and accounting questions that arose from the fight for the Equitable remained murky, even after the most intense investigation. Charles Evans Hughes admitted that sometimes he, too, found himself unable to trace the financial manipulations, which were designed to confuse and obfuscate. Researching this book took a year longer than I expected, as I tried to follow the money trail. What became clear was that the details were less important than the simple fact that the system was rigged; and that the same temptations and techniques are still at work, despite the subsequent legislation, oversight agencies, and journalistic investigations. It is not necessary to know precisely what happened in 2002 at Enron, Worldcom, and other companies; at the auction houses Sotheby's and Christie's in the 1990s; and at Drexel Burnham in the 1980s to recognize that money moves in certain patterns, or that corporate crooks can convince themselves that they are acting in the interests of their shareholders. The most substantial difference between the shell games of one hundred years ago and those that are still being played is that, for the most part, the maneuvers were legal in 1905 and are criminal today. One reason that we can prosecute the corporate cheaters now is that they were exposed at the time of the Equitable crisis. While the game continues, it is some comfort to consider that, just as a river may overrun its beds or be diverted, but still runs toward the sea, money streams toward the largest body of water, and there it is mixed with all the rest and then recycled.

Endnotes

The Hyde Ball and the events that followed have often been described with more enthusiasm than accuracy. I have attempted to correct errors by consulting contemporary newspapers and primary sources, comparing accounts, and sorting through the differences to find the truth. When I am not sure that the sources are accurate, I often write, "it was said that," "as it was described," or "according to rumors."

In addition to primary sources, I relied on the meticulously researched two-volume official history of the Equitable by the late R. Carlyle Buley, and the excellent more recent history by John Rousmaniere. Neither of these authors ever let me down. After the first citation, those sources are referred to in the notes as "Buley" or "Rousmaniere." The New York legislature's 1905 investigation of the insurance industry is referred to as "Armstrong," after the senator who presided. Other abbreviations: AXA: AXA Financial Archives; HBS: Harvard Business School Baker Library; NYHS: New-York Historical Society. NYT: *New York Times*.

Prologue

1. *Bulfinch's Mythology*, p. 873.
2. Tifft and Jones, *The Trust*, pp. 75–76.
3. Matthew Josephson's *The Robber Barons: The Great American Capi-

talists was originally published in 1934. John Steele Gordon, in the *New York Times Book Review*, Sunday, 2 June 2002, describes Joseph-son's book as "tendentious and intellectually dishonest," and remarks that using it as a source is "inexcusable." I agree. Gordon's most recent book is *A Thread Across the Ocean: The Heroic Story of the Trans-atlantic Cable.*

4. "Aftermath of the Bradley Martin Ball, Humors and Oddities," *New York World*, 14 February 1897.

5. Dunlop, *Gilded City, Scandal and Sensation in Turn-of-the-Century New York*, pp. 4–6.

6. Alex Kuscinski, *New York Times*, Sunday, 22 September 2002.

7. It was never certain that Morgan was a contender for control of the Equitable; however, he did buy the majority shares in 1909.

8. Rousmaniere, *The Life and Times of the Equitable*, p. 75.

9. Ibid.

10. Ibid, p. 79. In 1885, the amount raised nationally through all corporate bond sales was only $250 million, but between 1898 and 1905, the Equitable alone bought $200 million in corporate bonds.

11. *New-York American*, 29 December 1905, quoted in Buley, *The Equi-table Life Assurance Society of the United States 1859–1964*, pp. 696–97.

Chapter One
A DEATH: HENRY, 1899

1. Logan, "Building for Glory." *The New Yorker*, 21 October 1961.

2. Buley, p. 195.

3. Logan, *The New Yorker*, 21 October, 1961.

4. *The World*, 3 May 1899, p. 3.

5. Logan, "Building for Glory," *The New Yorker*, 21 October 1961.

6. Stern, Gilmartin and, Massengale, *New York 1900*, p. 145.

7. Buley, pp. 110–11.

8. The sculpture group did not wear well and was removed prior to Henry Hyde's death in 1899.

9. The house was not, as legend claims, swapped by Mrs. Plant in exchange for perfectly matched pearls from Cartier. The Plants did not own the house; they were tenants of William Henry Vanderbilt. He resisted the incursion of commercial establishments on "his" stretch of Fifth Avenue, but when the Plants moved out, he realized that he would not be able to keep the row strictly residential, and reluctantly leased the house to the jeweler. From a conversation with John Foreman, 2002.

10. Foreman and Stimson, *The Vanderbilts and the Gilded Age*, pp. 64ff.
11. Dr. Van Dyke was the minister of the Brick Presbyterian Church; the Fifth Avenue Presbyterian was temporarily without a minister.
12. *New York Press*, 4 May 1899, p. 3.
13. HBS, HBH to JHH, 21 September 1894. Case I, subgroup James H. Hyde.
14. Rousmaniere, p. 76.
15. Ibid., p. 61.
18. Ibid., p. 67.

Chapter Two
A LIFE: HENRY, 1859–1899

1. Buley, p. 293.
2. Ibid., p. xxviii, introductory quotation.
3. Trachtenberg, *The Incorporation of America: Culture and Society in the Gilded Age*, p. 6.
4. Buley, p. 67.
5. From undated pamphlet entitled "Truth in a Nutshell," AXA
6. Ibid.
7. Annie was born Anna Truesdell. Her father, Capt. Martin H. Truesdell, died in 1849 when she was four. He commanded a Hudson River twin -smokestack steamer, *South America*, and a portrait of him with the ship in the background was passed along to Annie, and then to James. By then Captain Truesdell had been so thoroughly forgotten that James sent a photograph of the painting to the New-York Historical Society to ask if they could identify the subject. Annie's mother, Jane, married Simeon Fitch, who owned a bluestone business, and a canal boat, sloop, and steamer company that transported freight on the Erie Canal and the Hudson River. Simeon adopted Annie, and she changed her name to Fitch. From a letter from JHH to the New-York Historical Society, 7 March 1950, courtesy of Lorna Hyde Graev.
8. Buley, pp. 181–86.
9. Ibid., p 131.
10. Ibid., p. 165, from the *Insurance Herald*, VI (1876), November 1.
11. Buley, p. 167, from the *Insurance Herald*, VI (1877), April.
12. From July 1905 newspaper reports on James Alexander's illness.
13. Buley, p. 197.
14. Ibid., p. 509.
15. *New York Times*, 15 October 1885, p. 4.
16. Buley, pp. 309–311.
17. *New York Times*, 25 February 1905, p. 9.

18. Geisst, *Wall Street: A History*, p. 111.

19. Rousmaniere, pp. 73–74.

20. Ibid., p. 85.

21. McCash, *The Jekyll Island Cottage Colony*, p. 1.

22. Buley, p. 509.

23. Ibid.

24. McCash, p. 79.

25. Ibid., p. 72.

Chapter Three
JAMES, 1876–1899

1. Buley, p. 511. Unless otherwise cited, quotations and specific information about this stage of James Hyde's life are from Buley, pp. 511–29.

2. Both quotations from George R. Leighton, "The Wall Street Violet," *Harper's Bazaar*, September 1951.

3. Strouse, *Morgan: American Financier*, p. 82.

4. Armstrong, Testimony of James H. Hyde, 2890–2891.

5. Buley, pp. 547–48, from James Hyde's address at fortieth-anniversary celebrations, summer 1899.

Chapter Four
THE FIRST MENTOR: JAMES ALEXANDER

1. Logan, "Building for Glory," *The New Yorker*, p. 152.

2. Armstrong, Testimony of James H. Hyde, 2890–91.

3. Speech by James W. Alexander, 1902. AXA.

4. Buley, p. 357.

5. Ibid.

6. Ibid., p. 516.

7. Details of the celebration from Buley, pp. 541–48.

8. From *The Proceedings at the Convention to Commemorate the Fortieth Anniversary of the Equitable Life Assurance Society of the United States*, New York, 1899. AXA.

9. Ibid.

Part II
THE RICHEST YOUNG MAN IN NEW YORK

1. Quoted in Martin Feldheim introduction, p. x, *The Gilded Age: A Tale of Today*, by Mark Twain and Charles Dudley Warner.

2. Krugman, "The Class Wars, Part I, "For Richer: How the permissive capitalism of the boom destroyed American equality." *New York Times Magazine*, 20 October 2002, pp. 62ff. Krugman adds, "Claims that

we've entered a second Gilded Age aren't exaggerated. . . . In 1998 . . . the 13,000 richest families in America had . . . incomes 300 times that of average families.

Chapter Five
THE GILDED AGE

1. Geist, *Wall Street, A History*, p. 19.
2. Ibid., p. 5.
3. Foreman and Stimson, *The Vanderbilts and the Gilded Age*, pp. 270–303.
4. Ibid., p 82. Shelburne is now a museum. In late 2001, it announced a staff cutback for purposes of economy.)
5. Patterson, *The First Four Hundred*, pp. 134–36.
6. Klein, *The Life and Legend of E. H. Harriman*, p. 97.
7. Amory, *The Last Resorts*, p. 90.
8. *Town Topics*, 10 March 1904.
9. Wecter, *The Saga of American Society: A Record of Social Aspiration, 1607–1937*, p. 374.

Chapter Six
A BACHELOR ABROAD, 1899

1. Craig, *Edith Wharton, A House Full of Rooms: Architecture, Interiors, and Gardens*, p. 134.
2. From *The Journal*, Lincoln, Nebraska, May 26, 1895, quoted in *Maverick in Mauve, the Diary of a Romantic Age*, by Florence Adele Sloane with Commentary by Louis Auchincloss.
3. Brandon, *The Dollar Princesses, Sagas of Upward Nobility*, pp. 88–90. The description of the de Castellane party may have been exaggerated, as party descriptions often were, but the atmosphere and sense of extravagance were accurate.
4. New-York Historical Society, folder Castellane.
5. Craig, *Edith Wharton, A House Full of Rooms*, p. 138.
6. Balsan, *The Glitter and the Gold*.
7. Buley, p. 485, from a letter from Henry Hyde to James Alexander, July 16, 1897.
8. Ibid., pp. 547-548.
9. Howlett, "Coaching in France with James H. Hyde," *The Official Horse Show Blue Book*, undated. Courtesy of Lorna Hyde Graev.
10. Richard Jay Hutto, conversation with the author, July 2002.
11. James H. Hyde, "The Charm of the Road," *Harper's Monthly*, May 1902, pp. 914–19.

12. In the 1905 fracas, Alfred Vanderbilt resigned from the Equitable board, but Bradish Johnson remained a director until 1918, and R.T. Wilson until 1919, long after James had left the company and moved to France. Alfred Gwynne Vanderbilt's first wife, Elsie French, divorced him in 1908, charging adultery on his private railway car with Agnes O'Brien Ruiz, the wife of the Cuban attaché in Washington. Alfred's former valet testified against him, and Elsie was awarded $10 million and custody of their son, William Henry Vanderbilt III. Mrs. Ruiz was divorced by her husband and later committed suicide in a London hotel. Alfred's second wife, Margaret Emerson McKim, was the heiress to the Bromo Seltzer fortune; she was married to a doctor who threatened to sue Alfred for alienation of his wife's affections, but they settled out of court. Vanderbilt's interest in horses continued throughout his life. In 1909, he rescued the National Horse Show by financing it, and was elected its president. Morris Howlett wrote in the *Horse Show Blue Book*, "More ribbons fell to Mr. Vanderbilt than to any exhibitor in the show ring." Alfred drowned when the Germans sank the *Lusitania,* and he gave his lifejacket to a mother with a baby. One of his sons with Margaret, Alfred Vanderbilt II, born in 1912, founded Pimlico racetrack outside of Baltimore. It was there that the famed horse Seabiscuit ran.

Chapter Seven
GAGE TARBELL: NEW YEAR'S EVE, 1899

1. Tarbell, "The Autobiography of a Life Assurance Agent," *Everybody's Magazine*, March 1903.
2. Ibid.
3. Ibid.
4. *Atlanta Constitution*, 26 March 1899.
5. Buley, 575, from John A. Garraty, *Right-Hand Man: The Life of George W. Perkins* New York, 1957, p. 45.
6. Strouse, *Morgan*, pp. 409–10.
7. Ibid., p. 546.
8. *The Pacific Underwriter,* 10 February 1900.
9. *New York World*, 1 January 1900, p. 1.
10. *New York Times*, 1 January 1900, p. 2.
11. Ibid.
12. Ibid.
13. *The Insurance Post*, 18 January 1901.

Chapter Eight
OF TRUSTS AND ESTATES

1. Buley, p. 210.

2. Francis Hendricks, *Preliminary Report on the Investigation into the Management of the Equitable Life Assurance Society of the United States, made to the Governor of the State of New York by the Superintendant of Insurance, as of 21 June 1905*, p. 7.

3. Buley, pp. 209–11.

4. *The World's Work*, March 1906, p. 7322.

5. *Picture Story of the Holly, Colorado Irrigated Country* (Omaha, Neb.: Payne Investment Co., n.d,). AXA.

6. Buley, p. 730.

7. As George Kennan explained in *E. H. Harriman, A Biography*, a book commissioned by Harriman's widow and published in 1922, "Control of any great insurance company carried with it control of a vast amount of money, and there are many ways in which such a corporation can be 'milked' . . . without actual criminality or flagrant dishonesty. Its officers . . . may establish a trust company, get possession of a large amount of its capital stock, and then favor it by depositing with it one, five or even ten million dollars of the insurance company's money at a very low rate of interest. If the trust company pays only two per cent for the use of such deposits, and then loans them out at five per cent, it obviously makes a large profit, and in this the officers of the insurance company share as stockholders of the trust company." pp. 407–408.

8. *New York World*, 11 June 1905.

9. Ibid.

10. $70 in cash, plus $140 at par for each $100 they owned at par.

11. Buley, p. 583, from chart of holdings as of 12 May 1905.

12. Hughes, *Report of the Joint Committee of the Senate and Assembly of the State of New York Appointed to Investigate the Affairs of Life Insurance Companies*, February 1906.

13. Armstrong, Testimony of T. C. F. Williamson, pp. 3128–29.

14. Klein, *The Life and Legend of E. H. Harriman*, p. 205.

15. Strouse, *Morgan*, p. 396. Banking was also having a growth spurt, with James Stillman's National City Bank increasing its capital from $4.2 million in 1895 to $15.5 million at the turn of the century.

16. Ibid, p. 543.

17. Buley, 573, from Darwin P. Kingsley, "The Financial Side of Life Insurance," *The Independent*, LII (1901), 19 December.

18. Kennan, *E. H. Harriman, A Biography*, p. 408.

19. Date approximate; according to Buley, "First notice in the Hyde papers of a syndicate operation by James H. Hyde is in a letter, Hyde to Alexander, 21 March 1902," footnote, p. 585.
20. New-York Historical Society, Hyde Collection, Depew folder.
21. Ibid., Depew folder.
22. Armstrong, Testimony of Chauncey M. Depew, pp. 3193–94.
23. Klein, *The Life and Legend of E. H. Harriman,* p. 32.
24. Ibid., p. 129.
25. Ibid., p. 329, quoted from Otto Kahn, "Edward Henry Harriman," in *Three Railroad Pioneers,* Stuart Bruchey, ed. (New York, 1981), p. 18.
26. Ibid., p. 115.
27. Ibid., p. 48.
28. Ibid., p. 112.
29. I am collaterally related to James J. Hill. My children are his great-grandchildren.

Chapter Nine
THE UNVEILING, MAY 1901

1. Malone, *James J. Hill, Building the Northwest,* p. 210.
2. *New York Times,* 3 May 1901, p. 5.
3. Ibid.
4. Strouse, *Morgan,* pp. 418–19.
5. Malone, *James J. Hill,* p. 215.
6. Armstrong, Testimony of E. H. Harriman, pp. 3104–5.
7. Ibid., pp. 3110–11.
8. *New York Times,* 3 May 1901, p. 9.
9. Klein, *The Life and Legend of E. H. Harriman,* p. 240, quoted from the *New York World,* 12 May 1901.

Chapter Ten
RIDING HIGH

1. Strouse, *Morgan,* pp. 409–11.
2. Ibid., p. 409.
3. Buley, p. 577.
4. Howlett,"Alfred Gwynne Vanderbilt. In Memoriam." from undated edition of *The Official Horse Show Blue Book.*
5. Ibid.
6. Undated clipping.
7. *Evening Journal,* 10 November 1901.
8. *Philadelphia News,* 1 November 1901.
9. Klein, *The Life and Legend of E. H. Harriman,* p. 332.

10. Buley, p. 632.

11. Armstrong, Testimony of James Hazen Hyde, p. 2269. Harriman continued to insist on secrecy, and, in the spring of 1905, as James Hyde testified, he "refused even to give the statement of the pool or those signing it to the superintendent of insurance." In fact, Hyde told Charles Evans Hughes, "Mr. Hendricks [the superintendent] clamored with me to clamor with Mr. Harriman for it." Neither of them was able to budge Harriman, and both Harriman and Schiff denied knowing anything about the details of the deal.

12. Havemeyer, *Along the Great South Bay*, p. 242.

13. *New York World*, 16 February 1905, p. 3.

14. *Brooklyn Eagle*, 13 November 1905.

15. New-York Historical Society, James H. Hyde to Annie Fitch Hyde, dated Paris, 17 October 1910.

16. *Town Topics*, 23 November 1905. The phaeton (pronounced fay-e-ton) was a four-wheel vehicle with a shaped, rather than a square, box, and was easier to mount than other carriages. The largest, version, the mail phaeton, had the same axles used on mail coaches and was drawn by four horses; the smaller sizes, in descending order, were the demi-mail, the Stanhope, the spider, the George IV, and several kinds of ladies' phaetons, sometimes with wicker bodies. Smaller phaetons were drawn by only one or two horses. Information courtesy of Mary Stokes Waller.

17. Merkling, Freeman, Fitzgerald, and Solin, *The Golden Horseshoe: The Life and Times of the Metropolitan Opera House*.

18. Collins, *Otto Kahn: Art, Money & Modern Times*, p. 70.

19. *New York World*, Sunday, 16 November 1902.

20. *New York Times*, 17 November 1902.

21. "The Joys of Four-in-Hand," *New York Sun*, 12 April 1903.

22. Clipping from unidentified newspaper in JHH scrapbook, titled "James Hazen Hyde, The Millionaire Whip and His Notable Guests on the Liberty's First Trip, 'Tan-ta-ra! Here They Come! Clear the Road for the Merry Company!'" Courtesy of Lorna Hyde Graev.

23. *New York Press*, 19 April 1903.

24. Ibid.

25. *Town & Country*, 21 March 1903

26. Buley, p. 593–594.

27. Ibid, p. 587.

28. Buley notes on HBS Hyde Papers, Case P-12-1903, Alexander trying to retire as a trustee of the H. B. Hyde Estate; Alexander memo for McIntyre, 23 December 1903.

Chapter Eleven
THE ELIGIBLE BACHELOR, 1903–1904

1. *New York World*, 16 February 1905, p. 3.
2. Teichmann, *Alice: The Life and Times of Alice Roosevelt Longworth*, pp. 132–33.
3. Ibid., pp. 133–35.
4. *New York Sun* 27 October 1903.
5. Auchincloss, *Theodore Roosevelt*, p. 24.
6. *Town Topics*, 24 November 1904.
7. Ibid., 26 November 1903.
8. Ibid., 24 November 1904. Elizabeth was not the daughter of Paul Morton, who became chairman of the Equitable in 1905.
9. Ibid., 22 December 1904.
10. Ibid., 12 January 1905.
11. "Afternoon Tea Chat," *New York Times*, undated clipping.

Chapter Twelve
NEW YORK AND PARIS, 1903–1904

1. Buley, p. 360.
2. Ibid., p. 682.
3. Buley notes on HBS Hyde Papers, Case P-12-1903, "Financial Affairs—Stock Market, etc., summer of 1903, Alexander to James who is in Paris, 17 July 1903."
4. Ibid., "Financial Affairs, August 1903, Alexander to Dear James in Paris."
5. Klein, *The Life and Legend of E. H. Harriman*, p. 332.
6. HBS, Hyde Collection, Box 13, 25 March 1904, Memorandum for Mr. Hyde from JWA.
7. Ibid.
8. Armstrong, Testimony of James Hazen Hyde, p. 2295.
9. HBS, Hyde Collection, Box 13, Folder 2, Equitable Life Assurance Society–New York.
10. Baudot, *Réjane*, Translations from the French by Patricia Beard. Information about Réjane in this chapter is based on François Baudot's essay, unless otherwise noted.
11. Klein, *The Life and Legend of E. H. Harriman*, p. 363.
12. Auchincloss, *Theodore Roosevelt*, p. 81.
13. Klein, *The Life and Legend of E. H. Harriman*, p. 365.
14. AXA Financial Archives.
15. *Pittsburgh Gazette*, 1 November 2001.

Part III
THE BALL
1. Patterson, *The First Four Hundred: Mrs. Astor's New York in the Gilded Age*, p. 86.

Chapter Thirteen
THE PARTY ERA, 1883–1905
1. The site where the house and stable were built are now occupied by Fort Tryon Park and the Cloisters Museum.
2. Wherever possible, accounts of the parties that follow are gleaned from contemporary newspaper articles and accounts written by people at the time. But because great parties invite exaggeration and fanciful reportage, the reader is advised to take the details as truer to the spirit than to the absolute facts.
3. McAllister, *Society as I Have Found It*, p. 234.
4. Patterson, *The First Four Hundred*, p. 24. Henry and Annie Hyde were not included in the Four Hundred, although Mary and Sidney Dillon Ripley were. It also does not appear that the Hydes were guests at Mrs. Astor's balls.
5. From conversation with Lorna B. Goodman, 2001.
6. Patterson, *The First Four Hundred*, p. 65.
7. Ibid, p. 8.
8. Unidentified newspaper clipping, 25 March 1883.
9. McAllister, *Society as I Have Found It*, p. 532.
10. *New York Sun*, 27 March 1883.
11. Richard Jay Hutto, in conversation with the author, July 2002.
12. *New York Times*, 24 January 1897, claimed, "It was proven by careful investigation . . . that the $100,000 which was expended by hosts and guests on the Vanderbilt fancy dress ball of 1883 circulated through all portions of the community."
13. *Town Topics*, 18 February 1897.
14. *New York Times*, 9 February 1897.
15. Ibid.
16. *New York Sun*, 12 February 1897.
17. *New York Times*, 3 February 1897.
18. *New York Times Supplement*, 21 February 1897.
19. Richard Jay Hutto, letter to the author dated 15 July 2002.
20. *New York Sun*, 12 February 1897.
21. *New York World*, 12 February 1897.
22. Ibid., 14 February 1897.

Chapter Fourteen
THE HYDE BALL: JANUARY 31, 1905

 1. *Town Topics*, clipping, undated, 1905.
 2. Some of the pictures of the Bradley Martin Ball were taken at the Waldorf, the rest were made by a photographer nearby, whose studio was open all night.
 3. Mitford, *The Sun King*, pp. 100ff.
 4. Cartwright, "James Hazen Hyde's Costume Ball," *Metropolitan Magazine*, June 1905.
 5. *New York Herald*, 1 February 1905.
 6. *New York Times*, 5 February 1905.
 7. *Town Topics*, undated clipping, February, 1905
 8. *New York World*, 6 February 1905.
 9. *New York Times*, 15 February 1905.
10. *New York Times*, 27 July 1959. The errors that have multiplied over the past century include minor misattributions of costumes; elaborations of decor, invented menus, and misinformation about attendance (In the June, 1905, *Metropolitan Magazine* story, the author writes, "Miss Alice Roosevelt came up from Washington to attend the dance. She wore a striking costume of white, with garlands of flowers, patches and powdered hair." Alice accepted the invitation, but decided not to attend at the last minute.) The "authoritative" statement that the ball cost $200,000 and that the Equitable paid the bill continues to appear in Gilded Age social histories.
11. White, Clare Nicholas, ed. *Stanford White: Letters to His Family,* "Letter from Stanford White to his wife, February 7, 1905."

Chapter Fifteen
THE WINTER OF DISCONTENT: FEBRUARY 1905

 1. *New York Times*, 19 April 1905.
 2. AXA.
 3. Ibid.
 4. Armstrong, Testimony of E. H. Harriman, p. 2360.
 5. Buley, p. 612 (footnote).
 6. Klein, *The Life and Legend of E. H. Harriman*, p. 329.
 7. HBS, Hyde Collection, carton 13, folder 39.
 8. Buley, pp. 612–13.
 9. Where quotations are not attributed, it is because they appeared in many contemporary newspaper accounts, as well as in Buley and in later government documents.
10. *Report to the Board of Directors of the Equitable Life Assurance Soci-*

ety of the United States, May 31, 1905 (hereafter referred to as "Frick Report"), p. 16.

11. *New York World*, 16 February 1905.

12. Ibid., 17 February 1905.

13. Buley, p. 616 (Many of these quotes are from notes Buley took from the Harvard Business School Hyde Collection. Buley credits the sources as having been filed in Case P-13, however only a few of the notes are currently in either case P-12 or P-13.)

14. HBS, Hyde Collection, carton 13, folder 7.

15. *New York World*, 18 March 1905, p. 7.

16. HBS, Hyde Collection, carton 13, folder 38.

17. Morris, *Theodore Rex*, p. 13.

18. Ibid., p. 127.

19. Rousmaniere, pp. 97–98.

20. *New York World*, undated clipping.

21. Buley, pp. 618–19.

22. HBS, Hyde Collection, carton 13, folder 36.

23. *New York World*, 4 March 1905.

24. *New York Times*, 16 February 1905.

25. Ibid.

26. Less than twenty years later, the story was still meandering on. In a 1928 biography of Frick, published only eight years after Frick died, the author wrote—erroneously—that when the "inside struggle for control of the Equitable . . . approached a climax [Frick] . . . joined with other prominent Republicans in trying to effect a solution by obtaining the appointment of Mr. James H. Hyde as Ambassador to France, but the best the President could be persuaded to offer was the Ministry to Belgium, which the young man promptly declined." Harvey, *Henry Clay Frick, The Man*, p. 299.

27. Buley, p. 619.

28. Ibid.

29. *New-York Herald*, 28 February 1905.

30. *New York World*, 17 February 1905

31. *New York Times*, 17 February 1905

32. *Town Topics*, 23 February 1905.

33. Buley, p. 607.

34. Ibid.

35. *New-York Herald*, 20 February 1905

36. *New York Times*, 25 February 1905, p. 9 col. 3.

37. HBS, Hyde Collection, Henry B. Hyde to James Hazen Hyde, November 1895.

38. Ibid., William McIntyre to James Hazen Hyde, 18 June 1898.

39. *New York World*, 26 February 1905, p. 2. The text of Section 36 of the law read, "No director or officer of an insurance corporation doing business in the State shall receive any money or valuable thing for negotiating, procuring or recommending any loan from any such corporation, or for selling or aiding in the sale of any stocks or securities to or by such corporation.

"Any person violating the provisions of the section shall forfeit his position as such director or officer, and be disqualified from thereafter holding any such office in any insurance corporation."

40. *New-York Herald*, 16 February 1905, p. 4.

41. *New York Times,* 18 February 1905, p. 5.

42. *New-York Herald*, 16 February 1905, p. 4.

43. *New York World*, 26 February 1905, pp. 1ff.

Chapter Sixteen
"THE EQUITABLE ROW": THE TURNING POINT, SPRING 1905

1. *New York Times*, 1 March 1905.

2. *Encyclopedia of the City of New York*, p. 199.

3. *New York World*, 5 March 1905.

4. *New-York Herald*, 22 February 1905.

5. Ibid., 3 April 1905.

6. *New York Times*, 7 April 1905.

7. *New York World*, 9 April 1905.

8. Buley, p. 625.

9. *New York World*, 29 March 1905.

10. *New-York Herald*, 29 March 1903.

11. Frick Report, p. 16.

12. *New York World*, 30 March 1905.

13. *New-York Herald*, 1 April 1905.

14. Ibid., 6 April 1905.

15. Ibid., 18 April 1905.

16. HBS, Hyde collection, carton 13, folder 18.

17. *New York Times*, 20 April 1905.

18. Buley, p. 638.

19. *New York Times*, 19 April 1905.

20. Ibid., 4 April 1905.

21. *New-York Herald*, 4 April 1905.

22. *New York World*, 16 April 1905.

23. *New York Times*, 19 April 1905, p. 2.

24. The following account and quotations are taken from the story in the *New-York Herald*, Wednesday, 19 April 1905, unless otherwise noted.

25. Ibid., 20 April 1905.

26. HBS, Hyde Collection, carton 13, folder 7, letter from M. M. Minton, n.d.

27. *New-York Herald*, 24 April 1905.

28. *New York World*, 23 April 1905. The Gogetic story is largely taken from this article in *The World*, except as otherwise noted.

29. *New-York Herald*, 24 April 1905, p. 3.

30. *Town Topics*, 27 April 1905.

31. *New-York Herald*, 21 April 1905, p. 3.

32. *New York Times*, 22 April 1905, p. 2.

33. *New-York Herald*, 20 April 1905, p. 4.

34. Buley, p. 636.

Chapter Seventeen
HENRY CLAY FRICK

1. Much of the detail describing Frick's life prior to his involvement in the Equitable crisis has been gleaned from the following sources: Martha Frick Symington Sanger's *Henry Clay Frick: An Intimate Portrait*; George Harvey's *Henry Clay Frick, The Man*; Samuel A. Schreiner, Jr.'s *Henry Clay Frick: The Gospel of Greed*; and Kenneth Warren's *Triumphant Capitalism: Henry Clay Frick and the Industrial Transformation of America*.

2. Harvey, *Henry Clay Frick, The Man*, p. 135.

3. Accounts of the sequence of events vary slightly.

4. Harvey, *Henry Clay Frick, The Man*, p. 142.

5. Sanger, *Henry Clay Frick: An Intimate Portrait*, p. 208.

6. Ibid., p. 212.

7. Harvey, *Henry Clay Frick, The Man*, p. 276.

8. Buley, p. 629.

9. Harvey, *Henry Clay Frick, The Man*, p. 365.

10. *New York World*, 16 April 1905.

11. Buley, p. 633.

12. Ibid.

13. Ibid.

14. Klein, *The Life and Legend of E. H. Harriman*, p. 337.

15. Ibid., p. 335.

16. Ibid, p. 336.

17. Buley, p 635 .

18. Armstrong, Testimony by E. H. Harriman.

19. Armstrong, Testimony by James Hazen Hyde.
20. *Report to the Board of Directors of the Equitable Life Assurance society of the United States at Its Meeting of May 31ª, 1905, of the Committee appointed April 6th, 1905 to "Investigate and Report Upon the Present Management of the Society,"* aka "The Frick Report." AXA.
21. Description of the tenor of the meeting and quotes from the *New York Times*, 3 June 1905.
22. Ibid.
23. *New York Times*, 4 June 1905.
24. *The World*, 4 June 1905.
25. *The World Sun*, 4 June 1905.

Chapter Eighteen
THOMAS FORTUNE RYAN

1. Ryan, "Why I Bought the Equitable," *North American Review* 198, August 1913.
2. "Like a Baby," Talk of the Town, *The New Yorker*, undated clipping, page 18
3. Ibid.
4. Numbers like these are inevitably estimates, and I have put them in quotation marks; the point is that Ryan was very rich—probably nearly twice as rich as J. P. Morgan.
5. Hellman, "Rummaging Around with the Ryans," *The New Yorker*, undated clipping
6. Ryan, *North American Review*, p. 162.
7. Ibid.
8. Morton quote from Buley, p. 662, footnote; Commissioner C. A. Prouty quote from the *New York Times* editorial, 2 January 1905, quoted from the same Buley footnote.
9. *New-York Herald*, 11 June 1905, p. 1.
10. *New York World*, 11 June 1905.
11. *New York Times*, 10 June 1905, from Buley, p. 659.
12. Ibid., 20 July 1905.
13. *New York World*, 29 October 1905.
14. Armstrong, Testimony of Edward H. Harriman, pp. 5135ff.
15. Armstrong, Testimony of Thomas F. Ryan, pp. 4566ff and 4799ff.
16. Buley, p. 658.
17. Buley, p. 659, Morton to "My Dear Charlotte," June 14, 1905, Morton family letters, copy in AXA Financial Archives.

Chapter Nineteen
SUMMER 1905

1. *New-York Herald*, 6 August 1905.
2. *New York World*, 22 July 1905.
3. Ibid., 23 July 1905.
4. Ibid.
5. *New York World*, 30 July 1905.
6. Morris, *Theodore Rex*, p. 539.
7. Danelski and Tulchin, eds., *Autobiographical Notes of Charles Evans Hughes*, p. 121.
8. *New York World*, 24 August 1905.
9. The Deacon rumor was published in more than one place; this account is taken from "Saunterings," *Town Topics*, 28 September 1905.
10. *Town Topics*, 14 September 1905.

Chapter Twenty
THE ARMSTRONG INVESTIGATION AND AFTER:
SEPTEMBER–DECEMBER 1905

1. *New York Times*, 1 October 1905, p. 4.
2. *Autobiographical Notes of Charles Evans Hughes*, p. 123.
3. *New York Times*, 1 October 1905.
4. Armstrong, Testimony of George W. Perkins, pp. 771ff.
5. *New York Times*, 18 September 1905.
6. Armstrong, Testimony of George W. Perkins, see note 4.
7. Strouse, *Morgan*, p. 546.
8. *New York Times*, 8 September 1905.
9. Ibid., 11 October 1905.
10. *Town Topics*, 26 October 1905.
11. *New York Times*, 8 October 1905.
12. "Editorial: Charles Evans Hughes," *McClure's*, December 1905.
13. *New York Times*, 9 October 1905.
14. *Town Topics*, 9 November 1905.
15. *Brooklyn Eagle*, 14 November 1905.
16. *Town Topics*, 23 November 1905.
17. Unless otherwise noted, quotations from James Hyde's testimony are from the Armstrong Investigation hearings, pp. 2200–28, 2343–72, 5135–64.
18. Armstrong, Testimony of Thomas Fortune Ryan, pp. 2343–72.
19. *Town Topics*, 21 December 1905.
20. J. P. Morgan had a particular interest in archaeology. He often went to Egypt, and he nearly died there. He was on a chartered boat, heading

up the Nile toward Deir-el-Bahri to visit the Metropolitan Museum of Art's expedition when he suffered a mental breakdown and became fatally ill. Traveling with one of his daughters, a personal physician, and his Pekingese dog, he returned to Shepheard's Hotel in Cairo. From there he was taken to Rome, where he died.

21. *New York Times*, 27 May 1909.
22. Known as the Hearst Medical Papyrus, after the family who supported the exhibition. "The Hearst Medical Papyrus," http://sunsite.berkeley.edu/APIS/medical.html.
23. James Hyde's account of this incident says only that he and JWA met at the Pyramids, that they passed each other on camelback, and that neither spoke to the other. The winter they met was probably 1908, the year the Reisner expedition began. With Hyde's Harvard connections, and Alexander's role as a former trustee of Princeton University, it is probable that both would have visited the site.

Chapter Twenty-one
PARIS, 1906–1917

1. Last will and testament of Henry B. Hyde.
2. New-York Historical Society, "Dear Ma," Paris, 22 February 1909.
3. James donated his correspondence to the New-York Historical Society. One explanation for his keeping the letters between him and his mother, and then making them publicly available are that he kept and catalogued nearly everything. It is also possible that, believing that Annie had treated him badly, he was willing to have what he called her "unfriendliness" on record.
4. New-York Historical Society, undated letter, stamped "Received 3 November 1908."
5. Ibid., telegram; date deduced from Annie's birthday and other correspondence.
6. Ibid., "My dear Ma," Paris, 5 November 1908.
7. Ibid., "Dear Ma," Paris, 11 November 1908.
8. Ibid., "Dear Ma," Paris, 30 November 1908.
9. Ibid., letter, Paris, 19 July 1909.
10. Ibid., "Dear Ma," from Steam Yacht *Emerald*, Smyrna, 24 June 1910.
11. *New York Times*, 23 September 1910.
12. New-York Historical Society, "Confidential. My dear mother," Paris, 11 March 1911.
13. Ibid., "My dear Mother," Paris, 6 April 1911,.
14. Ibid.
15. *New York Times*, 26 June 1904.

16. Wall, *Carnegie*, pp. 660ff.
17. Ibid., p 661.
18. *Boston Transcript*, 14 November 1913.
19. *New York Times*, "J. G. Leishman Dies; A Former Diplomat. Found Dead in Bed of Heart Attack in Hotel at Monte Carlo." 28 March 1924.
20. Idem.
21. Mme. Adams, to the author 22 June 2000.
22. From telephone interview with Professor Susan Cavan, who interviewed Henry Hyde extensively.
23. Codicil to Henry B. Hyde's will, dated June 16, 1896.
24. *London Times*, 26 November 1913.
25. New-York Historical Society, 28 November 1913.
26. The visitor was Louis Réau, a member of l'Institut de France, l'Académie des Sciences Morales et Politiques, a prestigious intellectual organization to which James would eventually be elected a member, an exceptional honor for an American.
27. The concept of the four continents began with the discovery of America by Christopher Columbus, prior to which Europeans believed that the continents numbered three.
28. *New York Times*, 1 December 1918.
29. Private family papers, courtesy of Lorna Hyde Graev.

Afterword
"THE AUGUST MOON": HENRY HYDE

1. Information about Princess Torre e Tasso courtesy of John Royall, from privately circulated family history; and from Richard Jay Hutto.
2. *New York Times*, 10 October 1948.
3. Hon. John Roper, letter to Henry B. Hyde on the occasion of his 80th birthday. Courtesy of Isabel Hyde Jasinowski.
4. Henry B. Hyde, unpublished, undated document, titled "JERSEY TRUST, Chronology of H.B.H.'s locations, personal activities, personal associations, and intentions from 1915 to date" Courtesy of Lorna Hyde Graev.
5. Ibid.
6. Cave Brown, *Wild Bill Donovan: The Last Hero*, p. 324.
7. *The Internet Encyclopedia of Philosophy*, René Descartes (1596–1650), utm.edu/research/iep/d/descartes.htm.
8. Henry Hyde, unpublished memoir.
9. *New York World*, April 1941 (precise date missing from clipping).
10. *New York Times*, 11 March 1941.
11. *American Weekly*, 25 November 1945.

12. Unless otherwise noted, information about Henry Hyde's OSS career is based on his unpublished memoir, on Anthony Cave Brown's *Wild Bill Donovan*, and on the kind assistance of John E. Taylor, whose bibliography, The John E. Taylor Collection: September 2000 at the National Archives and Records Administration, has been extremely helpful, as was Mr. Taylor.

13. Cave Brown, *Wild Bill Donovan*, p. 171.

14. Willets, *Sting of Glory*, p. 7.

15. Ibid., pp. 9–10.

16. Ibid., pp. 17–18.

17. Ibid., pp. 22–23.

18. Information beginning with the transport for the mission is largely gathered from Cave Brown, pp. 316–40.

19. Schlesinger, *A Life in the 20th Century*, p. 336.

20. *The Overseas Targets War Report of the OSS (Office of Strategic Services)*, vol. 2.

21. Letter from John Colville to Henry Hyde, to be read on the occasion of his 80th birthday, fax dated 23 October 1995. Courtesy of Isabel Hyde Jasinowski.

DENOUEMENTS

1. Buley, p. 708.

2. Letter on stationery from the Forest Inn, Summerville, S.C., signed William A. Day. Undated, but written after JWA's death. When Paul Morton fired Thomas Jordan, he appointed Day as acting comptroller of the Equitable. Day, who had served as assistant attorney-general of the United States, continued as comptroller, and was an Equitable director from 1907 until 1928. New-York Historical Society.

3. *New York Times*, undated clipping, mid-July 1909.

4. Wellesley College Archives.

5. Buley, p. 707.

6. Ibid., p. 680.

7. Strouse, *Morgan*, p. 605.

8. Post-1905 financial history of the Equitable is largely gleaned from Rousmaniere, chap. 8, pp 107–21, and chap. 21, pp. 304–21; and from a telephone interview with Richard H. Jenrette, former chairman of the Equitable, March 20, 2003.

9. The putative Harriman sale is not recorded at the Equitable.

10. Rousmaniere, p. 116.

Bibliography

Books

The Age of Elegance: The Paintings of John Singer Sargent. London: Phaidon Press Limited, 1996.

Alexander, William. *A Brief History of the Equitable Society: Seventy Years of Progress and Public Service.* New York: The Equitable Life Assurance Society of the United States, 1929.

Ames, Kenneth L. *Death in the Dining Room & Other Tales of Victorian Culture.* Philadelphia: Temple University Press, 1992.

Amory, Cleveland. *The Last Resorts.* New York: Harper & Brothers, 1952.

Armstrong, Hamilton Fish. *Those Days.* New York: Harper & Row, 1963.

Auchincloss, Louis. *The Vanderbilt Era: Profiles of a Gilded Age.* New York: Charles Scribner's Sons, 1989.

Baedeker, Karl. *Paris and Environs with Routes from London to Paris.* London: Dalau and Co., 1907.

Balsan, Consuelo Vanderbilt. *The Glitter & the Gold.* Maidstone, UK: George Mann, 1973.

Batterberry, Michael and Ariane. *On the Town in New York: The Landmark History of Eating, Drinking, and Entertainments from the American Revolution to the Food Revolution.* New York: Routledge, 1999.

Baudot, François. *Réjane: La Reine du Boulevard.* Paris: Editions KL, 2001.

Beer, Thomas. *The Mauve Decade: American Life at the End of the Nineteenth Century.* New York: Carroll & Graf, 1997.

Bernier, Olivier. *Pleasure and Privilege: Life in France, Naples, and America, 1770–90.* Garden City, NY: Doubleday & Co., 1981.

Birmingham, Stephen. *Our Crowd, The Great Jewish Families of New York*. New York: Harper & Row, 1967.

———— . *The Right Places*. Boston: Little Brown and Co., 1973.

Blanchard, Mary Warner. *Oscar Wilde's America*. New Haven, Conn.: Yale University Press, 1998.

Brandon, Ruth. *The Dollar Princesses: Sagas of Upward Nobility, 1870–1914*. New York: Alfred A. Knopf, 1980.

Brough, James. *Princess Alice: A Biography of Alice Roosevelt Longworth*. Boston: Little, Brown, and Co.

Brown, Anthony Cave. *Wild Bill Donovan: The Last Hero*. New York: Times Books, 1982.

Brownstone, David, and Irene Franck. *Timelines of the 20ᵗʰ Century: A Chronology of 7,500 Key Events, Discoveries, and People That Shaped Our Century*. Boston: Little, Brown and Co., 1996.

Buley, Carlyle R. *The Equitable Life Assurance Society of the United States 1859–1964*, vol. 1. New York: The Equitable Life Assurance Society of the United States, 1967.

Buley, Carlyle R. *The Equitable Life Assurance Society of the United States 1859–1964*, vol. 2. New York: The Equitable Life Assurance Society of the United States, 1967.

Bulfinch's Mythology: The Age of Fable, The Age of Chivalry, Legends of Charlemagne. New York: Thomas Y. Crowell Co., 1970.

Cable, Mary. *Top Drawer: American High Society from the Gilded Age to the Roaring Twenties*. New York: Atheneum, 1984.

Carnegie, Andrew. *The Gospel of Wealth*. Bedford, Mass.: Applewood Books, 1998.

Cashman, Sean Dennis. *America in the Gilded Age: From the Death of Lincoln to the Rise of Theodore Roosevelt*. New York: New York University Press, 1993.

Collins, Theresa M. *Otto Kahn: Art, Money & Modern Time*. Chapel Hill & London: University of North Carolina Press, 2002.

Craig, Theresa. *Edith Wharton A House Full of Rooms: Architecture, Interiors, and Gardens*. New York: Monacelli Press, 1996.

De Borchgrave, Alexandra Villard, and John Cullen. *Villard: The Life and Times of an American Titan*. New York: Doubleday, 2001.

De Marly, Diana. *Worth: Father of Haute Couture*. New York: Holmes & Meier Publishers, 1990.

Depew, Chauncey M. *My Memories of Eighty Years*. New York: Charles Scribner's Sons, 1922.

Donn, Linda. *The Roosevelt Cousins: Growing Up Together, 1882–1924*. New York: Alfred A. Knopf, 2001.

Dorsey, Hebe. *Age of Opulence: The Belle Epoque in the Paris Herald 1890–1914*. New York: Harry N. Abrams, 1987.

Dunlop, M. H. *Gilded City: Scandal and Sensation in Turn-of-the-Century New York*. New York: William Morrow, 2000.

Dwight, Eleanor. *The Gilded Age: Edith Wharton and Her Contemporaries*. New York: Universe Publishing, 1996.

Folsom, Burton W., Jr. *The Myth of the Robber Barons: A New Look at the Rise of Big Business in America*. Herndon, Va.: Young America's Foundation, 1996.

Foreman, John, and Robbe Pierce Stimson. *The Vanderbilts and the Gilded Age: Architectural Aspirations, 1879–1901*. New York: St. Martin's Press, 1991.

Four Americans in Paris. New York: Museum of Modern Art, 1970.

Gaines, Steven. *Philistines at the Hedgerow: Passion and Property in the Hamptons*. Boston: Little, Brown and Co., 1998.

Geisst, Charles R. *100 Years of Wall Street*. New York: McGraw-Hill, 2000.

———. *Wall Street: A History*. Oxford: Oxford University Press, 1997.

Gordon, Lois, and Alan Gordon. *The Columbia Chronicles of American Life 1910–1992*. New York: Columbia University Press, 1995.

Green, Harvey. *The Light of the Home: An Intimate View of the Lives of Women in Victorian America*. New York: Pantheon Books, 1983.

Gregory, Alexis. *Families of Fortune: Life in the Gilded Age*. New York: Rizzoli International Publications, 1993.

Handbook to Paris and Its Environs. London: Ward, Lock & Co., undated, early twentieth century.

Harvey, George, *Henry Clay Frick: The Man*, New York & London: Charles Scribner's Sons, 1928

Havemeyer, Harry W. *Along the Great South Bay: From Oakdale to Babylon, the Story of a Summer Spa, 1840–1940*. Mattituck, N.Y.: Amereon House, 1996.

Henry Baldwin Hyde: A Biographical Sketch. New York: The Equitable Life Assurance Society of the United States, 1901.

Hill, Professor Thomas E. *The Essential Handbook of Victorian Etiquette*. San Mateo, Ca.: Bluewood Books, 1994.

Homans, Abigail Adams. *Education by Uncles*. Boston: Houghton Mifflin Co., 1966.

Howells, William Dean. *A Hazard of New Fortunes*. New York: Meridian, 1994.

Hughes, Charles Evans. *The Autobiographical Notes of Charles Evans Hughes*. Ed. David J. Danelski and Joseph S. Tulchin. Cambridge, Mass.: Harvard University Press, 1973.

Jackson, Kenneth T. *The Encyclopedia of New York City.* New Haven, Conn.: Yale University Press, 1995.

Josephson, Matthew. *The Robber Barons.* San Diego, Calif.: Harcourt Brace & Co., 1962.

Kennan, George. *E. H. Harriman: A Biography.* New York: Houghton Mifflin Co., 1922.

Kete, Mary Louise. *Sentimental Collaborations: Mourning and Middle-Class Identity in Nineteenth-Century America.* Durham, N.C.: Duke University Press, 2000.

———. *The Life and Legend of E. H. Harriman.* Chapel Hill, N.C.: University of North Carolina Press, 2000.

Klein, Maury. *The Life and Legend of Jay Gould.* Baltimore, Md.: Johns Hopkins University Press, 1986.

Lessard, Suzannah. *The Architect of Desire: Beauty and Danger in the Stanford White Family.* New York: Dial Press, 1996.

Lewis, Alfred Allan. *Ladies and Not-So-Gentle Women.* New York: Viking, 2000.

Lewis W. H. *The Splendid Century: Life in the France of Louis XIV.* Garden City, N.Y.: Doubleday & Co., 1957.

Lindley, Clara Hill. *James J. and Mary T. Hill.* New York: North River Press, 1948.

Lord, Walter. *The Good Years: From 1900 to the First World War.* New York: Harper & Brothers, 1960.

McAllister, Ward. *Society as I Have Found It.* New York: Cassell Publishing Co., 1890.

McCash, June Hall. *The Jekyll Island Cottage Colony.* Athens, Ga.: University of Georgia Press, 1998.

McCash, William Barton, and June Hall McCash. *The Jekyll Island Club: Southern Haven for America's Millionaires.* Athens, Ga.: University of Georgia Press, 1989.

Malone, Michael P. *James J. Hill: Empire Builder of the Northwest.* Norman: University of Oklahoma Press, 1996.

Martin, Albro. *James J. Hill & the Opening of the Northwest.* New York: Oxford University Press, 1976.

Merkling, Frank, John W. Freeman, Gerald Fitzgerald, with Arthur Solin. *The Golden Horseshoe: The Life and Times of the Metropolitan Opera House.* New York: Viking Press, 1965.

Mitford, Nancy. *The Sun King.* New York: Penguin Books, 1994.

Morris, Edmund. *Theodore Rex.* New York: Random House, 2001.

Morris, Lloyd. *Incredible New York: High Life and Low Life from 1850 to 1950.* Syracuse, N.Y.: Syracuse University Press, 1996.

Nichols, Charles Wilbur de Lyon, *The Ultra-Fashionable Peerage of America: An Official List of Those People Who Can Properly Be Called Ultra-Fashionable in the United States*. New York: George Harjes, 1904.

Norris, Floyd, and Christine Bockelmann. *The New York Times Century of Business*. New York: McGraw-Hill, 2000.

O'Connor, Richard. *The Golden Summers: An Antic History of Newport*. New York: G.P. Putnam's Sons, 1974.

Our Times: The Illustrated History of the 20ᵗʰ Century. Atlanta: Turner Publishing, 1995.

Patterson, Jerry E. *The First Four Hundred: Mrs. Astor's New York in the Gilded Age*. New York: Rizzoli International Publications, 2000.

Platt, Frederick. *America's Gilded Age: Its Architecture and Decoration*. Cranbury, N.J.: A.S. Barnes and Co., 1976.

Preston, Diana. *Lusitania: An Epic Tragedy*. New York: Walker Publishing Co., 2002.

Pyle, J. G. *The Life of James J. Hill*, vol. II. Garden City, N.Y.: Doubleday, Page & Co., 1917.

Rearick, Charles. *Pleasures of the Belle Epoque: Entertainment & Festivity in Turn-of-the-Century France*. New Haven, Conn.: Yale University Press, 1985.

Rousmaniere, John. *The Life and Times of the Equitable*. The Stinehour Press, 1995.

Sanger, Martha Frick Symington. *Henry Clay Frick: An Intimate Portrait*. New York: Abbeville Press, 1998.

Schlereth, Thomas J. *Victorian America: Transformations in Everyday Life*. New York: HarperCollins Publishers, 1991.

Schlesinger, Arthur M., Jr. *A Life in the 20th Century: Innocent Beginnings, 1917–1950*. Boston, New York: Houghton Mifflin, 2000.

Schreiner, Samuel A., Jr. *Henry Clay Frick: The Gospel of Greed*, New York: St. Martin's Press, 1995.

Simon, Kate. *Fifth Avenue: A Very Social History*. New York: Harcourt Brace Jovanovich, 1978.

Sloane, Florence Adele. *Maverick in Mauve: The Diary of a Romantic Age*. Garden City, N.Y.: Doubleday & Co., 1983.

Smith, Jane S. *Elsie de Wolfe: A Life in the High Style*. New York: Atheneum, 1982.

Social Register: 1887. New York: The Social Register Association, 1986.

Spence, Clark C. *The Salvation Army Farm Colonies*. Tucson, Ariz. University of Arizona Press, 1985.

Spurling, Hilary. *La Grande Thérèse: The Greatest Swindle of the Century*. New York: HarperCollins Publishers, 2000.

Stern, Robert A. M., Gregory Gilmartin, and John Massengale. *New York 1900: Metropolitan Architecture and Urbanism 1890–1915.* New York: Rizzoli International Publications, 1983.

Strouse, Jean. *Morgan: American Financier.* New York: Perennial, 1999.

Sweet, Matthew. *Inventing the Victorians.* New York: St. Martin's Press, 2001.

Tadié, Jean-Yves. *Marcel Proust: A Life.* New York: Viking, 2000.

Teichmann, Howard. *Alice: The Life and Times of Alice Roosevelt Longworth.* Englewood Cliffs, N.J.: Prentice-Hall, 1979.

Tifft, Susan E., and Alex S. Jones. *The Trust: The Private and Powerful Family Behind The New York Times.* Boston: Little, Brown and Co., 1999.

Trachtenberg, Alan. *The Incorporation of America: Culture & Society in the Gilded Age.* New York: Hill and Wang, 1982.

Traxel, David. *1898: The Birth of the America Century.* New York: Alfred A. Knopf, 1998.

Twain, Mark, and Charles Dudley Warner. *The Gilded Age: A Tale of Today.* New York: Meridian, 1980.

Vanderbilt, Arthur T. II. *Fortune's Children: The Fall of the House of Vanderbilt.* New York: HarperCollins Publishers, 1989.

Wall, Joseph Frazier, *Andrew Carnegie,* Pittsburgh, Pa.: University of Pittsburgh Press, 1989.

Warren, Kenneth, Triumphant Capitalism, *Henry Clay Frick and the Industrial Transformation of America,* Pittsburgh: University of Pittsburgh Press, 1996.

Watts, Stephen. *The Ritz.* London: The Bodley Head, 1963.

Wecter, Dixon. *The Saga of American Society: A Record of Social Aspiration 1607–1937.* New York: Charles Scribner's Sons, 1937.

Wharton, Edith and Ogden Codman Jr. *The Decoration of Houses.* New York: Arno Press, 1975.

White, Claire Nichols, ed. *Stanford White's Letters to His Family,* New York: Rizzoli, 1997.

Willets, Ann. *Sting of Glory.* New York: Random House, 1954.

Wilson, James Grant, and John Fiske. *Appleton's Cyclopedia of America Biography.* New York: D. Appleton and Co., 1888.

Wilson, Laura. *Daily Life in a Victorian House.* New York: Puffin Books, 1993.

Woon, Basil. *The Paris That's Not in the Guide Books.* New York: Robert M. McBride & Co., 1931.

Periodicals

"American Characters: James Hazen Hyde." *American Heritage* (Aug.–Sept. 1981): 96–97.

Baker, Ray Stannard. "Railroad Rebates: What Rebates Are, How They Are Paid, Who Pays Them, and How They Affect Industry." *McClure's* (December 1905): 179–94.

"The Career and Achievements of Charles Evans Hughes: Republican Candidate for Governor of New York." *Harpers Weekly* (13 October 1906): 1452–53.

Cartwright, J. C. "James Hazen Hyde's Costume Ball," *Metropolitan Magazine* (June 1905): 305–19.

"Charles Evans Hughes: Editorial." *McClure's* (December 1905): 220–23.

"The Four Continents: From the Collection of James Hazen Hyde." New York: Cooper Union Museum, 1961.

Crews, Watson, Jr. "Wonderful Jimmy." *American Weekly*, (19 December 1948): 2.

Denison, Lindsay. "James H. Hyde: The Personality of the Young Man Who Controls the Equitable Life Assurance Society." *(The World's Work,* May 1905): 6204–6.

Dow, Joy Wheeler. *The World's Work* (July 1905): 6399–6408.

Hendrick, Burton J. "The Story of Life Insurance." *McClure's* (November 1906): 63–73.

"How May We Insure Our Insure?" *The World's Work* (April 1905): 6012–17.

Hutto, Richard Jay. "The Party of the Century." *Quest:* 52–57.

Johnston, Charles. "Men of To-Day: Charles Evans Hughes." *Harper's Weekly* (21 April 1906): 562–63.

Krugman, Paul, "The Class Wars, Part I," *New York Times Magazine,* 20 October, 2002: 62ff.

Lane, Linda. "Tragedies of Society." *American Weekly Magazine* (25 November 1945): 20–21.

Lefévre, Edwin. "Paul Morton—Human Dynamo." *Cosmopolitan Magazine* (October 1905): 569–76.

Leighton, George R. "The Wall Street Violet." *Harper's Bazaar* (September 1951): 305.

"Life Insurance: The Wrong Way and the Right Way." *The World's Work* (July 1905): 6349–53.

Logan, Andy. "Building for Glory," *The New Yorker,* 21 October, 1961.

"The March of Events." *The World's Work* (August 1905): 6557–58.

North, Douglass C. "Life Insurance and Investment Banking at the Time of the Armstrong Investigation of 1905–1906." *The Journal of Economic History* (Summer 1954): 209–28.

Porel, Jacques. "Fils de Réjane." *Town & Country* (Christmas 1961): 133–79.

"Life Insurance Corruption v. The Revelations and How They Came to Be Made." *The World's Work* (March 1906): 7317–23.

Ryan, Thomas F., "Why I Bought The Equitable," *North American Review* 198 (August, 1913): 161–77.

Surowiecki, James. "The Financial Page: Has Capitalism Killed the Mogul?" *The New Yorker* (10 July 2000): 25.

Tarbell, Gage. "The Autobiography of a Life Assurance Agent," *Everybody's Magazine* (March 1903): 280–86.

Government and Equitable Papers

Preliminary Report on the Investigation Into the Management of The Equitable Life Assurance Society of the United States Made to the Governor of the State of New York by the Superintendent of Insurance as of June 21, 1905, with Addendum Covering Matters Referred to Therein. New York: The Spectator Co.

Report of the Joint Committee of the Senate and Assembly of the State of New York Appointed to the Legislature, February 22, 1906. State of New York, Assembly Document 41. Albany, N.Y.: Brandow Printing Co., 1906. *The Overseas Targets War Report of the OSS (Office of Strategic Services),* Vol. 2. Introduction by Kermit Roosevelt. New York: Walker and Co. 1976.

Supreme Court, Appellate Division—First Department. November 1907. No. 1338. The People of the State of New York, Respondents, Against The Equitable Life Assurance Society of the United States and Others, Appellants. New York: Evening Post Job Printing Office.

Testimony Taken Before the Joint Committee of the Senate and Assembly of the State of New York to Investigate and Examine into the Business and Affairs of Life Insurance Companies Doing Business in the State of New York. Vol. I–9. Albany, N.Y.: Brandow Printing Co., 1905.

Equitable Documents, Speeches, and Papers from the AXA Financial Archives.

Alexander, James W. "The Ideal Company," a paper read before the National Convention of Insurance Commissioners at Columbus, Ohio, September 1902. The Equitable Life Assurance Society Historical Collection.

———. "The Hazard of Inexperience," a lecture delivered by James W. Alexander, President of the Equitable Life Assurance Society of the United States, Before the Students of the Yale University Course of Insurance, June 6, 1904.

Alexander, William. "How the Equitable, a Mutual Company, Came to Have a Capital Stock," unpublished document, 10 March, 1919.

———. *My Half-Century in Life Insurance.* New York: privately published, 1935.

The Equitable Life Assurance Society of the United States, Report of a Committee of Policy-Holders and Representatives of Policy-Holders." Hon. E. D. Morgan, Chairman. 1877.

Hyde, James Hazen. "Life Assurance as an Investment for Young Men." The Equitable Life Assurance Society Historical Collection.

"Parkinson, Thomas I., Member of the Newcomen Society, President of the Equitable Life Assurance Society of the United States. Equitable of the U.S. "What Henry B. Hyde Started in 1859!" New York: The Newcomen Society in North America, 1950.

Reddall, A.H., "The Equitable at the Turn of the Century." The Equitable Life Assurance Society Historical Collection.

"Report to the Board of Directors of the Equitable Life Assurance Society of the United States at Its Meeting of May 31, 1905, of the Committee appointed April 6, 1905, to Investigate and Report upon the Present Management of the Society."

Tarbell, Gage E. "Extracts from Monthly Letters to Agents of Gage E Tarbell." Equitable Life Assurance Society of the United States Historical Collection, undated.

Rousmaniere, John. "Toasting the Emperor: The Equitable, Jacob Schiff, and the Russo-Japanese War." Privately published manuscript, 1993.

Archives

AXA Financial Archives, New York, N.Y.

Baker Library Historical Collections, Harvard University Graduate School of Business Administration, Boston, Massachusetts.

The Widener Library, Harvard University.

National Archives at College Park, College Park, Maryland.

Newport Historical Society Library, Newport, R.I.

New York Society Library, New York, N.Y.

The New-York Historical Society, New York, N.Y.

New York Public Library, New York, N.Y.

Wellesley College Archives, Wellesley, Massachusetts.

Acknowledgments

*L*orna Hyde Graev, who started me thinking about this project, consistently supported my endeavors, made introduc-
tions, shared family albums and memories, and, for some months,
gave me a room of my own in New York. Without her I would never
have written *After the Ball*. Her determination that the book should
reach a wide audience and her efforts to get the word out set a standard for imagination, effectiveness, and organization.

Isabel Hyde Jasinowski was generous and helpful, in particular
guiding my understanding of the role of her father, Henry B. Hyde,
in the OSS, and the ways in which James Hyde influenced his son's
personality.

Jonathan Coss, the AXA Financial archivist, is warmly coopera-
tive and knowledgeable, and an invaluable asset to a company with a
long, fascinating history. This book would have been considerably
thinner without his assistance. Any errors I have made appear in
spite of his help.

At HarperCollins, Larry Ashmead was wise enough to believe in
this story, patient enough to wait until I got it right, and has been a
wise advocate. Susan Llewellyn cheerfully and supportively cured a
veritable plague of edits. Elizabeth Ackerman created a superb jacket,
conveying the elements of glamour, finance, scandal and tragedy.
Elliott Beard (to whom I am not related) designed the book with ele-

gance and sensitivity. Tami Beth Rock helped expedite matters with unflappable good humor and efficiency. Tim Brazier took on the publicity with assurance and creativity, and is a pleasure to work with. The marketing and sales departments used their considerable clout to back up *After the Ball* from the start, as did the senior editors at HarperCollins.

Laura Marmor, a brilliant editor and good friend, edited the manuscript, and helped the story flow with greater clarity. Peter Matson, my agent and friend, was, as always, ready to listen, comment, and encourage. Connie Petropoulos did a magnificent job of combing the newspapers and magazines of the Gilded Age and finding and photocopying material that fills a dozen loose-leaf binders. Kristin O'Brien came in at the end to help pull together the photographs and bibliography.

Anson Beard, David Braga, and Nancy Elting read the manuscript during the final editing stage and offered important suggestions and corrections. Richard H. Jenrette read the galleys and added his invaluable expertise to my understanding of the financial aspects of the story. Talking with him is a lesson in clear thinking.

Martha Frick Symington Sanger, author of *Henry Clay Frick: An Intimate Portrait* and *The Henry Clay Frick Houses*, loaned me a photograph of her great-grandfather, an extremely useful out-of-print biography, read the manuscript with an exacting eye, and provided valuable moral support.

John Foreman, coauthor of *The Vanderbilts and the Gilded Age*, walked me through turn-of-the-century architecture in New York, and gossiped with me about people who have been dead for a century but seemed to us as though they were just around the corner. Mary Stokes Waller invited me to visit the extraordinary carriage collection she and her husband, Harvey Waller have assembled, and provided many of the facts about the sport of driving that appear in these pages. Richard Jay Hutto allowed me to use family photographs of the Bradley Martin Ball, and was an infallible source of Gilded Age information. Paul Windels Jr. offered anecdotes, amusing company, and a look at photographs from his family's collection. John Taylor at the National Archives, researched details of Henry

Hyde's service in the OSS with efficiency and enthusiasm. Elizabeth Peters shared her boundless knowledge of Cairo in the early 20th century, and saved me from dressing James Hyde in the Lawrence of Arabia costume I had mistakenly imagined he would wear to the Pyramids.

My family always comes through with support and good advice: my mother, Sarinda Dranow; my children, Alex Beard and Hillary Beard; my daughter-in-law, Amy Craft Beard; my sister, Elizabeth Krysztofiak; my friend, Sam Beard; and my uncle, David Cowin. Jill and Dick Blanchard, and Molly Schaefer and Dan Slott provided places to write, read, sleep, eat, and enjoy their friendship while I wrote. Betty and Gary Lewis, my neighbors, got me out of the house to look at the landscape. Writing a book is a solitary occupation, but thanks to a host of friends, it was rarely a lonely one.

Index

Page numbers in *italics* refer to illustrations.